Bright

Particular

Star

Charlotte Cushman as Lady Macbeth

Bright
Particular
Star  *The Life*
& Times of
Charlotte
Cushman
by Joseph Leach

New Haven and London, Yale University Press, 1970

Copyright © 1970 by Yale University.
All rights reserved. This book may not be
reproduced, in whole or in part, in any form
(except by reviewers for the public press),
without written permission from the publishers.
Library of Congress catalog card number: 76-99829
International standard book number: 300-01205-5
Designed by Sally Sullivan,
set in Linotype Caslon type,
and printed in the United States of America by
The Colonial Press Inc., Clinton, Mass.
Distributed in Great Britain, Europe, and Africa by
Yale University Press, Ltd., London; in Canada by
McGill-Queen's University Press, Montreal; in Mex-
ico by Centro Interamericano de Libros Académicos,
Mexico City; in Australasia by Australia and New
Zealand Book Co., Pty., Ltd., Artarmon, New South
Wales; in India by UBS Publishers' Distributors Pvt.,
Ltd., Delhi; in Japan by John Weatherhill, Inc., Tokyo.

For Dorothy Ann

" 'Twere all one
That I should love a bright particular star
And think to wed it, he is so above me.
In his bright radiance and collateral light
Must I be comforted, not in his sphere."

—All's Well That Ends Well, I, i.

Contents

Contents

Illustrations

Preface

A century ago, a period when little serious American talent wrote plays, three dynamic stars brought a vigor, an excitement, a dimension to the art of acting that has not since been matched in this country. While recent biographies have treated Edwin Forrest and Edwin Booth, no attempt has ever been made to document fully the life of the solitary actress completing that bright constellation. Even now, Edwin Forrest's name is shadowy, and Booth's fame is coupled largely with the notoriety of his brother, John Wilkes. But Charlotte Cushman's name is vaguest of all.

Why have such names and talents as theirs faded so cold? The answer involves more than straight biography. Partly a fact of life in the theatre, their disappearance is at once a personal story and a commentary on the country that produced and adored them for a time, and then cast them from all memory.

That Charlotte Cushman rose from genteel poverty on a Boston side street to the pinnacle of international fame is a fact. That her circle included many of the period's most celebrated names is a fact. That she experienced many of the major events of her nation's history is no less true than the fact that for years after her death her grave in Mount Auburn Cemetery in Cambridge was, among all the famous graves, the one most often visited. She is the only actress yet admitted to the Hall of Fame for Great Americans. Yet to the public now and to most of those who stroll past her bronze bust in the Hall of Fame the name beneath it is shrouded in mystery. This is perhaps the most extraordinary fact of all.

The person who bore the name Charlotte Cushman merited a different fate. In Hamlet's charge to Polonius to see the players "well bestow'd," Shakespeare gave one guide for thinking about actors. "Do you hear, let them be well used, for they are the abstract and brief chronicles of the time." Polonius' reply is succinct, "My lord, I will use them according to their desert." Whether Miss Cushman's world used her according to her desert, whether one sees in her now some brief chronicle of her time or sees her strictly as herself, the impression stands that in its most powerful actress America appreciated for a time one of the shining figures that by their light illuminate the path for lesser men. As much as Emerson, Longfellow, or Thoreau, she was a brilliant blossom in the sudden eruption of talent that came to be called the flowering of New England. As such, she belonged to that early band of pioneers who accepted the challenge Emerson laid down for all Americans in 1837. "We have listened too long," he declared, "to the courtly muses of Europe." Too long had the American people timidly doubted their ability to create independently a culture worthy of world respect. Both as woman and as star, Charlotte Cushman relished all her life her strategic position in the campaign that eventually rectified that error.

Acknowledgments

In my attempt to revitalize Charlotte Cushman's name, I would be presumptuous and inaccurate to attempt to claim sole credit for whatever is worthy in the following book. As my source notes indicate, my search for the details of her career led me to widely scattered places. In every instance, I was greeted with courtesy and help. While I would wish to thank each of these people by name, space limitations force me to concentrate upon those whose assistance to me caused them the most trouble.

For reasons which they know well, I owe special thanks to Mr. and Mrs. Charles Van Brunt Cushman at Miraleste, California; Professors Ralph H. Gabriel and Norman Holmes Pearson at Yale; Helen D. Willard, curator of the Harvard Library Theatre Collection; Dr. John Broderick and Dr. C. Percy Powell of the Library of Congress Manuscript Division; Dorothy Mason at the Folger Shakespeare Library; J. S. Ritchie at the National Library of Scotland; Eleanor C. Westcott at the Charlotte Cushman Club in Philadelphia; Thomas de Valcourt at Longfellow House in Cambridge; Louis Rachow at the Players Club; June Moll and Frederick J. Hunter at the University of Texas at Austin Library; James Cleveland and Frank Scott at the University of Texas at El Paso Library; Jean McNiece and Robert W. Hill at the New York Public Library; Janet James at the Radcliffe College Library; Gladys E. H. Hosmer; Thomas Kilfoil at the Columbia University Library; Donald Gallup, curator of the American Literature collection at Yale, Professor Leon Howard at UCLA, Professors Napier Wilt and Joshua C. Taylor at the University of Chicago; Jean Preston at the Huntington Library; Phyllis Ball and B. M. Greeley at the University of Arizona Library; Mrs. Lesslie Stockton Howell; John Alden at the Boston Public Library; Frieda C. Thies at the Johns Hopkins Library; Warren G. Wheeler at the Massachusetts Historical Society; David G. Stowe, for his kind permission to use the Cushman materials collected by his father, Lyman Beecher Stowe; Fred Packard, Jack Carson, Edward Sherman, Grace K. Smith, Mary Lillian Collingwood, Hunter Faires, Andrew

Acknowledgments

Cairncross, Francis Fugate, Leonard Sipiora, Pauline Ramsey, and Haywood Antone. All these people have given me help far beyond whatever their roles as librarians, colleagues, or friends could possibly have seemed to require. At the Yale University Press Merle Spiegel and Kathleen Roberts have given me superior guidance.

For kind permission to quote from unpublished manuscripts I am deeply indebted to the following: the Yale University Library, the University of Texas at Austin Library, the Boston Public Library, the Johns Hopkins University Library, the University of Rochester Library, the Missouri Historical Society, the Folger Shakespeare Library, the University of Pennsylvania Library, the Massachusetts Historical Society, the Louisiana State University Library, the New-York Historical Society, the Harvard College Library, the Columbia University Library, the Charlotte Cushman Club, the Pennsylvania Historical Society, the Princeton University Library, the Woman's Archive at Radcliffe College.

Special acknowledgment is due to the Manuscript Division of The New York Public Library, Astor, Lenox and Tilden Foundations, for permission to quote from their Miscellaneous Papers, their Gansevoort-Lansing Collection, and their Theatre Collection. For permission to quote from various letters of Charlotte Cushman, I am indebted to the Trustees of the National Library of Scotland and to The Walter Hampden Memorial Library at The Players, New York. Finally, grateful acknowledgment is owed to the Howard-Tilton Memorial Library at Tulane University, the Sidney Lanier Papers, and to The Huntington Library, San Marino, California.

I am particularly indebted to former President Joseph M. Ray and Vice President Milton Leech at the University of Texas at El Paso for their interest and for granting me university funds to support my research. Dorothy Ann Leach merits far more than her husband's gratitude for the spirit that unflailingly encouraged my quest.

Joseph Leach

University of Texas at El Paso

Girlhood in Boston

(1816–1829)

A ten-minute walk can cover the distance from Boston's North End to the Parker House at the corner of Tremont and School. Though the route lies slightly uphill, though the traffic around Haymarket Square can cause delay, the course is short, the impediments insignificant. Charlotte Cushman took nearly sixty years to span that distance, but she filled her trip with detours and voyages and ascents that made her journey notable.

Her story begins with the country. Her blood came west on the *Mayflower* in the veins of Mary Allerton, whose marriage to Thomas Cushman took place in the new colony, Plymouth Plantation, in the year 1635. The Cushman–Allerton roots sprang from the bedrock of religious nonconformity in England. As agent for the Pilgrims, Thomas' father, Robert, had petitioned the Virginia Company for permission to settle on its territory in North America. He had petitioned King James I to give the settlers "liberty of conscience." Though James denied Cushman's request, he did allow the Pilgrims "so long as they remained faithful subjects to his Majesty" to be tolerated in their form of worship. Thus encouraged, Robert Cushman arranged the purchase of two ships, the *Speedwell,* a vessel of sixty tons, and the *Mayflower,* somewhat larger.

The vessels took to the wind off Southhampton on August 5, 1620. A compound of troubles forced the ships back to port, but on September 6, one hundred and two Pilgrims set sail once more on the *Mayflower.* Among them rode the Isaac Allerton family, including daughter Mary. Early the next summer Robert Cushman and his son Thomas sailed west on a ship called the *Fortune.* Men who looked after "great riches, ease, pleasures, dainties, and jollity in the

World," Robert had written in a pamphlet detailing the facts of American settlement, "I would not advise them to come there." But any man willing to spend his labors for the good of those who should come after, any man desiring to further the gospel among the poor heathens, contenting himself with such hardships as by God's providence should come upon him, "such men I would advise and encourage to go, for their ends cannot fail them."

Once arrived in Plymouth, Robert Cushman left young Thomas in the custody of Governor Bradford and returned on business to London; he died in England in 1626.

The "grave, sober, holy, and temperate" Thomas Cushman served as ruling elder of the church at Plymouth for forty-three years; Mary Allerton Cushman lived until age ninety, the last of the *Mayflower* "Adventurers." Passing years saw the circle of their descendants widen, Pilgrim roots become Puritan towns, Puritan towns become outposts of British commerce, British allegiance alter into American nationality and self-interest—until, in 1769, in the sixth generation from Thomas and Mary, Elkanah Cushman was born in Plymouth.

Elkanah's parents were people of humble means. When they died, Elkanah, who was thirteen, made the long walk up to Boston to seek his fortune. There he met Mary Eliza Babbit, whose line went back to Ireland. Her father, Erasmus Babbit, Jr., born in Sturbridge and graduated from Harvard, practiced law in various towns. Fond of music, blessed with an exceptional memory, he could "play upon the violin and sing 'from sunrise to sunset,'" with the inevitable result that his clients were few, his fees small. His marriage to Mary Saunders of Gloucester, whose family had blood ties with the Sargents, Winthrops, and Saltonstalls, had produced two sons, Winthrop and Augustus, and a daughter, Mary Eliza. Though Mary Saunders Babbit herself had a ready wit and abounding good spirits—and a talent for mimicry—she possessed an endless ambition, a drive that eventually made her despair of Erasmus' frivolities and small fees. In 1810 she moved with her children to Boston. Her daughter Mary Eliza was seventeen, a spirited girl with a broad square face, a fine singing voice, and notable skill as a reader.

To help meet expenses, Mary Eliza maintained a school until she married Elkanah Cushman in 1815; Elkanah was forty-six, a widower with a son and a daughter; Mary Eliza was twenty-two. On July 23, 1816, Elkanah and Mary Eliza Cushman became the parents of Charlotte.

By then, Elkanah had become an established Boston merchant and shipper. At one time he may have worked as a hairdresser, but his partnership in Topliff and Cushman brought his major income during Charlotte's early years. The firm manufactured ship-bread, which it transported and sold over a wide coastal area, at times as far south as the West Indies. Its warehouses occupied space on Long Wharf, the pier which jutted from the bottom of State Street nearly two thousand feet into Boston Harbor.

Charlotte's own roots were planted firmly on Richmond Street, later renamed Parmenter Street. The birth house, Number 110, was a typical Boston middle-class home of the period. White steps led up from the cobblestoned street to the door recessed in an arch. The three-story building topped out in a sizable attic, an ideal play place for children in winter. Wide-shuttered windows pierced its timbered front; its ends were dark stone.

Over the housetops behind, the spire of Second Church punctuated the sky from its corner on Hanover Street. Here, with the help of the ministers Henry Ware and Ralph Waldo Emerson, Mary Eliza firmly grounded her children in Unitarianism. The Cushman house was easily accessible to Long Wharf, a short walk downhill for Elkanah, a long circuitous expedition through exotic byways and secret paths for Charlotte.

An easy jaunt north led her to Old North Church; a half mile south and west past Mill Pond, which later became Haymarket Square, brought her to Boston Common, pasture for the community's cows, playground and battleground for its children.

Inside the Cushman house, the common or family room to the left balanced the dining room to the right, with the larder and kitchen behind. Seated on a low stool in that kitchen, Charlotte listened entranced to her Grandmother Babbit mimic a whole menagerie of animals. The sleeping rooms upstairs were sparsely furnished: plain sturdy chairs, a highboy, a bed or beds spread with thick feather covers, a sea chest or two for storage. The steeply roofed attic above the bedrooms extended to the four lines of the house. Its center was tall enough for a man to stand, for a tall girl perched on a chair to sing for the assembled neighbors.

During Charlotte's childhood when she and her family lived in the house on Richmond Street, and later at a succession of other ad-

3

dresses in the area, Boston emerged from its colonial status as an English-oriented seaport to an American blend of seafaring investment and industry. Charlotte grew up with the town, a place which foreign visitors for years would find reminiscent of London, with its brick and timbered houses, its Adams spires, long cobbled streets, irregular plan, its bustling waterfront, its street cries, and the sturdy English values of its people.

Whether Calvinistic in religion or frankly materialistic in business, Boston mingled its English past with its American present. It had not yet become a town noted for its art or intellect. If Washington Allston could sell a painting in Philadelphia for $3,500 in 1816, he could hardly reap a fraction of that figure in Boston. One irate Bostonian complained that Boston was consuming its wealth "in the profusion of the table, and other luxuries equally indicating a gross and depraved taste." In 1817 there were not over sixty thousand books in the entire city. When Gilbert Stuart died in 1828, he was buried in an unmarked grave on Boston Common.

In the years immediately following 1816 Boston perched solidly above its harbor, differing little from the town it had been in April 1775, when it saw the *Somerset,* British man-of-war, foretelling the end of English control. From the sea it rose a mass of stolid brick and granite, thrusting up from the center an irregular skyline of red towers and white spires, black chimneys and gabled roofs huddled around Charles Bulfinch's domed State House. Its rocky land connected with its back country by a narrow strip called "The Neck," which easterly gales and high tides flooded at times, leaving Boston at sea.

Hardly more than a country town in size, Boston was human-oriented—with scope for the energies of its adults, with elbow room for the frolics of its children. Its homes were largely the functional style of its Puritan past; bright gardens sparked its slate gray streets in summer. Firelight from its hearths, torchlight from its street flares, cut the winter dark. The town crier shouted the news along its narrow streets. From her infancy, Charlotte knew his jangling bell, his ringing report of some current event, whether an auction down on Long Wharf, the berthing of an overdue vessel, or an eminent death. The favorite of all North End children, the crier in June broadcast the word that the grass on Boston Common had just been cut, that the children must "Come and roll! Come and roll!" down the newly mowed slopes.

In that pasture, where Emerson as a boy tended the family cow,

Charlotte and her brother tended their own cow ten years later. She came to know well the route between Richmond Street and the Common as day after day she goaded the plodding animal over the stones, up the gentle sweep of Beacon Hill, through the gates onto the Common's green acres. The Common was fenced; the grass was usually lush. If the task required anything more than an occasional glance at the animal, it seldom interrupted the clamor and noise of play. The trees and stony outcroppings invited young imaginations to riot. The girls demanded the shade to play house in; the boys claimed the branches to swing on, the rocky points to hide behind as forts. For Charlotte, the greater fun lay with the boys. She neatly described her childhood pace on Boston Common: "I was born a tomboy."

The Common in winter offered its frozen pond for skating, its broad white slopes to the blades of a hundred sleds. Snowballs arc'd overhead. When trouble developed, Charlotte fired back snowball for snowball or hid in one of the icy forts, just as in summer she shinnied to the top of the tallest tree.

Born in 1818, her brother, Charles Augustus, was Charlotte's earliest friend. Together they explored the byways of Boston, raced breathless and laughing up Copp's Hill for the view through the ancient gravestones, squashed bare feet in the muddy shore of the Charles, bashed the skulls of Charlotte's dolls "to see what they were thinking about."

Charlotte burned with curiosity to see how things worked, to know how they were put together. The square-jawed girl with dark hair falling loose to her shoulders had no faculty for making dolls' clothes, but their furniture she could make skillfully. "I could do anything with tools," if not with a needle.

Out of sight of their mother, Charlotte and Charlie searched out the smells and noisy excitements along Boston's wharves. By the time she was six, often along with John Gibbs Gilbert, who had been born in the house next door, she knew the fun of clambering among the crates waiting for shipment, the rich smelling coils of oily rope, the bales of teas and spices. One of her favorite games was leaping, joyous and terrified, out over the chasm of water that lay between the wharf and the deck of some swaying vessel.

One morning she misjudged the distance. Screaming, she fell head first into the icy water. Panic-stricken, the boys stood helpless, watching the terrible thrashing, then the grayish bubbles that marked the place where Charlotte had disappeared.

Before Charlie could run for his father, an older boy suddenly came running, stripping off shirt and shoes, and dived in. In a few moments, he reappeared with Charlotte, gasping and choking, under one arm. He hauled his dripping burden onto the dock. Crying, she could not speak; her teeth chattered. When he saw she was not hurt, he went his way, leaving a pair of dockhands to carry her to her father.

Elkanah reprimanded her, then wrapped her in a large jacket and sent her home. Opening the door to the sneezing girl and her wide-eyed brother, Mary Eliza would have meted out heavier punishment if Charlotte had not immediately developed a heavy cold. But the girl needed no firmer rebuke. She would always remember that terrifying incident.

On March 17, 1822, a second daughter was born to Elkanah and Mary Eliza. Susan would grow up the "pretty" sister, the dainty one of the two. Before Susan, Charlotte had only barely suspected the value of personal beauty, but she soon learned that her little blue-eyed sister could set off gales of compliments with the merest tilt of her delicate chin, the slightest cut of her eyes. Charlotte herself had never garnered any such praise. If the fact dismayed her at first, it soon translated into the broader swagger she injected into her games.

Playing with Charlie and the boys, Charlotte wasted no thought on her looks—or on the quiet little Susan content at home with her dolls. Whether playing bandits among the rocks and trees or skating on Frog Pond, she led the group. To invent a plan was to put it into action; to imagine a game was to play it—with Charlotte appointing the captains and laying out all the boundaries.

She had a passion to imitate everything—the gibberish she heard from a swarthy sailor on Long Wharf, the dour Bostonian riding by stiff and officious in his black coach. Around the fire on winter evenings, she could match Grandmother Babbit in mimicking voices and gestures and faces, especially when Charlie or Susan cried out, "Now be a pig, Charlotte! Now be a lobster! Now be old Miss Gaines!"

As time passed, the family came more and more to relish the quick laughter she could set off with the subtlest change in her voice, her royal air in sweeping the crumbs from under the table or grandly poking the fire. For upstairs, to their helpless grief and distress, Grandmother Babbit now lay dying of cancer.

The circle at Mary Eliza's knee was complete by 1825, when another son, Augustus Babbit, was born. Just as Grandmother Babbit had once amused Charlotte with songs and imitations, Charlotte now delighted this tiny brother with her own oinks and whinneys and squeals. As he grew out of infancy, little Augustus' high spirits delighted his elder sister. Though nine years divided them, Charlotte felt a special bond with this brother. She saw in Augustus a mind and fertile imagination like no one else's in the family. She knew from the start that this "was by far the cleverest of my mother's children."

Charlotte's mimicry did not always find such a happy audience as Augustus. When the Reverend Mr. Henry Ware, minister of Second Church, came to call, she watched him, his chin in his hands, resting his elbows on the table. Over the teacups, his easy talk with Mary Eliza proceeded pleasantly until Charlotte began mouthing his words. When Mary Eliza saw her, she reprimanded her sharply: "Take your elbows off the table and your chin out of your hands; it is not a pretty position for a young lady!" If Ware recognized the parody, he gave no sign, though he could hardly have missed it.

The reprimand did nothing to spoil Charlotte's interest in Henry Ware. She early formed a deep attachment for the minister and for the venerable hall where he preached. No longer fashionable or wealthy, Boston's Second Church had an age of history behind it; from its curved mahogany pulpit Increase and Cotton Mather had thundered their Puritan warnings. Its rectangular tower had rung out the knells and tolls and joyous peels of a whole community's biography. By Charlotte's time, the church had become solidly Unitarian. The good Mr. Ware preached the liberal view of a reenvisioned Christianity, challenging his hearers to see proof of God's love in the unity pervading God's creation, the harmony open to the simplest understanding. At his death, Charlotte wrote a monody expressing her grief.

Though Henry Ware's sermons were filled with sunshine, the workaday mood of Boston was otherwise. The dour negations of the earliest Puritans still shadowed the daily life of the town. Sundays were serious, a matter of blue-law control. In many families there was no Sunday cooking, no pleasure reading, no play. Sundays were for church attendance, for Bible study and prayer. In spite of their growing worldly interests, many Boston hearts still pondered the age-old Calvinist question: "Am I doomed to burn forever in Hell?" still firmly certain that God tolerated mankind's whims only at His pleasure.

The Boston of Charlotte's early youth had only one theatre. Built at the corner of Franklin Avenue and Federal Street in 1794, when the town finally lifted its official opposition to drama, the Federal Street Theatre stood a monument to the community's slowly altering values. An elegant structure with a projecting arcade wide enough to shelter arriving carriages, it had spacious saloons and Corinthian columns throughout its interior. Though some years would pass before Charlotte attended her first performance, she early sensed the excitement that surrounded the pros and cons of theatre. If "entertainment" stood at the heart of Boston's dilemma, its theatre sometimes raised additional questions.

Like other American cities of the period, Boston sensed in the English stars who appeared on its stage the snobbery of Mother England toward the new country struggling to break its European strings. "English managers, English actors, and English plays . . . must be allowed to die away among us, as usurpers of our stage," Whitman would later write in his Brooklyn *Eagle*. Native theatres could lead the fight against despotism, could scorn all bigotry, all affectations, avarice and "unmanly follies."

With just such follies, Edmund Kean had enraged Boston in 1821 by his refusal to play to a small house, though that house demanded a show, not its money. Four years later, when the arrogant Englishman dared to appear in Boston again, the crowd exploded into an angry mob. Shouting and hooting, it broke windows and doors and pelted Kean on stage. For all its pious doubts about "entertainment," a city's image had been insulted, a nation's stature had been scorned.

Charlotte may have witnessed the riot. At all events, theatre was news in her formative years, whether as an arena for international rivalries or as a bright facade on Federal Steet where glamor sold for the price of a ticket, where the charm of costume and disguise and the stories spelled out by the fabled men and women occupying its boards came home to Charlotte on the lips of her young Uncle Augustus Babbit, who attended it regularly.

For Charlotte, Babbit's accounts became the material for playlets of her own. The front steps at 110 Richmond Street were her stage during the middle years of her childhood. She was a schoolgirl now; by now she was feeding a bottomless appetite for words, pantomime, and stories fleshed out and dressed in the skirts and shawls from her

8

mother's storage chests. With Uncle Augustus encouraging her, she needed only the tall front steps or the attic at the top of the stairs. The parts she played and the gestures and costumes appropriate to them were as delicious now as her earlier forays over the hills.

The holidays of her youth fed her hunger for drama and display. The Fourth of July was a frenzied medley of bells and echoing cannons from Beacon Hill, ringing orations and flags, military parades with fifes and drums along one side of the Common, games and foot-races whirling the dust, and great showers of fireworks streaking the night sky. For days afterward, Charlotte and her friends would still be translating the day's sparkle and tempest into mimes and speeches.

Charlotte may have started school as early as four. At the time, Boston sent its young to public schools taught by middle-aged "dames" —who might or might not be suitably skilled. Charlotte's childhood neighbor, Mary A. Livermore, who became the most popular female lecturer of her day, recalled the dreary school which Charlotte probably attended. It was "kept" by Ma'am Adams, a shrewish tyrant who dozed in her chair, took snuff, drank tea—or nipped Santa Cruz rum from a bottle stowed in a cupboard. The room was furnished with hard benches, so high that the feet of the children dangled in midair. If a bench tipped over, as it often did, the class set up a savage howl for sheer joy at the noise. If the dame dropped off to sleep, the room broke into pandemonium; the children darted about the room, throwing their spelling cards out the window, sometimes even dashing into the street. When Ma'am Adams awoke, she tore through the room brandishing a switch, raining its stinging blows on bad and good alike.

From such a primary school, Charlotte moved on to grammar school, probably the Hancock on Hanover Street. Here boys and girls were taught separately, never playing together during recess, never using the same stairs or doors. They sat stiffly on long benches before tall desks; no child was permitted to slump against the desk behind. The schoolroom windows flooded light directly in the children's eyes. A blazing fireplace at each end attempted to warm the room. Despite the discomforts, good teaching occurred in such hostile surroundings, and Charlotte developed an early skill as a reader.

For Charlotte, these childhood years held a sort of primal joy in being alive. Recognizing the high-spirited child she was, her mother held her in check with a loose rein; Mary Eliza's own penchant for song and laughter understood the penchant for joy in the child. If there was a watchword for Charlotte's early childhood, the word was "laughter."

The sound of that laughter became precious in the Cushman household in 1825, the year of Augustus' birth, the year the family's income began suffering serious decline. Though the times favored success in merchandizing and shipping, Elkanah's business methods exposed him to difficulties he could not wholly control. On the long voyages to the West Indies, Topliff and Cushman's sales agents could make the difference between the firm's realizing high profits and total loss: once out of Boston harbor these supercargoes controlled all financial arrangements. On their own, they decided profit margins and terms of sales. Conducting its business by such means, the company suffered almost inevitable mismanagement and fraud from its supercargoes. Topliff and Cushman was too small a firm to weather for long a string of such losses.

The impact of the business decline came home to Charlotte when her parents faced the fact that straitening family circumstances required a move to humbler quarters. Reluctantly, they left 110 Richmond Street in 1825. It was the first of a series of uprootings that would take the family over the next ten years to Centre Street during 1825 and 1826, to Spring Street in West Boston during 1827, to 161 Court Street during 1828, and to other places—most of them still adjacent to Second Church and Long Wharf—one even across the river in Charlestown.

Sadly regretting the moves, Mary Eliza became in the process the pivotal point for her family. However deeply her face might reflect her troubles, the children found their security in her. As the mother took on more and more responsibility, the father figured less and less in the family's routine. Charlotte's masculine contacts during this period were her brothers and her Uncle Augustus, seldom her father, whose age and fiscal worries by now prevented his being the strong responsible head he might have been. Elkanah drifted as the family moved. As his children grew, his business dwindled. With a wife so much his junior, with a family of children at least twenty years younger than the son and daughter of his first marriage, he found the rhythm and pattern of their lives more and more difficult.

It was young Uncle Augustus Babbit, only thirteen years older than she, who first took Charlotte to the theatre. What her father lacked in spark and interest, this uncle possessed abundantly. Handsome, careful of his dress, Augustus usually sported a tall, white wing collar and neckcloth when he was not garbed for his trade, the sea. He encouraged Charlotte with prizes for her studies, especially music and penmanship. Like his parents and his sister, Mary Eliza, he delighted in music and singing; he had a special interest in theatre. When the Tremont Theatre was built in 1827 to compete with the venerable house on Federal Street, Augustus Babbit underwrote part of its cost.

In the theatre season of 1826–27 the great English tragedian, William Macready, made his first American tour. A top star at London's two legitimate theatres, Drury Lane and Covent Garden, Macready played a resoundingly successful engagement at the Park Theatre in New York and moved from there for a brief run as Coriolanus at the Boston Theatre, beginning on October 30.

The experience was totally new, totally arresting for Charlotte. The actor she saw was not handsome; his features were far from distinguished—but he outweighed the limitations of his face with the intellectual power of his acting, the flash of his incomparable blue eyes.

At his debut the year of Charlotte's birth, Macready had transported London with his "paroxysms of passion," the wild transitions of his eyes. Gradually his experiences in Covent Garden and Drury Lane had developed in Macready his own "school" of acting, an attempt at naturalness that substituted sheer violence for the classical posturing of an earlier day. He had retained the broad gestures of Sarah Siddons and John Philip Kemble, but he had tempered them with more natural speech. By 1826, Macready's "style" placed him among the greatest of English actors. Walt Whitman's later description of Macready's magnetism on stage detailed the effect Charlotte witnessed as a child. Merely walking down the stage, Macready was a king, not solely because he wore a crown and a scarlet robe; his total envelopment in the role "dilated his heart with the attributes of majesty"; royal authority flashed from his eyes. He walked with a slight roll, each shoulder thrusting forward alternately; he spoke with a particular catch of his breath at moments of greatest intensity. The sound might degenerate to an almost cough-like rasp, but Macready could suggest with it the highest reaches of passion. His electrifying pauses at such moments were the secret of all his skill, the essence of his power.

At her first exposure to such artistry, Charlotte drank in the wonder, the force of language she now heard for the first time. She went home from Macready's kingly performance alive to new ideas for games. Her attic could become the Boston Theatre; a chair or two could suggest the stage. With her friends from school rounding out the cast, she herself could play Macready. In the attic plays she began devising, she almost always reserved a masculine part for herself. The stuff in her that relished climbing trees on Boston Common, leaping from Long Wharf to the deck of some anchored vessel, was translating itself into the characters she enjoyed playing at home. She soon discovered that Macready's reading skill at the Theatre could challenge her at school.

In reading class, it came her turn to read a speech from John Howard Payne's *Brutus*. Before, she had been shy and bashful about reading aloud, afraid of her own voice. But as she now worked haltingly through the passage, her tongue suddenly loosened. She finished the lines, reading with such force that the teacher promptly sent her to the head of the class. It was a moment of artistic birth, too slight to be recognized at the time, but in the thrill that surged through her, she sensed a new capacity within herself. Years later Charlotte looked back at the child marching proudly and a little uncertainly to the front of the room and knew that at that moment the faculty had been born that became her ruling passion.

Until then her only strength at school had been arithmetic. She had a small medal to prove it, a prize her teacher had given her one day for especially good work with the figures on her slate. Charlotte had packed the medal away, against the day when Uncle Augustus would sail again into port. Now, as she moved up in the class, she heard a boy grumble, in puritanical envy: "No wonder she can read. She goes to the theatre."

It was true. Augustus Babbit was seeing to that. As a stockholder, Babbit not only held an interest in the theatre's profits; to lighten his sister's trouble, he took Mary Eliza to the theatre whenever his ship was in port. She came to know William Pelby, the theatre manager, and the bewigged and painted people backstage, and Charlotte often accompanied her. Through Uncle Augustus, Charlotte had open entrée to all the plays.

It was on such an occasion that Charlotte first heard the operetta *Bluebeard*. Now in her early teens, she organized a group of girls to produce a version of it in her attic. With neighborhood children and their mothers for audience, Charlotte sang and played the swashbuckling role of the lover Selim, garbed in what passed for white Turkish trousers, a tight-fitting jacket, a red sash at her waist and

12

a straight red feather stuck in her hair. A wooden sword slapped at her side. Charlotte's dash and command in the role overshadowed the girls who played Fatima, Irene, and Abomelique, especially at the moments when she leaped to a chair and sang out, with wide Macready gestures, "Fatima, Fatima, Selim's here!" in a voice that was already attracting attention.

Singing had long been a natural part of her games, of her simple household chores. She could shout as loudly as her brother Charles; she could out-sing all the children she knew. Now her voice was maturing into a rich contralto. By late 1828, the Cushman finances had sunk so low that Mary Eliza, with some of her own mother's spirit, concluded that she herself would have to shoulder the major load. But taking this stand was not easy; opportunities for women to work outside the home were strictly limited. She thought of teaching a school, but Elkanah's elder daughter, Isabella, had already left to manage a home of her own, and Mary Eliza's own children were too small to fend for themselves. Nor could she work in a shop. If she considered sewing flannel shirts at home on consignment from some "slop-shop" in Ann Street, the six cents per shirt she could earn discouraged her. She determined at last to move the family to a bigger house, one as ample as possible for their needs, but one especially suitable for boarders. The house she finally chose stood at 327 Main Street in Charlestown.

The family move came just in time. Working agreements between Elkanah and his partner had always rested on the shakiest unwritten foundations, but in the midst of all their growing troubles, relations between them now took a calamitous turn. Feelings became so bitter that Topliff grabbed all the firm's remaining assets and forced Elkanah into bankruptcy. Creditors took over all his property, even the family furniture.

If Charlotte resolved to seek revenge the dismal day she saw the household goods passing piece by piece out of the house—and Mary Eliza's paying guests along with them—her angry grief matched that of her sister and brothers huddled in the skirts of their weeping mother. With this failure, Elkanah Cushman's moral fiber left him; from then on, he hovered vaguely in the background of his family; he became a shadowy figure removed, in Charlotte's thinking, to the sidelines of life.

But the loss worked differently on Charlotte and her mother. By some means, they rallied their spirits; Mary Eliza recovered her paying guests. She could not guarantee ease and comfort for her children. The most she could attempt in the sudden maturity facing them was to instill in them some sense of their own resources.

Pondering the family's difficulties, Charlotte considered her own position. Her voice might indeed have some promise. Boston's church choirs were always looking for soloists. And though the work seldom paid directly, it brought trained singers into contact with people able and willing to pay for vocal instruction. Decent opportunities otherwise were slim. Of one thing she was thoroughly certain: a lifetime of boardinghouse keeping was unthinkable. For Charlotte, it was an early end to childhood, but perhaps she could sing her way.

For the Good of the Family

(1829–1835)

Charlotte found it easy enough to dream of a life built on song, but singing her way out of drudgery, singing the family into new ease and comfort, was hardly a Cinderella affair. To begin with, she must develop whatever talent a teacher might find in her. And locating such a teacher, with the meager fees her mother could pay, only complicated the dream.

Mary Eliza decided to ask a family friend, a retired sea captain named John Mackey, a straight question: Could a young lady's trained voice bring her a living? Captain Mackey and Jonas Chickering had recently founded a piano factory in Boston, and Mackey was in a position to know. His reply was positive. Even in a town where openings for women, especially in the arts, were severely limited, Charlotte ought to be able to make her way in some church connection. She could use a piano in his warehouse for practicing, and his young protégé, George O. Farmer, could pass on to her the rudiments of singing he was learning from John Paddon, the best voice teacher in town.

Charlotte began her informal lessons with Farmer in 1829, just as her formal schooling was ending. At thirteen she had mastered the practical skills—reading, writing, and arithmetic—that Boston expected its girls to know. Though "slower" females might remain in class until sixteen, the Boston School Committee made no provision beyond the basic subjects; public school could offer them nothing more. For Charlotte, age thirteen was a turning point. She might proceed to a denominational academy or a private school that taught the elegant manners of polite society, but Mary Eliza's practical values, even given the means, hardly imagined such hopes for Charlotte. Charlotte's further education—whether practical, philosophical, or moral—would have to come from the world of experience beyond the schoolroom walls. Better to look to her work with George Farmer as a step toward a solid trade than waste any dreams on elegance.

Under Farmer's elementary lead, her progress soon brought her a choir position at Second Church, where the pulpit was undergoing a change. To succeed Henry Ware, the long-beloved pillar on Hanover Street, the congregation had called young Ralph Waldo Emerson to be junior pastor. Emerson's narrow shoulders, large feet and hands, and eagle-like features soon became a familiar sight to the new girl in his choir. Every Sunday for three years she followed his highly untheological sermons, his slow evolution from liberal Unitarianism into the Transcendental speculation that eventually took him out of the ministry in 1832. In his ordination sermon on March 11, 1829, Emerson confessed his own humility: "I come to you in weakness, and not in strength. In a short life, I have yet had abundant experience of the uncertainty of human hopes."

Disavowing any role as an "ecclesiastical policeman," Emerson made his point through quiet illustrations: religion was nothing limited or partial; it had universal application; its interests were all mankind's. Charlotte heard him develop his idea of compensation, the perpetual balance of opposites, sweet and sour, young and old, "the wings of Time are black and white, Pied with morning and with night. Mountain tall and ocean deep Trembling balance duly keep." She heard the earliest stages of his doctrine of self-reliance: "the good man reveres himself, reveres his conscience, and would rather suffer any calamity than lower himself in his own esteem." One sermon interested her particularly: "A trust in yourself is the height not of pride but of piety, an unwillingness to learn of any but God himself." The self was to be trusted, for in God "the self must be perceived." What moral or intellectual excellence man ever gets out of this little plot of ground "you call *yourself,* by the sweat of your brow—is your portion."

However long such germinal ideas might take to sprout, they were not lost on the attentive girl in Emerson's choir. By the sweat of her brow, Charlotte's portion seemed increasingly to lie in music, and Emerson soon noticed the "plump, round, rosy" girl behind his pulpit singing out the joyous words of a song like Wesley's "New Year's Hymn." Unmusical himself, Emerson took a special delight

16

in the force and authority that radiated through Charlotte's voice as it ranged upward now from a full contralto.

That voice was one of Emerson's few joys between 1829 and 1832 while he struggled to shepherd his flock on Hanover Street. From the sidelines, Henry Ware offered him little help, for the turns Emerson's ideas were taking raised serious doubts about his real interest in a formal ministry. "How little love," Emerson's journal noted in October 1831, "is at the bottom of these great religious shows; congregationalism and temples and sermons,—how much sham!" If his people ever faced the truth about Unitarianism, they would discover that its strength was largely negative. The objections it raised against proud, ignorant Calvinism were about all the strength it had. The creed at Second Church was "cold and cheerless" until controversy warmed it with "fire got from below." Not more than ten people, Emerson was certain, ever truly came to hear the sermon. "The singing, or a new pelisse, or Cousin William, or the Sunday School" were the "beadles that brought and the bolt that hold" the silent faces in church each Sunday.

If the singing was an attraction, Charlotte could claim part of the credit. And for payment she gained more than fresh ideas in Emerson's choir. Her experience paid off in a heightened skill and poise, and it carried over into a new role she assumed at home.

Late in the day or between chores, she would take her stand on the front steps where neighborhood children had gathered to hear her sing. At fourteen, Charlotte discovered before this realest kind of audience a hint of a latent ability. She first tasted on her mother's steps the delight that could come from swaying a crowd's emotions. Like Whitman, noting the lonely cry of the bird, "the solitary guest from Alabama," Charlotte's own sense of her personal destiny may have awaked from that early hour, "now in a moment I know what I am for."

And stranger things were happening all around. Her childhood neighbor and playmate, John Gibbs Gilbert, had already made a theatrical debut; the tall young man was already becoming one of the country's favorite comedians.

But except for her songs and her secret wishes, life at present was grim enough. Boardinghouse keeping was no easy role, even with

Charlie old enough now to share the continual chores. At eight Susan was a pretty child, too small to help with the burdens. At five Augustus delighted them all with his sunny smile, but he could do nothing more practical.

The constant worry on Mary Eliza's brow darkened the household. The sound of her sobbing upstairs, pacing and pacing her worries, troubled Charlotte's sleep. That worried pacing in the room over the kitchen begot the urge in Charlotte, at fourteen, to save the family. Now physically mature, she was five feet six, tall for the day. Her face was plain. Her chin projected; her jaws were square like her mother's and Grandmother Babbit's. Her wide mouth turned down. Her nose was too blunt to offer any lift to her heavy expression. When she saw her face in the same glass with Susan's, she grimaced. Her one source of pride was her long dark hair, which she brushed morning and night to maintain its sheen. True, her blue eyes radiated sober intelligence, but whatever beauty sparked her face now was the rare smile that broke the mask when she looked at Augustus.

For two years Charlotte's closest friend outside the family had been young Charles E. Wiggin, son of a former employee at Topliff and Cushman. At fifteen, Charley had come back to Boston and taken a room at Mary Eliza's. Charlotte's struggles to beat her difficulties were deeply admired by Charley Wiggin. If the two saw some things differently—Charley's Baptist training only slowly let him relax and enjoy the theatre—he could celebrate and encourage whenever good fortune came Charlotte's way.

Such a stroke was Charlotte's "concert debut" on March 25, 1830, in a recital arranged by George Farmer and the new manager of "The Hall" on Franklin Avenue, Algernon S. Chase. After a guitar solo, a flute duet, and a trio singing "Sweet Home," an anonymous "young lady," said the program, would sing "Take This Rose," "Oh, Merry Row the Bonny Bark," and "Farewell, My Love." The newspapers ignored the recital, but for Charlotte the night was a milestone. Facing her family and a goodly crowd of her neighbors, she made it plain that her weary routine as a scullery maid had no connection at all with her ambitions.

Emerson's sermons surely suggested that any pattern could be broken if necessary, even crushing frustrations like a family's poverty. To be sure, her voice needed more training, but it already covered the darker contralto tones nicely, and at times it opened out into the brighter range of a full soprano. Her songs during the public recital gave Mary Eliza renewed hope that Charlotte could eventually lighten the troubles of them all. Charley Wiggin was there to applaud and approve.

Back in Emerson's choir loft, Charlotte attracted the interest of another friend of her father, Robert D. Shepherd. The power of her voice and her sincerity struck Shepherd so deeply that he offered himself as her patron: the girl deserved better instruction. George Farmer's own teacher, John Paddon, might be persuaded to accept her as a pupil. After deliberating with Mary Eliza, Paddon formally "articled" Charlotte for a period of three years. Under the contract she would serve an indentured apprenticeship; her work in Paddon's home would pay for her lessons. Though she could no longer help with the labors at home, her efforts with Paddon clearly promised more practical ends.

Something in the hard work Paddon demanded struck a favorable note in the eager daughter of English Puritans. Under her humorless new teacher, Charlotte drove herself hard. The regimen Paddon demanded quickly revealed the promise in the voice, the character in the singer. Singing the difficult Italian and English music he set before her, she soon surprised even him. For nine months she followed his exacting routine, and her progress might have continued indefinitely if another turn had not come in her life.

Early in 1833 an invitation arrived from relatives in New York. Could Charlotte come for a two-week visit? The Samuel Judds could give her a well-deserved break in all her labors, and she could return home newly refreshed for more. Paddon and Shepherd readily approved her making the journey, and Mary Eliza saw no reason to stand in her way.

Safely arrived in New York, Charlotte noticed immediately the city's quicker pace, an obvious difference from Boston's sedate routine. As the English Mrs. Trollope saw it, New York rose from the sea like Venice "in the days of her glory." With a population of 250,000, the metropolis of the New World stretched four miles north from the tip of Manhattan. In its Battery it boasted one of the world's most beautiful promenades; Broadway ran its full length between public buildings and sprawling hotels bordered by trees and grass and shops, their interiors lighted at night with gas. If another newcomer, Fanny Kemble, correctly observed an unkempt air about the place—the grass in City Hall Park that looked a bit shaggy around the white picket fence enclosing the park, the broken brick sidewalks, and the many pigs rooting free in its gutters—New York still sported a remarkable air. Men stepped aside to let a lady pass. Dress styles among the rich were entirely French; coiffures were elaborately frizzed in the French manner. On the sidewalks fruit markets displayed their wares in bright-colored mounds. Swags of dress goods draped the fronts of the shops.

Visitors like Mrs. Trollope and Fanny Kemble might note a strongly anti-British feeling among the brisk New Yorkers, but to Charlotte the city's main concern centered on its own material progress. Its newer dwellings used a warm brown stone from New Jersey, decorated with bright green window blinds. Inside, the furnishings were equally rich; the silk upholsteries and marble tables, the porcelains and mirrors were surely as fine as London's. Omnibuses with names like Lady Washington, Lady Clinton, Lady Van Rensselaer rolled through the streets. Private carriages behind spotless teams were handsomer than anything Boston could offer. Hackney coaches plied the major thoroughfares for twenty-five cents per mile.

At the Judds' urging, Charlotte's two weeks stretched into three months. Near the end of her sojourn, they broached a disturbing idea. In view of her happiness in their household and their easier life, in view of her complete captivation of them, would Charlotte consider their legally adopting her? Looked at practically, the notion had much in its favor, but the matter created in the seventeen-year-old girl a troubling dilemma. There was no doubt about the greater ease and comfort, and there was little doubt about the advantage to Mary Eliza with one less mouth to feed, one less child to worry over. And there was another advantage.

If she really expected her voice to prove her salvation, New York could offer attractions that Boston could not possibly match. Its developing taste for opera was one case in point. And its warmhearted support of the drama was another. Though the Judds were firmly opposed to the theatre themselves, Charlotte discovered early the great excitement that centered in New York's Park Theatre, where visiting stars like Charles and Fanny Kemble regularly played. Charlotte may even have seen the elegant Fanny, "better than merely beautifully," in her round of popular roles; years later she recalled her "young hero worship" of the new star.

For the Good of the Family

Only lately, New York had created a special reason for Charlotte's wishing to stay. A fully fledged opera theatre had just opened its doors at the corner of Leonard and Church Streets. The Italian Opera House foretold a long step ahead in the cultivated life of New York. Boys at its entrance met arriving carriages with the cry, "Buy a book of the opera! English and Italian!" White-vested ushers moved quickly among its aisles and the velvet chairs in its boxes. The audiences sparkled in full dress and jewelry. When the conductor tapped his baton, forty men took up their instruments, the curtain rose grandly, and the performance, Rossini's "La Gazza Ladra" perhaps, began.

With professional opera now playing to full houses in New York, the musical tone of the city seemed sure to rise steadily. Choir singers and voice teachers could see a bright day ahead with the Opera House magnifying the whole community's feel for music. Compared to New York, what could Boston now offer? Charlotte dreamed no dreams of herself on an opera stage, but if her voice held any promise at all, could she afford to go home? Yet, down deep in her heart, could her homesickness be ignored?

The question focused her uncertainty. After her three-months' absence, did she still have a place with Paddon? An articled agreement was not lightly ignored. And did she still want it, with the rather uncertain future it offered? In her dismay, she could not answer the question alone. Mary Eliza would have to decide.

The months that led to the turmoil in Charlotte had brought her mother similar concern. In the end, Mary Eliza's sense of family dictated her stand. Formal adoption into the Judd family was out of the question. Later, Charlotte would be old enough and free to decide for herself the best route toward the life she finally wanted. But for now Charlotte must come home to the family and meet with them all whatever fortune offered. When the word came, Charlotte felt no grave disappointment.

Back in Boston, she found her old singing teacher furious. His eyes sparking fire, Paddon demanded to know how so careless a pupil could dare expect further interest from him. He cancelled the articled agreement. Miss Cushman's foolish memories of New York, he said curtly, could compensate for the loss.

The problem now was to form a new plan, and in forming it Charlotte established a basic pattern for her life. Facing a problem meant defining the result she wanted, then building a strategy. The pattern whispered a certain Emersonian optimism, the echo of pulpit ideas at Second Church. Where others called defeat inevitable, Charlotte would face defeat and call it momentary delay.

At home, the floors still had to be swept, the beds aired and shaken, but there was no greater reason now for Charlotte to accept a lifetime of mopping and scrubbing than there had been at the start of her lessons with Paddon. On that, she and her mother agreed. The girl must find a new teacher.

Leaving Manhattan, Charlotte had not guessed that New York's new zest for opera might excite the country at large. But the names of Joseph and Mary Ann Wood entered her life in Boston just after the celebrated English singers had made triumphant debuts at New York's Park Theatre. When the Woods followed their widening fame north to Boston, Mary Ann needed for her two concerts a finer piano than the battered piece backstage. To find one, she and Joseph went to Captain Mackey's warehouse where Charlotte still practiced. To Mackey, Mary Ann mentioned another problem: could he suggest a local contralto who could sing a couple of duets with her?

Next afternoon, Charlotte made her way nervously to the Woods' suite at the Tremont House. Climbing the stairs, she felt suddenly foolish. How could she dare sing for the best English singers, so the papers said, ever heard in the United States? But during her audition, she relaxed a little. They were not formidable people. At the piano their coach, James G. Maeder, let her set her own pace. From her chair by the window, Mrs. Wood smiled encouragement. When she finished singing, the Woods and Maeder all cried their praise. Pressing her hand, Mrs. Wood insisted she must train her voice for opera. A gift like hers must not be wasted; such talent demanded training—and the most serious respect. Leaving the hotel, Charlotte could still hear Maeder's thundering assurance: "such a voice properly cultivated" could lead her to "any height of fortune I coveted."

Rushing home with the news, visualizing the future, Charlotte was suddenly happier than she had been since her earliest childhood. Throughout the Woods' stay in Boston, she met them almost daily for similar talks. She became Mary Ann's constant companion on strolls down the bustling sidewalks of Tremont Street, along the shady paths of the Common, with Mary Ann emphasizing again and again her certainty that Charlotte must set her sights toward a career higher than choir work or coaching. She must groom her voice for the stage.

For the Good of the Family

The concerts with Mary Ann Wood only strengthened a resolve now growing inside her. About Mary Ann herself, Boston waxed ecstatic. "If that woman will sing a dirge over my grave," cried the *Transcript,* "I will cheerfully die tomorrow." And Boston did not miss the compliment Mary Ann paid to one of its local daughters; the light from the English star brightened the name of the girl who shared it.

Boston's praise for Mary Ann Wood was a slowly evolving sign that new days were at hand for Cotton Mather's old city. In 1834 Boston stood at the threshold of a forty-year period when it would become America's literary "Parnassus." In that "brief but golden day" it would call itself the hub of America's intellectual universe. The wealth its ships brought home, the profits its industries reaped became the gold to support a Brahmin class; the money that spilled over fed a broad middle core, still loyal to its godly doctrine of hard work, but able now to afford with the fruit of its labors the finer pleasures. With a population of sixty thousand, Boston ranked in size just under New York, Philadelphia, and Baltimore. The Boston and Worcester Railroad, which extended only as far as Newton in 1834, would push to Lowell, Worcester, and Providence the following year. In residential areas that now extended eastward toward Pearl Street and Fort Hill and westward along Franklin and Tremont Streets, Boston's new middle class housed itself behind Georgian and Grecian facades, turning its back on the somber timber and stone, the negations of its Puritan past. The new Brahmins themselves moved more and more onto Beacon Hill and Beacon Street facing the Common. With Harvard to lead Boston's intellectual advance, its Unitarian ministers to preach the virtue of the enlightened mind, "improvement," particularly "self-improvement," became a Boston watchword.

At long last, "improvement" could mean artistic refinement. And a local bookseller like James T. Fields could build a succesfsul career publishing poetry and fiction that an earlier Boston would have tossed aside as wicked impracticality. By the time of Charlotte's meeting with Mary Ann Wood, Boston's enlightened citizenry could dare to encourage a local hopeful to train her voice for a larger place than a bench in a choir.

Opportunity for Charlotte knocked in another form as well. At the end of the Woods' engagement, the "remarkably fine" gift James Maeder saw in Charlotte and the wide opportunity he saw for himself in a city only beginning to sense its musical possibilities prompted

23

his decision to remain in Boston. A man of great charm, lavish with his means when he recognized talent, Maeder would take Charlotte as an articled pupil.

If the term had sour overtones, the system still offered advantages. Now Charlotte could aspire to real prominence on a concert or opera stage. Now the family could hope for an end to their money troubles. There was one factor, however, that Charlotte had not counted on.

More accurately, it was a succession of factors. For all the pleasure and release Mary Eliza had found at the Tremont Theatre with Augustus Babbit, for all the delight she took in good theatre, she was at heart devoutly Puritan. She could enjoy theatre at a safe distance, but she could not live with it. Applauding skilled players on a stage might be one thing, but seeing one's own daughter planning a life-time career among them was quite something else. Singing on stage, a painted face among the painted players, was hardly the life she had pictured for Charlotte when it first occurred to her that the girl's voice might be the family's redemption. Surely her daughter could see the chasm that lay between family need, its reputation, and the theatre as the core of her life.

For no matter how surely Boston itself was changing, the town still had its doubts about theatre. Weren't all stage people unthink-ably scarlet? Wasn't every actor's path mired with threat and temp-tation? In this risky business, could Charlotte possibly stay clean, liv-ing forever on the wave of a crowd's adoration?

Charlotte respected the argument; she knew her town well, but her mother's warnings were premature. The Woods had only sug-gested the stage; her voice still had to be trained. The day it might bring her fortune lay far, far ahead.

In all the clamor, a quieter voice now demanded a hearing. Here in her late teens, Charlotte confronted her personal affections. In the five years and more that Charley Wiggin had boarded at her table, he had become a valued friend and confidante. And dining across from her, Charley knew the family hopes that centered in this eldest daughter. Only now did he confess his own hopes. Strolling out on Long Wharf one late afternoon, Charley begged her to forget all about an opera career and marry him.

Charlotte let her gaze drift out over Boston Harbor; then she shook her head slowly. She was not ready for marriage. She was not sure she would ever be. Besides, she told Charley, nobody could tell about a career until he had tried it. Watching the light die in his

24

eyes, she reassured him. She needed more time. Like her mother's, Charley's fears were premature.

Charley Wiggin did not struggle for Charlotte's favor alone. A quick introduction at church perhaps had led young Charles Spalding to come to the boardinghouse almost daily, and by late summer, 1833, he was writing his cousin about Charlotte. She was not like most girls, he wrote, people who could seem brilliant only under the best of circumstances. Her natural zest was her charm. "She does not follow where others lead the way. She is the pioneer who opens the pathway." She never deceived. "Gay, volatile, and even reckless," she had a gift for discerning character. "I wish with all my heart that wealth and honor and high society might be bestow'd by me, to make her happy."

If this friendship led to a formal engagement, as one report claims, Charlotte's "charming" impulsiveness dismayed the boy's family. When she took a stagecoach out to meet them, she arrived seated on top between two young men. The mother of her fiancé greeted her warmly, commenting on her good luck in finding acquaintances on the same coach. "Acquaintances?" Charlotte laughed. "I never saw them before, but I am going to ride with one of them tomorrow."

When the new friend galloped up next morning leading a horse for Charlotte, she tucked up her skirts, leaped into the saddle, and raced off after him. An hour later she was back, with the friend lost a mile behind in her dust. Pondering this forward, headstrong, young person, Spalding's mother was too astonished to comment.

In time the friendship cooled, though in May 1835, when Spalding died after days of violent headaches, his father wrote Mary Eliza that his son had often alluded to Charlotte in his more lucid moments. When Charlotte sent him the miniature Charles had given her, the father wrote gratefully and enclosed a lock of the boy's hair.

Whatever grief Charlotte felt at losing a friend, at eighteen her notions about herself and her purpose were too unformed to make her mourn the loss of a lover. She might find her personal mission later. Her responsibility to the family might include marriage; eventually she might place marriage at the logical center of her life, but during her training with James Maeder she could make no permanent promises. If Charley Wiggin or anyone else came to seem right later, later there would be time. If the alternative happened, so be it. Time itself would tell.

When the Woods returned to New York, Mary Ann maintained

a steady interest in Charlotte's progress. "I am sure, my dear Charlotte, that I need not tell you how I miss you," she wrote on January 23, 1835, "and how happy I shall be to see you again, and trust you will follow my advice by practicing steadily . . . as I am most *anxious* for your success." In the margin Charlotte penciled, "The happiest day of my life [was] while reading this letter."

If Charlotte blossomed under Maeder's instruction, her contact with the man himself was no less happy. Where John Paddon had been a sober taskmaster, Maeder had a temperament like her Grandmother Babbit's, a genial wit and a sunny outlook that became even more delightful after his marriage to the young English singer, Clara Fisher, in December 1834. Clara's had been a celebrated name on the English stage ever since her debut in 1817, at age six, in Drury Lane's "Lilliputian" production of *Richard III*. Acting and singing in America had brought her additional fame, particularly in juvenile roles; her singing of "Home Sweet Home" often moved her audiences to tears. By the time she met Charlotte, she had formed a theory of acting that could apply to singing as well: never attempt to act until you can read well enough to convey the meaning of the words without moving the hands. The skills and insight Charlotte learned from both the Maeders served her well the night in April 1835 when she took her first determined step toward an operatic career.

In the time that led to that evening, Charlotte held firm to her vision. Real as her mother's objections were, they could not dash her hopes that talent and hard work—and a strong sense of moral uprightness—could make their way in the musical theatre. Certainly, she could see no moral lack in the Maeders or the Woods. Was there reason to conclude, from an assumption based on little evidence, that the stage inevitably corrupted? To oppose the assumption took courage in Boston, but in doing it, Charlotte remembered again the heady ideas she had learned at Emerson's pulpit.

Whatever thoughts Emerson might have expressed about a life in opera, he had admonished Boston to rethink a whole spectrum of subjects. Consistency to the old Puritan hobgoblins was a foolish consistency indeed; the sun shone brightly today, lighting all regions of the human intellect and sensibility. Boston must reexamine its morals. To Charlotte, bred a Unitarian and challenged in her most formative years by the young minister at Second Church to think her own thoughts, the force of his reasoning was clear. She must seek her own harmonious place in God's perfect scheme. If God created voices and the hearts to make them sing, he had blessed the arts and the stages that afforded them expression.

Within a year Emerson would publish his Transcendental manifesto, his conviction that never in history were the skies brighter than now; his *Nature* would fling the challenge to all conservatives. Sustained by such logic, Charlotte found in Maeder's connection with the Tremont Theatre and his personal interest in her talents a clear enough reason to see herself on the musical stage.

So ran the drift of her thoughts and her debates with Mary Eliza the spring of 1835. In Mackey's echoing warehouse and in her sessions with Maeder she groomed herself for various singing roles, particularly the part of Countess Almaviva in *The Marriage of Figaro*. Mozart's difficult opera had been known in New York since 1824. It had been performed in Boston, and to choose it now for a debut involved an almost impossible risk. To go well, it required a perfect ensemble; every voice needed to be a superior instrument. But in spite of its problems, Maeder was convinced that Charlotte was ready for it on April 8.

She herself was less certain. The dream of using her voice in some form of stage art appealed now more strongly than ever before, but the desire was nothing if the gift it required was lacking. Mary Eliza held her peace. Her objections stood firm, and as surely as Charlotte dreamed of a sparkling future on stage, her mother prayed that the debut would somehow redirect her daughter toward more proper ends. Temporary failure in public now would be a small price to pay for missing a lifetime of grief later.

The night before her debut, dread and misgiving troubled her sleep. Details of the ordeal ahead raced through her mind. Was her voice ready? Was Maeder correct that she could handle a soprano role, even though Almaviva's top notes were considerably higher than her natural range? And since this was opera, not a recital, would her acting be good enough? Here in the dark the debut ahead seemed like nothing but pitfalls.

At dawn, she threw off the covers and dashed into her clothes. She tapped on Charley Wiggin's door. Would he go for a walk with her? She had to do something to steady her nerves. The walk through the dim streets calmed her a little. By night, after a day packed full with a last-minute costuming and a rehearsal, she felt better, though still so tense that she begged Charley to walk with her again, this time across the river and up the hill to the Tremont Theatre.

Moving up Tremont Street past the burying ground and King's Chapel, past School Street to the theatre's Grecian facade, Charlotte completed a circle she had begun eight years before, an excited little girl with her Uncle Augustus. The night they had seen William Macready in *Coriolanus* neither she nor Augustus could have imagined the step the nervous young woman was now taking.

Lanterns swung in the wide arches over the theatre entrance. The tall columns extended upward into an ornate triangle that disappeared in the darkness above. Crowds would soon be massed at the doors, eager to hear Clara Fisher sing Susanna. And even if Charlotte's own friends and family filled only a row or so, the *Advertiser and Patriot* had spread a hopeful word that eased some of her fears: "She is said by the best musical judges to possess an extraordinary voice of great compass, rich, flexible, and sweet."

At the door she thanked Charley and told him good-bye. He wished her a wistful "good luck," knowing that any success she achieved tonight might spoil his own hopes. Then she moved through the shadows backstage to the dressing room and began struggling into the heavy costume. Clara Fisher and the others in the cast wished her well. And then she stood ready in the wings, counting the minutes of the long first act, feeling a tightness in her throat before she could make her first entrance at the beginning of Act II.

The nearly twelve hundred faces that watched Charlotte's entrance saw an eighteen-year-old girl struggling to hide her timidity and fear. As Almaviva she had a difficult task: she not only must sing well but must try somehow to ease herself so fully into the character that the audience would forget the singer. Hopefully, while she was singing, she would forget about herself.

She did not wholly succeed. In *"Porgi amor,"* when Almaviva laments that the Count no longer loves her, her notes were so quiet that the back corners of the hall could not hear. And she had trouble remembering her proper position in the scenes. Maeder and Thomas Barry, the theatre manager, had showered her with so many details that at times she felt on the verge of panic. But encouraging smiles from Clara Fisher helped settle her fears; scene followed scene more easily once she realized that the eyes of the audience were not always riveted on her, ready to note her slightest error. But her costume gave her real trouble, and nobody else could help. The whirlpool of heavy drapery around her feet threatened to trip her each time she tried to move, to act as well as sing the Countess' tearful emotions.

In spite of her fears, the long performance was interrupted again and again with cheers. Though they were mainly for Clara, Charlotte tasted the sweet delight of knowing that some were also for her. When her voice rang out in the happy ensemble at the end of Act IV, her fears and doubts had disappeared in a bounding inner gladness that, while she might not have wholly succeeded, she had not wholly failed. The applause at the final curtain sounded sweeter than any music she had heard.

She left the stage elated. The stormy applause had not been simply polite. It was more than a friendly gesture toward a local girl who promised to make good. When Mary Eliza and Susan and Charlie pushed into her dressing room, their faces reflected her own joy that she had safely leaped her first hurdle. Mary Eliza said nothing to spoil the victory, though on Charley's face Charlotte caught the shadow of a warm friend's happiness mixed with a lover's dismay.

In the days that followed, the papers loudly echoed Charlotte's own joy. One critic complained that she put less energy into her part than "it would bear," but Charlotte blamed that on her heavy costume. "There is but one opinion expressed in and out of the house," cried the *Atlas,* "Miss Cushman's success was brilliant." Her voice, in spite of her youth, was superior to that of any other American heard thus far in Boston. "She does honor to her teacher, Mr. Maeder." In spite of obvious nervousness, her acting had a "very respectable character." With her "good person," she held the stage with a proper grace and dignity. If Boston had enough musical taste to appreciate a really fine singer, the young lady would become "deservedly a great favorite." To the *Pearl* and *Literary Gazette,* the much she still had to learn was splendidly matched by the great knowledge she already had. As an actress she showed much promise. And a newspaper notice from faraway New York opened her eyes a little wider to her possible future. "A Miss Cushman is doing wonders at the Tremont, in opera," reported the *Spirit Of The Times.* "If she should succeed at the Park, Mr. Manager Barry will make his fortune—perhaps." New York, it seemed, was far from a closed issue.

In the height of her new celebrity, John Paddon took an ad in the *Transcript* to say that while he was happy in Miss Cushman's success, that while he had joined her other friends at the Tremont to cheer her efforts, he must state for the record that he had already given her much instruction "before any such name as Maeder was heard of in this city." No one could possibly think that a voice could be brought to stage quality in a few short months. Miss Cushman had studied only briefly with Maeder, and it was easy to see how little credit he could claim. Paddon considered himself "the *substantial cause*" of Miss Cushman's success.

Paddon might better have swallowed his injured pride. Charlotte herself stilled the mild tempest that broke out in the Boston press. Maeder, she stated, deserved full credit. Paddon himself had said that when she broke her articled agreement he saw no promise in her. Paddon finished the paper byplay with another paid note in the *Atlas*: "I only feel for Miss Cushman a very sincere, and indeed *anxious* desire for her success."

The debut on April 8 led to another appearance in the same role on the thirteenth, again to high acclaim, "less embarrassed" than on the first occasion. On the twenty-first and twenty-second, before she felt fully ready, Maeder presented her in an opera version of *Cinderella,* but here her efforts failed. The *Pearl* found her music "imperfect"; she needed more study before she could hope to compete with "stars"; as an actress she needed "grace." On the fourth of June, after more hard work and redoubled efforts, she sang Julia Mannering in an opera version of Scott's *Guy Mannering: Or The Gypsy's Prophecy.*

Throughout the summer, her spirits stayed high, if somewhat less than joyous after her drubbing as Cinderella. She had found the profession in which she wanted to work. And the labor it demanded was still worth the cost. She filled her days vocalizing with Maeder, learning new roles, anticipating the day when the Woods would return for a fall engagement in Boston. Her gratitude toward the Woods was boundless. On October 6, Charlotte was the Countess Almaviva to Mary Ann's Susanna. Neither the *Advocate* nor the *Atlas* fully applauded her performance; the *Atlas* could see "but little improvement in her singing and none in her acting," though it was "no faint praise to say that she appears well even beside Mrs. Wood."

By late fall Maeder knew that in Charlotte he had a promising find, a singer of professional caliber. Why not take her with Clara and him to fill a singing engagement in New Orleans? Charlotte had already anticipated his question. Life on an opera stage was clearly a matter of constant travel. One willingly accepted the vagabond life it required.

But Maeder's question was difficult. Her mother would have strong opinions, though she would have to admit now that Charlotte's voice had promise, that it was indeed a practical instrument that might bring financial rewards for them all. And just as truly, in her singing she had something valid to offer. Heads could shake and objections could thunder, but she would proceed with her plans. If it gave any comfort to Mary Eliza, she would prove once and for all that working on the stage she could still stand firmly on the side of morality. Her mother must throttle her fears.

And for the last time a problem centered in Charley Wiggin. Years later a New York paper failed to name the young man, but if the story was true, Charlotte broke once and for all Charley's hopes that she would give up this "unwomanly proceeding" and marry him. The only clear road she saw for herself—and for the good of the family—was the long road south to New Orleans and the public stage. Charley would watch her movements from a distance, he would marry a local girl and succeed in other ways, but he would never become fully reconciled to the loss he suffered when the opera stage outbid him for Charlotte's affection.

Whatever pain her decision cost her, marriage to Charley Wiggin had no place in Charlotte's dreams by late fall, 1835. When James and Clara Maeder persuaded her to cast her lot with theirs, she set her sights on the warm southern clime of New Orleans where new adventure and the truest test of her self-reliance waited.

Finding a Place in New Orleans

(1835–1836)

Already the biggest hurdle was passed. Without changing her mother's views, the long talks between them had only confirmed Charlotte's determination to be a singer. If Unitarianism had prepared her for anything, if Emerson had expressed any truth, she saw herself now, standing calm and unruffled, in a universe of uncertainties. The intuitive voice within her seemed to be indicating her proper place.

Still, logic and intuition could not scatter all the clouds in her heart the afternoon in late November when she took her long farewell of Mary Eliza and Susan, her tall brother Charles, and the large-eyed, unsmiling little Augustus. She begged them to write, then cried that there was really no cause for tears; in a few months she could send home money enough to take them out of the boardinghouse forever. Then bundles in hand, she made her way up the gangplank, turned, and smiled a little too cheerfully down to the huddled figures struggling to return her smile. The hope of later reunion would have to sustain them all.

But in Mary Eliza, deeper fear trembled. Catholic New Orleans was hardly civilized; in morals and outlook it stood a universe away. Even worse, it was diseased. In October 1832, yellow fever had carried off five thousand people; one-sixth of the city had died. In the summer of 1833 fever had killed more thousands. Every city could expect to pay some annual toll to pestilence, but New Orleans seemed uniquely sick. How could Charlotte expose herself to such risks, the family to so much worry, so far away?

Charlotte had faced the big question. She regretted the family's worry about her, she understood fully their sense of loss as she told them good-bye, but the family must bear in mind its responsibility to her. She must do what she must. Her judgment and the temper of the times said go. Wealth at the end of the rainbow, free land at the end of the trail had long been popular refrains along the eastern seaboard; their echoes extended at least as far back as the Puritan "Adventurers" pushing into the wind off Southhampton, and as far ahead as the white lines of wagons plodding westward beyond the Appalachians and the Mississippi. It took stuff to brave the journey: the destiny in it could not be denied.

With her own determination fully intact, Charlotte pioneered by taking her stance on the swaying deck of a tall ship named, interestingly enough, The *Star*—even if doing so was a little strange. The few young women who left home in the 1830s usually went as wives, armed like their men with high hopes and long rifles. Single girls at nineteen rarely imagined themselves in such a parade. It would be years before Charlotte would see anything peculiar in her forthright shouldering of her family's load. Like the old Puritans, she mingled her hopes for new freedom with a stern conviction. If this trip had much to do with freedom to live as she wanted, it had much to do with duty. The will of God and the duty to those at home looking to her for help sat squarely upon her.

The *Star* docked in New York for only a day. Charlotte considered making a quick farewell to the Judds, but knowing their views toward theatre, she thought better of it. Later she wrote to Sam Judd, "I feared for my reception and would rather not have seen you at all than braved your unkindness to me," though the Judds had never been unkind, only concerned lest she make a fatal mistake. This business of becoming a stage person, of facing up to one's destiny, exacted its toll.

Leaving New York, Charlotte first felt the rhythm peculiar to all actors, the continual round of departures that sets their measure, the perpetual journey that becomes for them their only settled place. For Charlotte, this break with all the world she knew determined her destination, the sparkling new stage of the St. Charles Theatre now nearing completion in far-off New Orleans. Aboard the *Star,* Charlotte noted her fellow passengers, some like herself recruits for the new St. Charles: James and Clara Fisher Maeder and their infant; the young Louisa Lane just beginning her own career; and several Italian musicians.

For nine days, the *Star* trailed its easy wake over the swells around Cape Hatteras, then through the Florida Straits into the Gulf toward the mouth of the brown Mississippi. Entering the Balize, the *Star* met another ship with other recruits direct from England, the soprano Mrs. Gibbs and the comedian Latham. At the docking, a flurry of happy congratulations tore through all the St. Charles people; their chatter about the promising times ahead only heightened Charlotte's own tense elation.

Descending the plank, she saw a harbor at once like Boston's and once like no other place in the world. For a Long Wharf, New Orleans had a vast three-mile levee holding in check the Mississippi's lazy flood. It could service a whole flotilla of merchant ships; dozens of strangely flagged and painted vessels plied their business directly along it; storehouses and cotton presses stretched in a long busy line. Steamboats squatted at anchor, more elaborate than any Charlotte had seen plying the Hudson to Albany or the waters of Long Island Sound. Pushing and heaving among them, crude rafts and low-slung arks from the upper river and its tributaries hugged the water line. Boatmen in fur caps and buckskin poled their makeshift crafts among the larger vessels. Sweating black slaves sang in time to the rhythm of the heavy loads they swung in an endless line from ship deck to drays waiting on the docks.

In the flat green city that stretched beyond the levee, Charlotte sensed immediately the distance she had covered. Her voyage out of Massachusetts Bay had left behind, along with the familiar chill of New England's winters, its tight-lipped restraints and material push. A casual air here swayed the palms; dwellings and shops nestled in tangled vines and climbing roses. In this heavy air, where the forty thousand people of New Orleans moved easily along the low-curbed streets, New England's sharp-edged convictions had little place.

Charlotte soon discovered that though Americans had been making their inroads in New Orleans apparent ever since 1803, housing themselves under spreading oaks and magnolias in the Garden District, pushing their commercialism into the character of the town, they had scarcely loosened the ties New Orleans still maintained with its older culture. Corn pudding and roast beef found little favor; tastes still ran to light sauces and fine wines. Back home, Boston thrust its Georgian towers skyward from the top of its rocky hills, but New Orleans basked in the heavy sun of its gardens, the rain dripping from the green iron of its verandahs.

The new St. Charles Theatre was meant to accommodate the city's American interests and the vast wave of English-speaking transients that flowed into town each winter. When Charlotte arrived, the influx from the plantations and the hinterland upstream had already begun. In the course of a winter as many as forty thousand temporary faces might swell the crowds on New Orleans streets. Sharp-eyed Yankees, large-boned Kentuckians, loud Texans, and tall Virginians compounded a drama that erupted almost nightly in some sidewalk fracas, some altercation in a saloon. Among them swaggered the effete Louisiana planter, redolent of the air of old France, with his mannered confidence, his finely balanced temper. Indians skulked around the coffeehouses and markets. To the Irish comedian Tyrone Power, the special flavor of life in New Orleans was its blend of characters newly arriving each autumn.

This was the crowd that Charlotte came to know best in New Orleans. The public she observed was largely masculine. The women of the parlors, the ballrooms, and promenades were beyond her reach and her notice. She would see the female population in fleeting glimpses, moving under male escort and peering seductively from behind their lace veils in the dark boxes at the St. Charles.

In this hedonistic city, she came only slowly to know anything beyond the neighborhood of the St. Charles. The theatre set her boundaries; her quick daily walks to and from work and the tall garret she rented in a house nearby spelled her major contacts with the life so clearly opposite from that of Boston. But Mary Eliza had been right about one feature of New Orleans. Even the shortest walk exposed one to the most incredible smells. Stagnant gutters and ditches ran through all its streets, the breeding ground no doubt of every kind of pestilence. And indirectly word would reach her about the passions that quickly flowered, then as quickly withered in pistol smoke under the giant oaks of City Park or in the garden behind the Cathedral.

Faced with the subtle charm and temptations of New Orleans, Charlotte did not forget her reason for coming. At nineteen, she might sense the wide gulf between her own healthy square looks and the enticing grace behind the lace veils, but her Yankee practicality looked beyond this life of pleasure toward the profit it could bring. From whatever idle amusement she might give New Orleans as an opera singer, she hoped to reap a more practical joy. The path to fortune and happiness for her was the narrow line of hard work at the St. Charles.

In a sense, her contract at the St. Charles was the fruit of another man's labor. James H. Caldwell, once a leading English comedian at Manchester and Bath, had emigrated to America in 1817, but his work at the Charleston theatre had created difficulties. His quarrels with the manager had led to a duel, the duel had set off a riot that wrecked the theatre, and Caldwell had fled to New Orleans. Here he had amassed a fortune, become a social leader, and was just now realizing his greatest dream, the building of the finest theatre in America. He still acted occasionally, but by now his major interest centered in the business aspects of theatre and his franchise to light the city with gas. The love of his life was divided between his lavish new playhouse and the actress, Jane Placide, for whom he had erected it.

The house had few equals. Abroad, only the opera houses in Naples, Milan, and St. Petersburg could match it. Built at a cost of $325,000, an incredible sum for the day, soaring dramatically above the adjacent buildings, its tall Corinthian and Doric columns set it abruptly apart. Its parquet floor, the four tiers of boxes, and a high gallery for Negroes extending almost to the domed ceiling could seat four thousand people. Its private boxes, the only area for women, were richly curtained and finished in mahogany. A massive gas chandelier weighing over two tons shed brilliant light through thousands of cut-glass drops. Charlotte could only gaze up at the light and the vast reaches of the theatre and feel amazed.

On December 1, 1835, the date set for her New Orleans debut, the theatre was not wholly finished. Rains had delayed the work repeatedly; one incredible deluge had lasted ninety days. A temporary chill and lack of cheer filled it. It was not an easy place for a debut. Nor were the high standards New Orleans demanded an easy challenge to face.

In spite of its casual air, New Orleans brooked no compromise in its art. Its sophisticated Creoles had long ago set one of the most exacting standards in the theatre world, and that standard had carried over into its English-speaking audiences. Once seated, once the curtain had lifted, they held themselves silently attentive. No "society buzz" vied with the voices on stage; except between acts, there was no visiting from box to box. Before such people an actor had little chance to conceal a bungled sentence, a slurred phrase, a fault in timing. Not until the end of a scene did the crowd express any reaction. If it approved, its bravos rang splendidly; its delight was inspiration to the actor. But its disapproval could paralyze; its cold silence could terrify even a veteran.

Another factor in New Orleans life was no less disturbing. For all its interest in current affairs, its concern for cotton and slave prices and the business picture in general, its fascination with the Washington and New York scenes, and the bitter campaign currently raging beyond the Sabine in Texas where American settlers were struggling for freedom from Mexico, New Orleans paid careful heed to its theatre critics. It followed religiously the highly articulate voices of the *Bee* and the *Picayune,* opinions that could make or break a beginning career.

Charlotte's earlier fears in Boston did not begin to match the icy dread that surged through her now, alone on this gigantic stage. No papers had given her any comforting advance publicity; no Charley Wiggin was on hand to commend her to the theatre; no friendly support smiled up at her from a full row of friends and relatives. In her mind a single thought stood uppermost. This one first night could make or break her hopes for a whole season—and the bright dreams of a whole family. Young as she was in the theatre, her run at the Tremont had taught her that every appearance on stage brought new unknowns, a fresh chance to triumph, a new chance to fail. Audiences guaranteed nothing. By the rules of the game, she would stand this night on her professional merits alone.

Almost in panic, she had one slight comfort. She was opening in a familiar role, the Countess Almaviva. And she had the warm wishes of Clara Fisher Maeder as the Cherubino and of Mrs. Gibbs as Susanna.

The men in the audience—the planters and merchants, the transients not yet settled down for a break in their high-life in town—and the stiff formal groups in the boxes sat through a performance that left few of them happy. If they did not shout down her embarrassingly bad efforts, neither did they applaud. Charlotte's taut nerves, her short breath, her heavy movements in her costume brought her almost to the verge of collapse. Her top tones came out incredibly shrill. The final curtain mercifully ended a fiasco.

The silence in Charlotte's own records of the night matched the silence of her first New Orleans audience, but the papers of December 4, after her second attempt in Mozart's opera, give more than a clue to the reason. The *Bee* praised Clara Maeder for her acting and gave mixed praise to Mrs. Gibbs for a voice that was soft and sweet though deficient in volume, but for the newcomer, Charlottle Cushman, it expressed only derision. For all the weakness of Mrs. Gibbs' voice, it was "greatly superior to that of Miss Cushman, who made the worst countess we have had the honor of seeing for some time." Mrs. Gibbs was "a second rate singer," but Miss Cushman was only "bearable."

37

Facing such bitter words, Charlotte's silence veiled her calamity. She was contracted for an entire season, but who could say if her later efforts would elicit happier reactions in this appalling city? She might yet find her bearings on this formidable stage—using whatever talent she had thought she had—but logic could not ease her disappointment. The future that had glowed so brightly in Boston now lay at her feet.

Later reports would declare that in New Orleans Charlotte lost her singing voice gradually, but from the first the *Bee's* criticisms tell a different story. The promise she had shown in Boston had disappeared completely by the time she made her bow at the St. Charles. If it was nerves, if it was the change in climate, if it was the newness of the barn-like theatre, or the soprano role that Maeder had cast her in—when strictly speaking she had always been a contralto—the odds were stacked against a brilliant beginning. While the chance to sing with the best theatre orchestra in America might have offered encouragement, it had only increased her fears. The twelve hundred seats of the Tremont had seemed a reasonable limit to carry, but the four thousand seats and the towering height of this palace-like theatre had proved something else. After a third lamentable performance on December 10, Caldwell withdrew *The Marriage of Figaro;* the ability of Charlotte Cushman and the other singers had proved no match for the theatre's lofty expectations.

Though Charlotte's lamentable efforts that first night foretold her early end as a singer, she tried valiantly during the remaining five months of her contract to please in other singing roles. On December 5, she sang the Princess of Navarre in Isaac Pocock's *John of Paris.* On the sixteenth, she was the Patrick of O'Keeffe's *The Poor Soldier.* Sympathetically, James Murdoch recalled seeing Charlotte's first appearance as a singer forced to tax her uncertain powers in too large a hall. But dressed in her soldier costume, Charlotte impressed Murdoch with her "fixed and determined purpose," a subtle clue that she still had other resources.

The papers remained unsparingly caustic; were this Miss Cushman not a pupil of Maeder, on whose recommendation Caldwell had employed her, "she would not be thrust forward in and out of season." The *Bee* granted Charlotte some acting ability, particularly in her hoarsely rendered recitations, but "we would as soon hear a peacock attempt the carols of a nightingale as to listen to her squalling caricature of singing." Seldom in tune, she possessed neither "taste nor skill."

As for the Maeders, for all their earlier confidence, they could not conscientiously argue that the papers were wholly wrong. But James Caldwell, more sympathetic than the papers, was not so easily swayed. He kept her busy, halfheartedly learning other singing parts. Throughout the weeks that led up to New Year's, she seldom left her garret room except to appear on stage. The Christmas revelry down in the streets only heightened her own despair, studying alone at the top of the stairs.

On January 4, 1836, she sang Lucy Bertram in *Guy Mannering.* In New Orleans no critic took it seriously enough to comment. On January 8, she recited the dramatic reading, *The Standard of Liberty,* recalling Andrew Jackson's New Orleans victory against the British in 1815. In this she achieved enough success to merit repeating it on January 16. She played a nonsinging Lady Freelove in Colman's *The Jealous Wife* on January 20. A week later Caldwell gambled again on her singing voice as Clymante in Dimond's opera, *My Native Land.* On February 5 she sang "Rise, Gentle Moon" in a musical medley by Gilbert. As Gillian, she sang several brief songs in a play called *The Quaker.* She played Margaretta in *Rule a Wife and Have a Wife* with the English star, Thomas Cooper, and the company's tragedian, James Barton, also a transplant from England.

Those labor-filled weeks added up to a long wistful struggle against almost impossible odds. Only blind determination and a certain honesty made her keep working. Her living and the small sums she contrived to send home to Mary Eliza depended on her playing the roles assigned, however much she might tell herself that the *Bee*'s stings foretold unavoidable failure. In rare odd moments, she eked out her small income by copying "lengths" of parts for other actors. During the long months of the spring of 1836, stricken with the bitterest homesickness, she tried to prepare herself for the day when she must return in defeat to Boston.

She tried and failed again on April 11. Though her role as one of the wicked sisters in Lacy's *Cinderella* called for no important singing, the *Bee* laughed at her. "Miss Cushman can sing nothing . . . in mercy to the audience," in justice to herself, she should limit herself to acting parts, in which she could perform "with success."

If newspaper venom ever affected the course of an artistic career, the *Bee*'s hostility on April 12 spelled the beginning, not the end, for Charlotte. Unbeknown to Maeder, whose goodwill she had come to doubt in New Orleans' repeated scorn of her voice, she pondered what other recourse she might have. Gathering her courage, she went to James Caldwell. Though a shrewd businessman and a master manipulator of the people in his employ, the owner of the St. Charles gave her a sympathy born of grief. Jane Placide had recently died; his own hopes for the time ahead had vanished in disappointment. In the face of Charlotte's sour reception, Caldwell might have cancelled her contract; he might have sent her home to Mary Eliza's knowing looks and the willing arms of Charley Wiggin.

Instead, Caldwell gave her advice: "You ought to be an actress, and not a singer." She should study some straight dramatic parts. Explaining her problem, he commended her to his tragedian, James Barton. Barton took her in hand.

In later years Clara Maeder and Charlotte would remember differently the incidents leading to the night of April 23, 1836. To Clara, Charlotte's difficulties were due to the girl's own willfulness: the work of practicing her singing roles was too "arduous"; she was "badly stage-struck." But Charlotte, just as surely, would blame her difficulties in part upon Maeder, for forcing her into roles too high because he needed "the upper register of my voice, which as his wife's voice was a contralto, it was more to Mr. Maeder's interest to use than the lower one." Whether Maeder was to blame or not, Charlotte's loss of her singing powers was a step toward a brighter day. In place of the singing voice that had promised such high rewards, a powerful speaking voice had gradually emerged, a voice that could range from the deepest baritone to a delicate treble.

Barton had already noted Charlotte's penchant for acting. Since there was always room in the theatre for an energetic young woman who could speak lines intelligently, Barton echoed Caldwell's own counsel: "You're a born actress; go on the stage. You cannot fail; you must succeed." Charlotte had already proved her ability as a dramatic reader. Barton was soon to appear in *Macbeth;* perhaps Charlotte could play opposite him.

If the thought of attempting an exacting role like Lady Macbeth dismayed her, it did not prevent her from setting to work immediately. Except for a brief respite on April 18 and the following two nights to play Helen MacGregor in *Rob Roy,* a straight role she played in a man's Scotch bonnet and a brace of pistols, she kept herself closeted in her room, pouring over her lines.

The challenge was large. Ever since Mrs. Siddons had taken the role to new heights in the late eighteenth century, the part of Lady Macbeth had been considered the acme of the tragedienne's art. Long an admirer of the Siddons–Kemble school of acting, Barton's scholarly notions of stage art, his studious habits, his retiring nature, his gentlemanly manner put Charlotte at ease; under his guidance, she took heart. Perhaps, if she had any future, it lay on the legitimate stage, as Barton and Caldwell and the ill-tempered *Bee* suggested.

Together in her garret room, Barton and Charlotte worked again and again through the heavy rhythms. Barton remembered seeing the great Mrs. Siddons. Her Lady Macbeth had been infinitely feminine. Deeply in love with her husband, insanely ambitious for him, she had been a subtle wife who ruled her mate with a caress, spurring him to crime and violence with a kiss. But Barton was too perceptive a student of Shakespeare to insist upon this as the only reading. The character inevitably took its coloring from the actress. Barton saw in Charlotte a strongly aggressive, vitally healthy young woman with a husky voice who would appear ludicrous aping the gentle conception of Mrs. Siddons.

More perceptively, Barton sensed in the girl a depth of emotion, a force that had not yet "found" itself. Under his lead, Charlotte must channel her feelings into the very heart of the role. But for the worried girl from Boston, still wearing her reserve like an armor, forgetting herself was hardly so simple. Charlotte hesitated; Barton insisted. Without revealing herself, she could not hope to bring Lady Macbeth alive. Still she held back; Barton demanded: she must open herself wide. In her worry, Charlotte doubted that she had any such hidden reserves.

The moment had arrived for desperate measures. Barton may have recalled Edwin Forrest's narrow escape from a shark, an episode that had occurred some years before while Forrest was en route from New Orleans to Philadelphia. During a sudden calm, Forrest had peeled off his shirt and dived into the sea, circled the ship, then lay back treading water. But a frantic cry of "Shark!" had set him thrashing wildly toward the anchor chain; he had pulled himself up to safety just in time, then had lain breathless on deck staring up into a circle of terrified faces. But Forrest, instead of panicking, had taken the moment as a chance to learn something about basic emotions. Lying quietly on deck, he had calmly considered the span of feelings that had swept over him; recalling these later would increase his skill as an actor.

Forrest's experience involved a practical technique, an early suggestion of Stanislavsky's "memory-of-emotion" system, and Barton had already discovered its value. He would put it to use now on Charlotte. Hurling out every imaginable rudeness, belittling her

41

"puny" efforts as an actress, scoffing at her "ridiculous" hopes to make her mark in anything, Barton put her into a towering rage. At the top of her lungs, crying between the words she thundered back at him, she vented all the passion and fire she had in her. While she stormed and wept, Barton stood back observing. With his experienced eye, he saw what he had long suspected. The girl had all the physical and mental attributes of a fully fledged tragic actress. Her expressive face and ringing voice registered every quality necessary in creating a living character on stage.

When Charlotte had cried herself out, Barton admitted his miserable trick. And collapsed in her chair, she recognized that she had just gone through an effective lesson in acting. She had seen for herself, at long last, the proof of her own emotional powers. In Barton's confidence and in her own discovery she gradually sensed an awakened belief in herself.

Ever since Elkanah's defeated withdrawal from the family, she had known that any achievement she might make must come through her own efforts. Now in April 1836, she could look back over her bitter failures as a singer at the St. Charles and know she was not really broken. She could tell herself now that Barton's trust was more solidly founded than Maeder's; deep in her own artistic conscience she sensed a keener certainty. Fate often chose puzzling ways to open doors.

From Barton, with an occasional assist from Caldwell, Charlotte received the broad foundation of a permanent technique. During the months at the St. Charles she had watched one of the grand exponents of the Siddons–Kemble school of acting, Thomas Cooper. His style had blended a dignity of manner with an elegance of diction that translated into majesty on the stage. Like Sarah Siddons herself, Cooper acted from a theory that saw in art a purpose to elevate nature, to exclude the ugly, to exalt the ideal. Grandeur was its key; grand declamation and statuesque posture and movements were its structure.

Charlotte had seen a hint of the theory in William Macready, but now, under Barton's repeated drillings, she comprehended its larger aims. The mind-battering sessions with him, their repeated readings of Shakespeare's rolling periods were the only real acting lessons she ever received. She would always observe carefully another actor's individual tricks, the means he used to achieve certain effects, but never again would she undergo such disciplined training in the craft of acting, in vitalizing a character into form and motion and sound.

One detail about playing Lady Macbeth Charlotte failed to mention until the day she was due to perform. Partly because she had immersed herself so deeply in learning the lines, partly because she feared the consequences, she waited until the last afternoon to mention to Caldwell that she had no costume. Later performers would escape the eleventh-hour distractions of supplying their own costumes and makeup and wigs, but in the theatre of Charlotte's youth, actors solved such problems themselves.

And Charlotte had no costume; on her slender means she had no real way to acquire one. Fearing his wrath, but hoping the late hour would prevent his assigning the role to anyone else, she took her problem to Caldwell at the end of the last rehearsal. Caldwell tempered his annoyance with some dismay. The papers had already broadcast the word that tonight Charlotte Cushman would appear as a dramatic actress, as Lady Macbeth, "a character which she has been studying under a competent teacher." The performance could hardly be cancelled. She must dress herself in some sort of makeshift. The other important house in New Orleans, the French Theatre, often gave *Macbeth* in translation. Perhaps its Lady Macbeth could help. Caldwell dispatched his tall slender actress with a note to Madame Clozel, but at the latter's dressing room door she met a surprise. Clozel was short and enormously stout; her waist measured nearly seventy-two inches.

Sensing immediately Charlotte's tearful alarm, Madame Clozel gave out a great laugh, threw out her arms, and ushered her in. She unwrapped her own costume, shook out its folds, and then set to work lowering hems, basting wide tucks, adding dark draperies to hide the quick stitches. The result would hardly bear close inspection, but from the proper stage distance it would serve. As a final touch she threw several large folds of point lace and some strands of white wax beads over the shoulders.

April 23, the Bard's anniversary, took on a new meaning this spring of 1836. Whispering a prayer that tonight she could prove, once and for all, her claims for an acting career, Charlotte swept on stage in her heavy dark draperies and bone white beads, her tone suggesting a dawning awareness that the witches' prophecy for Macbeth's destiny held a clue as well for his lady's.

An actor's lines on stage match only rarely his real feelings and thoughts as he moves through his paces, but Lady Macbeth's early lines paralleled the thoughts that had surged for days in the determined young actress reading the letter. For Charlotte, it remained for this performance as Lady Macbeth to show if "the valor of her tongue," the power of her speech could spell her success; but she was hardly into the evening before she sensed that some turn of events was shaping. Playing her big scenes squarely at the point where the dim rays of the footlights converged in a focus, remembering that all the big effects had to be centered there in order to register at all in the vast house, she played the role as she and Barton conceived it, a passionate figure of towering gestures and ringing, declamatory tones.

While her careful diction paid due regard to the standards of Mrs. Siddons, Charlotte rejected completely the divine Sarah's feminine concept of the role. This Lady Macbeth embodied a virile determination to cower her weakling husband into total obedience. In Charlotte Cushman, New Orleans saw Lady Macbeth become the dominant goading force in an essentially masculine play, hands clutching a pair of daggers, eyes blazing an obsessed ambition, chin set firm to the task ahead, overriding completely Macbeth's own moral doubts.

From pit to highest gallery the St. Charles saw the young woman become a monumental compound of fierce intensity and organ-like tones, determinedly pressing her aims, failing at last in a maze of sleep. Alongside this torrent, Barton's noble Macbeth was a pale thing scarcely seen.

An electrified audience saw "a pantheress let loose." Charlotte's ragtag costume had become queenly robes, blackly regal wings appropriate to the dark outlines of the character. Many in the audience saw the wife of Glamis become real for the first time; the written lines of a poet had become the flesh and fire of a Queen. Long before the final curtain, Charlotte realized that the great waves of applause welling up around her now presaged for her the brightest possible future. Her curtain bows accepted the frenzied cheers. And backing again through the break in the curtains, her hand grasped firmly in Barton's, she took a higher acclaim amid the actors assembled on stage.

Suddenly, James Barton knew the bounding joy that comes to the patron when his protégée is recognized. Almost from the start, he had seen the promise that had enkindled the ovation still roaring beyond the curtains. Now, madly elated, he pumped Charlotte's hands, then dashed off through the people crowding around her, wildly crying, "I knew it, I knew it, the greatest living actress on the stage."

It was too soon for Charlotte herself to grasp the full impact of the ringing applause and Barton's glorious words, but already the world had taken a different stance. She could later dismiss this first performance with a terse "And thus I essayed for the first time the part of Lady Macbeth, fortunately to the satisfaction of the audience, the manager, and all the members of the company." But at the time, the frenzied approval all around her foretold an end to homesickness and soul-distress. Just as surely as she had found her speaking tongue in school long ago in Boston, she had now found her artistic instrument, the tool to forge out, in a chaotic world, an ordered place for herself and her family.

The *Bee* would still remind its readers that Miss Cushman's limitations in opera were "pro-di-gi-ous!" but it cheered her success in Shakespeare. She should confine herself now to straight drama.

Charged now with a vigor born of new hope, she proved again on May 12 her skill as a quick study in *The Tempest*. Two nights later she played Lucretia Borgia in a play replete with murder and matricide, another chance to exhibit her special powers. On the sixteenth and seventeenth she spoke a prologue to *The Martyr Patriots;* on the nineteenth she was Fatima in *Bluebeard* with Clara Maeder— recalling the childish delight she had found on the makeshift stage in Mary Eliza's attic. Next night, "by particular desire," she appeared again as Lady Macbeth and received as her personal benefit a percentage of the box office take in addition to her salary.

A week later the season ended. Her theatrical apprenticeship, her commitment to Maeder and Caldwell, was over. Though her days and nights had been constant study and acting, at times she had glimpsed the gaudier life Mary Eliza had feared. But while her mother might question Charlotte's ability to judge, New Orleans had not corrupted her; the ramparts of her moral convictions had held. Her sturdy good health had withstood whatever threats lurked in the city's malarial air. Free now to return to the patterned life she knew in Boston, she was equally free to pursue Barton's leads toward legitimate acting in New Orleans or somewhere else. Like the new Texas that had only last month broken its ties to Mexico, she stood now at an important crossroads and faced her freedom.

She decided against New Orleans. Yet her times South, as Whitman himself would phrase it, forever affected her outlook. Boston and New Orleans would stand as factions always at war in man's makeup, his vertical sense of practicality conflicting with his horizontal sense of pleasure. The dilemma did not greatly trouble her, other interests gave her graver concern, but in the later roads she traveled, the later cities she chose, her standards implicitly blended the two. Puritan restraint and Creole geniality, she discovered on this first long break with Boston, were the double facets of her own nature.

She did not really wish to return to the home and hearth of her childhood. Her Boston past had already become a prelude to ampler ranges. During these agonizing months in New Orleans, she had discovered more than an acting talent and a speaking voice. She had sensed, without any chance to savor it, a taste for richer living. If Boston and New Orleans stood as hubs of their own diverse systems, she had learned that somewhere between sober propriety and heedless abandon centered the good life for her.

On June 1 she wrote Sam Judd in New York. She would sail tomorrow on the *Edward Bonaffe* for Philadelphia; from there she would come directly to New York by the twenty-fifth. She wanted to see the Judds again, despite their hostility toward the life she had chosen, to thank them again for their kindness and to take whatever steps were necessary to establish herself in the role of dramatic actress.

4

Debut in New York

(1836)

Like young Elkanah when he set out for Boston in 1782 to seek his fortune, his daughter Charlotte set out in 1836 for New York, a city now numbering 270,000. To her credit she had intellect, experience, and, compared to her father, a much brighter claim toward fame. Arriving in New York, she suffered no doubts; her mission was as clear as it had been since the St. Charles' roaring acclaim had rescued her from the brink of despair and had launched her forth with new hope. With a confidence wholly unlike her vague uncertainties when she first made her way up its streets in 1833, Charlotte arrived in Manhattan knowing exactly what she wanted to find. With the *Bee*'s printed assurance that the sheer blaze of her talents had already conquered the most blasé of foes, she felt fully ready for the best New York could offer. She sent a quick note to Edmund Simpson, manager of the Park Theatre.

Overlooking a broad, tree-lined expanse, Simpson's playhouse was the second Park Theatre to stand on the site. Since 1821 it had carried on a tradition of excellence established in 1798. Behind the arches of its tall classic facade, the Park accommodated 2,500 spectators, an encouraging fact to one who had just made her mark in a house nearly twice as large. In addition to its excellent stock company, the Park regularly presented top foreign stars. Charles and Fanny Kemble had first appeared here in 1832. Tyrone Power, Charles Kean, Charles Mathews and his wife had all added their names to the long list of talents that the Park, over the years, had presented to the New World. Surely, if a newspaper's good report and a girl's bounding confidence meant anything, Simpson could soon add Charlotte's name to his fabled list.

In 1836 Edmund Simpson stood at the height of his long career
at the famous theatre. An able actor, Simpson worked skillfully behind the scenes, running the theatre's business and locating and encouraging new talent. But although he constantly sought new faces,
and although Charlotte's confidence gave her courage to seek him
out, neither fact turned the immediate trick with Simpson. Her brief
success in New Orleans, much as it interested him, could not open
his doors. To Charlotte's note, Simpson returned a courteous, if
disappointing, reply: Would Miss Cushman care to give him a
chance to observe her work? He would be pleased to offer her a
chance to act on trial.

To Charlotte, flush with her Southern victory, Simpson's reply
seemed, in her words, "a great slight"; his attitude was insulting.
Surely with the plaudits still ringing in her ears, she might have
expected a warmer reception than this.

Broader experience would have given her better counsel. But in
her first brush with reality in New York, Charlotte now read a note
from Thomas Hamblin, manager of the Park's inferior rival, the
American Theatre, popularly called the Bowery. On the strength
of a word from James Barton, himself just arrived from the South,
Hamblin had sought out Barton's young protégée to ask if he might
watch her rehearse. If Miss Cushman were as able as her patron
insisted, Hamblin believed he could make her a favorite.

Charlotte moved more quickly than wisdom dictated. Simpson had
not rejected her; as a businessman he had merely appeared less eager
than she had wished. Too new to the ways of job hunting, she ignored
the obvious advantage of having any place at the Park, with its excellent acting school, over a top position in a second-rate house like
the Bowery. She dispatched a note to Hamblin at the Bowery: Miss
Cushman would be pleased to discuss his terms.

Hamblin's Bowery dated from 1826; for a time, its 3,500 seats
had made it the largest theatre in America; in scope and elegance
it had outshone the Park. But time and the English actor who had
managed it since 1830 had brought changes. Under Hamblin, the
Bowery had come to deserve its nickname, "The Bowery Slaughter
House," from its round of bloody, thundering spectacles. Hamblin
brought to his work a strong sense of fair play and a business acumen
surprisingly good for a former comedian at Drury Lane, though his
flashing eyes scarcely suggested his kindly nature. At her tryout for
Hamblin, Charlotte moved to stage center to run through scenes

from *Macbeth,* Rowe's *Jane Shore,* and Kotzebue's *The Stranger,*
poised from her days at the St. Charles.

Hamblin watched and listened. The girl's choice of cuttings proved
she had range. Her resonant voice could carry to the highest seats
in his house. Most important of all, she had "presence," that inde-
finable quality every manager hoped to find in a new actor. She had
a vividness that might pay off in any number of ways before audiences that always demanded display and color. And the girl's face,
for all its lack of beauty, took on a kind of splendor during the
strongly passionate reading, an incandescence far more impressive on
stage than beauty alone; her awkward body quivered with a passion
almost electric. In no sense had Barton overstated the case; he had
hardly suggested the girl's remarkable gift. When she had finished
her demonstration, Hamblin summoned her to him. Would Miss
Cushman accept a three-year contract?

A few days later Hamblin's agent brought her the contract. Dated
to begin on July 30, it guaranteed a salary of $20 per week for the
first year, $30 per week for the second, and $40 for the third. She
could keep one-third of all moneys received the nights of her benefits. Subject to her Bowery schedule, she might act at other theatres
as well; her salary would continue. Her first run at the Bowery
would cover the month of September. To bind the matter, since Miss
Cushman was under age, she must supply the name of a person to
whom it could be drawn.

Once Mary Eliza signed the contract, Charlotte could look confidently ahead, professionally and legally committed to a life shaped
to her talents. Without further dreaming, she could aspire now to a
long life of action on a field more joyful than any other. If New
Orleans saw her artistic birth, New York would see her hope's fulfillment.

Immediately, Charlotte wrote home her good news. Since the
boardinghouse had never brought more than a bare subsistence, why
should her mother continue the struggle? Why not break up the
household and move with the children to New York? Charlie could
find some sort of job in a store, Mary Eliza could manage the house,
and they could all live splendidly on Charlotte's small salary. In
the Bowery section near the theatre, she found herself temporary
quarters.

To fill her days until the family arrived, she set to work on her
costumes. More accurately, she busied herself with plans, for in her

costumes centered a problem. Typically, the contract made no mention of wardrobe; she was to supply her dresses and accessories. This much she knew. But here in this aloof city, where she knew almost no one (the Judds would be no help at all), how could a beginner stand the stupendous cost?

Costumes and their part in production costs spell one of the major differences between the theatre of Charlotte's youth and that of a later age. Producers would eventually note that in any man's reasons for attending a theatre the beauty and interest of the costumes figured importantly. The effect of a play was partly its visual impact. In time the budget to dress the actors would become the concern of a show's producer. But such a change would come too late for Charlotte's good at the Bowery. At Hamblin's house, one assumed that the actor's performance outweighed his garbed appearance—so long as his clothes suggested the character.

But the high cost of the trip from New Orleans and her present living expenses left Charlotte no money to buy them. When she approached Hamblin hesitantly and told him her problem, he offered a hand. He would supply her the necessary costumes; she could repay him at $5 per week. She borrowed enough money to dress the characters she had demonstrated at her audition. To stretch her wardrobe further, she searched through a street of secondhand shops near the Bowery for odds and ends she could afford. She picked up a few lengths of bright-colored silks, a skein of gold thread, and some trinkets, until she had collected a great bundle of useful articles.

By mid-August when the family arrived, she had an eye on a job for Charlie; she also had her lines fully in hand. Things were off to a splendid beginning. Susan would remain in Boston with Elkanah's older daughter, Isabella, until Mary Eliza could be sure that the move was sound. And little Augustus—Charlotte had not realized how much she had missed him until she saw him bounding down out of the coach, his cap flying, his arms spread wide, crying her name.

Experience had already taught her that life seldom moved steadily forward, that prudence sometimes demanded an alternate plan. The strain of seeing the family established, the pressure of learning lines for a full month of one-night appearances had built up so much by late August that she decided one morning to drop everything and take a long walk in the country. Walking had always released her tensions in Boston. But this time she overextended her energies. By mid-afternoon she found herself in the village of Harlem, five or six

50

miles from home, aware only now that she was nearly exhausted. For young men driving gigs or sulkies, the jaunt up to Harlem through wooded fields and farmsteads was a popular sport; in the cool of the evening they could cover the distance "along the north avenue" at incredible speeds up to twenty miles an hour. But in the August heat, covering the distance on foot was another matter. She staggered home, sick with a blinding headache, high fever, and chills.

Her illness became a three-week bout with "rheumatic fever." Reading about herself in the New York papers gave her pale comfort: "The Bowery has opened with a fine *corps dramatique:* . . . we are promised a young lady, whose first appearance was made in opera, but who is said to evince a most magnificent talent for 'the muse that the gifted Siddons wooed.' This is Miss Cushman." Horace Greeley's *New Yorker* noted that Charlotte Cushman would soon make her debut before the Bowery's partons, "a candidate for a portion of their favor, which . . . cannot be too lavishly bestowed; for in addition to her professional merits, she has many private virtues which need only to be known, to give her strong claims" to community respect. Miss Cushman should become "a general favorite." And the *Spirit of the Times* was equally encouraging. "There is a Miss Cushman coming out here, who is said really to possess considerable talent. We shall see, as she is engaged for three years." To share the billing in the course of the season would be "no less a magnet than Ann Waring," Mr. Blakeley, the Harrisons, Mrs. Herring, and Mr. Cony's dogs, Hector and Bruin. "We had some hopes," sighed the *Spirit,* "of the *Park* and the *National* until we heard Hector and Bruin were engaged at the Bowery."

But flattering newspaper words, plus the dubious support of a pair of trick dogs, were little help while her fever continued to rage. She had to get well; she must manage somehow to appear on stage; her run would expire in four weeks. Every day missed was a day's income lost. Other actors were booked for the period beyond; to make her mark any time soon in New York, she had to take her place on the boards. When someone brought her word of a new treatment for fever, a course of medicated vapor baths, Charlotte leaped, however weakly, at the chance to try it. She could see little to lose.

Within a week, she was back on her feet, strong enough to run through a short rehearsal, to give a final touch to her Lady Macbeth costume, to stand ready—almost too late—for her opening night in New York. Only one of her contracted four weeks remained. If success in the theatre was largely a matter of talent and luck, it was also partly a matter of nerves, basic health, and unflagging optimism. She needed them all in the short, nervous hours that preceded her debut.

The glittering building Charlotte entered Monday evening, September 12, 1836, was an imposing structure, a complex hall in a "fireproof" exterior stuccoed to resemble marble. On its square, classic front, massive Corinthian columns and lanterns towered over the sidewalk and the short flight of steps approaching its doors. Above its elegant entrance soared a colossal carved eagle, measuring twenty-five feet between the tips of its gilded wings.

But the Bowery's cool, Greek-revival appearance hardly suggested the tenor of shows that rattled its rafters inside. Charlotte's Lady Macbeth was an appropriate choice for a Bowery debut. Her reading could splash all the blood, could volley all the thunder anyone within its hearing demanded. Tonight, she was the same, hard-driving, unsubtle power she had been in New Orleans, though now, in spite of her nerves, she was far from a naïve beginner. Hamblin himself played Macbeth, with the beautiful Ann Waring as Lady Macduff. Her beauty might have foretold a long career, but the plain-featured Charlotte Cushman was slated for the brighter future. No direct word appeared in print against Charlotte's appearance, but the press made much of Ann Waring's abounding grace, her delicate movements, the charm of this "very attractive young lady."

Charlotte would learn to accept in print a blatant fact. In a profession that worshipped physical beauty, she could never hope to see her own looks receive any praise. She would make her impression, instead, with whatever force she possessed and the organ tones of a matchless voice, the power of a mind sure of itself on stage.

Sweeping through her debut, an almost sexless embodiment of will determined to push Macbeth toward his dreams, she would make her mark with talent—she must leave to other hands the spells a beauty could weave. If Hamblin's Macbeth demurred in the plan to murder Duncan, Charlotte's Lady Macbeth, first cousin to a Medea, lashed him forward. In spite of her recent illness, the energy she unlocked suggested she could drag, or lift, the broken-down Macbeth from the stage, could "pitch into him" with her clenched hands and muscular arms, could replace her words with blows.

While this Lady Macbeth lacked the polish it would later acquire, Charlotte forcefully depicted a blind obsession steadily building its strategy. Later critics might praise the "deep, thrilling, pitiless tones" of her voice, the "wild, roving, inspired glances" of her eyes as she invoked the angels of crime, but her first Bowery audience recognized in the vigorous newcomer a magnetic authority, able with voice and slashing gesture, "with the horror of her infernal purpose, fiend-driven and inspired of hell," to chill a listener's blood. The echoing reaction caused the *Spirit of the Times* to herald the arrival of this "Boston girl" and wish "her success with all our hearts."

As she later recalled, "I succeeded beyond my expectations and those of the manager," an understatement of the fears and physical weakness that had plagued her during the long weeks preceding the debut. Now with her final curtain, she could relax a little. She had broken the ice confronting a newcomer, and if the applause meant anything, she had carried the day in the one city in all America where victory most counted. For once, she could relax in the knowledge that affairs for the Cushmans now shone with a radiance.

The following night, September 13, she played two other characters, Mrs. Haller in *The Stranger* and Helen Macgregor in *Rob Roy,* women vastly different from her Lady Macbeth. On Saturday, September 17, she was Patrick in *The Poor Soldier* and Alicia in *Jane Shore* with the beautiful Ann Waring. She had entered the contracted routine of a professional career. By the end of her grueling first week at the Bowery, although her hopes were high at her New York reception, her energies were correspondingly low; she fell prey again to chills and fever. Too honest to take home the wardrobe she had not fully paid for, she left it locked safely away at the theatre. With the little strength she had left, she staggered home again to meet Mary Eliza's grave concern.

The following Wednesday, September 21, Ann Waring suffered serious injury in a fall from a high platform. And the next evening during a performance of *Lafitte, The Pirate of the Gulf,* fatal calamity struck the house itself. Hamblin had spent $5,000 on this production; he had filled his stage with a large cast, brilliant scenery, broad action and noise, the rattle and fire of muskets, even a cannon's blast, but his attention to authenticity spelled his downfall. Perhaps from a spark in the shooting, a fire broke out early the next morning. Immediately it tore through the vast interior; a passerby saw flames already eating through the building's roof. When the firemen arrived, the Bowery was one seething mass; above the flames and ashes, the gilded eagle soared for a time, then crashed in a great shower of sparks. Firemen rushed in all directions with axes and futile buckets of water, while a hundred Bowery employees stood helpless as their goods dissolved in flames—musicians lamenting their instruments, carpenters their tools, actors their costumes and properties. In an hour, nothing remained of the Bowery but steaming embers and its proud Corinthian columns. The "fireproof" exterior had gone down in flames.

In that hour, more than a famous theatre had fallen. Sick in her bed, Charlotte learned of her own bitter loss: her costumes with the bill against them still unpaid, her three-year contract, her family's immediate hopes. All had vanished in the smoke and ashes.

In times of calamity, Mary Eliza was hardly a woman to record her thoughts. As a person, she emerges only indirectly through reference in Charlotte's own writings, but the early morning when the frantic cries brought word of the Bowery's burning, she could hardly have kept herself from Puritan speculation. Back in Boston, she had counseled her daughter as best she could; she had pointed out patiently the risks Charlotte ran in choosing a stage career. While she had scarcely feared so literal a downfall as this for the girl, she was not surprised. To enjoy the theatre was not to ignore its pitfalls. The fire was a judgment. Throughout America, theatres often succumbed to flames. On this same site, two Bowery Theatres had gone down in fire. Twice now, Charlotte had suffered dire setbacks, the loss of a singing voice, the loss of a legal contract. How much more clearly could one expect God to speak? Was it not time now for Charlotte to redirect her ambitions, time for them all to return to Boston?

Charlotte could not easily shrug off her mother's argument. In despair she could admit that doors opened and doors closed as signs of God's perfect will. Her talent had been recognized in the city where talent was appreciated. But in God's judgment was her acting talent the merest delusion? Was she to throttle her ambition in some pale compromise with ease and comfort, some mindless return to the simple sphere of her childhood, to lead a conventional life empty of any excitement but satisfactory, perhaps, in other ways?

With the Bowery's end, the complications had become too great. Years later a friend would report a statement Charlotte made at this time. If Charley or someone else "had come forward then and offered me a home I would gladly have accepted, and would have led my life untroubled by ambitious dreams, unsuspecting of the divine afflatus within me."

One wonders. By now she had already discovered the "divine afflatus." Already she was fully certain of her own genius. For all the comfort she might take in the knowledge that Charley Wiggin was waiting in Boston, she could not, for reasons related to honesty, go back to him. In her dawning awareness about many things in her makeup, she could hardly give Charley the domestic devotion he needed; she could not offer him the fully committed heart and body that marriage required.

Just now, whatever the future held for her genius lay buried under the Bowery's smoking ruins. She could only pray that time would open another lead.

5

Testing Time in Albany

(1836–1837)

In her despair, Charlotte might have interpreted the dour signs exactly as Mary Eliza read them, but moving the family back to Boston, facing the ordeal of moving them anywhere else, would take money she did not have. Within a week, she knew she could not alter her plans. She would remain in New York, regain her strength, and watch for another chance.

That chance came within a few days when the Franklin Theatre in Chatham Square announced a benefit for all the Bowery people, a performance of *Aladdin of the Wonderful Lamp* on September 21. Back on her feet, her hopes partially revived, Charlotte would play Aladdin. And Simpson's people at the Park gave their own benefit and sent all the proceeds to Hamblin's actors. Two weeks later Charlotte played Patrick in *The Poor Soldier* in another Franklin benefit. In the meantime, E. Burke Fisher, editor of the *New Yorker* magazine, had written letters about Charlotte to Francis Wemyss of the American Theatre in Philadelphia and to Lewis Godey, editor of a new women's magazine, asking if either man could help a young lady, with a dependent family to support, who had already made quite a name for herself in New York.

Charlotte herself appealed to William Dinneford, manager at the Franklin. Regretfully Dinneford could offer her nothing permanent in New York, but she might write his partner, W. R. Blake, who managed the Pearl Street Theatre in Albany. In a few days a reply arrived from Blake, offering her a five-week contract. She was tempted to turn it down: ideally, she should remain in New York where she could accept at a moment's notice whatever job might open. But Albany was not really so far away, and a few brief weeks there would help her surmount her troubles.

Immediately after the Franklin benefit on October 7, she led Mary Eliza and Augustus aboard a sidewheeler for the long ride upstream past the wooded hills of the Hudson. Charlie Cushman would remain at his clerking job in New York. Susan was still in Boston with Isabella.

The town they reached in the late afternoon was a strongly Dutch city of some 30,000. Perched on a high outlook over the river, Albany impressed them immediately with its steep cobbled streets, the pinkish red bricks of its gabled houses, and its Greek Revival state house. Its handsome Pearl Street Theatre was one of its special prides. Greek like the state house, it had become famous throughout America for its stage equipment, its elaborate refreshment room, its ladies' boudoir, and its large punch room that extended the width of the building. Under Blake's direction, the Pearl was among the most prosperous theatres in the country; his acting company, one of the most artistically sound. Charlotte was not long in discovering her good luck in landing a contract with it.

She found temporary lodgings at the Rising Sun Tavern on Pearl near the theatre. A few days later, after she had enrolled Augustus in a boarding school, the Greenbush Classical Academy, she and her mother moved to simpler rooms at the Republican Hotel.

When she reported for work, Blake gave her the happy news that the famous English actor, Junius Brutus Booth, would be the Macbeth for her opening night, October 11. Ideally, Booth's superior talents could serve her well, but Blake put her on guard. Junius Booth had a luminous power; long past his prime, he could still flash the genius that had gained him fame. But there was no predicting him. The stumpy little man who could disport himself like an emperor when he was sober sometimes forgot his lines, sometimes even forgot to appear. Charlotte must be ready for anything on stage with the erratic Mr. Booth, especially if he had slaked his thirst at a saloon en route to the theatre.

Charlotte would later dismiss the old actor as a first-class "mountebank," but for her first night in Albany, Booth remained on his good behavior. At the final curtain, when "the tall, thin, and lanky girl" and the imperious little veteran with the flashing eyes took their bows, raves and cheers poured over them.

If Mary Eliza listened to the ovation at the Pearl dreading some new calamity, Charlotte wasted no time on such gloomy thoughts. Albany's plaudits were all she needed to reaffirm her determination. Acting was the rightest possible life for her. She set to work with a vigor, learning the long list of roles she must act during her weeks in Albany.

Her efforts did not go unappreciated. Because of her opening night hit with Booth, because she cheerfully tackled a new part almost nightly, Dinneford and Blake extended her contract. The Albanians pronounced her "a real steamboat and no mistake"; the "Boston girl" would succeed "as she deserves," reported the *Spirit of the Times*.

On October 31, she gave a clue to her broader talents. After her benefit as Count Belino in *The Devil's Bridge,* she delivered an original poetic eulogy, a tribute to Albany's firemen, inspired no doubt by her own unhappy loss in New York. The applause for her poem set her head spinning with an added range to her plans. Why not try augmenting her income with an occasional venture in writing? She sat down immediately and penned a vaguely autobiographical story, "Extracts from My Journal: the Actress," and sent it to Lewis Godey.

When Godey published Charlotte's sad little tale in February 1837, its popularity suggested a practical move. Writing for publication could serve a double purpose. She could add to her income, and just as important, the papers and magazines carrying stories and poems "by Charlotte Cushman" could spread her name before the public.

This early contact with Godey's indefatigable lady editor, Mrs. Sarah Josepha Hale, began an enduring friendship—one based on each woman's admiration for the other's talents—though Charlotte's straightforward handshake with the world seemed strangely at odds with Sarah Hale's own gentle creed: Delicacy is woman's chief characteristic; after the Fall, "Divine Goodness mercifully exalted her sex to conserve the moral virtues of humanity and thus become the 'glory of man.' "

In pages that glorified woman as the moral custodian of the universe, Charlotte's little story about the grieving actress seemed perfectly at home, perfectly attuned to the magazine's Victorian notions of womanhood. But when Charlotte wrote the story, it was a question of money, and she herself would never conform to the quaint restrictions the good Mrs. Hale recommended. The small girl who had once swung with the boys from the trees on Boston Common was not lost in the woman, now in her twenties, who could dazzle

Albany audiences one night as a demure, proper, young lady, and the next as a swashbuckling hero bedecked in tights, doublet, and a flashing sword.

National recognition in the *Spirit of the Times* delighted her—it was good to be called "a very clever actress"—but the paper did not rest the matter there. Strangely enough, Mordecai M. Noah in the New York *Evening Star* had described her as a young lady of "notable beauty," but such a breech of truth was too much for *The Spirit*. In reply to Noah, the *Spirit* hooted, "As to her being 'lovely,' and all that sort o' thing, it's all a bam." In its outcry, Charlotte took another basic lesson in how to react to personal attack. Once she established herself in Albany, she could usually count on a favorable word about her acting, but it was a rare paper indeed that ignored her appearance.

A few weeks later, still jesting, the *Spirit* printed the plaintive lines received from a reader in Batesville, Arkansas: "I would like to see the pretty Miss Cushman, for Maj. Noah discourses so eloquently about her beauty that I am half in love with her." In the pain the comment caused her Charlotte could remind herself that such notice, for all humor the *Spirit* saw in it, was nationwide publicity.

When the Albany *Microscope* rose gallantly to her defense, she saw in the whole affair at least a flattering interest. "The 'Boston girl' seeks not to make people 'drunk' with beauty nor pierce tender hearted whiskerandos with the artillery of bright eyes." The young actress now at the Pearl aimed at nobler things—at excellence in her lines and eminence in her profession. The *Microscope* challenged any paper in the country to know more about the matter; it had watched her performances nightly.

Pretty or not, during her five busy months in Albany, Charlotte managed to fill her leisure moments with active participation in Albany society. She had chosen her hotel wisely. At the Republican her Yankee shrewdness sparkled almost as brightly as her dramatic talent on stage. With several New York legislators boarding at the hotel she spent long afternoons around the fire in the lobby, debating political questions, weighing the pros and cons of such things as eventual statehood for Texas and England's galling arrogance toward America. For the men, Charlotte's bright talk was a novelty, and it gave them new insight into the backstage life of the theatre, where decency and respectability could obviously flourish, if this young Miss Cushman was a fair example. And it did her no harm at all to let it be known that she was a distant cousin, through the Babbit line, of the Governor, William L. Marcy. Charlotte soon found herself, to Mary Eliza's profound relief, a great favorite in Albany society. She later recalled the special kindness of the government people. "More of the [legislators] could be found at my benefit than at the Capitol."

Still, Charlotte's most impelling routine centered in her work. Like Edwin Forrest, who had sprouted his own wings at the Pearl, she found there her most fundamental experience as an actress, her first real occasion to apply the instruction James Barton had given her. From the chance to act with talents like Junius Brutus Booth, she could note at close hand a broad range of acting techniques. Among the people in the Pearl company, acting was a serious, professional dedication, and by observing their work and their stable temperaments, she formed an attitude that became her most valuable tool. Though the Pearl was not really a drama school, it gave her the practical, exacting regimen she needed.

For one thing, she learned how to study in Albany. Since theatre language is the language of sound, Charlotte saw in the matter a method of study. To memorize her lines, she learned never to look at the page. Having skimmed through the play, she listened while someone else read her speeches aloud. When Mary Eliza, as her first backstage assistant, read a passage slowly and distinctly, she repeated whatever words she could remember. Then after listening carefully to the speech read slowly again, she repeated it. By the third reading, the speech was usually etched in her mind. From the start, in repeating her lines, she emphasized the "action" words; in practice sessions with Mary Eliza she tried to visualize the proper gestures and motions. After all, a play's stage "business" lay implicit in the words, though the actual blocking could wait for rehearsal, for the inspiration of physical motion linked to the other actors.

Here at least, her early work with Clara Fisher Maeder served her well; Charlotte remembered Clara's conviction that no actress had a right to appear on stage until she thoroughly comprehended the play's language. Learning her words easily, she developed the habit of considering every possible connotation. Her almost scholarly scrutiny of every facet of meaning—"her excellence in her lines," as the *Microscope* noted—explained in part her resounding success in Albany. Once having learned a role, she rarely forgot it.

While her work went well at the theatre, while Mary Eliza contented herself at the hotel, Augustus sent happy letters from school, in which he made plain the tender bond he felt for "My dear, darling sister." When she offered to buy him a present with the earliest money she made in Albany, she was delighted he wanted a horse; she would have chosen the same.

About Augustus, there was no argument. He had always been her favorite, and he always would be. Now that ways were opening at last for her to put the family on a sound footing, her hopes and plans for Augustus gave her life the most meaning. This brother would make his mark.

Susan was another matter. Until now, she had posed no special problem. She was the younger sister at home, the girl who brightened her limited world with a quiet charm, a fineness of feature that contrasted strongly with Charlotte's own sturdy looks. Susan's dark hair framed a face of almost patrician beauty. Of late, her deepset eyes, her graceful chin and fragile nose had come to make the thirteen-year-old girl arrestingly attractive.

Practicality had dictated that Susan remain in Boston with Isabella until family affairs were settled. The decision had seemed sensible at the time, but it created difficulties. A friend of the family— though Elkanah himself did little for the family's wellbeing, he had a ready supply of willing friends—Nelson M. Merriman, offered himself as Susan's benefactor. He could help Susan financially; with his ample means, he could take her under his care and educate her, would willingly adopt her, if the family consented.

To Mary Eliza, adoption was no more thinkable now than it had been in Charlotte's case with the Judds, but Merriman's financial offer did meet an immediate need. She accepted it gratefully and relaxed, assured that all was well with Susan in Boston. But in due course, word came that Merriman's health was declining. On his sickbed, he devised a plan that caused Charlotte and Mary Eliza the deepest concern. Fearing an early death, Merriman wrote to Mary Eliza that he knew only one way to make certain that Susan received, after his death, the property he wanted to give her. Laws being what they were, he could make Susan his major beneficiary only if she was his widow. To protect the girl's practical interests, would the mother consent to the marriage?

The letter was troubling. Charlotte and Mary Eliza read it more than once to make certain they understood it. Marriage was hardly a matter of money. Even if Merriman died soon, the thought of Susan's marrying a man as old as her father, even a sick old man wishing her nothing but happiness, was difficult. Mary Eliza paced her room at the Republican. She had no word from Susan to indicate the girl's own feelings. At last she knew she must hurry to Boston to verify all the details. In Boston, Mary Eliza was dismayed to find that her stepchildren, Elkanah's elder son and daughter, thought well of the plan, even though young Susan declared that she herself was repelled by the whole idea. A presentiment of trouble delayed Mary Eliza's decision.

The plan did have a practical side. At last, Mary Eliza let expedience overrule her sentiments. With no enthusiasm on the part of the bride, the marriage of Susan Cushman, age fourteen, to Nelson M. Merriman took place in Trinity Church, Boston, on November 4, 1836.

The story begins to read like a melodrama when Nelson Merriman's health improved miraculously soon after the wedding. In a short time, his normal vigor returned, and young Susan found herself trapped in a marriage she hated to a man who had lied. Another sad fact became clear soon afterward. One morning Merriman told Susan he must go to New York on business. He had hardly left town, however, before an army of creditors came pounding on his door. Susan could only face them, more dismayed than anyone else at the sudden turn her fortunes had taken. The months stretched ahead without any respite to her fears, or to those of Charlotte and her mother in Albany.

At the Pearl, Charlotte attempted to bury her own concern for Susan in the steady excitement of her work. In rapid succession she played a variety of roles.* Though most of them were flimsy concoctions, she found in each one an opportunity to test her resources, to plumb the range of her talents, from broadest farce to tragedy. Far from the inhibited beginner who needed the trick of a James Barton to unleash her feelings, she felt as easy in one night's pratfalls and laughter as she felt in the next night's hush and stifled sobs. Whether a power-bent, crown-obsessed Lady Macbeth or a Louise in *Norman Leslie,* by January 1837, she had become an immense

* Helen Macgregor in *Rob Roy,* Alicia in *Jane Shore,* Henry in *Speed the Plough,* Floranthe in *The Mountaineers,* Mrs. Haller in *The Stranger,* Mrs. Lionel Lyn in *Married Life,* Joan in *Joan of Arc,* Margaret in *Margaret of Burgundy,* Jack Horner in *Greville Cross, or The Druids' Stone,* Louise in *Norman Leslie,* Emilia in *Othello,* Alvedson in *The Two Galley Slaves,* Lucy Clifton in *The Fiend of Eddystone,* Henry Germain in *The Hut of the Red Mountain,* Portia in *The Merchant of Venice,* Julia in *The Hunchback,* Tullis in *Brutus,* Jorilda in *Timour the Tartar,* Belvidera in *Venice Preserved,* Roxanna in *Alexander the Great.*

favorite. She thrived under the rigorous schedule, content with the busy life she had chosen.

In February, she played George Fairman in *The Liberty Tree, or Boston Boys in 1773.* In keeping with its theme, at the play's end she paid tribute to the great Edwin Forrest, who was reaping just then a remarkable success in London. Forrest's Drury Lane debut in October 1836 had met an ovation, however deep his fears had been that his American citizenship might create a bitter reception.

If many English hearts still carried memories of the American Revolution and the War of 1812, England had much to learn about the ambitious people who had fought her. Happily, Forrest's commanding performance in the American play, *The Gladiator* by Robert Montgomery Bird, had thrown Drury Lane into a delighted uproar. Something in the American's style suggested a debt to the great Edmund Kean, a debt incurred when Forrest had acted with Kean in Albany. And William Macready joined the ovation with praise for the actor's manliness and power. When one man stood up and shouted, "Welcome to England!" the audience took up the cry.

Forrest thanked them for their kindness; he noted his satisfaction that "England and America were joined by the closest goodwill, that obviously the more enlightened portion of their population was superior to any feeling of national jealousy." None too accurately, the London *Age* returned the sentiment: "We cannot conceal our gratification at finding that the country which has received with so much hospitality . . . every British performer who has visited its shores, should at least have given us an opportunity of returning the compliment."

Forrest's English reception set off rejoicing throughout the sensitive United States, and Blake fostered Charlotte's wish to deliver a eulogy to the actor on the stage where he had made a high mark.

> Friends of the drama! Patrons of the stage
> From laughing beauty on to graver age,
> You all remember one, who last stood here,
> Basked in your smiles, or wrung perchance a tear
> As from his lips the tide of feeling prest,
> And in his bearing Genius stood confest!
> I mean the *Forrest of our native land.*
> . . . .
> He sought to grasp the sceptre of his art
> That he deserv'd to win; all know full well

That he *has* won it, England's praises tell.
The Ocean Queen, Great mistress of the age,
Has bowed before this wonder of the stage.
She bends to genius—you his virtues scan.
She hails the Actor—you reward the Man.

In her work and in social flings Charlotte may have found time for romance. Years afterward she described an Albany friendship that caused her grief for a time. She never identified the man, never divulged much about him, but in her references to him, she declared that her affections had gone deep—at least deeper than anything she had felt for Charley Wiggin or Charles Spalding. He was a young man "in a higher position of life, who . . . seemed the impersonation of all that was elegant and refined." He courted her; she was almost swept off her feet. She let herself imagine a future with him —until the day she discovered that "his intent was *not* honourable, nor his purpose marriage." She broke off the friendship at once. During her remaining days in Albany she scrupulously avoided meeting him.

Describing the friendship to Geraldine Jewsbury many years later, she recalled that when she saw him approaching she hid herself as he passed. To Miss Jewsbury's comment, "You were strong!" Charlotte answered, perhaps a little nostalgically, "I, strong! Child! I was as weak as water, but I was kept from harm."

Later, Charlotte recalled the affair as a serious matter indeed. "There was a time in my life of girlhood when I thought I had been called upon to bear the very hardest thing that can come to a woman." But a short time had shown, "in the battle of life which was before me, that this had been but a spring storm, which was simply to help me to a clearer, better, richer, and more productive summer." Without this early trial, "I should never have been so earnest and faithful in my art." In the spring of 1837 there was ample time ahead to test the permanence of her decision; the fact did not preclude a later change of heart.

By the first of April, after the five-week initial engagement with Dinneford and Blake had blossomed into a seven-month run, Charlotte was ready to bid Albany farewell. And the Albanians were prepared, however reluctantly, to send her off in a shower of praise. The months she had worked among them had brought steady delight at the Pearl, especially on the nights when she had tackled an unlikely role like Romeo.

Her playing the love-sick hero had resulted from an accident back in New Orleans, a happenstance that had pushed her into the tights and doublet of Patrick in *The Poor Soldier* when a regular actor had not been available. She had hardly seen the step as fortuitous; that night, she had merely filled a gap in the St. Charles company, unaware that she was adding a unique quality to her career. The skill she had brought to the role stemmed in part from her child-hood. If her games on Boston Common and Long Wharf had taught her a masculine swagger, if the roughening change in her voice helped her affect a masculine tone, her playing male roles became a pattern before she or anyone else intended it. By the end of her Albany sojourn, upstate New Yorkers knew Charlotte Cushman as an able young actress especially adept in "breeches parts," so skilled in male impersonation that no one seriously objected to a woman's daring, in Victorian America, to change her skirts for the revealing costumes and aggressive demeanor of men.

At her farewell to Albany, an audience that had believed her fiend-driven Lady Macbeth saw her now as an impetuous youth afire with love for Juliet. Her Romeo's love-sick speeches to Friar Lawrence rang completely true. His supple gestures, his leaps over the garden walls, his impassioned words, the flash of his sword driving at the "Furious Tybalt" carried such conviction that few in the audience remembered that a woman's skill lay behind them.

Actors in women's parts seemed normal enough to Shakespeare. On stage, Edward Kynaston had impressed Samuel Pepys as "the loveliest *lady* that ever I saw." To see Kynaston as Evadne in *The Maid's Tragedy,* Charles II waited patiently until the actor was "properly shaved." In similar fashion, decades before Charlotte, a parade of actresses had skillfully played men. Mrs. Siddons appeared as Hamlet, and recent times would see the Dane portrayed by Char-lotte Barnes, Fanny Wallack, Eliza Shaw, Alice Marriott, and Mrs. Emma Waller. Even Clara Fisher Maeder had attempted the role. Albany's "enthusiastic applause" for Charlotte's Romeo was all the encouragement she needed to make him one of her standard roles.

Her final Romeo in Albany ended to great and ringing applause. She was making her way through the wings toward her dressing room, tired but fully content with her labors, when one of the act-ors rushed toward her, grasped her hand, and pulled her back on stage. As she entered, the curtain rose, the cast struck up a farewell song, and stagehands brought forward a large floral wreath to place on her head. Reporting the scene, the *Advertiser* commented, "Miss

Cushman is about leaving us, but we hope only for a short time, as we feel she has no warmer or dearer friends than the Albanians."

In this small world of the Pearl Street Theatre, Charlotte rose from her bow—smiling at the cheering faces, the friends from the Republican Hotel, her colleagues, the social "names" she had come to know during past months—feeling an inexpressible joy at having found her place, a lifelong role for her talents. But above that joy would tower two emotional hurts that had little to do with the Pearl: "the first spring storm and hurricane of young disappointment"—the abortive love affair, such as it was—and the earth-shattering word that came from Augustus' teacher a few days after her farewell to Albany. On the ninth of April Augustus had sent down a note from school: "If the weather is good and the road is good, Mr. Bulkley talks of going east and I shall go with him." The time was spring vacation; the destination, a short distance over the line in Vermont.

"Oh, how I wish I could see you once more before you go to New York," Augustus had written.

The trip to Vermont had seemed sensible. Winter was breaking. Augustus would be safe with his teacher. Riding his own horse, he should come to no harm. Then the terrible report reached her in Albany.

In high good spirits, at the end of the holiday, Augustus had galloped off down the road toward home. The farmer who witnessed the accident wrote: "I was crossing the road from the house to the barn. I observed a little boy coming down the road a short distance from me on a high spirited horse. The boy appeared to be frightened and reined his horse very tight." The farmer had passed on into his yard, but "as I turned around, I heard him cry out once. . . . About twenty rods from me the horse jumped three or four times after I seen him. Before the boy fell, he pitched backward over the right hip of the horse head foremost."

"I went to him as quick as I could. He lay on his left side with his face turned into the mud. I took him up in my arms. . . . Before I got him to the house, I perceived that he breathed and I think groaned once or twice." The farmer had bathed him with camphor, but three quarters of an hour later, the boy had "died as one falling into a calm and peaceful sleep." The report ended: "I do not know as there can be any blame attached to any one."

Reading the words, Charlotte felt the world "liquefy" under her feet; "the waters went over my soul." It was slim comfort to know that Augustus, "the cleverest of my mother's children," the brother who had been "the delight of my young eyes," had died without long suffering.

Two days later, when the coffin arrived back in Albany, Charlotte took the jacket Augustus had worn in the accident and packed it away. In the jacket centered all the bitter remorse Charlotte felt at having given Augustus the horse that killed him.

She placed the body in a vault against the day when she could decide on a proper place for burial. Then, mothering her grieving family, she left Albany immediately.

Walking Lady at the Park

(1837–1838)

Family tradition had always maintained that "Cushman" meant "cross-bearer." In her despair, Charlotte could not dispute the claim. Nor could Mary Eliza. Charlotte knew by heart all her mother's reasons for hating the stage. Nor could she meet her mother with reason for reason why she should remain on it, when Mary Eliza found it the evil cause of their woes. Charlotte could not blame the theatre. Grief was a thing to expect anywhere, a threat to face with whatever moral courage she could muster.

She would spend no time debating her course, though in one sense she was as Calvinist as any Cushman. Not even her mother could scoff at her faith in labor. She would *work* her way out of her grief; she would commit her thoughts and efforts to the tasks at hand. If her heart had less incentive now that Augustus was dead, her mind held a new vision. "Knowing very little of my art as art," she would seek to place herself in a position where she could "learn it thoroughly."

Susan was married; she might even be happy some day. Charlie was self-supporting; her mother was secure. The family's needs were met. A few months short of her twenty-first birthday, Charlotte was free at last to answer a voice deep inside her. Outside of a possible marriage some day, she could center her course now on her own aspirations. She sat down immediately and wrote Edmund Simpson at the Park. She would take any position Simpson could offer, even a "utility" place in his company. His quick reply offered her twenty dollars a week as "walking lady," the contract to begin with the new season in September.

Walking Lady at the Park

The work would be heavy. The Park was famous, even notorious among actors, for its constant change of bills, a system that had gained it a dubious reputation for plays sometimes under-rehearsed, performed by actors always overfatigued. Yet the price was small for the glory one might reap on its fabled stage. Against its simple settings—usually a series of painted wings and drops, a rear wall obscured by canvas, and the simplest furnishings—one could easily bury one's grief in bodily and mental exertion.

To keep busy meanwhile, Charlotte would take a short run at the National, the once proud Italian Opera House that had promised so much for New York's musical tastes in 1833. Badly located in a disreputable neighborhood, it had reluctantly faced the fact that its only hope lay in legitimate drama. Reopened as a theatre in 1835, the National now courted the crowds with its high quality bills and the brilliant lamps and gaslights it had erected from the corner of Broadway down Leonard to its doors. Charlotte took quarters for herself and Mary Eliza at 77 Bowery.

It is regrettable that dramatic criticism was only sketchily developed in the America of 1837. Without recorded words of the critics, Charlotte's early career lies obscured in vague notices, advertisements, and short mentions of her name in theatre gossip columns. A decade would pass before critical journalism would become a serious craft. Yet for all her apparent early obscurity, the three years she now began were her busiest and most productive.

The show went on strikingly well with this first reappearance in New York. As a "lady-actor of gentlemen," she was perfectly favored in looks, voice, and manner. To the New York *Courier*, "a casual observer would have found some difficulty, on Saturday evening, in realizing the fact that Romeo was played by a girl." With a little more fire in the impassiond scenes, a little more emphasis to his grief, Romeo would have been "faultless." But if Charlotte had emphasized the real grief she felt, the performance might have dissolved in a flood of tears. Three nights later she scored again as Patrick, a broad leap from the sublime of Romeo; two nights after, she was the Count in *The Devil's Bridge*.

Accounts debate the circumstance that first assigned her Meg Merrilies in Scott's *Guy Mannering;* in Charlotte's own recollections names and places contradict. But her appearance as the weird gypsy on May 8, came hardly a month after Augustus' death, when a last-minute illness in the cast forced her on stage.

If Charlotte remembered the broad outlines of *Guy Mannering* from her appearance in it as Julia in Boston in 1835, she had paid little attention to the nondescript old hag who dominates the last twenty minutes of the play. But when a knock at her door brought word that she must appear that evening as Meg, she had no choice. The play was already advertised; no one else was available. Too late for any real study or proper costuming, too late for any rehearsal, Miss Cushman must make the effort; she might carry the book if she liked. Two years backstage had made Charlotte familiar with emergencies. Now, too much the trouper to panic, she listened carefully while Mary Eliza read her the lines. Inspiration on stage might suggest the proper business.

Though this dramatized version of Scott's novel had been popular in Scotland since 1816, it was a flimsy play. *Guy Mannering* lacked any real interest beyond the forceful Meg herself. Immediately sensing this, Charlotte determined to inject whatever spark she could into the humdrum story of Henry Bertram, heir to the Ellangowan estate in Dumfries. As a child of six, Henry was kidnapped and smuggled to Holland by the wily lawyer plotting to get his property. Now grown, thinking his name is Brown, Bertram serves with the British army in India, falls in love with the daughter of his commanding officer, follows her to England, and eventually arrives in the gloomy, robber-haunted neighborhood of Ellangowan Castle. His disheveled old gypsy nurse, Meg Merrilies, recognizes him and succeeds in restoring his claims to Ellangowan.

In haste, Charlotte contrived some rags for a costume, but the lines themselves gave her no clue to the character. The second act curtain was up; she was standing in the wings before the dialogue gave her a lead:

"This moor, ye must know, is not in great reputation. There's thieves and gipsies haunt it . . . there's an old woman, Meg Merrilies, the queen of 'em, that deals wi' the devil, they say, and can make 'em do any thing, if she but lifts up her finger."

"What does Meg Merrilies say; she, whom we must all obey?"

"She say! Why, she *doats;* . . . she's turned tender-hearted, and swears she'll hinder us from lifting a finger against the lad of Ellangowan, and that if we attempt to keep him from his own, we but fight against fate!"

In the words "she doats" Charlotte found the character. The tattered gypsy was suddenly a weirdly bent, hollow-eyed, shriveled crone clutching a crooked staff in skeleton fingers, still endowed with a tenderness for the child, now grown to manhood, whom she has just seen return. At once, Charlotte was aware that Meg Merrilies must horrify but elicit a deep pathos as well.

At her entrance, Charlotte darted from behind a tent, advanced silently, then gazed at the young man. When Bertram turns and discovers Meg looking at him, he says in fright, "My good woman, do you know me, that you look at me so hard?" At this point, the mood of the play changes. It is suddenly Meg's show, every action and lilt in meaning colored now by the impact of the gnarled old hag.

John Braham, the English tenor, was Henry Bertram to Charlotte's first Meg, and his reaction suggests the shock that carried over the footlights. Where Braham had expected to see the healthy young woman he had met backstage, he started in sudden fright at the wizened face, the demented eyes glaring at him through shredded gray wisps of hair, the wrinkled skin and twisted bones held rigid. After a hurricane-like swoop to the middle of the stage, she stood up suddenly tall, breathless, gripping her forked staff, staring.

When Braham finally managed to stammer, "My good woman, do you know me, that you look at me so hard?" Charlotte's hollow tone curdled his blood: "Better than you know yourself."

"Your manner is wild and oracular enough; come, give me a proof of your art."

"If, with a simple spell, I cannot recall times which you have long forgotten, hold me the miserable impostor. Hear me, hear me, Henry —Henry Bertram!"

Meg then croons the lullaby she had often sung to Bertram as a child. Singing it, Charlotte made no effort to recapture the force of the voice she had lost in 1835. Her tones emerged now in sounds that trembled and broke with feeling.

> Oh, hark thee, young Henry,
>   Thy sire is a knight,
> Thy mother a lady,
>   So lovely and bright
> The hills and the dales,
>   From the towers we see,
> They all shall belong,
>   My dear Henry, to thee.

At the curtain, Charlotte rushed off to glance again at her lines. A knock at her door informed her that Braham wished to speak with her. Had Braham come to reprimand her for misinterpreting the lines? A utility actress could hardly dare take such liberties.

But the little man grasped her hand, smiling. "Miss Cushman, I have come to thank you for the most veritable sensation I have experienced for a long time. I give you my word, when I turned and saw you, a cold chill ran all over me." He could assure her, had she done such work on a London stage, her future would have been made. Braham's compliment, the accolade of England's most popular tenor, was no idle praise, and Charlotte accepted it gratefully.

Braham's praise came at a fortunate time. If the theatre was to be her life, if the world outside was too much the pawn of circumstance, it was comforting to know that London, the capital of the English-speaking theatre, might one day sing the praises of "the Boston girl," who lived almost solely now for the life she could know at work.

The prominence Charlotte gave the part from the first displayed the growing assurance she now felt on stage. Tempered by sadness, strengthened by personal conviction that the center of the stage was her rightful place, more and more she would make her work a matter of artistic creation, a proof of the creative spark within her, evidence of her power to change the suggested outlines of a character into a fully realized personality. If James Murdoch, the actor who had witnessed some of her ups-and-downs in New Orleans, could dismiss Scott's character as a "dramatic nondescript," if another could call it a "melodramatic monstrosity," the actress with range and active imagination she was now becoming could turn the "nondescript" into a figure almost classic.

Charlotte's remaining weeks at the National carried the afterglow of excitement she felt at the success of her Meg Merrilies. An added delight was the chance to act at least four times with James W. Wallack, the handsome transplant from England, who had seen in his youth Mrs. Siddons, Edmund Kean, and John Philip Kemble. To act with him was to sense a little the brilliance one might have witnessed in the fabled people themselves, to study the effects Wallack remembered and used as patterns. With Wallack she was Elvira in Kotzebue's *Pizarro*; she was Romeo to Wallack's Mercutio, Gertrude to his Hamlet. On the seventeenth of May, she again riveted all eyes upon herself as Meg Merrilies.

The change of characters and the rapid preparations would have dismayed a talent less fully committed, but in the steady round of work Charlotte found the salvation her grief required, the buoyancy her sensibility relished. It was a different matter for her mother.

Lacking any heartfelt commitment to life outside her own feelings, Mary Eliza suffered in private. The small quarters they occupied held her locked in grief. It was Charlotte's need of her help that eventually paved the way for Mary Eliza's return to practical life. As they had worked together in Albany, so they worked together now. While Charlotte listened carefully, her mother gave her her lines, reading and rereading them aloud until Charlotte had mastered them. The daily routine distracted them both from sorrow.

Personal griefs aside, the summer of 1837 was a difficult time for any person wresting a living from a public luxury like the theatre. By the end of Charlotte's run at the National, the American economy was deep in depression. Panic hung like a cloud over all theatres. The New York gentleman Philip Hone complained in his diary: " 'Gold and silver we have none,' and there is no *change* either in our prospects or our currency."

A general panic in stocks resulted in sudden bankruptcy for men who had thought themselves unassailably wealthy. On New York sidewalks, sales of rich furniture and other elegant household effects became common. When New York banks suddenly suspended payment and other banks in the country followed suit, unemployment reached calamitous proportions. Major cities saw "bread" riots. Every man tensed himself for the next financial blow.

As a relative beginner in the theatre, Charlotte felt the pinch as deeply as anyone else. With no assurance of steady work until fall, she learned as well as any actor the direct connection between general prosperity and the fortunes of life backstage. Fortunately, work for her soon opened in Boston. Beginning the thirtieth of May, she served notice to the Boston public who remembered her as a promising young singer at the Tremont that she was now back among them, an established actress with success to her credit.

Her few days in Boston did nothing to alter her plans. Charley Wiggin could still offer marriage, but marriage had little place just now in the major dream of her life. And Charley and the rest of her friends in Boston soon realized that the uncertain girl who had made a tremulous operatic debut at this same Tremont Theatre had vanished in the confident young woman now burning with dramatic intensity. To Boston's astonishment, her somber words, her throbbing language could drive home in great hammerings of sound Lady Macbeth's self-absorbed determination. The melodius singing voice was now veiled forever in declamatory speech that rang to the farthest tiers. She amazed the town with her range, control, and forthright

73

conviction, whether as Portia in *The Merchant of Venice,* as Madge Wildfire in Scott's *Heart of Midlothian,* or the comic Henry in *Speed the Plough.*

Watching the girl's astonishing versatility one man in the audience, Colley Grattan, the British consul, went home and contrived a play expressly for her. The playwright's lines that accompanied it underscored the compliment it implied: "I would give much to see you *look* Aline, though there is nothing in the words of the part worthy of you."

After Boston, she was ready to tackle new country. She retraced her route to New York and Albany, then ventured west on a packet boat on the Erie Canal for the long slow trip to Buffalo, where she had contracted a brief engagement. The journey behind the three-horse team plodding the towpath through New York state's remote hinterland took more than a week. Lazing away her days as the empty scenery moved past, she found ample time for reflection, perhaps the occasion to write poetry. Her sonnet, "There Is No God," expressed an Emersonian faith that would have found encouragement in the quiet landscape, a promise that temporal griefs could be met.

"There Is No God"

"There is no God"—the skeptic scoffing said—
 "There is no power that sways or earth or sky;"
Remove the veil that folds the doubter's head.
 That God may burst upon his opened eye!
Is there no God? You stars above array'd,
 If he look there, the blasphemy deny;
Whilst his own features in the mirror read,
 Reflect the image of Divinity.
Is there no God? The purling streamlets flow
 The air he breathes, the ground he treads, the trees,
Bright flowers, green fields, the winds that round him blow,
 All speak of *God;* all prove that *His* decrees
Have placed them, where they may *His* being show;
 Blind to thyself, behold Him, *Man,* in these!

At Buffalo, she played briefly at the Eagle Street Theatre, then moved on to the high adventure of a sailing voyage to the small town of Detroit, far to the west in the new state of Michigan. Charlotte arrived August 8 in Detroit, a dusty muddle of 10,000 people, with "not a paved street in it, or even a foot-path for a pedestrian." She settled herself at the makeshift National Hotel, where in a forthright bid for favor from the local newspaper, she invited the editor of the *Free Press* to call. At a reception at the home of Governor Stephen T. Mason, she met an English literary light, whose friendship she enjoyed for the rest of his life.

Captain Frederick Marryat was then barnstorming through the United States gathering material for a travel book. Charlotte counted her meeting with the short, sturdy little man in Detroit one of her high moments. Marryat's eyes twinkled with a bounding wit; in his blue coat with yellow buttons, his white naval-cut vest tied loosely with a black handkerchief, his ruddy face bright and intelligent, Marryat could talk as brilliantly as a comic character in a Sheridan play. Unfortunately, the book that came out of his travels was hardly so charming. His *Diary in America* (London, 1839) was anything but complimentary to the life and scenes he witnessed. The most extraordinary national libel the press of England had yet given to the world, one American journal called it, while another decried such British arrogance that looked only at the surface of American society, saw the worst, and concluded that England and English institutions surpassed everything American. "Sam Slick," T. C. Haliburton's popular "Down-Easter," voiced the American sentiment toward travel writers like Marryat: "I seldom or never talk to none o' them, unless it be to bam 'em. They think they know everything. . . . I wouldn't give a chaw of tabackey for the books of all of 'em tied up and put into a meal-bag together."

But Charlotte saw a charm in the English wit, despite the tilt of his English nose. At the Governor's reception and during the days that followed, they exchanged verses. A flirtatious game sprang up between them. On his voyage back to Buffalo, Marryat continued it in a playful letter: "Should you observe a tremulous motion in my handwriting, do not ascribe it either to love or to having indulged last night in too many mint juleps." The true case was that the steamboat, "like most of the inhabitants of the waters, waggles his tail as he goes along."

Marryat had been thinking over their meeting. "A certain young lady was a little affronted when we met," wrote Marryat, "but if I did not know the way to her heart, I did to her head and she was easily pacified. I told her that [I was] aware of her determination to remain single and not to be the slave of one when she could reign despotic over thousands. I ascribed any man as insane who would trust himself more than 24 hours in her company, without prudentially resorting to absence as a cure for the wound already inflicted by her brilliant eyes." He ended his letter with the hope that when they met again, Charlotte would give him a poem. "It will keep you out of mischief till I come back. . . . Farewell, and be a good girl, if possible."

The jaunt out to Buffalo and Detroit and her little encounter with Marryat were pleasant enough, but Charlotte never lost sight of the fact that during this summer of 1837 she was biding her time.

When late August came, Charlotte was back in New York, thrilled again at the bustle of life about her, the constant urge in the air, the city's opulence. Life along these streets was a digest of all humanity, a portrait of man en masse, as Walt Whitman would soon describe it. To Lydia Maria Child, "the enterprising, the curious, the reckless, and the criminal" in New York made life a perpetual game.

Negro beggars lined the curbs along Broadway, their hands outstretched, while street vendors cried at intervals: "Hot corn! Hot corn! Buy my lily white corn!" After dark, children still roamed the streets, "prolonging the task of selling something" to avoid starvation. Wherever one looked, advertisements demanded attention. Even the sidewalk pavements carried the names of shops and the wares they sold. Marryat called them "horizontal tombstones."

A stroll up Broadway and a right turn at City Hall Park led Charlotte along Park Row to the front of a dirty white building, "which," said Whitman, "you internally set down in your mind as the most villainous specimen of architecture you ever beheld." This was the famous Park Theatre. Across from it, in its open tree-planted park, stood City Hall, "a redundance of marble tracery and ornament." A little beyond was Tammany Hall and the notorious Five Points, the gloomy slum that festered in New York's east side.

This was to be Charlotte's neighborhood for the next three years. She would learn its cobblestones and crannies. She would stroll its streets without fear, seeing in the life all about her the stuff of a million dramas, recognizing in the faces the features of all the emotions she could ever hope to suggest on stage.

And she would soon learn not to be put off by the Park Theatre's "contemptible aspect." Inside, it was elegantly white and gold. The Irish comedian, Tyrone Power, found it, with its three tiers of boxes and its horseshoe form, as handsome and well appointed as any theatre outside of London. Three great oil chandeliers, "a wonder of the age," lighted the 2,500 seats where New York's brightest society congregated in the lower boxes, where less elegant faces and prostitutes peered down from the higher galleries.

Quickly at home on the Park's broad stage, Charlotte felt none of the fears that had troubled her at her Boston and New Orleans openings. She was now a contracted professional, a name that had already achieved national publicity. Settling herself into her appointed place in the Park's company, she learned quickly the rapid routine that Simpson, the Park's plain-mannered, well-meaning manager, and his partner, the irascible Stephen Price, once manager at Drury Lane, demanded. Here she would work with the brightest names of the English-speaking stage, for it was a rare week that Simpson and Price did not present a visiting luminary from Europe. Tyrone Power and Edmund Kean, Charles and Fanny Kemble, and William Macready had begun their American tours on its boards. And in the regular company, Charlotte found ample challenge to her best efforts. Peter Richings, for one, an English actor of the old Siddons–Kemble school, gave her constant contact with the tradition she had first encountered in her hectic sessions with James Barton.

At the start of her season, Charlotte had only one serious misgiving, and it had nothing to do with art. She had received incredible news from Susan. Unthinkably, the young Mrs. Nelson Merriman was pregnant. And following a pattern that Charlotte now knew to expect, for reasons she could hardly appreciate, her mother and Susan looked immediately to her for help. For a time a bitter debate raged inside her, but the chilly resentment suddenly ceased when later word arrived from Susan that her husband had suffered a "loss of reason" and, mumbling something about going south on business, had abandoned her in Boston. Charlotte now knew what she had to do. In New York, she and her mother could help ease the girl's troubles; their quarters at 86 Frankfurt could accommodate her and the child. In a few days the unhappy Susan arrived.

A larger meaning was not lost on Charlotte herself. She saw no incentive at all toward marriage. If it held any advantage, any great extension of the good that life could offer, she could see little proof. The men she had known thus far were millstones around the necks of the women forced by circumstance to suffer them and the offspring they quickly ignored. Her career was totally absorbing, and it left little time or inclination to ponder the good of any romance—if love should ever challenge the odds in her mind against it.

77

As she had hoped, her work pressed heavily enough to outweigh all other concerns in her thoughts, all the grief in her heart. If the Park's playbills guaranteed anything, if it was a rare play that ran two nights in succession, it was a rare actor who did not appear almost nightly. She could find no cause to complain. The grueling stock company routine was sound training, even if it forced one to start on the lowest rung of the ladder.

In their company, Simpson and Price maintained an exact hierarchy. Rank brought position in the cast and definite assignment of talent. The leading man played protagonist roles in tragedy and the more serious ones in comedy. The light comedian played fine gentlemen. To the first old man fell the prominent elderly characters that in youth would have been assigned to the leading man. The walking gentleman took the parts of dashing young men; the utility man and utility lady were jacks and jills of all trades. The leading lady played the starring female roles in serious plays, though she might command the better comic parts as well. The walking lady ordinarily played ingenue roles.

Charlotte was the walking lady at the Park, though Simpson recognized her versatility early and used her more often as a utility lady. As such, in the course of a season she could display the whole range of her talent. Her first year at the Park, she played old women, young men, chambermaids, tragic queens, and comic ladies.

Her three-year stint began on August 26, 1837, with one of her standby roles, Patrick in *The Poor Soldier*. George C. D. Odell, the indefatigable historian of the New York stage, would later see a "preposterous" irony in the fact that a woman of Charlotte's talents made her debut at America's foremost theatre in a part that gave her so little scope. But in 1837 Charlotte still had the highest levels of fame to achieve, and her art was hardly the finely tooled instrument that time and labor might make it.

Next day the *New Yorker* hailed her arrival: in the light of Miss Cushman's "histrionic advantages, combined with her musical taste, we predict that she will become a general favorite." Talent, not beauty, would be her fortune, for Miss Cushman was no pretty face with no intelligence behind it, and audiences could rejoice in that knowledge.

Charlotte understood the intention. Praise was welcome wherever praise rightly belonged. But at twenty-one, the word that even suggested a hint of beauty in her face would have sounded sweet. The hunger for that word would never leave her.

Walking Lady at the Park

Pretty or not, true daughters of Boston were practical above all else. Good looks would have been a blessing, but although the face in her glass showed no trace of girlish charm, it had acquired in late months a womanly integrity and poise. Beneath the dark chestnut hair she now wore in a middle part smoothed over the ears and knotted in back, the great blue eyes reflected confidence and a burning energy. The jaw line would never be beautiful—her chin projected, her nose was "retroussé"—but the smile radiated vivid health and zest. In the years Charlotte could now envision at the Park, she would grasp every chance to prove the insight and intellect her face suggested. True life was seldom a matter of mere surface charm.

On such a foundation she would attempt a career among the dedicated professionals in Simpson's company. However jealously they guarded their rank in the billings, they laid aside all questions of status in the greenroom, partly because they recognized quickly Charlotte's obvious gifts. W. H. Chippendale and his wife, John Povey, William Creswick, and Peter Richings were especially friendly. And William Fredericks made her almost a protégée. The big Irishman's resonant brogue could ripple and snort in conversation, but on stage he could fill the theatre with his classic purity of tone. What James Barton had been to her in New Orleans, William Fredericks soon became in New York, suggesting a bit of business, commending a reading.

Charlotte found additional help in the steady procession of visiting stars. She studied closely as George Handel Hill, the famous "Yankee" impersonator, went through his paces in *Knight of the Golden Fleece*. Playing opposite him, Charlotte fully appreciated "Yankee" Hill's skilled professionalism, a comic whose slapstick set off gales of laughter because he had calculated every effect. As Sy Saco, or Solon Shingle, or Sam Slick, or Solomon Swap, Hill's shrewd, wily stereotype of the Yankee peddler was internationally famous, suggesting in the bargain that Yankee character epitomized American character in general. His recent acting triumph in England had delighted the British and further confirmed their notion that Americans, whatever else they might be or become, were tricksters who needed watching.

Charlotte studied an even better performer on September 19. The legendary Edwin Forrest, the man whose success in England had in-

79

spired her eulogy in Albany, appeared at the Park as King Lear. Unquestionably a star of the first magnitude, Forrest's promise had been apparent to Edmund Kean as early as 1825. "I have met one actor in this country," Kean remarked at a banquet, "a young man named Edwin Forrest, who gave proofs of a decided genius for his profession, and will, I believe, rise to a great eminence." The night Charlotte first acted Cordelia with Forrest brought her the keenest thrill she had known as an actress. The magnetic force in the man carried over into the girl who observed his every gesture, listened keenly to his reading of every line.

Forrest was blessed with a magnificent voice embodied in a gladiator's physique. "The million" claimed him. Forrest had crudities of style, his roarings and bellowings could shake the rafters, but he could make an audience weep and shudder. He could seem so real on stage that a critic compared his acting to the "blare of trumpets and clash of cymbals," to the "thundering surges of the sea." In Edinburgh, his reading of Hamlet's line, "My father's brother!—but no more like my father than I to Hercules!" had caused a Scot in the pit to cry: "Hoot, awa', mon! Dinna talk damned nonsense! Ye are just Hercules himsel'!"

Offstage, the great Edwin was no less impressive, though his unpredictable temper made him a good deal less easy to like. The polished gentleman, the man of intellectual dignity, moral refinement, and strength, could suddenly become—without warning or provocation—"a creature of uncivilized bluntness and untempered brutality." An unfortunate actor who once stumbled through his lines caught the full blast of Forrest's rage:

"You are a butcher by trade, are you not?"

"No, sir, I am an actor."

Grabbing him by the collar and dangling him at arm's length, Forrest cried: "An actor! You are not, sir; you are a butcher. Go resume your calling, kill sheep, kill oxen, kill asses, if you must, but never kill Shakespeare more."

Charlotte's first brush with Forrest at the Park left her unscathed. "This wonder of the stage," as she had called him in Albany, fully deserved all the honors England and America had showered upon him, "a combination and a form indeed, where every God did seem to set his seal to give the world assurance of a Man!" After *Lear* she could still sing his praises.

Nor would she ever discount his power to dominate a part, to invest it so fully with his personality that audiences trembled with his electrical effects. In the bombastic, inflammatory, herculean Mr. Forrest, his meticulous care with words, his almost physical manipulation of them, Charlotte could recall the earliest acting advice she ever received, the admonitions of Clara Maeder and James Barton to let the role breathe and *move* with its words. To these earlier guides, and now to Forrest, Charlotte owed some credit for the fact that she soon became the best reader in the Park company.

Playing Cordelia to Forrest's Lear was like being engulfed in a cyclone. *King Lear* was the actor's show from start to finish; Lear was his greatest role. And Charlotte learned, like all the actors who ever appeared with Forrest, that everything else in the play was secondary, mere stage business meant as a frame for the star. When Lear's delirious prayer to nature reverberated through the theatre, lightning seemed to flash all around him. To appear with Forrest was unforgettable, but to Charlotte it was a little like not being on stage at all: she learned immediately where the enraptured eyes of the audience centered.

A few nights later she was Nahmeokee to Forrest's brave Indian, Metamora. Since 1829 the actor had appeared repeatedly in John Augustus Stone's sad tale of the noble red man who refuses to "forsake the home of his fathers and let the plough of strangers disturb the bones of his kindred." Forrest had personally commissioned the play, the role suited him perfectly, and it had brought him a fortune —though so little profit to Stone that the playwright had drowned himself in the Schuylkill. As Metamora he could posture and declaim all over the stage. Poised like bronze on a rocky crag, his legs planted firm and his arms held high, Forrest's roarings could vibrate the stage.

In the final scene when Metamora has lost all his warriors, when his child has been murdered, he and his wife, Nahmeokee, hear white men approaching. Knowing the end has come, Metamora embraces Nahmeokee, then quickly stabs her. As he lowers her body to the ground, one thought gives him comfort: "She felt no white man's bondage—free as the air she lived—pure as the snow she died!" Though few eyes ever wandered from Metamora, a *Herald* reporter commented next day: "By the way, Miss Cushman played the Indian wife remarkably well. Her qualifications are eminently suited to such brusque characters."

On October 19 Charlotte played another brusque character, Goneril to Forrest's Lear. On November 18 she was Laura in Sargent's *The Genoese* with Josephine Clifton, an American actress who had recently scored in London. The aura that surrounded Miss Clifton's beautiful head, her great kindness, strengthened in Charlotte an idea that had been slowly forming. She remembered John Braham's praise of her Meg Merrilies. Had he spoken honestly about her chance for success in London?

Another English visitor in New York recognized her qualifications for London. "In one of my evening rambles about the city," the unnamed observer wrote, "I found myself passing the Park Theatre, and I was moved to go in." In the part of Emilia, "I saw a large-sized, fair-complexioned young woman, not of handsome, but of impressive presence." Her denouncing of Othello after his murder of Desdemona was "electric." Her power and passion made Emilia the dominant role in the scene. Adding his own cheers to the rapturous applause, "I knew that there was no ordinary artist in this then comparatively unknown young woman."

Soon, one of Charlotte's regular fans at the Park was the Knickerbocker wit, Fitz-Greene Halleck. At forty-seven Halleck made a career of observing New York's passing scene. Charlotte knew to expect him in the same seat almost nightly, sitting with one hand cupped behind a partly deaf ear, noting every movement on stage. His quick eye, his ready applause often greeted the sudden flash of genius he detected in a new actor. Park Theatre people knew to watch him. His approval could brighten any newcomer's chances. Charlotte never discounted the value of his support.

Charlotte's life was now almost totally committed to the Park and its people. Though no one could yet call Charlotte Cushman a star, she was secure enough now to pass along some of the help that had come her way. An aspiring playwright, Adrien de Montfort, appeared at her door. Would Miss Cushman read one of his plays? The youth's earnest tone, his eagerness, matched a familiar feeling. She invited him in, gestured him to a seat, quickly read his manuscript, then laid it aside. The language was good; the tone, impressive. But the play lacked dramatic effect. "The quiet home dramas would have little chance of success in our day," she told him. "The public require stronger food, I might almost say unnatural stimulant."

But Charlotte encouraged him, "Some day or other, when I can find time, I will give you a plot for a play, and you may make another trial. I think that a dramatic version of the story of some of the 'Spartan Mothers' would give *you* an excellent opportunity to write, and *me* to act. I reverence the characters of these noble women to whose greatness we have not given due recognition." In the meantime, she gave de Montfort a note to an influential friend —Fitz-Greene Halleck, perhaps—who could help him publish his stories.

But although Charlotte made friends in the Park company, she also made enemies. The passions she could detonate on stage occasionally exploded behind it. For a reason not clear in the record, a scene painter touched off her wrath. She was "terrible" to him, "a tiger when her passions were aroused, capable of anything." When the report reached his friend, William James Stillman, he himself gained her ill will. Later, when Stillman had met her, he was firmly convinced that Charlotte's fury at times stemmed mainly from an impatience with some man's ineptness, some masculine "stupidity" blocking her way. But such storms were rare, though intense while they lasted.

When occasional free time allowed it, she rambled alone through New York's teeming streets. The free Negroes captured her interest, their airs and clothes and manners reflecting the white airs and postures about them. In place of the Park, the blacks had their own theatre, the African Grove at Bleecker and Mercer. In the townhouses where she was a guest, conversation centered more and more on the pros and cons of abolition. In 1838, the fear was steadily growing that slavery would one day devastate the country.

With the Judds (once she had made plain her determination to keep on acting) she exercised her talent for conversation. National concerns held the floor: the ever-rising tide of pioneer migration beyond the Cumberland and the Mississippi, the reports coming in from Texas, new towns springing up along the frontier. For all his exaggerations, her friend Marryat was right in saying that America was changing so rapidly that he "who would describe America now" would have to correct himself in ten years, for "ten years in America is almost equal to a century in the old continent."

Charlotte kept a steady eye on theatre news pouring in from the South and West. New playhouses were opening in St. Louis; Galena, Illinois; Dubuque, Iowa territory; Iberville, Louisiana; Columbus, Mississippi; Huntsville, Alabama; and the small village of Chicago expanding like a mushroom at the tip of Lake Michigan. The ambitious little hamlet, Houston, was celebrating in verse its own attempts to found a permanent drama: "To other climes, our native drama long hath been indebted," but in these changing times "here let genius dwell and tuneful lyres, with proud ambition strung, raise high their notes, to native music sung." To every American Charlotte's age, the country's financial pains could scarcely discount its unquenchable hopes. And for Charlotte at the Park, top theatre in the city where America's driving ambitions centered, the promise seemed boundless.

"Miss Cushman and Her Sister"

(1838–1840)

If the remaining years of Charlotte's contract with Simpson and Price could teach her valuable lessons, only time would tell if her profits would include more money. Good sense might recommend that she tackle willingly every role the managers assigned, the present varied use of her talents might seem to promise the future she wanted, but for herself a deeper truth was made plain. In stock companies, even the best ones, walking ladies took most of their gains in experience.

At home where idleness hung heavy on Susan's hands, Charlotte suggested a new interest to speed the months until March. Too awkward now to assist with the household chores, Susan could help Charlotte learn her new roles. Throughout the winter, a new camaraderie developed between them. Feeding Charlotte her lines, Susan discovered in herself a real flare for reading, a born sense of phrasing that injected new excitement into the study routine. On the fourth of March, 1838, Susan Merriman gave birth to a healthy boy. She named the infant Edwin Charles, though Charlotte promptly nicknamed him Bub. In the fatherless household, the baby's arrival brought the three women an immediate joy, but their uncertainty tempered into a long-range concern that was not always best for the boy. Three mothers were more than any child needed.

In May, Forrest returned to the Park, ready to overwhelm his audience again in a new comedy, Bulwer-Lytton's *The Lady of Lyons*. In the play the proud Pauline Deschapelles has rejected various suitors, including a former Marquis. Resenting the slight, Beauseant persuades Claude Melnotte, son of Pauline's old gardener, to masquerade as a Prince and trick the girl into marriage. After the wedding, remorse overcomes the young husband; he confesses the ruse to Pauline and has the marriage annulled. The rest of the play gives Pauline ample opportunity to prove that she really loves Claude. At the end, they remarry.

With Forrest as Claude, Charlotte had little to do as his mother, but she made the part "interesting and prominent." Walt Whitman was deeply impressed: Charlotte put "more genius" into her Widow Melnotte than any number of foreign stars could hope to inject.

A few weeks later, *The Lady of Lyons* served her better. On June 10, when one of the loveliest English actresses ever seen in America, Ellen Tree, came to the Park to play Pauline, Charlotte was again the mother. But by the twenty-eighth, she had gained enough support from Simpson and Price to attempt Forrest's own role as Claude. A fine house received her Claude "exceedingly well." The *Spirit of the Times* would not swear that Forrest and Ellen Tree had ever set off louder applause.

Charlotte began the new season in August 1838 as Hero in *Woman's Wit*. The *Spirit* hailed "the exquisite taste" of her performance: Miss Cushman's rapid advance would surprise no person aware of the "unwearied assiduity with which she has devoted herself to the cultivation of her talents." Her prospects were "brilliant." Gratifying words indeed to begin a new season. At home, her mother and Susan were well, little Bub flourished in the circle of maternal attention, and Charlotte herself had never felt more secure.

In the maturity her busy years were bringing, Charlotte was discovering the normal price success exacts from the professional artist. Striving to win, he seldom knows total victory in a subjective medium like acting. No matter how skilled he may be, he cannot always please the multitude. A case in point was James Gordon Bennett's complaints in the *Herald*: If Miss Cushman ever hoped to become a really popular actress, she must alter her style, rid herself of a general looseness, a "helter skelter, random, devil-may-care manner on stage." Said Bennett, "She plays with her part, but she does not play it."

While the comment provoked her, it gave little help. To her knowledge, she had no particular style, no mannerisms or tricks, no hollow gestures or stock expressions. She was playing too many roles to use any stock technique. Still, Bennett's word was a thing to consider, especially in light of her growing hopes not only to merit New York stardom but eventually to storm the gates of London.

Truly, no one could hope to please everyone. The day Bennett took her to task in the *Herald,* Porter eased her pain in the *Spirit*: "It is characteristic of Miss Cushman to give herself to the study of her parts, however beneath her rank, with all industry." Whether barmaid or chambermaid, heroine or clown, she played her parts with "care and fidelity." Her constant study was bringing her "increasing excellence and popularity." Ahead of her surely lay substantial rewards, "a high salary and good benefits."

Charlotte was not the first or the last to find the critics a puzzling lot, no matter how inept they might be. Unable to please them all, too busy to worry, she redoubled her efforts. Audience acclaim was, after all, the truest reward, and when the acclaim was like that shouted by a vigorous young reporter from Brooklyn, she took heart. "Who has seen her Evadne, in *The Bridal,* but acknowledged the towering grandeur of her genius!" wrote Walt Whitman. "In the simple utterance of her shrieking 'yes! yes! yes!' as she swings down to her brother's feet, was one of the greatest triumphs of the histrionic art, ever achieved!" For young Whitman, "in the twinkling of an eye—in the utterance of a word—was developed the total revolution of a mighty and guilty mind—from pride, defiance, anger, and rioting guilt, to an utterly crushed state of fear, remorse, and conscious vileness!" He could swear he would never forget "the surpassing beauty of that performance!"

Throughout the fall of 1838 and into the winter, as her success at the Park continued, Charlotte sensed a growing disquiet in Susan. With Nelson Merriman out of Susan's life forever, there was little to fear on that score. The girl had no obligation to him, no compulsion to go back to him should he ever appear. Susan's dissatisfaction finally came out in a serious talk. As a mother with a child's needs on her hands, she could accept no more charity from Charlotte. She must begin to pay her own way.

But Susan was soon to discover, as her mother had years before, that jobs for women were still not easy to find. And what were her capabilities? Suddenly inspired, Charlotte suggested that Susan herself attempt a stage career. In the practice sessions at home, feeding Charlotte her lines, the girl had already revealed a certain talent. Charlotte could coach her, could guide whatever real gifts might become clear in directed study. Captivated, Susan set immediately to work on the promptbooks Charlotte brought home, imagining the day when she herself, at stage center, might reap applause.

To date, the public could agree that Charlotte had already made three roles particularly her own: Romeo, Lady Macbeth, and Meg Merrilies. They had become hers the minute she first appeared in them. She soon added a fourth to her list.

Dickens' new novel, *Oliver Twist,* had scarcely hit American book-stalls before Simpson and Price had a dramatized version ready. The plight of an appealing orphan seemed surefire at the box office, especially against such disreputable types as the evil Fagin, the Artful Dodger, Bill Sykes, and his companion, the ragged, uncouth Nancy.

All along, Charlotte had found Edmund Simpson completely amicable, but in Stephen Price she had found a puzzling antagonist. She was not alone in her troubles; to a man, the Park's actors knew Price as a boastful, greedy opportunist. Sooner or later, the whole company had come into conflict with him. When Charlotte's own strong convictions stood up to him, sparks flew.

Near the first of February, 1839, Price announced his casting for *Oliver Twist,* the play to be ready in a week. The disreputable Nancy fell to Charlotte. She dared not show her fury at being assigned so sordid a role; the mere thought of it repelled her. But against Price's ill will, she knew she was helpless. "I dared not refuse, nor even remonstrate, for I knew he wished to provoke me to break my engagement." Her only choice was to make the best of the matter, to try to outwit Price's determined attacks against her. The problem called for strong measures, for in spite of its crudity Charlotte saw in the role a spark of pathos. Immediately, she devised a plan.

She made it clear to Mary Eliza that she must be gone a few days. Before leaving, she admonished Snsan to keep up her study, to be ready for the day when she could seek an audition with Simpson. She then put on her most nondescript clothes and picked her way through the dingy streets to the notorious Five Points, fit slum for a Fagin's gang. In a miserable den called "Mother Hennessey's," which catered to prostitutes and bums, she rented a room.

Next morning, she wandered the filth-littered streets, listening intently to the raucous voices and street cries, watching the shifty faces, eager to catch every feature of poverty and hunger. One old hag, resenting Charlotte's interest, tried to attack her. When another old woman became violently ill in a saloon, Charlotte took her to Mother Hennessey's and cared for her until the woman died in the night. Before breathing her last, she gave Charlotte all of her possessions, a ragged bonnet, her threadbare dress, and her shoes. Next morning Charlotte packed the items in a tattered basket, scratched through a trash heap until she located a large rusty key, then made her way back to the theatre.

Small wonder, perhaps, that the play that opened on February 7, 1839, elicited an almost terrible fascination. Dickens' scene and his people had been translated exactly to the stage, "in all their wretchedness, in all the squalid misery of their lives . . . forever skulking uneasily through the dirtiest paths of life, with the great black ghastly gallows closing up their prospect, turn them where they might." The despicable Nancy lacked all refinement. In every ugly detail she was the wretched women Charlotte had observed in Five Points, though through her acting Nancy the creature became a fully realized human being.

When Peter Richings as Sykes said, "A dolly-mop, eh, Fagin? And here she comes with a bonnet, apron, basket, and street-door key complete," Charlotte entered, swinging her great rusty key. While her lines called for her simply to cross and signal to Oliver, she moved stealthily around the crowd, crossed the stage, then recrossed, shot a look of sympathy at Oliver, thrust her tongue in her cheek, and then exited.

Throughout the play she dominated her scenes; the sympathy was hers as much as Oliver's. To one observer, Charlotte put "pages of despair into the simple act of battering her ragged old hat on a nail in the wall, sitting down, rocking to and fro, and biting the tip off a stick." Dickens' abandoned outcast, a girl who might have remained a tigress of the slums, became in Charlotte's portrayal a feminine sensibility blotted and trampled by human cruelty, slowly discovering a sense of honor and decency.

Part of the trick was the costume. The tattered hat, the shredded apron, the dirt-colored shawl, the disheveled dress, the red boots—all were spoils of her visit to Five Points. But the acting was also an import from the seething, festering streets nearby. Charlotte had seen Nancy's counterparts on every corner. It was no difficult trick to suggest the girl's bitter hopelessness when she tries to defend Oliver against Fagin and Sykes:

Nancy: Let him be then, or I shall put that mark on some of you that will bring me to the gallows before my time!
Sykes: You're a nice 'un—to take up the humane and genteel side!—a pretty subject for the child to make a friend!

Nancy: God help me! I am—I am; and I wish I had died in the streets before I had lent a hand in bringing him to where he is. Ah me! he's a thief from this night forth—and isn't that enough without more cruelty?

Fagin: Civil words.

Nancy: Civil words, Fagin! Do *you* deserve 'em from *me?* Who taught me to pilfer and to steal, when I was a child not half so old as this? You! I have been in the trade and in your service twelve years since, and you know it, well—you know you do!

Fagin: And if you have, it is your living.

Nancy: Ah! it is—it is my living! And the cold, wet, dirty streets are my home! And you're the wretch who drove me to 'em long ago, and that'll keep me there till I die.

Brandishing her stick, Nancy rushes at Fagin, but Sykes grabs her and squeezes her so tightly she faints, while hatred and horror play in her face.

In Nancy's final scene, Charlotte took the character to its pathetic limit. Sykes enters the dark bedroom, determined to punish her for plotting against Fagin and himself.

Nancy: It *is* you! I am so glad.

Sykes: It is. Get up!

Nancy: You've put out the light; but no matter, the day is beginning to dawn, and I'll open the window.

Sykes: Let it be! There's light enough for what I've got to do. (Seizing her arm and dragging her to center)

Nancy: Oh! Tell me what I've done—I—I won't scream or cry; but speak to me and tell me what I've done.

Sykes: You know! You were watched tonight, and every word was heard!

Nancy: Then spare my life, for the love of heaven, as I spared yours! (Clinging to him) You cannot have the heart to kill me! I will not lose my hold! You cannot throw me off! Oh, stop before you spill my blood! I have been true to you—upon my guilty soul! . . . I will hold you till you kiss me and forgive.

Sykes drags her off the stage, then a scream is heard, then a fall, and Sykes reenters, pale and trembling. "There is blood upon these hands and she is dead." The next instant, Charlotte dragged herself back into view. Keeping her face away from the audience, calling pitifully to Sykes, begging him to kiss her and forgive, she sounded "as if she spoke through blood."

The *Spirit* had raves for Charlotte's "inimitable truth and great power" as Nancy. "She makes it the most effective character in the play." In spite of her fears about the repulsive part, wholly against Stephen Price's intentions, Charlotte's Nancy became an immediate hit. Walt Whitman labeled the reality of her acting "appalling," the most "intense acting ever *felt* on the Park boards." And as late as thirteen years afterward, Francis Wemyss, the Philadelphia theatre manager, still recalled her Nancy's "powerful impression." She repeated the role sixteen times that season. And to Charles Dickens' regret, sourly complaining that he never made a farthing from a stage version of his books, Charlotte's Nancy established an American theatre vogue for Dickens.

Dates in the record vary, but within a few nights excitement again hit the Cushman household. With a successful audition behind her, Susan Cushman made her stage debut as Laura to Charlotte's Montaldo in Epes Sargent's play, *The Genoese*. For Charlotte, the preceding weeks had conjured up her frenzied days in New Orleans, when she had labored and prayed with Barton. Like her sister, Susan was a quick study, though here their resemblance ended. Susan's gentleness fitted her for roles Charlotte could never consider, the supple, romantic ingenues requiring the grace she herself lacked. And that fact would save trouble. Booked in the same company, the sisters need never compete for the same roles.

If Susan's debut set off no volcano of cheers, the Park's regulars found in this "pretty" Cushman ample talent for an acting career. At home, new happiness reigned. At last the sixteen-year-old mother could venture out of her shell. A contracted professional, she could peg her sights toward building a life for herself and her child, on a starting salary of $12 a week.

Charlotte's keenly honed memory, one of the many acting tools she developed during these busy years at the Park, gave her a happy lift in September 1839, when John Howard Payne came to call. She confessed her debt to her eminent visitor; now, fourteen years after her self-conscious tongue had loosened while reading aloud Payne's lines from *Brutus* at school, she could credit the course of her life to that simple schoolroom exercise. The joy she had discovered that day in words clearly pronounced and projected had never left her.

The time had come for repayment. Just now Payne had a playwright's interest in Texas; its recent struggles had fired his imagination. He had finished a Texas play; he was working on a Texas novel. *The Banished Son,* he wrote after the meeting, "is now entirely in the rough, and requires remodelling throughout; but you will make out the story. I purpose making Texas the scene of refuge and making the villains some of the Mexican marauders there." It should make a popular play.

Payne had Charlotte in mind for one of its derring-do roles. The Texas subject should brighten its appeal. Charlotte recognized the flattery in Payne's visit; the friend of Southey, Coleridge, and Charles Lamb had come to solicit her help. His song, "Home Sweet Home," had long been famous; his *Brutus* was one of the most arresting plays yet written by an American. But Payne had his difficulties. Without the help of an established actor or a "foreign stamp of approval" on his work, no American playwright stood much chance of finding his works succeed at the box office. His only real chance at profit lay in making a direct sale to a manager or being commissioned to write a vehicle for a star.

Payne had brought four unproduced plays to Charlotte. Might he have her reaction? Did they stand a chance with Simpson and Price? "They are trusted to you in perfect confidence; and under a reliance that no one else will be permitted to see them."

Payne was correct that a Texas subject brightened a play's appeal. For more than ten years, "G.T.T." soaped on a man's front window fully explained his sudden absence; he had "sloped," "Gone to Texas" to seek his fortune or escape the law. Reports filtered back to the States playing up these Texans as renegades, frontier braggarts who might settle down one day and become civilized men, but present evidence for such was scant. Too busy fighting the wilderness, the Texans cared little for critical opinion. Translated onto the stage, who could say just how popular Payne's *Banished Son* might become, with Charlotte Cushman playing the lead?

Next day, Charlotte returned three of Payne's manuscripts with "thanks for the pleasure they have afforded me." She would keep the fourth a day or so longer, "but would not allow the day to pass without making a part of my promise good." Whatever help Charlotte managed to give the eminent Payne, his visit marked a progress in her own career. If "theatre" meant "actors" in the public mind, Payne sought her help as an actor whose light shone with increasing brilliance.

It occurred to her late in the season to seek advice about her own ambitions. After a performance of Shakespeare's *Henry VIII,* probably the first time Charlotte played Queen Katharine, she asked William Chapman, Lord Sands in the play, what chance she might have at success in England. A man of many talents, Chapman had just returned from a career in England and on the Mississippi showboats. His opinion would be based on solid experience.

Chapman's reply was immediate. "Extraordinary gifts" like hers were wasted in the "trivial" parts Simpson repeatedly gave her; by all means, Charlotte should go to London and let her talents be known.

Chapman's advice needed thinking. At twenty-three she could dream, but an actual voyage to London and a debut before an English audience required something more. In New York a walking lady's salary might keep body and soul together, but it could hardly do more —certainly not cover the cost of an ocean voyage, however practical the investment might be. She could begin her plans now, but time must give her guidance. Meanwhile, with whatever help she could offer, Susan had a name to establish, and she herself must appear to her best advantage on occasions like July 5, 1839, the day the playbills announced, "The President of the United States will honor the theatre with his presence this evening."

From a flag-draped box the President's party watched Charlotte rollick through an important new role, Lady Teazle in *The School for Scandal.* With the country's shaky finances, with his popularity hitting a new low almost daily, Martin Van Buren needed entertainment. Charlotte's Lady Teazle brought the President momentary relief from his cares, for unlike the rural belle imitating the haughty Lady Sneer and Mrs. Candour whom Miss Abington had created at Drury Lane in 1777, Charlotte made the part "fresh and hoydenish." The President applauded her pouting and quarreling, her wheedling and coaxing Sir Peter. Her success in the part and Van Buren's delighted responses brought her many new admirers.

Susan's own acting, some two weeks later, confirmed all opinions that the younger Cushman possessed no mean talent herself. With

Charlotte as Emilia and George Vandenhoff as Othello, she charmed the audience with her fragile, almost willowy, Desdemona. At the curtain, Charlotte and Susan returned to stage center and, in a low-sweeping bow, acknowledged the applause together. Throughout the 1839–40 season the sisters regularly appeared in the same plays.

If the playbills caused trouble between them, there was no sign of it. In the heavy black letters tacked on the Park's front doors, "Miss Cushman" always meant Charlotte; Susan was "Her sister." If the younger of Mary Eliza's daughters resented this second billing, she had more important things on her mind. Stardom might be vital to a burning talent like Charlotte's, applause an indispensable element, but for Susan, now that she had qualified for the work, her best reward was the steady income it brought to the household on Frankfurt Street.

However much new talent fears a critical press, during these early years Charlotte needed more perceptive appraisal than New York papers usually gave. From the start, William T. Porter's *Spirit of the Times* had ranked among her most loyal supporters. In 1838 Porter had trumpeted the word, "We cordially congratulate herself and friends upon the brilliant prospects before her." Porter's goodwill was heartening, but a person striving constantly to improve found little help in such comments.

His notice on March 1840 was more to the point. Porter confessed his reluctance to fault anyone so "ambitious to excel," but the sooner Miss Cushman, an actress of decided talent, learned that force and command did not solely depend on violent gesture and angry tone, the sooner she would achieve "the perfection for which she strives." As Mary Stuart, she had "over-acted." The towering Queen had been leveled to "something between a scold and a vixen." Let her not misunderstand; his rebukes were meant in all kindness, but Miss Cushman must remedy a serious defect which had increased along with her "confessedly superior" powers.

The reprimand brought no joy, but she could agree she had much to learn. Throughout the spring, as she and Susan continued to appear almost nightly, she maintained a firmer control. They were Mrs. Page and Mrs. Ford in *The Merry Wives of Windsor* on April 23; they were Gertrude and Ophelia on the twenty-fourth; their benefit with Charles Kean in *Macbeth* on May 8 brought one of the best houses of the season. Porter published his satisfaction; the size of the crowd was "a most deserving and eloquent tribute" to the talented sisters.

"Miss Cushman and Her Sister"

Back in April, when Simpson announced Kean's forthcoming run at the Park, the greenroom had tingled with suppressed excitement. The son of the fabled Edmund would undoubtedly shed a luster recalling his father's brilliance. Though few in America had forgotten the great Edmund's arrogance on his tour in the 1820s, few debated his rank as one of the world's superstars. His arresting looks, his carriage, his magnetism had made him a legend. His son Charles was expected to fill his shoes.

Unfortunately, young Charles possessed hardly a diluted version of his father's gifts. Charlotte gave him her utmost support as Goneril, but she found little brilliance in the man. His acting was filled with calculated effort; his voice had a peculiar rasp and nasal huskiness. In spite of Kean's limitations, Charlotte brought much credit to herself in his presence. James Parton, as a child, saw her Goneril to Kean's Lear and "hated her—making no distinction between her and the part she played." After only four nights at the Park, Kean succumbed to severe laryngitis and moved on to Boston where further calamity befell. He was standing in the wings ready to enter, when a counterweight fell from the flies and killed a man standing on the spot Kean had just vacated, spattering the actor with blood.

Near the season's end, a question arose. After three years of service to Simpson, Charlotte was certain she was worth more than the $20 guaranteed in her contract. And she was no less certain that Susan deserved a raise. What increase for them did Simpson have in mind? She would expect $5 more for herself and at least a token increase for Susan. Simpson debated: Miss Cushman must realize that these perilous times made box office receipts unpredictable. But to Charlotte, perilous times were the soundest argument why good service deserved reward. After a heated argument Simpson stood firm at $20 for Charlotte, $12 for Susan. Outraged, the Cushman sisters decided not to rejoin the niggardly Simpson in the fall.

August 12, 1840, was Charlotte's final night at the Park. Taking her bows, she could look back proudly, if wearily, on a period of almost total growth—in spite of Simpson's tight-fisted control of her income. That earlier August when she had first moved into the focal point of these footlights, she had been a fledgling with everything to gain in a top professional company. But now, if she had not yet achieved real fame, she had become an artist. She had kept her ambitions clear. In three years at the Park she had played more than 120 different roles, ranging from leads to the humblest, unnamed faces.

Practicing her art, she had learned a practical lesson. Never again would she humbly submit to a manager's every dictation. At the Park, if she had sometimes "over-acted," she had often been overworked. She had been foolish to make herself so generally useful. And while her compliance had attracted Simpson's healthy regard, the fact had not weighted her pocket. She had discovered that Simpson and Price, like any practical managers of the time, kept useful people down, "lest they should feel their own strength" and oblige their employers to hire two or three people instead of one—or else pay that one more money.

Appreciation by others was partly the value one placed on oneself. Confident of her gifts, fully aware that her work at the Park had accounted for more than its share of customers, she resolved now never again to undersell her own wares. If leaving the Park made her worth "painfully apparent" to Simpson, he had no one to blame but himself. She left Simpson's company now to become leading lady at W. E. Burton's new National Theatre in Philadelphia, a chance at last to plant her banners on the highest ramparts of her profession.

An Artist's Growth in Philadelphia

(1840–1842)

Shortly before Charlotte led her family onto the train, she dashed off a note to Sam Judd: "The recollections of your kindness will ever be fresh in my heart." For whether they knew it or not, ever since 1832 the Judds' hopes for her happiness had spurred her best efforts, even if they could never approve of her career. At age twenty-four, the day she turned her back on New York in July 1840 and headed toward Philadelphia, she needed their confidence. For all the force and command others might see in her, the authority in her manner could hardly belie the trembling in her heart.

Leaving New York, she could relax in the knowledge that in the move she had everything to gain professionally. Out of it might eventually come stardom. But what of the family? Would Burton's promises justify the flurry of the past few weeks, the pain of tearing up roots only slowly put down. And what of her own feelings? Facing the new uncertainties, could her courage withstand another possible onslaught of "judgments"?

Safely arrived in the Quaker City, she sensed immediately a difference in atmosphere. With a population of 90,000 Philadelphia seemed hardly more than a large town; it maintained a poised air that New York had long since discarded. Nestled in Quaker dignity around Independence Hall, Philadelphia was a cluster of red and white houses, whose "perfect silence and solitude" impressed Charlotte now, as they had impressed the newly arrived Fanny Kemble eight years before.

The Philadelphia Charlotte came to know centered its enterprise on the docks along the Schuylkill. Its red brick sidewalks were seldom crowded; its housewives took vigorous pride in the polished brass rails and scrubbed marble steps at their doors. In Captain Marryat's opinion, a newcomer could easily believe that any day of the week he had arrived on was Sunday. At night, except when the theatre doors stood open, the silence of the narrow streets was broken only by the occasional sound of a carriage passing.

Charlotte quartered her family—Charlie had quit his job in New York—at the Washington House in Chestnut Street, "for less than we could keep house, and in a first class hotel at that," she wrote Sam Judd. From the hotel, a short walk each morning would take her and Susan to rehearsals and, under Charlie's escort, performances each night.

Every time she walked that easy distance, Charlotte knew the thrill of seeing her name carried high on the daily playbills tacked to the front of Burton's new National. And the theatre itself imparted a similar thrill, with its new paint and shiny brass, its clean curtains. On August 31, when Burton dedicated his new house—"the first in the Union," he called it—Charlotte parted the heavy drapes to deliver some lines she had written herself, a hopeful prologue to the new season. And then, playing Lydia Languish to Susan's Lucy in *The Rivals,* she began this latest chapter in her career.

The week following, playing six different roles, she made it clear to Burton and all the company that she would bend every effort to make her mark. On September 1 she was Ellen Rivers in *The Patriarch and the Parvenu;* on the second, Gabrielle in *Tom Noddy's Secret.* Three nights later she shocked the Quakers with her tattered Nancy; on the seventh she was Beatrice in *Much Ado;* the eighth she played Smike in *Nicholas Nickleby.*

By now, the daily grind and nightly change of characters was so standard a life for a stock company actor that Charlotte thought little of it—beyond her steady sweet taste of top billing. On the twenty-seventh she played Mrs. Page to James H. Hackett's Falstaff and left Hackett himself reeling from her determination to succeed. To Hackett, the young actress had faults, but there was no gainsaying her promise—and her probable victory. "There is nobody strong enough to question her right, after she has made up her mind," he said.

Throughout September and October, she and Susan "bloomed and flourished." Most nights found them together on stage, though Philadelphia soon saw in Charlotte's magnetism a threat to Susan's conventional grace. Backstage, some even detected a show of temper in Susan that might stem from resentment. By late in the month, Charlotte wrote Sam Judd that she had made "a decided hit." It was not bragging to say that among the Philadelphians "I have established myself at once a favorite." If she envied the ovation Baltimore had just given the English dancer, Fanny Ellsler—admirers had drawn her carriage through the cheering streets—might she not hope, some far-off day, to hear similar cheers for herself?

In her leisure hours Charlotte often found herself in the studio of James Hamilton, Philadelphia's celebrated marine painter, and when rehearsals allowed it, she spent mornings cantering out to Hamilton's country home in time for good conversation and breakfast with the admiring fans and moneyed patrons that circulated around him. The horseback jaunts relieved tensions that sometimes built up on stage, and she found in the bright talk at Hamilton's table a welcome outlet for a mind that teemed with ideas. And no less important, contacts to be made through Hamilton were a matter of "minding the main chance." If any trait in her had become uppermost by the time she finished her contract in New York, it was alertness for practical openings. At this point, Charlotte made certain that Fanny Kemble should enter her life.

Niece of Sarah Siddons, brilliant star in her own right, Fanny Kemble's name excited the dreams of any actress. Following a stunning debut at Covent Garden, she and her father had crossed the Atlantic in 1832 to reap an acclaim no less incredible on American stages. Up to that time, Fanny was the most brilliant actress ever seen at the Park; her Julia in *The Hunchback* had created the wildest sensation. Marriage in 1834 to the very eligible Pierce Butler of Philadelphia had led to her retirement in "Butler Place," a house of great style set at the head of an avenue of trees in suburban Germantown. But as a pampered wife, Fanny had not found happiness. Even before the marriage, her friend Catherine Sedgwick had foreseen trouble. "Steeped to the lips with genius," Fanny had glorious faculties, delightful accomplishments, and, alas, "half a hundred faults." Pierce Butler was an amiable sort but "infinitely inferior" to her.

For all her talent, by 1840 Fanny knew she could never play the submissively proper wife Butler wished to exhibit to Philadelphia society. Her British disdain for American "provincialisms," her determination to speak out and write as she pleased, to ride horseback whenever and wherever she liked made her a difficult mate for a conservative like Butler. In letters home to England Fanny confessed herself "a stranger here, and fear I shall continue to do so until I die." Her enormous confidence puzzled Philadelphia's matrons, though Whitman early confessed that her New York performances inspired parts of his *Leaves of Grass*. And when Emerson came to know her at her summer home in the Berkshires, he found her "marvelous." Charlotte echoed the sentiment. The glamorous Fanny was a compound of everything desirable. Perhaps flowers could open her door.

A thank you and a friendship with Fanny immediately followed: "I am very much obliged to you for giving me such a very agreeable acquaintance," Fanny wrote. Charlotte's horseback rides to Butler Place were soon returned by Fanny's regular attendance at Charlotte's performances. The friendship flourished, despite Charlotte's occasional disbelief that the niece of the Divine Sarah could possibly interest herself in Charlotte's efforts. Flowers from Fanny brought firm reassurance: "You are quite mistaken in your reading of my countenance this morning at church. I had not the pleasure of seeing you, being rather short sighted. Had I done so, I am very sure the greeting I should have been happy to offer you would have satisfied you. . . . I am at home always from one o'clock until half past four or five and again in the evening from eight til ten, and either morning or evening should be very glad to receive you any day and every day as often as your inclination prompts and leisure serves you to visit me."

Fanny's visits highlighted the fall, though the night of December 19 brought special excitement at the theatre. Burton gambled his entire resources on a production entirely new to the American stage. Set in an immense Rhine grotto, his *Naiad Queen* featured a hundred thinly clad girls draped about the stage on gigantic shells painted gold and silver. From time to time these Lorelei maidens bestirred themselves and plunged into an immense pool at stage center. At the height of the scene the figure of Charlotte Cushman slowly emerged from the water and expanded into a wide open flower. In another scene the maidens became warriors, with Charlotte as their drillmaster leading them through a lavish display of military precision.

Philadelphia found Charlotte as the Naiad Queen "fresh and imposing" in her helmet of white ostrich plumes, breastplate of gold scales, flesh-colored tights, and red sandals. Brandishing her shield and her battle axe, she dominated the show; one fascinated male frankly confessed, "Such a display of ladies legs no mortal man could resist the opportunity of seeing." For her success on opening night, "the theme of praise on every tongue," she could exact from Burton a certain regard befitting her popularity.

Burton's investment paid off, but throughout the season, with the country's money still tight, his theatre delicately balanced between slender success and failure. Charlotte sensed the difficulties. "Theatricals are assuming a most dismal shape—nothing but *trouble* from all parts of the country," she wrote her friend Mrs. William Creswick. So far the National was doing a paying business, "yet rumour says we are going to close."

For Burton she could feel little sympathy, despite her appreciation of his skill as a comedian. Like managers she had met before, the man had a miserly streak that spoiled him. "I was compelled to go to N.Y. last week on business and asked Mr. Burton's permission to leave me out of the bills one night. I did not go at that time, but waited until my name was out of the bills, and was gone two days. When I sent for my salary, I found it was *all* the week deducted for those two nights. Pretty good that, and so it has been ever since I have been in Philadelphia, and he has insulted me in every possible way."

To make matters worse, things were not well at home. Susan and Bub had been sick for a month with scarlet fever, though both were slowly improving by the end of January, and Charlotte herself had been far from well. It was some comfort to know that her worth to Burton was not completely unrecognized. Bennett's New York *Herald* congratulated the Philadelphia National on having some of the best actors in the country: "It would be impossible to find any superiors in their line to Charlotte Cushman, Peter Richings, and Burton himself."

By February, business at the National was "I blush to say . . . bad, bad, bad." She poured out her troubles to the Creswicks: "For eleven weeks we have been upon two thirds and for the last three weeks no salary at all. Last Saturday Burton closed the season and reduced the salaries of all who remained. I have withdrawn Susan altogether from the Theatre. I remain myself under a reduced salary."

In desperation, she sought legal advice but found that if Burton chose he could "keep me out of any money until next September," when her contract expired. "So I have had to give it up as a bad job. I shall remain until I can better myself and then go. I have been most heartily disappointed." The only bright note was Tyrone Power, who "is playing with us for three nights." Susan was ill again, "Baby is very poorly and I—I am as thin as Job's turkey." To eke out expenses, she sold an article to the New York *World* and a poem, "The Peasant Boy," to the Philadelphia *New World*.

And now Charlotte suffered additional worry over her father. In

Boston, Elkanah was "quite infirm and miserable." For years he had lived in a small house on Commercial Street with his daughter Isabella Weld and her husband. Charlotte's recent business trip to New York had been to arrange for a loan, on Elkanah's behalf, from Sam Judd. The matter was embarrassing, but the fact was "that Mr. Weld is ashamed to let anybody know that he will not support father, as he is quite able to do it, and therefore refuses." Elkanah's needs, at age 72, could not have come at a more difficult time.

By spring, the picture brightened somewhat when desperation prompted her move with Burton to the National Theatre in New York. The family remained in Philadelphia against the day when Charlotte could see her way more clearly. Out of the ragtag remnants of companies left stranded by the perilous times, Burton assembled a powerful list of actors for his New York house. Several nights in April and early May, Charlotte delighted full houses as she snapped her Rhine maidens through their military paces, though the *Spirit* was not impressed with Charlotte's own part in the show: "It is a sad pity that a clever woman like Miss Cushman should be wasting time and a strong intellect in show pieces."

Be that as it may, intellects still had families to feed, and finding this further proof of her worth to Burton was comforting. For his high-handed treatment of her in Philadelphia, she levied upon him his portion of humble pie. She delighted in delaying rehearsals until Burton sent a cab to fetch her in style.

She held firm to her job, though affecting the grand lady with Burton did not help her income. By late May she sold Bennett some articles but had to go into debt nonetheless. Putting up her wardrobe as security, she borrowed $150, then persuaded the lender to release some of her costumes by giving him a thirty-day note. "I thank God that is off my mind for a time."

If Charlotte ever learned of Hackett's opinions about her "obsessive" determination, she proved him right in late May. By now there was no way to explain calamities. One met adversity and stood firm. When she heard the frantic cries, she held herself ready. The National Theatre was ablaze. Her job and her costumes gone again, now deeply in debt, she could only assume a twisted smile. And now a letter from her cousin, Winthrop Babbit, reached her from Boston the middle of June. "This day at 20 minutes before 8 o'clock departed this life your Father." In her small quarters in New York, in the midst of her suffocating worries, Charlotte struggled to feel the proper filial grief. But tears came slowly now, when for all practical purposes her father's death had been an accomplished fact for years. Elkanah's passing, like the flames that devoured the National, were part of an old story, a narrative punctuated with the ups and downs of experience.

To recoup some of her loss Charlotte made a trip in July to the wilds of Pennsylvania, to Lancaster, "eighty miles in an inland town, playing on a stage 6 feet by 10 to a parcel of Germans who do not understand one single word of English." But half a loaf was better than none, and in a drape of velvet and a makeshift fur she could palm herself off as Lady Macbeth before the staring eyes. For the fall, aware at last of her worth, Simpson was offering her good reason to return to the Park—at $50 a week—"but I am too terrified to decide." Burton was opening a new house and wanted her to join him, "but he has so swindled me that I am afraid of him." She confessed to the Creswicks, "I wish I knew what to do."

The thing to do was accept Simpson's offer. By August she and Susan were back at the Park, ready with *Midsummer Night's Dream,* a play not seen in New York in fifteen years, with Simpson's playbills expressing the humble hope that admirers of Shakespeare would extend "their patronage to an undertaking somewhat hazardous and requiring more than ordinary skill and attention." When Charlotte stepped on stage as Oberon, the ovation that greeted her return was the most heartwarming response she had ever received.

Once the play was underway, the applause for Susan was no less sincere. The *Spirit* happily celebrated the fact that both sisters displayed a poetic feeling "for which we were quite unprepared": Charlotte had never enunciated her lines so well, and Susan's Helena was "decidedly the most effective personation in the whole cast." On succeeding nights they played to full houses, the only difficulty at the Park being a "rude and unladylike" Miss Clarendon, who "poutingly" rejected Charlotte's offers of help during rehearsals.

In spite of the country's depression, his own healthy box office encouraged Simpson to gamble again on October 11, when he brought out Dion Boucicault's new comedy. *London Assurance* marks a dramatic change in American staging. Breaking all convention, Simpson discarded the simple painted backdrops and wings normally used and dressed his stage as a drawing room furnished with rich carpets, ornate furniture, and works of art; as an Elizabethan garden with statues, walks, and a distant view of Gloucester; as a morning room with a wide view through great French windows over the lawn. Never before had an American audience been offered so elaborate a spectacle.

In such a setting, *London Assurance* had a better than average chance of success, but it would have made its mark regardless. As Lady Gay Spanker, Charlotte did not appear until the third act, but from that point she dominated the action. Exuberant, aggressive, self-assured, her Lady Gay's domineering control of her pip-squeak husband was the comic heart of the play. If her effects met mixed reactions—some found her face "greatly against her"—her vivid acting and the elaborate staging filled the house for an unprecedented three full weeks. Whitman was so impressed that he ranked her Lady Gay with Junius Booth's Richard III and Forrest's Metamora: "I cannot conceive anything finer"—though later, in his novel *Franklin Evans,* the play itself seemed "one of those flippant affairs that pretend to give a picture of society and manners among the exclusive . . . the most nauseous kind of mock aristocracy tinging the dialogue from beginning to end."

Whitman's enthusiasm for Charlotte's acting did not reflect everyone's. The editor of the *New World,* Park Benjamin, labeled Charlotte's Lady Gay a "blustering hoyden," an ill-bred, "loud-talking Amazonian." For reasons not wholly editorial, Benjamin preferred Miss Clarendon, who played Grace Harkaway. Simpson had originally cast Susan in that part, but Benjamin had pressured Simpson into substituting his good friend by threatening to turn the full force of his paper against the expensive production. Simpson acceded and the pretty Miss Clarendon played.

But Miss Clarendon did not please. The *Spirit* said she lacked "force," and Bennett's *Herald* said bluntly, "The audience bore the affliction as a man does the rheumatism." Outraged, Benjamin fired off a letter to Barry, Simpson's stage manager, accusing Charlotte of having written the *Herald* strictures: if there was any virtue in a New York audience or the New York press, Charlotte Cushman should be hissed from the stage.

No less angry, Charlotte immediately returned the fire: "You accuse me of being the author of an attack upon Miss Clarendon in the *Herald.* Most positively do I deny this, and *dare you* to the proof." Mr. Benjamin's "private feelings" for the lady had made him forget himself; his indignation was cause for "wonder and astonishment."

As for being hissed from the stage, "I think you have business of more importance."

Bennett printed the exchange in full: "Park Benjamin has organized his troops for hissing tonight. Poor Charlotte Cushman! To set herself up on two straight elegant limbs, in opposition to Park Benjamin and his 'notice.' "

But Charlotte felt no need for anyone's pity. Night found the Park full to the chandeliers. When Max Harkaway announced Lady Gay's approach across the lawn, loud cheers—not hisses—greeted her. Her speech to Meddle the Lawyer, "Harkee, Mr. Meddle, if you don't be quiet, I shall horsewhip you," left no doubt she could as readily horsewhip Benjamin the editor. At the curtain, bravos called for "Charlotte Cushman!"

Bennett's paper happily reported, "The dashing Charlotte will not neglect to make many points" out of Benjamin's cowardly attack. Whitman tossed off her attacker as a "vain pragmatical nincompoop," no more a critic than a "witless ape."

Flush with her victory, Charlotte knew that the play's New York success—and the healthy publicity Benjamin's anger had brought it—guaranteed its success throughout the country. Always alert now for practical opportunities, she wrote Noah Ludlow and Sol Smith, theatre manager in St. Louis: "I know of a marked copy of 'London Assurance' which has been doing wonders for us. Knowing that it will be an impossibility to procure a copy on acct. of the anxiety of the parties in possession to keep it, I have thought that perhaps you would be glad to obtain this." The St. Louis men could have it for fifty dollars. Simpson, of course, must hear nothing of it.

The dust settled quickly; Charlotte and Susan appeared on November 20 as Lady Blanche and Lady Anne in Sheridan Knowles' *Old Maids,* carrying the major burden of a "dull" play. Though "without them, it would hardly have been heard through," Washington Irving found Charlotte "in the garments of the 'opposite sex,' very cheerful" and worth the applause. Susan expressed "deep feeling and force" in her "sweet and flowing elocution."

In December, when they played in *London Assurance* in Philadelphia, the garden scene featured real grass, real flowers, and real orange and lemon trees. In Boston Charlotte had the added delight of appearing on stage with her childhood friend, John Gilbert. She was back in Philadelphia on February 1, 1842, when Boston lavished a testimonial dinner on its celebrated visitor, Charles Dickens. For the occasion, Joseph M. Field regaled the diners with a poem, beginning,

Remember wot I says, Boz
    You're goin' to cross the Sea;
A blessed vay avays, Boz,
    To wild Ameriky;
A blessed set of savages,
    As books of travels tells;
No Guv'nor's eye to watch you, Boz,
    Nor even Somivel's.

Dickens himself closed the friendly affair among "the savages" on a rather more serious note, the matter of an international copyright. America had great writers who would live for all time, as did England. But, said Dickens, "I hope the time is not far distant when they, in America, will receive of right some substantial profit and return in England from their labours; and when we, in England, shall receive of right some profit and return in America for ours." Without adequate copyright protection no country could ever develop and keep a literature of its own. Dickens offered a toast: "America and England, and may they never have any division but the Atlantic between them." Charlotte could only confess that Dickens spoke of matters to which her Meg Merrilies and Nancy had contributed.

The spring before, when the National burned, an idea had circulated among Charlotte's New York fans that she deserved her own theatre. Nothing had come of the thought, but in March 1842 the *Sun* reported, "A popular theatre is soon to be erected in the most frequented part of Broadway, and placed under the management of that universal favorite, Miss Charlotte Cushman." When Whitman got wind of the venture, he cheered Charlotte's efforts in his *Aurora* and noted the impact of Dickens' visit: "Let us have an international copyright law, and we shall have a national drama, and literature also." The citizens of this great republic must be more just to themselves. "Let us respect our own capacities and not hide our lights under bushels."

Bennett pledged the full support of the *Herald*. To push the project herself, Charlotte flooded the mail with letters. Several features in the plan recommended it. As her own boss, she could avoid the mistreatment she had always resented from managers like Burton and Price, she might increase her income, and if her dreams truly materialized, she might make the difference Whitman predicted. "Having heard of your liberality as connected with a fondness for the arts," she wrote Campbell P. White, "I have ventured to solicit your valuable aid and influence." Surely, among the other true arts, the drama had stood too long neglected in America. Was it not shameful that P. T. Barnum could lead New York astray with his freak shows when such better things were possible in a legitimate theatre? Men of taste and refinement like White must help raise the American theatre "from its present glooms."

As late as June, Bennett was still hopeful: "A new theatre, by the friends of Charlotte Cushman, is to be built near the Tabernacle on the ridge of Broadway. The ground is secured and the subscriptions filling up." But again the plan fizzled; "the present gloom" would continue. Charlotte and Susan accepted a run in Trenton. The western New Jersey town had no theatre; plays were given in a hotel ballroom. To attempt *Romeo and Juliet* with no balcony, without any stage equipment was a tall order, but when the Trentonians insisted, the hotel manager suggested a makeshift: Juliet could stand on a chair; a bedspread or quilt held in front could suggest the balcony rail. The manager himself would hold one end of the quilt; the Negro bellboy, the other.

The performance began; candles were quickly blown out. Capulets and Montagues took over the acting area. For all the make-do, it appeared that the show might work out. Then the balcony scene was in progress. But just as Susan was saying, "At what o'clock tomorrow shall I send to thee?" a bell sounded downstairs in the lobby. Suddenly, the boy's grin appeared from behind the quilt, and a voice said, "I's sorry, Miss Cushing, I hear my bell ringing. I is obleeged to let my side of de house DRAP!" And down it went.

The audience fell into gales of laughter, and the manager quickly declared an intermission. Laughing, Charlotte and Susan took refuge in a bedroom until the show could go on, with the bellboy's reshouldering his side of the house.

By August, Philadelphia seemed a likelier place than New York to pattern a program around her own name. The Walnut Street Theatre needed a manager, and E. A. Marshall, the lessee, offered the job to Charlotte. Her competition would be another female manager, Mary Elizabeth Maywood, recently appointed at the Chestnut. In Marshall's view, a healthy excitement might be built up in Philadelphia if the theatres could be matched against each other as the personal projects of two determined women.

On the second of August, 1842, Charlotte wrote to Chippendale in New York. "I have made arrangements with Marshall for the next season. He is now the *only paying man* and consequently one to seize upon in desperate times. What do you say to joining me next season?" Together, they ought to be able to do something handsome. Hard as the times were, "you can make more capital out of the Philadelphians in one year than you can of the New Yorkers in six."

At the Walnut, she took over a top-quality company that included some old friends: William Fredericks, J. M. Field, Peter Richings, E. L. Davenport, and her former mentor, Clara Fisher Maeder, now returned to the stage as a fully committed actress. The reunion with Clara was a sort of measuring point, proof of how far she had come since her opera debut in Boston. The house itself at the corner of Ninth and Walnut was "beautifully clean, white, and very nice," buttressed by a respectable tradition that went back to 1809. The 1,300 seats in the pit were padded in red plush; there was a large balcony and elegant boxes on each side. The stage was a full forty feet wide and eighty feet deep.

A Woman's Heart and Mr. Macready

(1842–1843)

 Opening night, September 22, Charlotte left no doubt in the crowded house about her determination to succeed, whether tonight as Mrs. Racket in *The Belle's Stratagem* with Clara Maeder as Letitia, tomorrow night as someone else, or throughout the season as the most energetic theatre manager Philadelphia had ever seen. If hard work and shrewd planning could promise victory, she would need no such word as "failure."

To make her intentions clear to the public, a few nights later she stood before the curtains to deliver her manifesto as a manager. "Theatrical representations were once given in this city, in a manner and style that secured the constant attendance of a respectable and cultivated audience," not merely the people of fashion who came to see some favorite star. Happy families filled the boxes; the pit listened with delight to innocent amusement. So it could be again, "and shall be if my efforts can make it so." Her plays would afford "healthy morality and generous sentiments." And to avoid offending Philadelphia's Sunday morals, she would ring down her Saturday night curtain no later than eleven o'clock to give her clients time to be home by Sunday.

To help celebrate the new venture, Fanny Kemble sent her a note and a package. In the process of making a temporary break with Pierce Butler, Fanny had recently found at the country house the girdle and headband she had worn as Julia in Knowles' *The Hunchback*. "I do not know whether you would have any value for it on that account, but it has occurred to me that perhaps you might, I send it to you. If you do not care for it, you can but toss it into the Walnut St. wardrobe." Other notes and more costumes followed.

"I am going to the Yellow Springs," wrote Fanny, "where I shall be very glad to see you if you come down." But Charlotte was much too busy as actress and manager to think of any such pleasure. When George Vandenhoff arrived from England to play a run in October, it was Election Week and business was off, but Vandenhoff was immediately impressed with Charlotte's "rude, strong, uncultivated talent," if not always her accuracy. In *Hamlet* she shocked him with her reading of Gertrude's line: "What wilt thou do? thou wilt not kill me?" instead of "thou wilt not *murder* me?" When he noted the error, she felt "abject," though too harried with business correspondence to worry for long.

If her double duties made her sometimes "negligent" in rehearsals, as it seemed to Vandenhoff, success at the Walnut now required her to keep a constant eye on the till and ledger. If her Nancy seemed altogether too "fearfully natural," too "horribly real," she was merely channeling her efforts where they could do the most good. If Vandenhoff found Susan a pretty creature without "a spark of Charlotte's genius," though so popular with the young men that he could rank her the best walking lady in America, Charlotte could welcome the report primarily for what it meant to business.

As for Susan, there was further cause to be happy these days. When Nelson Merriman's Philadelphia relatives learned how shabbily he had treated his wife, they offered to pay the full costs if Susan would sue for divorce. The decree was granted on grounds of desertion, and within a few months word came that Merriman had died "somewhere in the Far West."

At her desk, Charlotte pursued her managerial labors. While Forrest was appearing at the Walnut in late October, she wrote her concerns to Chippendale. "Dear Chip. Your kind letter I rec'd duly, and should have answered immediately but have been crowded with study, with Forrest. If it will suit you better, we will not play you until Friday, 'Road to Ruin' and 'Dr. Bilworth,' or not in the farce at all unless you wish it. 'The Pretty Girls' is doing capitally, and we wish to run it as long as possible. Have you ever played Strickland's part in 'King O'Niele,' General Count Dillon? I want to do it on Saturday, it is not long and very good. I suppose I may put you in for it with some one of your farces. I want to keep 'She Would etc.' for my night next week. 'The Maniac Farmer' I will do as soon as you get here as you like. We will do 'Wild Oats,' 'Love Chase,' 'The Beaux Stratagem'! Will you play in the latter, and what? Next week after you come you can put me up to many things for our mutual benefit, that in the hurry and confusion of business I don't think of. 'Jack Cade' did very well last night $500 odd. We shall do 'London Assurance' week after next. I wish I could get hold of 'West End.' If by any chance you get hold of a copy of 'Love's Sacrifices,' let me have it *immediately if not sooner*. Tabitha is well but outrageous with Forrest, who does not lord it with *me* as usual but lets her have it *all*. Charles, Mother etc. etc. desire kindest remembrances.

And believe me, Dear Chip,

I will have a room for you,   Yours truly,
   but am sorry you don't come to us.   C. S. Cushman"

Later in the fall she prevented John Brougham, the Irish comedian, from running afoul of the blue laws. As "The Irish Lion," he had just taken his seat on stage and started a speech when he saw the curtain descending. He wheeled toward the wings, crying, "Is the house on fire?" But Charlotte, gesturing her regrets, came forward and explained that in Philadelphia, late Saturday night, laws were laws. For her trouble, Bennett's *Herald* soon had comforting words: in Philadelphia "Charlotte Cushman takes the lead in talent and respectability."

To relieve the mounting tedium, Charlotte cultivated another Philadelphia friendship. After morning rehearsals, when time permitted, she stopped at the home of a young writer, Annie Brewster, for talk over a cup of tea, to read with her the current play's passages aloud. To Annie, "the deep contralto voice of my friend" had in it "a sweet tenderness"; Charlotte herself seemed a Miranda from an Enchanted Isle. And to Charlotte, the mornings were not just a break in her heavy routine. Through the readings with Annie, she found a new pleasure in her profession. Until now, she had studied her lines as an actress, ever alert to the staging and movement implied in the words. But with Annie, plays suddenly became literature. Reading the lines, when sudden new insights came she would cry, "It is a new world!"

Phrases in Shakespeare took on new meanings; new references became clear. The talk often lasted into the afternoon. During a performance, her mind still tingling with the new light, she would dash off a note to Annie at intermission. At other times, they read aloud Lessing's criticisms of acting; in Annie's opinion Charlotte made Lessing's *Dramaturgie* a Bible.

By spring 1843, Charlotte had to confess to herself—if no other—
that the shoe of theatre management pinched severely. The country's
money ills seemed dead set against her, and however much she regretted the fact, she often found herself unable to pay her actors their
weekly salaries. And among some of the men, she heard the word
"domineering" applied to herself. To the public, a female theatre
manager might seem novel, but to male workers backstage, the com-
mands of a woman were irritating. She sensed especially W. R.
Blake's resentment and the bristling hostility that welled up in her
when, playing opposite her in comedy roles, he always seemed to receive the major share of the calls. She confided her griefs to Colley
Grattan in Boston.

Grattan gave her his sympathy, but her talk of "quitting the profession in a year" was foolish. "I expect to see you stand very high
indeed in it by that time." Charlotte was perhaps tinged by a "sensi-
tiveness" too common among actors. "Beware, not of jealousy,"
Grattan warned, "for I am sure *you* are above its reach, but of over-
anxiety to please those whom the ardor of your temperament leads you
to overestimate."

There were other irritations. Philadelphia theatres had their loyal
supporters, but theatre people had no cause to rejoice at their treatment in public. In church, where one surely expected a welcome,
Charlotte's status as actress created a scene. When she and Susan and
Charlie attended the First Unitarian Church one Sunday in April,
the pewholder they were to sit beside objected so strongly that the
head usher noted the matter in his diary. "When I told him it was
for Mr. Cushman for himself and sisters, he objected at once to going
into church with persons who were employed upon the stage." Deeply
offended, the pewholder left the church, and his wife moved to another seat.

The pain was especially intense in light of Mary Eliza's headshak-
ings and doubts. And Blake's ridicule had grown worse. The company was aware of what Blake labeled Charlotte's "social ambitions."
When word got about that Susan had joined a certain female "status"
organization, the greenroom smiled to Blake's questions about associations designed to promote actresses into "the upper ten sphere,"
about "the female sacred button-hole society." Blake could act, unfortunately, or Charlotte would have fired him. Socially ambitious or
not, she expected some credit for a certain nobility of purpose.

A Woman's Heart and Mr. Macready

Probably through Fanny Kemble's insistence, Charlotte made her way to the portrait studio of Thomas Sully, cousin of Pierce Butler. Then at the height of his fame, Sully reigned the supreme portraitist in America. The man whom Gilbert Stuart had blessed in Boston, whom Benjamin West and Sir Thomas Lawrence had encouraged in London, Sully wielded his brush year after year to record the notable faces that came to his door. More than once he had painted the tempestuous Fanny Kemble.

The portrait he painted of Charlotte fully explains his popularity. From his English mentors Sully had learned a valuable trick: by softening chin lines and cheeks he could emphasize any beauty he found in the eyes. In the picture Sully delivered on April 27 Charlotte saw a vibrant, appealing, young face with great luminous eyes, a softly molded jawline and chin—all of it flushed with a sunny brightness and undeniable feminine charm. The picture was stunning, but it was hardly a portrait. She wrote Sully a playful note; he had worked wonders with "my unfortunate 'Mug.'" "I have established it in my mind," as a settled fact, at last, *"that I am beautiful."* Such an error explained, did it not, her un-Yankee-like mistake in overpaying one of the installments on the $80 fee she owed him?

Much as Sully's brush flattered, Charlotte's time in his studio brought even happier results. His family welcomed her as one of their own. A friendship with his daughters, Blanche and Rosalie, brought her almost daily to the Sully house. Rosalie had inherited a fair amount of her father's talent. Two years younger than Charlotte, gentle in temperament where Charlotte was strong, Rosalie Kemble Sully was a painter in her own right. Between them soon flowed an intuitional understanding. The hope of friendship that had so attracted Charlotte to Fanny Kemble and the interest that had brightened so many of her mornings with Annie Brewster now became almost totally centered in the young woman whom she would soon call "beloved."

Charlotte's diary—one never intended for publication—details the progress of the profound attachment. Its penciled pages refer again and again to daily visits to Rosalie, to Rosalie in the front room, to Rosalie in the upstairs parlor sitting "beside me" on the sofa, to

Rosalie at church, in her painting room "working away as for her life," stopping now and again to look at an unfinished canvas on her stand. For Charlotte, Rosalie's miniature portrait of her became a special treasure.

When Charlotte established the family at 277 S. 8th Street, she took separate quarters for herself in suburban Clover Hill, to Mary Eliza's strong disapproval. Rosalie became a regular visitor. At Clover Hill, Charlotte surrounded herself with a growing store of books and music, her painting and miniatures, and her pet cardinal.

The affection between them sustained Charlotte through a difficult spring and summer. Receipts at the Walnut dropped steadily; in spite of her labors to decorate the bills with attractive names like Forrest, Junius Brutus Booth, Yankee Hill, John Brougham, Yankee Dan Marble, James Hackett, and Josephine Clifton, the money did not come in—hands held it for needs more vital than nights at the theatre. At the Chestnut Miss Maywood had already given up any attempts to make a go of her management. To Vandenhoff, returning to the Walnut in April to play Mercutio to Charlotte's Romeo, the season of 1842–43 was one of the worst known. Even the Park had had to drop its prices. And if Vandenhoff correctly sensed a mood in the staid Philadelphians, Charlotte's playing Romeo did not enhance her personal position among them.

The whole idea of a woman's playing a masculine role repelled Vandenhoff. She had "unsexed" herself to no purpose "except to destroy all interest in the play, and all sympathy for the ill-fated pair." The only good point in "this hybrid performance" was her skill with a sword, a trick Vandenhoff claimed credit for teaching her. In killing Tybalt and Paris she looked neither man nor woman; her passion was "epicene."

Was Vandenhoff specifying the cause of a later heartache in Charlotte's friendship with Rosalie? Charlotte's vague diary notations and an inference in one of Rosalie's letters suggest an affectionate regard between them that was not universally approved, though the written endearments that passed between them said nothing that might not have appeared in any number of Victorian expressions of female friendship. Elizabeth Barrett liberally sprinkled her letters to Mary Russell Mitford with such endearments as "Love me, Miss Mitford." And many of Jane Welsh Carlyle's letters to various women sound no less oddly romantic to a later age.

However deep the attachment, to the parties involved the friendship was the brightest note in their private lives during 1843 and 1844. In Rosalie Sully Charlotte found her emotional needs totally fulfilled. Without the sustenance she found in Rosalie, her resounding failure as manager of the Walnut Street Theatre would have been more difficult to take.

On July 10, 1843, she took her last bow as full manager. She had tried to play her managerial cards adroitly, she had given the job her full energies, she had acted with all the power she possessed, but the till inevitably measured a theatre's success, a manager's effectiveness. By its charts she had failed. To replace her, W. R. Blake became her "assistant," a word used in the papers to protect her feelings. She would serve under him only so long as she could tolerate him, acting in the company he would manage alternately at the Walnut and the Chestnut.

Free of the Walnut's burdens, Charlotte knew by fall that in her latest setback good luck had again protected her. The English tragedian William Macready, the man whose acting had so thrilled her in childhood, the man who with Edmund Kean and John Philip Kemble composed the great triumvirate of English actors, sent word in October that when he played in Philadelphia, he wished Charlotte to play opposite him.

Charlotte confided her fears to Annie Brewster. Underlings in his cast suffered a special kind of stage fright, knowing the Macready temper, the tenseness on stage that put him off balance if a breath was misplaced, a syllable wrongly emphasized. Philadelphia had heard of his terrible treatment of Mrs. Sloman at the Park. Dressed in black velvet, point lace and pearl beads, she had made the appalling mistake of catching her pearls in Macready's costume during the murder scene in *Macbeth*. The string broke, the beads fell dribbling across the stage, and the sound had infuriated Macready. As soon as he had delivered his final line, he had thrown the terrified actress off the stage.

For his Philadelphia opening, Macready would play Macbeth to Vandenhoff's Duncan and Charlotte's Lady Macbeth. In a sense, the chance to perform with the fabled star was cause for joy. Had this not been a dream ever since Uncle Augustus had led her into Macready's regal presence at the Boston Theatre on Federal Street?

But to appear with him now would lay her open to the most explosive temperament on the English-speaking stage, to an ego that fed by aggrandizing itself, to a suspicious introspective nature that left all comers convinced that the only play Macready ever approved of was a five-act monologue written solely for himself. The fact was well known that Macready despised the acting profession; he had a snob's contempt for its greasepaint and pretense—and other actors.

To withstand the strain before Macready arrived, Charlotte busied herself with reading about him, especially about his techniques. His mirror practice was famous. "I know that in gesture I do not excel," Macready had once explained, "and facial expression is what I principally depend upon." At home, hands tied behind him, he practiced before several large mirrors that would play up any tendency to exaggerate, all as an effort "to keep the features, perhaps I should say the muscles of the face, undisturbed, whilst intense passion would speak from the eye alone."

Charlotte told Annie Brewster a few days before the Macready run, "I mean to prepare Lady Macbeth in that way." But she soon gave it up as a bad job. "If I act that way when Macready comes, I'll kill myself." Mirror-pointing might work for Macready, but "it plays the mischief with me."

At the Chestnut, the night of October 23, Charlotte made her first appearance with William Macready. The hand that held Macbeth's letter trembled, but the voice that read it was firm, her manner controlled. And before Charlotte sensed the fact herself, the audience noted the strong resemblance between her face and Macready's. Except for his hair, bunched over his ears in "Newgate knockers," Macready and Charlotte might have been brother and sister. He had the same depressed nose, the same chin, the same broad brow that had always been Charlotte's own private grief. During an early performance, so ran a story, when a child in a box asked his father which was Macready and which was Miss Cushman, the father replied, "whichever you please, my little dear!" Even Mary Eliza confessed to an eerie feeling when she saw them together.

The resemblance did nothing to spoil Macready's own appreciation of Charlotte's acting. Watching the sleep-walking scene from the wings, Macready nodded approval, and at a backstage party afterward, he toasted his "quondam murderous consort's health." The words brought blessed relief. Relaxing, Charlotte commented, "My Lady Macbeth has improved somewhat since I acted it in New Orleans at my debut. Then I wore a dress which you, Mr. Macready, could have worn, and could have cut off from the superfluous skirts enough to make me a gown."

Later that night Macready wrote in his journal, "Called for warmly, and warmly received. The Miss Cushman who acted Lady Macbeth interested me much. She has to learn her art, but she showed mind and sympathy with me; a novelty so refreshing to me on the stage." And next morning, Charlotte voiced a newly refurbished dream. "I mean to go to England as soon as I can. Macready says I ought to act on an English stage and I will."

Before Macready left Philadelphia, he contracted with Charlotte to support him in Boston. "She would be glad to go for $50—it would be worth my while to give it." Unfortunately for Charlotte, the work in Boston did not materialize. The theatre manager's daughter had already been appointed when she arrived. Uncertain of the next proper step, she stayed on in Boston to watch Macready work. The note she sent to him at the Tremont House regarding his Othello put the actor's famous ego on guard: "Shall I tell you that I *feared* for you," Charlotte wrote, "that when you raised your hand to your head, I was prepared to see you faint in reality from the violent reaction? I was in agony . . ." She explained the poem she had enclosed by saying: "What folly you will think me guilty of in writing to you as I do, but you are kind in indulging my whims. . . . God bless you, dear sir, and believe me, I am ever your grateful Charlotte Cushman."

All of which was too much for the suspicious Macready. "I am in a strange country," he told his diary, "and I think it is only a duty to myself to be strictly circumspect. I have not the slightest purpose, dream, or intent of wrong or folly. . . . Wrote to her, promising to see her tomorrow, which I will do in the common room."

When she sent him flowers and more of her poems to read—her verses on Babington's conspiracy impressed him as "very powerful and clever"—he called on her next day, again in the common room of the Tremont House. "Talked with her a little and took leave of her most kindly, but without the slightest indication that our acquaintance is to become more intimate. She kissed my hand, but I was only kind." He paid her the $50.

About her poetry, Charlotte had little cause to apologize. Though they were frankly efforts to pad her income, they were scarcely the awkward work of a mere dilettante. Fitz-Greene Halleck's poem "Forget-me-not," in the *Knickerbocker* in July 1843, challenged from Charlotte a serious reply. Halleck's lines had concluded:

There is a flower, a lovely flower,
  Ringed deep with Faith's unchanging hue;
. . . .
Yet deep its azure leaves within
  Is seen the blighting hue of care;
And what that secret grief hath been,
  The drooping stem may well declare.
The dew-drops on its leaves are tears,
  That ask, 'Am I so soon forgot?'
Repeating still, amidst their fears
  My life, my love! forget-me-not!

Published in October, Charlotte's "Lines to Fitz-Greene Halleck"
read:

Like to the flower when autumn comes
  To seek its folds with chilling breath,
And winter's earliest whisper roams
  Its heart among, to tell of death;
Thus on man's heart, as o'er the flower,
  Falls tears, with grief and anguish hot,
And speed the cry to Heaven's high power,
  Forget-me-not! forget-me-not!

Now, in Macready, she had a subject that interested her even more,
and she soon used him in verse.

For December, she agreed to a killing task. She would return to
Philadelphia to continue acting at the Chestnut and the Walnut
but would go by train to New York every second day to appear at
the Park with Macready. The New York appearances brought mixed
results. Appearing at all with an actor of Macready's fame was an
advantage, working with him would broaden the technical knowledge
of any young actress, but the tiring pace of the long train ride every
other day, plus Macready's wholly unpredictable temper, kept her
nerves at high pitch. As Louisa Lane Drew later recorded, acting
with him gave one the pleasant sensation of knowing that "you
were doing nothing that he wanted you to do, though following
strictly his instructions. He would press you down with his hand on
your head and tell you in an undertone to stand up!" Charlotte had
already tasted such irritants in the ego of Edwin Forrest. The two
"grandeurs" had much in common.

Still, Macready's scholarly skill outshone all other acting she had ever seen. His Macbeth was a great general, "devil-ridden by his imagination," haunted from the time he sees the "air-drawn" dagger, allowing it to rise slowly, a dagger of the mind, turning its handle "inexorably to his hand." Gripping the dagger stained with Duncan's blood, he spoke in halting, electrifying whispers, the storm outside matching the storm inside his agonizing brain. With his cry, "Wake Duncan with thy knocking: I would thou couldst!" with his crazed eyes averted from the dagger, he let himself be dragged from the stage, leaving his audience terrified. To Charlotte, Macready's Macbeth radiated an indescribable "splendor."

Watching him work and catching his shadings gave her new light on Lady Macbeth. And from it all, she later realized, acting became on its highest level a scholarly effort to distill into form every hint of a role's meaning, every fugitive impression.

When Macready was happy, bliss reigned backstage. But let a supporting actor garble a rhythm or delay a cue and frenzy descended. Charlotte watched Macready's temper boil over on stage when a fearful novice bearing the dread news about Birnam Wood momentarily froze.

"My lord—my lord—" he began, "my lord—my lord . . ."

"Go on, sir—go on, sir," Macready hissed.

"My lord, as I did stand my watch upon the hill, I looked toward Birnam, and anon . . . anon . . ." Despite the prompter, the messenger's words stuck in his throat. Macready had been working himself up for the great point of the scene but at last broke out in fury, "Liar and slave!" and struck wildly with his truncheon. The messenger fell to his knees, shrieking, "As I did stand my watch upon the hill . . ." Sensing the truth, the audience set up a delighted roar. "Get off, sir! Get off!" Macready spat through his teeth. When the trembling actor sprang to his feet and bolted, the audience dissolved.

For Charlotte, the episode carried a lesson in acting. Macready's skill might have saved the scene and, incidentally, exhibited his artistry. Instead, unable to remove himself from the character, he lost the scene. Charlotte took note of the error.

And she held herself tensed for the moment when the Macready rage might vent itself upon her. Hopefully, she would give him his just deserts, like the brave actor whose fame had spread when he dared to oppose Macready in *Hamlet*. When Claudius insisted on dying at stage center where Macready as Hamlet had expected to die, Macready had grunted audibly, "Die further up stage, sir. What are you doing down here, sir? Get up and die elsewhere!" But Claudius had sat bolt upright and replied clearly, "Look here, Mr. Macready, you had your way at rehearsal, but *I'm King now, and I shall die where I please!*"

Charlotte kept her own counsel about Macready's faults. His lapses of temperament were unforgiveable; his mannerisms annoyed. As Macbeth, his listening to the witches with his mouth open wide made one long "to pitch something into it." And his pauses—suspensions in the rhythm meant to suggest thinking—sounded at times like stuttering. With Fanny Kemble, Charlotte could label Macready's style of speaking poetry a matter of ignoring all punctuation and "chopping it up into prose."

But, in the long view, one could learn from such an actor: habits of articulation and movement, other refinements that could spell the difference between adequacy and authority—in short, a style that owed much to the classic art of the Kembles. Had not Macready acted with Sarah Siddons herself and exposed his own style to "the impulsive intensity" of Edmund Kean? To this combination, he had added a mannered formality that, no matter how obvious, could sway an audience at his will.

Following Macready's lead, preparing a role now became patient study, careful analysis of text and characters, a probe into subtleties beneath the surface which she had never before suspected. Charlotte soon realized that, in order to gain his favor, adopting a style reminiscent of his own was mandatory. Macready demanded almost worshipful imitation. In her own case, good fortune altered the imitation into a style appropriate to her own temperament, though audiences seeing her work with Macready in Philadelphia and New York were not long in seeing a resemblance deeper than facial. A certain "trick of face," a tendency to quiver her "r's," a similarity in gait and gesture and voice tones almost as deep as Macready's added new authority to her acting. About Macready's voice a London critic had written: "While the highest pitch of declamation is still vibrating on the ear, the loud tone abruptly stops, and falls precipitately into the deepest colloquial whisper." The fact that Charlotte's voice had suddenly become a ringing instrument of much broader flexibility and range, striking the ear now with a new virtuosity, was a debt she owed to Macready.

A Woman's Heart and Mr. Macready

The Macready whisper was a trick that, handled intelligently, kept attention at its peak and wrung every possible effect from a line. Charlotte also found in Macready a model of word control. "I fail," he insisted, "when I allow my tongue and action to anticipate my thought." Valuable leads, indeed, for any disciple to follow.

But Macready's spitefulness and jealousy were something else. Macready wrote in his diary on December 4: "Rehearsed the play in a wretched state; Miss Cushman, who had her part when I was in Philadelphia, reading!—knowing nothing of what she had to do! How can there be artists when this lady, one of the most intelligent and ambitious, so entirely disregards the duties of her calling?" If he throttled his spite, his disgust was obvious, particularly when the performance itself went smoothly, with Charlotte letter-perfect in her lines.

She wrote her mother ecstatically: "In great haste I write only a few words, with a promise to write again tonight after the play and tell you all particulars of my great and triumphant success of last night,—of my reception, of being called out after the play, and hats and handkerchiefs waved to me, flowers sent to me, etc." In the *Spirit*'s report Macready had been "well received," but Charlotte had been cheered "enthusiastically."

The cheers for Charlotte were lost on Macready: "Looked at some American Saturday papers, which state that Miss Cushman more than shared the applause of the audience with me. If it was so, I never heard one hand of it. She is an intriguante, I fear, a very double person." His diary's scorn continues two days later, "Acted Melantius fairly; called for. They called for Miss Cushman here, who gets puffed in the papers, very absurdly"—the *Spirit*'s praise on December 16, for example. Miss Cushman "appears to more advantage than any lady who has graced the Park boards for many years."

The irritation Charlotte sensed in Macready stemmed in part from reactions like those of a visiting Englishman watching this run at the Park. "Even with this great and cultivated artist she held her own. She had not his experience, but she had genius. There were times when she more than rivalled him; when in truth she made him play second." At times she threw such energy, physical and mental, into her performance "as to weaken for the time the impression of Mr. Macready's magnificent acting."

To punish her, when Charlotte asked Macready to play for her Saturday benefit, he refused. "I have thus fixed Miss Cushman." But aware now of his scarcely veiled hostility, Charlotte airily dismissed his thrusts. She showered him with detailed flattery. "Your Werner is to me painful in the extreme, although so beautiful! It seems to harrow every feeling of the heart, good and bad, and it is this which causes pain." The expression on his face caused a "heart-sickness." The spirit actuating his conceptions "was caught from the death sigh of an Angelo or Da Vinci."

But by the end of her New York run with Macready, she could no longer hide her resentment of his arrogance, and she wrote him accordingly. Macready replied from Baltimore: "I assert, and, if my assertion heeds confirmation, will prove, that I never have by word or act been wanting to you in delicacy and consideration, nor in manifestation of kindly feeling, since I have had the pleasure of knowing you," though in his diary he expressed other sentiments: "Letter from Miss Cushman—oh! I do not like thee, Dr. Fell!"

Facing a Major Decision

(1843–1844)

The difficult days at the Park had seen no love lost between them, but in justice to Macready's skill as an artist—and recognizing a salable idea—Charlotte penned her sentiments for the press. Her poem in the *Anglo-American* saluted the worthy artist, if not the prickly man:

> Macready, if my muse seem all too tame,
> To sketch aright the thoughts I would reveal,
> Let not the heart be censured, for the blame
> That hand may not indite the half I feel;
> For, as I write, across my memory steal
> The seasons when I in thy conquests shared
> And know how vain, yet earnest was the zeal
> With which I strove, although all unprepared.
> To compass the proud, my wild ambition dared.
> Long after thou hast left us, men will speak
> Of thine all matchless skill, thy well stored mind
> As kindling memories about them break
> The spells, which erring prejudice would wind;
> Then will thy name be in all hearts enshrined
> Thy genius well-remembered; and thy name
> Placed among those wonderous teachers of mankind,
> Who ever may a world's high reverence claim
> And e'en midst change of time be still revered the same.

Irksome as she found the man, honesty forced her to admit publicly that her contact with the difficult Englishman had opened to her "a

mine of depth and power," though speaking practically, it seemed to
have done little else. Back in Philadelphia, she wrote a troubled letter to Chippendale describing the incredible aftermath of her run
with Macready: "I am more closely quartered in money matters
than I have been in the last two years—They did not pay me at all
at the Park and I have not had a cent since my return . . . I am
almost crazy—no salaries paid here for *four weeks.*" When Macready
concluded his American tour, he took back to England the magnificent trove of $30,000. Charlotte could not dispute the rumor that
the actor's name should be spelled "Magreedy." Such were the wages
of stardom.

To eke out pennies, she sold more poems. Magazines and papers
like *The Ladies' Companion, The Knickerbocker, The New World,*
and *Graham's* published her verses on subjects ranging as widely as
the recent death of Henry Ware, Jr., her old minister at Second
Church; Oliver Cromwell at the coffin of Charles I; and the austere
Shakers she had visited near Albany.

Backstage, in the rare interludes when Macready had relaxed his
arrogance, Charlotte had mentioned the increasing woes of Fanny
Kemble, blaming Pierce's "fickleness and infidelity." But Macready
had talked with the incorrigible Fanny in Philadelphia: "I have
seen enough to satisfy me there has been enough at home to drive a
loving heart from home," he told his diary.

Now Fanny poured out her marital griefs to Charlotte. "I was
coming to see you today as your appearance in church on Sunday
made me aware of your return to town. Your good wishes are not
lost, for such prayers are twice blessed and the kindness and consideration you show for me will, I hope, be repaid to you a thousand fold
at your need, which I sincerely hope may never be such as mine. Thank
you thank you for your sweet flowers. They are the *only* bright
things which will belong to this birthday of mine except the thought
that one year more of trial and difficulty is past."

Throughout the spring of 1844, Charlotte did her utmost to come
to Fanny's aid, siding completely with her in the bitterness infecting
the Butler household. In letters and notes that passed between them,
Charlotte offered her help, for in staid Philadelphia, before Fanny
could hope to divorce Pierce Butler and retain custody of her daughters, she would have to present full proof of his infidelities. Charlotte
volunteered to collect the evidence. The correspondence divulged no
details as to the means, but a firm contradictory note now entered
Fanny's letters. To Charlotte, any recourse was worth considering,

but Fanny felt otherwise. "I have very little doubt that I understand what you would advise, but there is but one means by which I am to be helped and that is by proving of evidence such as would furnish me with a plea for a divorce in the event of Mr. Butler's taking my children from me."

Later, Fanny was even firmer. "From the tenor of my last two notes to you you must have perceived that I had entirely given up all expectations of arriving at the evidence which you have so positively held out to me as within your power to obtain for some time past. I supposed such evidence would be obtained without an extraordinary difficulty. I am now perfectly convinced of the contrary and have only one request more to make of you, which is that you will from this time forth consider that I no longer desire or authorize you to pursue the enquiry for me." Still later, "I wrote to you, as I now again write to request that you will give up all further efforts in my behalf. What will become of my affairs I do not know, but I am well satisfied that neither you nor I have any power of altering them for the better."

As Fanny well knew, evidence of Pierce's adultery must be "specific and incontrovertible," and she was equally sure, long before Charlotte ceased her efforts, that such evidence was not easy to locate. In the end, Fanny thanked Charlotte for her goodwill, but goodwill could not produce the necessary facts, and she concluded that there was no chance whatever for her by legal proceedings, "and illegal ones I dare not take."

The offer of help that began as a gesture of friendship on Charlotte's part finally became a bone of contention that broke up the friendship. Hurt and impatient, Charlotte forced herself to sit idly by while Pierce Butler squeezed Fanny out of the marriage and proceeded to sue her for desertion. When Fanny's household disintegrated and custody of her daughters went to their father, the feeling remained strong in Charlotte, justifiably or not, that Fanny had rejected her offer of help from some basic mistrust—or, just as unthinkably, from some appalling unconcern for family solidarity. The wound would be slow to heal.

In the long run, Charlotte's concern for Fanny Butler receded into the background of her joy with the Sullys. On January 7, 1844, her diary noted: "Went to church. F. B. not there. . . . Went tonight to see Sully. Sully told me what F. B. said of my acting. It is much to be praised by her." She kept up her daily visits with Rosalie, and when a January acting tour through New England developed, she mailed a steady stream of letters back to South Fifth Street.

The tour itself was a chore to be gotten through as quickly as possible. In Providence, the resident company, a "miserable half starved" lot, was so drunken and ignorant that, playing with them, she wanted to laugh one minute, cry the next. The one bright note of her stay there was a Mrs. Church she saw at dinner. "The loveliest woman I ever looked upon . . . such eyes, such hair, such eyebrows, mouth, nose, chin . . . What a lucky thing I am not of the other sex, for a heavy mortgage would have been made upon her from this hour. As it was, it almost deprived me of appetite for my dinner."

Before she left Providence, she could agree with some of Fanny Kemble's and Macready's strictures against the profession. She had to fight the manager for the paltry sum coming to her. Appearing on stage with such churlish people as these, she felt a deep despondency. "What poor fools we are, what dolts, we sip of the lees of degraded humanity in preference to the eternal rest of the grave." When Fanny had expressed disgust at all of it, "how unjust I was."

By February, she was acting again at the Walnut, happy that *The Democratic Review* had taken her long poem, "The Poor Debtor." In March, Rosalie brought her a miniature she had painted of Fanny Kemble, and Macready, in a gentlemanly mood, wrote from Mobile to thank her for her poem about him in the *Anglo-American*. "You preserve the insect in amber."

In May, when letters from Macready urged her to support him again at the Park, she swallowed her dislike of the man and took the train for New York. En route to rehearsals, she lost her purse with $23 in it, a major calamity. But compliments from Macready and, surprisingly, a Lady Macbeth performance he thoroughly approved brightened her spirits. When he again advised her to go to England to act for an audience whose opinion really mattered, she listened carefully. Her poem, "There Is a God" surely expressed her elation when it appeared in *Graham's* in June. Back home for another brief stint at the Walnut, where she played Aldabella in *Fazio* on June 14, she filled her days with happy visits to the Sullys.

The matter of going to England was a subject to discuss with Rosalie. During the late summer, Charlotte debated all the pros and cons involved in the journey, the cost involved, the separation from this closest friend of her heart. She could not possibly finance the trip out of her earnings, much less leave any reserve at home against family emergencies. Still, she could not ignore Macready's advice. At twenty-eight, she knew full well that, for all her good work with stars like Forrest and Macready, only a name and fame made in London would ever bring her full stardom and a commensurate salary at home.

At last, she made up her mind to go. To gather her courage, she gave up her place at Clover Hill and turned over all her books, her cardinal, and her folios of music to Rosalie. Seated with Rosalie on the upstairs sofa in the house on Fifth Street, Charlotte gave her a ring and a bracelet, pledging through tears her eternal fidelity.

She dried her tears with thoughts of England. Lavish as the idea sounded, it occurred to her that she would need a personal maid. In the new country—if luck smiled on her—there would be a constant round of arrangements to make, appointments to keep. There would be no Mary Eliza to maintain any household routine. The Negro girl she finally located was, at fourteen, the personal aide she needed; Sallie Mercer's "anxious forehead," her "conscientious eyebrows" promised the kind of help she required. When she told her she planned to take her to England, the girl delightedly agreed, though her mother complained bitterly for a time, frightened, like Mary Eliza, lest she never see her daughter again. And privately, Charlotte's own fears of the voyage and the uncertain events to follow gave her no peace.

About Sallie herself, she had little doubt. Her good sense and intelligence could handle complicated instructions. "Dear Sallie," Charlotte could write, "Give the enclosed letter to Mr. Charles and ask him to put it in the Post Office before afternoon. Ask him to take Mr. Budd's note to his boarding house before 2 o'clock. You take the note to Mr. Thayer over to his house. Then go to Mrs. Oat and tell her to go down to Sully's with a linen lining to fit Miss Blanche to a habit waist. Tell her she must make her figure which is a *bad one* look first rate with lots of padding, and she is to say *Miss Cushman* sent her and then she must be fitted. Tell Mrs. Oat to go this morning if possible and I will settle with her for it. I want my blue wrapper and my belt. Get my things ready to take to Baltimore on Sunday afternoon. I do not know that I shall be in until Sunday morning. I wonder if Mrs. Oat could fit me on Sunday morning. If she can't, never mind. Never mind sending my habit out. Put some clean cuffs in it and have it clean for Baltimore.

Yours, Charlotte."

But training an intelligent maid was only one of a thousand de-

127

tails to solve before she could sail. There remained the question of money, cash enough for the voyage and for the time she must wait in London for income. She sent letters asking for loans. "I have been for a long time," she wrote one prospect, "hoping and wishing to go to England," to study under some of the great masters, since "it will be putting me in the way of making much money when I return to this country, for the support of my family who have for many years been dependent upon my weekly stipend." If Mr. Gregg could lend her 100 pounds, he would put her "in the way of future affluence." In Boston, Colley Grattan cheered her efforts but begged her to consider England only a training ground and not be discouraged if it fell short of her hopes.

Playing with Macready again in September in New York and Philadelphia reaffirmed another reason for wishing to triumph in England. Macready's British arrogance was not lost on his audiences. "Looked at the papers—the coarse vulgar wretches that are the editors!" he told his diary. "How my inmost soul sickens with loathing at them, the vulgar brutes. An American editor is a creature *per se*— agh!" That arrogance was no less apparent to Charlotte. If her plans succeeded, one day she could dispense with such annoyances and claim for herself a billing at least equal to his—and a salary greater than the $50 per week she had so far received.

During this final run in Philadelphia, she nurtured a further reason for going to England, one not easily voiced. Edwin Forrest had chosen to play at the Walnut at the same time Macready was holding forth at the Arch. If the two bombastic egos were not frankly competing against each other on some vague patriotic, political grounds, Philadelphia audiences soon saw in their performances a challenge to their national pride.

The English Macready versus the American Forrest became almost a battle cry, though in his curtain speech Macready gracefully thanked his audience for the warm reception, in spite of "some unworthy attempts that have been made to excite against me and my countrymen engaged in this profession on the plea of being foreigners."

The speech was courteous, but for all her debt to Macready, Charlotte acknowledged a private determination to prove the full weight of her talents to the blasé country whose disdain for things American

Macready made painfully real. Unlike many Americans, she had not made a project out of collecting the slurs and slights that England steadily volleyed across the Atlantic. But if she felt no hostility toward Britain, she felt no particular love either. Going to England might make her famous; it might make her rich—and it might open England's eyes.

Still the disciple of Emerson, convinced like him that America had humbled herself too long in praise of Europe's tired muses, she saw her course clearly. After "farewell" performances in Boston, Philadelphia, and New York, leaving her audiences firmly assured of her genius, hopefully reaping enough cash to finance most of the cost of the voyage, she would then head determinedly east. She would prove once and for all that talent could flourish west of the Atlantic as well as along the complacent banks of the Thames.

En route with Macready to Boston on September 28, 1844, Charlotte pumped him for all possible information and insights. At the Melodeon Theatre she appeared with him for three weeks in a series of plays she hoped would fully display her superior range: Queen Gertrude, Lady Macbeth, Goneril, and Emilia. Before the brightest lights of Boston—Charles Sumner, Longfellow, Lowell, Joseph Story, and Daniel Webster—she did her best to show what a Boston girl could do alongside London's Macready.

Critically, Boston approved. It found her Emilia "a new revelation." Her withering contempt for Iago, her "grandeur of tone," almost buried Macready's Othello. The audience recalled her with cheers.

On the twelfth of October, before her announced good-bye to Boston, she wrote Macready her thanks for his encouragement, for the model he had been in her work. On the fifteenth she attended his farewell party to the one American city he liked, and she looked forward confidently to the next evening when Macready would assist at her benefit. With him in the cast she could pocket a sizable sum for herself. But with evening, word came that the wily Macready had already sailed for England.

His absence spoiled the house she had needed. Whatever explained his sudden departure, the support she had given Macready throughout the run should have reaped a better harvest, though one familiar with Macready's temperament could guess that applause for his leading lady had wounded his jealous pride. Her farewell to Boston might have been a "bumper"; Boston might have seen the event as a turning point in the career of a native daughter and bid her Godspeed. Instead, Charlotte said good-bye to a half-empty house. Aggrieved at the slight, outraged at Macready's shabby dismissal, she left Boston the next morning with a mere pittance in her purse, consoled only by the packet of letters from Boston friends to introduce her in England.

She made a quick farewell to Philadelphia in *The School for Scandal,* playing to an audience little better than Boston's. She said good-bye to the friends she had made during her busy years since 1840, to the actors at the Walnut and the Chestnut and the Arch, to W. R. Blake, whom she still could not like, and to Annie Brewster. Rosalie and Sully himself would see her off in New York. For her sheaf of introductory letters, W. E. Burton wrote a statement commending her to Benjamin Webster, manager of London's Haymarket Theatre, calling her "undoubtedly the best breeches figure in America."

In the desk she had recently moved back to the house on Eighth Street, she left a supply of writing papers. Her mother and Susan must write her often and not worry about the high cost of overseas postage. They must write small, and if they paid the fee as far as Boston, she would pay the balance due on all letters forwarded. At the last minute, Charlie and his mother decided to go with her to New York, Charlie to look for a better job, now that Charlotte's leaving Philadelphia ended one good reason for staying. Susan stood solemn, on the brink of tears, holding six-year-old Bub tightly in hand, while Charlotte spelled out her plans to send back any good play scripts she could acquire, with the hope that Susan could do something really good with them for herself at the theatre. Charlotte knelt quickly and whispered something into Bub's ear about bringing him lots of presents. From the grimy train windows she took a last look at Philadelphia's familiar red bricks and white towers.

Once in New York she sought out an erratic old star. Could Junius Booth advise her about making a name in England? Booth was direct: Never play Nancy. It was a great part, one of her best, and she had made it. But she must never act it in London. "It will give you a vulgar dash you will never get over." If she determined to follow Booth's advice, she would not scrap the whole invention either. Perhaps in London she could salvage some of the business and reuse it as Meg.

For her New York farewell on the twenty-fifth at the Park, Simpson booked Vandenhoff to play Benedick to her Beatrice, but like her other farewells, the house was disappointingly small. Little went right with the performance. In her nervousness, in her chagrin at the empty seats staring up at her, Charlotte garbled an entire scene. Coming off, she cried, "For heaven's sake, what have I been doing?" Vandenhoff answered: "Knocking the fourth and fifth acts together."

And the box office dampened her spirits. Of the total $416.75, she and Vandenhoff could share only after $200, and she had to pay Vandenhoff $12.50 outright. In her diary she called it "scandalous swindling," though the *Spirit* next morning rallied her hopes a little. "This lady is about to visit England in a professional tour, which her varied talents must render lucrative. No actress can claim higher standing among the performers of America."

If that were true, she could only conclude that American audiences had a poor way of showing it. On that note, she was ready to sail. Mostly through loans, she had amassed $600 in cash; she had arranged a letter of credit for $200 more as a hedge against failure and had paid $150 for tickets for herself and Sallie.

On Saturday morning, October 26, still smarting from her poor send-off, she said good-bye at the hotel to Sully, who gave her a copy of Dickens' *Martin Chuzzlewit* to read on the voyage and told her her visit to England would make her proud of America. And then it was time to part with Rosalie—"on whom my soul doats," she told her diary—smiling through tears but suddenly remembering to press into her hand a penciled admonition to keep her spirits up, the months would pass quickly if they pointed their thoughts toward the joyous reunion to follow her London triumph.

Down at the busy East River dock, the family cried more tears than she wanted; it was plain to them all that, for all her wisdom in wishing to seek her fortune abroad, uncounted risks lay between this day and the distant time they could hope to see her again. And their recent loss of Uncle Augustus to these same waves lay like a stone at the bottom of their hearts. Charlotte tried to allay their fears, in spite of the deep dread that suddenly overcame her.

Mary Eliza broke free momentarily, remembering the apples she had brought to ward off Charlotte's seasickness. And then she and Sallie were up the plank of the steamboat that would take them out to the Narrows to board ship for England. If omens meant anything, she had chosen her vessel well, a 1,000 ton sailing packet named the *Garrick,* sister ship to the *Siddons.*

Vandenhoff's reports about the *Garrick* shored up her courage as she and Sallie stepped onto the ship's creaking deck. His westward passage in September two years before had been "thirty days of calm, dreamy enjoyment," the ship had skimmed the waves like a swan, while he had casually leafed a novel.

131

The deck under Charlotte's feet tilted suddenly, and the long ragged line of Staten Island began falling away. The happy shouts from the other passengers only deepened her own despair. When she peered over the side, the same gray water that had frightened her in the fall off Long Wharf frowned up evilly. Too late to change her mind, she could only stand miserably at the rail, already "wretched" with the "memory of all that I had left, pouring upon me words of regret at the steps I had taken and, although not feeling the effects of the sea, still my mind firmly made up come what delights might, I never would take another voyage from home."

She stayed on deck until seven, numb to the cold, oblivious to the first call to supper, bracing herself against the endless roll. At last, unable to stand, suddenly ill, she went below to a frightened Sallie and the musty stateroom, with Longfellow's "Hyperion" lines beating a rhythm in her head: "Look not mournfully into the past; it comes not back again. Wisely improve the present, it is thine. Go forth into the shadowy future, without fear, and with a manly heart."

An American Comes to London

(1844–1845)

In her long talks with Rosalie, in all her efforts to leave the family comfortable, Charlotte had buried her sadness at parting under a brimming confidence. But events of the last few days—her disappointing farewells, the small cash they had brought, Macready's rudeness—had eaten away at her certainty. Suddenly, her calm assurance vanished.

Her first day out of New York, she "rested in bed all day, part of the time asleep. The rest crying, Oh God how miserable I am. My thoughts of home, instead of bringing me comfort at the recollection of the love borne to me, rendering me only more wretched that I had left, as it were, comfort at home for uncertainty, perhaps unkindness —at all events, no friends. My constant exclamation, Why did I leave home."

Reading helped, but then thoughts of Rosalie poured over her, "Such wretched thoughts that it were better if I could not think . . . I hear her sigh for her absent friend. I feel almost her arms about me and then weep again, till I almost wish I could sleep away 6 months." The weather only made matters worse; a squall had sprung up when they cleared the Narrows, and no one could predict how long the blowing might continue or how severe it might become.

Conditions below were no help. During the slow days that followed, she stayed on deck as long as the light lasted, then went "with an aching heart and an irresistible dread" of the night to come to her berth in a cubbyhole awash with bilge water and bad air.

In the daily misery of nausea, of fear of the days ahead, of loneliness, "The one bright spot of my existence, the one hope that bids me toil on" was her certainty of Rosalie's affection. "Shall I ever make sufficient money to have her with me always? . . . Only my God can know how dear, how very dear she is to me."

Again and again, on the ever-tilting decks of the *Garrick,* she reproved herself. Why had she not contented herself with "moderate competency" at home, instead of inviting "this frightful uncertainty, this longing doubt which at last may end in disappointment, and which from the ridiculous prejudice of most of the audience I am going to is more than probable?"

Five days at sea, she still could not eat. When Sallie forced her, she managed a toasted cracker and tea. On the seventh, she forced down a mutton chop and sat up on deck until seven, chatting with Captain Trask and Mr. and Mrs. Bliss, some newlyweds from Troy. But rough weather and sudden nausea sent her below again.

Later, in a sudden burst of sunshine, she made her way back on deck and spent some time talking with Mrs. Bliss, an amiable little Presbyterian and not too rigid, "and whether she means it as a compliment I do not know, but she said that she thought that people in my profession were very different from what she finds in me." When night came on, she felt able to accept an invitation to dine with the Captain, "a true upright intelligent Yankee, generous in principle and straightforward in action."

But by Friday the 8th of November, the weather had turned. "Cloudy and stormy, blowing very hard from the east." Unable to stand the terrible rocking in her stateroom, she had just taken a seat near the wheelhouse when a great wave, breaking over the side, washed *"seat and me* and two sailors entirely over to the other side of the ship, and but for the rolling up of that side we should have gone over." Blinded by the water, she thought she was overboard. "No more than I expected." "I never was so frightened in my life, nor, even when overboard off Long Wharf, more wet."

In calmer weather, she picked up the book Sully had given her, but soon threw down "the most stupidly uninteresting book" she had ever tried to "wander" through. In *Martin Chuzzlewit* Dickens had pulled no punches. Two summers before, irritated by America's cool concern for an international copyright, he had written to Marryat his intention of giving "the eagle a poke under his fifth rib." And reading the book, when a character suggests the American eagle should be drawn "like a Bat, for its short-sightedness; like a Bantam, for its bragging; like a Magpie, for its honesty; like a Peacock, for its vanity, like an Ostrich, for putting its head in the mud and thinking nobody sees it," cities that had wined and dined the young Mr. Dickens raised an agonized cry. "All Yankee-doodledom blazed up like one universal soda bottle," reported Thomas Carlyle. For Charlotte, reading beyond the first few pages had only strengthened her fears. What kind of reception might she expect in a country that could write and relish such libel?

On the fifteenth, on a sensibly steady deck again, she could stand up, ready to shake her fist—and her seventy letters of introduction— at all her fears. Lines from Browning's "Paracelsus" penciled into her diary gave her courage:

> What though
> It be so?—if indeed the strong desire
> Eclipse the aim in me?—if splendor break
> Upon the outset of my path alone,
> And duskest shade succeed? What fairer seal
> Shall I require to my authentic mission
> Than this fierce energy?—this instinct striving
> Because its nature is to strive? . . .
> . . . .
> Be sure that God
> Ne'er dooms to waste the strength he deigns impart!

In place of despair, determination flamed anew: she would write her name beside the fabled Sarah Siddons'.

As the ship neared the Irish coast, the fog thickened again, and the English on board began "smacking their lips as if they recognized the taste of their own native air, off here three hundred miles from their homes." She could understand their eagerness. "If I was within 1,000 miles of Philadelphia, I am sure I should imagine that I could scent Philadelphia air." But if this was a fair specimen of English weather, "Great Heavens, what a state of *density* I shall constantly be in."

For the next two days the white mist persisted, but Charlotte was too busy writing to notice. Soon, she could dispatch letters home from Liverpool. "Sallie has been a great comfort to me. . . . So far, I am very glad I have taken her."

And then, on Monday morning, November 19, a shout went up. She laid down her pen, rushed up on deck. Close alongside, brown against the murky sky, were the Welsh mountains "that I have heard so much about, in plays so often acted upon." Greatly relieved, she could scarcely imagine that, after all this way, she would be in England by nightfall.

Once in the warm Adelphi hotel, the letters waiting for Charlotte put her at ease. Oddly, Macready had sent down three times to see if she had arrived. Edward Stirling wanted to know her terms for a short run at Covent Garden; Benjamin Webster offered her an engagement at the Haymarket after Christmas. But Macready was most insistent. Since his arrival from America, he had assembled a troupe to act briefly in Paris; Miss Cushman must join him immediately. James Barton, her old mentor, had sent word that he would help her in any way, that in spite of a crippling illness he now managed a theatre here in the West Country. Suddenly bewildered, she sent off a note to Barton asking for counsel.

Could she trust Macready? She would rest a few days in Liverpool, then decide. Barton warned her to beware. She wrote Macready accordingly; he wrote back, annoyed. She replied and then received "a letter quite ill-tempered, saying I was taking an irrevocable step." Next morning, Macready's agent arrived from London and tried to persuade her. But she stood firm. Prudence suggested that any plan beyond this point demanded the most careful attention to every angle, though it was heartening to know that opportunities stood open.

"I suppose I may make some friends," she wrote her mother. "Kiss dear Bub for me and tell him when his Aunty comes home she will buy him beautiful presents, so he must not forget her."

In the meantime, Sallie could see to the only needs she had at the moment. She could amuse herself whenever the weather lifted by watching the people of Liverpool stream past her window, many wearing respirators against the greasy smoke and fog, curious characters that might have come straight out of Dickens. She could stroll the cobblestoned walks and brush against the crowds in the ferry boats, sensing a new dimension of life she saw suspended in the stolid faces she passed.

Americans knew nothing about tragedy. It had no place in their national scheme, because they had never experienced it. To them fearing death seemed little more than a temporary ignorance, a blindness that would disappear as the logical mind studied the faults in man from which an obsession with death sprang. But here Charlotte observed a more sedate manner, an acceptance of things, of the world as God made it for man to inhabit as best he could, brightening it, spicing it, leavening it with whatever skills he had, but never expecting to alter its ineluctable cycle of life and death and life rekindled again. Charlotte looked at the pinched, sun-banished faces of Liverpool and observed a quiet acceptance of this fact.

She could enjoy further good talk before the grate with the Blisses, who urged her to come with them for a week's journey north to the Scottish Highlands; in case anything prevented her acting later in Scotland, it would be a pity to miss seeing Edinburgh. When Old Tarkington, who used to keep door at the Walnut, appeared at her hotel with a cheery welcome to England, she decided to leave Sallie with him and his wife and go.

Their coach sloshed through the ruts between high dark hedges roping the gentle swell of Lancashire, past Manchester with its church "over 700 years old," past Glasgow's iron foundries, through the bleak Scottish hills to Edinburgh. To a veteran Lady Macbeth, coming to Scotland was a little like coming home. Edinburgh was a mass of "tall, ancient houses, heaped densely together," a magnificent sweep of great trees and gardens, grim stone, Holyrood House, bright woolen kilts, and fishwives in short blue shawls shouldering large dripping baskets.

Almost prayerfully, Charlotte sought out the Theatre Royal where Siddons had made her debut, where John Philip Kemble and Edmund Kean had played, and gazed up respectfully at Sir Walter Scott's marble statue in its Gothic tower on Prince's Street.

As she had hoped, her letters to people in Scotland took her among some of the "wealthiest and most delightful" hosts, who drove her about with liveried coachmen and footmen to incredible country seats, ancient halls with roaring fires on the hearths, park-like green slopes with stone walls, dotted with long-haired cattle and sheep. "I never was among people who were so kind."

En route to Newcastle-upon-Tyne, she thrilled to the sudden blast of a hunting horn when a fox, a baying streak of white hounds, and red coats and black bowler hats bounded past. The vivid scene might have been a hand-tinted print by John Leech, an illustration straight from the sporting pages of the *Spirit of the Times*. At Yorkminster she heard the boys' choir chant the service "splendidly." And relaxing in her hotel, she saw in the papers that Macready had met with some small accident "which prevents his going to Paris as soon as he expected, ha! ha!"

Back in Liverpool, she found people equally kind. "I am engaged three deep when I come back here to stay any time." She had not dreamed of such splendor or elegance of manner, "and by the very right kind of people to make me in every way respected well." At the theatre she saw Ellen Tree, dreadfully fallen off except for a few stage tricks—Susan acted with far more spirit. If Macready's pet, Helen Faucit, was no better in London, Charlotte suddenly felt she had less to fear.

For sixty-two cents she bought a copy of a new London comedy that could do wonders for Susan at home, "if she only has the courage." Susan must show it to Blake, point out the fine part in it for him, and "don't let him take the book away," lest he copy it and assign somebody else to the role. If Blake liked the play, Susan could be the original Lady Alice in America, "which will be as good as Lady Gay was for me," and she must insist that Charlie was to have full rights to copy the parts and sell them to the other actors. If Blake would not meet such terms, Susan must offer the play to Burton, "as I promised him, so don't let him know how they came." To her mother, she had advice about Susan: "Don't let her be at all frightened at any original part she gets and make her throw dash into everything she does."

For Friday, December 6, she made a diary notation: "Left at 11 for London, passing through Birmingham. Country seemed beautifully cultivated, but now very desolate and dreary. No season for travelling, was very cold and uncomfortable. Arrived in London at 9, drove to my lodgings, very cold, had tea, went to bed after folding and sealing letters of introduction. Slept very cold," the old fears and depressions of the voyage suddenly heavy upon her.

Martin Chuzzlewit had freshly affirmed her awareness that, in British thinking, being American did not clearly mean blessed. It was no comfort now to recall that people from her distant part of the world were still ranked here, in the main, as priggish upstarts battering gauchely at the front doors of the world when the proper approach suggested hat in hand at the service entrance. She could recall the New York *Globe*'s quoting an amused English opinion in 1842: there were only four ways to think about Americans—as typical youth affecting manhood, as young John Bull working with his coat off, as a child growing too fast for his strength, as a safety valve for European monarchy. Life really began when one had arrived on a more sober plane of maturity, when one discovered that urge and drive and hot-bloodedness were only means to greater capacities. Americans knew only the means.

Next morning, outside her window at the Maurice Hotel in Covent Garden, Charlotte took her first long look at the city of all her hopes—pushcarts and fruit stalls, mounds of bright flowers and cheeses aswirl among the early morning traffic and hawking cries of London's major market, heavy lories pulled by the thundering hooves of great Clydesdales, bent figures shouldering sides of meat and crates of oranges, and here and there ragged old women cowering in doorways, hands outstretched for a farthing. In the distance, under a pale winter sun, soared the grimy white dome of St. Paul's.

Away from Covent Garden, the streets widened and straightened, pushcarts and fruit gave way to gleaming shop fronts and heavy doorways bright with polished brass. The row of mansions along Picadilly facing the Green Park immediately reminded one of the Beacon Street houses along Boston Common, except for their size and grandeur. To Bostonian eyes, the Park itself was much like the Common, except for its lack of spreading elms, the pleasant slope down from the State House, and the far-off country view.

But even Boston had no Hyde Park and Kensington Gardens, one vast sweep of paths among groves of trees, and certainly no Buckingham Palace, the great gray stone facade visible through the trees and iron grating. Away from its parks, however, London was mostly a tangle of noisy, crooked streets, a gigantic cluster of chimney pots and dingy red brick and yellow stone gasping for air and sunlight.

More to the point, Charlotte had not come to London for sightseeing. At a red box on the corner, she posted her London letters, then returned to her room to gather her thoughts. The thing she most wanted was a starring engagement, if only a night or two, in a bill that would prove to London the stuff she knew she had in her.

But despite the favorable notices she sent them, neither Stirling at Covent Garden or Webster at the Haymarket could offer her such a prominent chance. When J. M. Maddox at the Princess's in Oxford Street responded the same, she thought of Macready's summons to Paris. For more than a week she bided her time, accepted some invitations extended in reply to her letters, then convinced herself that out of her dwindling funds the cost of a trip to Paris might be a wise investment. Acting there with Macready might help open these obdurate English doors.

By the nineteenth, she had braved the choppy waters of the Channel aboard a small Folkestone packet, passed a night at Boulogne and, through the small windows of a clumsy diligence, seen Normandy's countryside flow by. Traveling twenty-four straight hours, she arrived via the Porte St. Denis in Paris.

She took her time about notifying Macready. She would see first the Palais Royal, the Tuileries, Notre Dame crowded among the tall jut-fronted houses and turrets on its island, the noisy Place de la Concorde and the spot where the guillotine had stood, and the Jardin des Plantes. Outside the walls, she would climb the crooked streets of Montmartre. She would stroll through the hooded booths along both sides of the Pont Neuf. And then at the Salle Ventadour she would confront the wily Macready.

It was not a happy time for Macready. His Paris run had gone fitfully. Parisians following his Shakespeare with *libretti* failed to give him the unbridled applause he needed. Worse, most of the critics were devoting their praise to Helen Faucit, whose tall, queenly beauty was immediately effective in Paris, even though her English remained unintelligible. In calmer times Macready himself might write poems to the "dove-like softness" of Helen Faucit's eyes, but true to form, he could not tolerate her as a rival.

Macready immediately welcomed Charlotte as the replacement—or competition—he most needed for the tall dark lady who dared to reap an undue portion of the applause. But Charlotte soon guessed his motives. When Macready made clear his plans, she remembered Barton's advice. The matter had to be weighed. She already knew the glamor of Helen's name among the English. The brightest name on the British stage was hardly a proper person to challenge boldly so early in her campaign. Faucit was not only an attractive actress; she was highly popular in British society, a favorite person as well as a favorite star. To replace her in Macready's company was to risk casting herself in a most unfavorable light. She thanked Mr. Macready, but she could not accept his offer.

She made her way back to London, wiser to the ways of London theatrics, newly resolved to begin in earnest the round of calls that would lead, if all went well, to a London debut under her own name. The days ahead were crucial. She would accept no engagement not likely to bring her full, individual recognition. Her trip to London had come at too high a price to settle for anything less. In the meantime, she and Sallie could subsist on a mutton chop a day and whatever stale muffins they could afford.

Another American had recently visited Paris. Edwin Forrest had sought an interview with Macready to arrange an appearance with his Paris company, but for reasons never explained, Macready's manager had blocked the interview, and Forrest had left Paris highly incensed, blaming the rebuff on Macready. Now in London, contracted for a run at the Princess's Theatre, Forrest sought out Charlotte to support him, beginning with Emilia in *Othello*. "I cannot begin with Emilia," she replied.

Forrest's plan was attractive, but in the attention centering on him, she herself would lose. When the headstrong actor urged the matter, she as strongly declined.

When the Princess's manager added his own petitions to Forrest's, she stood firm. Rumor had already reached her about Maddox. Though he put on good shows, honesty was hardly one of his long suits; among the profession he was notorious for his tricky dealings. Forewarned, she would appear with Forrest only if she could make an independent London debut in a play of her own choice one night before.

Forrest at last saw a shrewd advantage in timing Charlotte's appearance ahead of his own. American financial troubles and the Oregon Question had recently created serious anti-American feeling, and London could vent its spleen on the unsuspecting Miss Cushman before he risked his own skin.

To Maddox, however, the large-boned actress seemed almost ludicrous. Politically excited or no, who would pay to see such an ugly unknown? He stood firm.

A London doctor, a friend of Dickens, who had heard about Charlotte, urged J. H. Siddons, editor of a drama paper, to meet "a promising American actress of the highest type." When Charlotte admitted the editor to her rooms, her intelligence and good humor struck him immediately. Despite her large brow and strong jaw, this young woman could indeed be a new asset on the London stage. Wishing her well, he went straight to Maddox. "You villain," cried Siddons. "We have just seen a lady who will be a bright particular star in the cloudy firmament over which you preside." Maddox must sign this Miss Cushman before Webster or somebody else discovered her.

But Maddox countered, "She's not good looking." "You're a fool, Maddox. You must give her a trial." Siddons himself would guarantee that critics from the important papers covered the debut.

Next day Charlotte came to Maddox's office, armed with letters likely to change his mind. Still—as George Vandenhoff recounted the story—"the little Hebrew was obdurate as Shylock." The time had come for desperate measures. Rising to leave, Charlotte suddenly knew that she must give Maddox a full taste of her real acting skill. Reaching the door, she turned. "I know I have enemies in this country; but. . . ." She cast herself on her knees and, raising a clenched fist, cried, "so help me! I'll defeat them!" uttering this with all the passion and energy she had ever poured into Lady Macbeth. As Maddox later reported, at this point he said to himself, "Helho! s'help me! she's got de shtuff in her!" And he watched her thoughtfully as she gathered her skirts and swept out his door.

Early next morning, low in spirit, fearing she had overplayed her last hand, she saw Sallie standing at the window, then watched as the girl turned and a smile broke on her face. Sallie beckoned her to the glass. Below, walking up and down, collar turned up against the chill, was Maddox, too early to call, apparently killing time until he could decently knock. Charlotte relaxed. "He is anxious. I can make my own terms."

The chance to debut at the Princess's brought a special advantage. Named to honor Victoria before she became Queen, the Princess's was one of London's smaller, more intimate houses, a late arrival in the surge of new theatres that in 1843 had ended the Drury Lane–Covent Garden monopoly as the only legitimate theatres in London. Under their control, acting in the huge drafty houses had become stereotyped into great sweeping gestures and ringing tones, characterizations painted in only the most vivid colorings. For a newcomer, a debut in one of these "national" houses would have been doubly difficult, doubly traumatic before the endless dark sea of faces.

At the Princess's, actors could play to a more human scale, to an audience framed in a Louis XIV decor. Three tiers of white and gold boxes surrounded a pit set with benches. An air of lightness and whimsy sprang from the lilting scrolls, the gilt and red tassels that made the Princess's not only one of the best designed, but also one of the most beautiful theatres in Europe.

The agreement Charlotte reached with Maddox starred her as Bianca in Milman's *Fazio* the night of February 13, 1845, followed by a limited run with Forrest at seven pounds ($35) per night. The single night without Forrest would give her a chance to display her own talent without risk of being overshadowed by anyone else. To celebrate the bargain, she and Sallie went to the French Theatre to see Queen Victoria in one of her rare theatre attendances. "Saw lots of Lords and Ladies and the Duke of Cambridge go to the Queen's box."

Charlotte's contemporaries saw an irony in the play that she, the descendant of old Robert Cushman, chose for an English debut. A mixture of guilty lust and miserly intrigue, *Fazio* was the work of a respected clergyman, Henry Hart Milman, lately an Oxford Don and soon to be Dean of St. Paul's. For an actress to sway an audience, to prove her high pitch of feeling, the role of Bianca offered exceptional opportunity; each of her scenes is "a passionate explosion."

But there were difficulties involved. The morning of the thirteenth, when Charlotte arrived on time for rehearsal, she found the company had already started, totally indifferent to her success, the actor assigned to play opposite her being the least concerned of the lot. And the costumes and scenery disappointed her greatly, shabby makeshifts and cast-offs from a dozen plays. When she complained, Maddox asked in some ill humor if she expected to set the world afire.

Now was no time, however, to moon over slights; she had concerns more vital than any ill will or indifference in the cast. As evening approached, her nerves tightened; her throat contracted in sudden hoarseness. At the last minute, at Sallie's urging, she rushed out to have a doctor "burn" her throat with nitric acid to relax the pain. And then it was time to go to the theatre.

London had known Milman's play for years, critics considered it old-fashioned, but Charlotte was determined to give it new luster, though the quickening fear that swept over her as she made her way to the dressing room suddenly left her amazed at her temerity in daring any such madness in this jaded city, a London that had already seen in Mrs. Siddons and scores of other performers the best of all possible acting. What could she offer them now, except a quaint, American accent and a kind of naïve eagerness?

During the overture, Sallie brought the disturbing word that the chilly house was still nearly empty. When the curtain finally rose, Charlotte's nervous view of her first London audience was a scatter of listless faces and rows of empty black benches in the pit.

In the Milman story, Bianca and Fazio live in a small house in Verona where Fazio tirelessly experiments hoping to find the trick of changing iron to gold. When a rich miser stumbles into their garden and dies, Fazio steals his keys, rushes to his home, appropriates his money, then reports that he has found the secret. Hearing the news,

Aldabella, "a proud loose wanton," appears, flirts with Fazio and finally seduces him. Bianca notes a change in her husband, but realizes the truth only slowly. Enraged and jealous, she notifies the Duke of the real source of her husband's wealth. The Duke throws Fazio into prison. Though Bianca has assumed that Fazio will be freed once he has restored the money, the Duke sentences him to die. Wild with remorse, Bianca pleads with her friends to intercede with the Duke; she buries her pride and begs Aldabella for help. But Aldabella, aware now that Fazio's wealth was a hoax, only laughs. Crazed and grief-stricken, powerless to aid her foolish husband, Bianca dies of a broken heart.

As a vehicle, *Fazio* had already served Charlotte well. As Aldabella in August 1839 at the Park, she had excited "rapturous" applause; to the *Spirit of the Times* her "magnificent" energy clearly explained Aldabella's fascination with the weak-minded alchemist. Could she create a similar rapture tonight as the suffering wife?

Skeptical eyes in the audience watched the unknown American feel her way into her role. During the early scenes varied opinions registered: Miss Cushman was an actress "of a somewhat round and capacious face, of a somewhat masculine figure, and of a grave voice." Miss Cushman had a nose that compared to Macready's and a "voice nearly as deep." If this Miss Cushman was as notable an American player as rumor and the playbills reported, why was she hiding her light under Milman's threadbare play? In spite of her "brilliant and expressive eyes," Miss Cushman, in sum, had little to offer the London stage.

But in the quiet, early scenes, Charlotte had little to do. The audience took no more than a passing interest in Fazio's experiments. During the first interval, disheartened by the patter of applause, she slumped at her mirror while Sallie fussed with her drapery, straightened the tow-colored braids, and tried to find words of cheer.

In the next scenes, after Fazio had taken the miser's money and begun his illicit affair, Charlotte sensed a rising excitement in the audience. When Bianca understands at last the change in Fazio, she felt her face flash a sudden "horrible enlightenment" that began registering on the silence beyond the footlights.

"Fazio, thou hast seen Aldabella!"

In the pit, Westland Marston saw Charlotte's acting at this moment take on an almost religious devotion, a passion that suddenly fired the whole play. Bianca's jealousy became an "electric explosion." Pleading with Fazio not to see Aldabella again, ranging from bitter hatred to tender love, she seemed totally absorbed in each emotion. More and more earnest, speaking more and more quickly, she built up the feeling that if reason failed, her volley of words might thunder Fazio to his senses. Her breast rising and falling as though ready to burst, Charlotte seemed the enraged embodiment of despair.

In the next scene, begging Aldabella to intercede with the Duke, Bianca raised trembling hands, burying her pride in a tearful plea for kindness, then sank huddled under Aldabella's scorn, "the abject degradation of a proud heart naturally strong," suffering disgrace to wipe clean the slate of her guilt.

In the trial scene, pleading for Fazio's life, Bianca's repeated words "Giraldi Fazio, Giraldi Fazio" came out stern and remorseless at first, but melted as grief changed them into a "tremblingly sweet refrain." When she learned that Fazio must die, she threw herself at his feet, imploring forgiveness. The audience tension that had been building during this crucial scene suddenly welled up and broke loose in a storm of applause.

Charlotte's electrical effects were not merely a matter of acting. At the end of the scene, she felt herself so completely overcome with the passion of the scene and with sheer nervous agitation that she could only lie still for a time, too weak and disturbed to respond to the ringing "bravos" that burst over her. When she finally gathered her strength, she rose and beheld an ovation. Hats and handkerchiefs filled the air, roaring cheers rocked the Princess's from pit to topmost gallery, from aisles to whiskey seats. Applauding men stood on the benches; those in the boxes waved and shouted. In a sudden wave of relief, she knew that her English career was assured.

When the frenzied ovation finally allowed her to leave the stage, Charlotte rushed past her fellow actors in the greenroom, now clapping their own acclaim. Upstairs, she fell through her dressing room door to Sallie's elated, "You've got 'em, missus, you've got 'em."

Acting the prison scene was child's play now. When Bianca promises Fazio she will forgive Aldabella, though too numb to grasp his meaning until the death bell rouses her, the audience saw Charlotte stand suddenly rigid, staring unconscious into emptiness. When Fazio spoke a last grim word, Bianca gave no sign. When the guards led him away, she stood tensely immobile. Then as the ringing finally registered, she looked around in slowly returning sanity, comprehending now the full impact of her loss. Leaving the scene, she seemed neither to walk nor crawl; an invisible hand seemed to draw her into a "bottomless gulf of despair."

Rushing to the Palace to confront Aldabella with the terrible news, Bianca seemed a maniac turned loose in the Duke's ballroom, teeth clenched, hair flying.

Crying the words, shredding her tumbled locks, rubbing her temples, Bianca seemed to be trying to exorcise "the agony of a demented brain." Pressing her heart, Bianca sank to the floor, a dying heap. The scattered house exploded.

Gathering her drapery about her, Charlotte rose to take the cheers and bouquets, assured like Browning that God "ne'er dooms to waste the strength he deigns impart." After this night, could any grief ever challenge her joy in having found her place?

The Fruits of English Victory

(1845)

So the ordeal was over. There was nothing to do now but acknowledge the compliments of the newly respectful actors backstage, shuffle off the heavy costume, and let Sallie hand her into a cab for the ride back to her rooms. So much had happened so quickly that the only thing she wanted now was the dark oblivion of her own small walls.

By the time she had arrived there, she was dissolved in tears. Miserable, more lonely than she had ever been, filled with sudden revulsion at the foolish life she had chosen, she could only cry weakly in her chair while Sallie cooked her a chop and forced her to gulp it down. She scratched a laconic line in her diary, "Acted in London, triumphantly successful, flowers, etc."; she managed a few quick lines to Mary Eliza and Rosalie, then fell into bed coughing, with her throat on fire.

At dawn, a knock at the door brought a note from Maddox.

My dear Miss Cushman,

I heartily congratulate you on your splendid success last evening, and it affords me the greatest satisfaction in being able to convey to you the most unqualified approbation of some of the most able critics of the day of your performance of the character of Bianca. I assure you it is to me a most pleasant task to state that I was never more delighted,

Very truly yours,
J. M. Maddox

The papers accompanying the note rang with Charlotte's praises. The London *Herald* cried: "Miss Cushman is tall and commanding, having a fine stage figure. The expression of her face is curious, reminding us of Macready, . . . But that is nothing; she soon proved that she was a great artist on her own account. . . . It may be easily foreseen that her career in this country will be a most brilliant one."

The *Times* added its own raves: "The great characteristics of Miss Cushman are her earnestness, her intensity," her power to dart rapidly from emotion to emotion, "as if carried on by impulse." In the play, at the instant when Bianca suspects that her husband's affections are wavering, "Miss Cushman's career was certain." For real, impestuous, irresistible passion, "she has not at present her superior." If the London *Era* felt she needed to "smoothe off some of the angles, and give a polish to the stone which here and there indicated some of its native roughness," the fact remained that "she is a great acquisition to our stage."

As Charlotte would soon discover for herself, the London *Sun* expressed an opinion that rapidly swept over London and all of England. "America has long owed us a heavy dramatic debt for enticing away from us so many of our best actors. She has now more than repaid it by giving us the greatest of actresses, Miss Cushman. . . . Since the memorable first appearance of Edmund Kean, in 1814, never has there been such a debut on the boards of an English theatre. She is, without exception, the very first actress that we have." England had ladylike, accomplished *artistes,* but between them and Miss Cushman stretched a wide and impassable gulf, the gulf which divides talent, even of the very highest order, and genius. "That godlike gift is Miss Cushman's."

Reading the words, Charlotte knew she could now face the world, calmly assured that her own name was indeed added to the rarefied list of Americans who had journeyed to Mecca and received its accolade: James H. Hackett in 1827, Edwin Forrest and George H. Hill and Josephine Clifton in 1836, and now in 1845—if the *Age and Argus* spoke truly—Charlotte Cushman, "the best importation from the New World that we have yet had amongst us."

After such praise, contrary views hardly mattered. In the *Examiner,* Macready's friend, John Forster, complained that Miss Cushman's artistry was obscured "by a cloud of mannerisms and inelegancies." The *Spectator* found Charlotte's stage deportment "ungraceful," her attitudes "inelegant," her movements "angular," her style "rude and violent." But throughout London, playbills soon fluttered the magic words, "The Modern Siddons," and drawing rooms echoed,

148

"the sensation of the year," "the greatest English speaking tragedienne of her time."

She wrote home her excitement to Mary Eliza. "By the packet of the 16th I wrote you a few lines and sent a lot of newspapers, which could tell you in so much better language than I could of my brilliant and triumphant success in London. I can say no more to you than this: that it is far, far beyond my most *sanguine expectations*." If she had failed, she would not have hesitated to tell her mother her griefs— "for no one could have felt more with me and for me"—so now she would not hesitate to tell all her triumphs. Together, all her stage successes in America could not come near her success in London. "I only wanted some one of you here to enjoy it with me, to make it complete."

With her debut safely behind, she could turn her thoughts now to the immediate days ahead. Macready, back in England for a tour of the provinces, had missed her debut, but her interview with him in Paris had left her no reason to expect his goodwill. Her success could only increase his hostility. On Monday, February 17, she played Emilia to Forrest's Othello. The play had been announced as an "immense attraction," and though for Charlotte it seemed an anticlimax after her debut, for Forrest it was a chance to show London anew the impelling power of an actor willing to challenge Macready.

The evening brought him total dismay. At his every appearance, the applause could not mask an ominous, snakelike hiss. And it could not be lightly dismissed as anti-American hostility, for unbridled cheers greeted Charlotte. There was no mistaking Forrest's obvious fury at her when the performance was over.

The papers next day brought no relief to him. Charlotte had "electrified the spectators by her outbreaks of passion, and malgré her personal disqualifications," her unfortunate looks, "it is clear that she is hourly making fresh way in the estimation of the public." As for Forrest, Macready's "parasite" John Forster took him to task for his plodding delivery, his annoying pauses. The next Sunday, the *Times* added further injury; Forrest's Othello was very good, but it showed "little genius." Reading Forster, Forrest blamed Macready for the whole adverse reception, though Charlotte was not long in sensing that he included her in some fancied conspiracy against him. His resentment became almost a "mania," linked somehow to his awareness of Macready's interest in her. At one curtain when the audience cried, "Cushman! Cushman!" Forrest sat blackly sullen backstage. When Maddox demanded that Forrest take her out for her bow, Forrest exploded. "Damn Miss Cushman, she can go to Hell!" Charlotte gladly pushed her way through the curtain without him.

In Forrest's temper, Charlotte saw a clear threat to her own position. She begged Maddox to break her engagement with him, to bill her on Forrest's alternate nights so that London's obvious preference for her would not so pointedly discredit the actor. Delighted by all the fireworks, Maddox refused. After *Macbeth* on the twenty-first, the *Illustrated London News* condensed its scorn for Forrest into a cryptic "Miss Cushman is the chief attraction of the evening," inflaming forever the actor's hatred for this female who insisted on electrifying the crowd with her own carefully created "points," her own elaborate pauses and "freezings" under the applause. So, for all her wish to avoid entrapments, Charlotte had both egos, Forrest and Macready, solidly ranked—albeit separately—against her.

She could feel no sympathy for Forrest. "Susan will not be sorry to hear that Forrest has failed most dreadfully," she wrote Mary Eliza. "In *Macbeth* they shouted with laughter and hissed him to death. It appears, when he was here before, old Stephen Price quashed all the critics by keeping all out of the Theatre except those who would speak well of Forrest. Now he has no such support. The papers cut him all to pieces." But Susan must watch how she reported the matter; coming from Charlotte, "it *would sound badly*." When Edward Everett, American minister to the Court of St. James, extended her a flattering invitation to dinner, she politely refused: "The Forrests were invited and I would not meet them." When the onorous run ended at last, Forrest was convinced she was "not a woman, let alone being womanly," and she was equally certain that Forrest was "a butcher." Nothing would ever persuade her to act with him again.

Offstage, she had other interests. In letters to Philadelphia she poured out her joy—"No American has ever succeeded as I have" —and her misery—"I feel so sick for home that I don't know what to do." If some of the family could only join her, perhaps the loneliness would pass. "I think I should feel a great deal better if I had

Charles with me. . . . I am going into the provinces after the 1st of May and should so like to have him with me."

Back home, the family had had full report of her progress. The *Spirit of the Times* had reprinted the London critics and the acclaim that continued to shower upon her. And to the *Spirit* the matter was deeper than an actress' personal victory. Porter's paper could now see in her triumph a new phase in British–American cultural relations. In Charlotte's success, America's pride had been touched. Like a fighter on a battlefield, "Our Charlotte" had shown the disdainful Britons the true worth that could come out of the colonies. "Our Charlotte" had stormed the ramparts of arrogance and opened humility's eyes.

On the strength of such American reports, Philadelphia friends would surely lend Charlie his passage money. He could get a packet ship in New York direct to London. "God knows how long I remain here, it depends upon circumstances entirely," and if Charlie disliked the move, he could go home whenever he liked, "but he would be a great comfort to me now." The soreness in her throat had deepened into a persistent cough—she had had her throat burned nine times already with nitric acid—and she had little money, too little to send home copies of the newspaper reports about herself: "every newspaper costs me at the rate of 12¼ cents." But closer contact with the family would make her much happier. "Please," she wrote Mary Eliza, "write me nice long letters, and tell me all, but don't find fault with me or reproach me for anything. I do the best I can and I love you all more than you think I do."

Her best suffered no lack of praise in London. About her Rosalind in *As You Like It* on February 27, one paper wrote, "If ever we looked upon, heard, conceived Rosalind, it was upon that occasion. If we ever listened to the playful wit, the sweet mocking, the merry laugh of Rosalind . . . her merry eye, her arched brows, her changing looks, it was then and there." If Helen Faucit's Rosalind was all wit and mirth and beauty, "Miss Cushman *was* Rosalind." With the American actress on stage the whole *corps dramatique* at the Princess's seemed to play better. "Her genius embraced the whole stage"; together with a few other such men and women Miss Cushman could work "a notable revolution on the English stage." With Forrest out of the way, Maddox extended her contract. He did not offer to raise her salary, and Charlotte broached no question about it.

At a different theatre, she might have exacted a price to match her sudden fame, but now was no time to move, to risk any delays in appearing. There was a certain security in acting almost nightly before an audience willing to make its way to the Princess's rather out-of-the-way location. She stayed on for an almost unprecedented eighty-four nights to play Bianca, Rosalind, Mrs. Haller, Lady Macbeth, Emilia, Beatrice, and Portia. On March 4, when the curtain ended her performance of Mrs. Haller in *The Stranger,* the London *Times* had "hardly ever known such audible weeping in an audience."

Of her Julia in *The Hunchback,* the *Illustrated London News* was certain "no actress since Miss Fanny Kemble has rendered the part in so admirable a manner," partly due to Charlotte's new skill at makeup. If good acting and makeup could make Garrick look six feet tall, Charlotte had mastered a trick at her dressing table that could soften some of the plain heaviness in her face. As Julia she looked "lovely and elegant, even *espiegle*." When London society began opening its most prominent doors to this new American sensation, Charlotte began savoring the highest delights and expenses of fame.

Arriving on the twenty-seventh of April, "as handsome as any nobleman over here," Charlie Cushman found his sister surrounded by an admiring throng. She had taken new quarters at 92 New Bond Street; for three pounds a week she had a drawing room, a bedchamber, a storeroom for her trunks and costumes, a place for Sallie, a private water closet, and a small additional room for Charlie. She had hired a grand piano.

Since her hit, people almost vied with each other to see who could shower the most attention upon her. "I have been so crowded with company that upon my word of honour I am almost sick of it." During the days, she had to fight for privacy. Breakfast was seldom finished before visitors came calling. It was a rare day that found her in a room with less than six people. At times, to free herself, she resorted to tricks—"Must rush to rehearsal." Edward Everett sought her again for breakfast; she must accept an invitation to come any time. Robert Browning's friend, Mrs. Jameson, wanted to meet her.

Success was wearing, but the attention was sweet. London society was so much freer, more natural than any she had known at home, blessedly untroubled by her profession. "The playbills that are out about me would astonish the nerves of the quiet Philadelphians." As an American, she could feel perfectly at ease, not at all apologetic like some of her countrymen for differences in dress and pronunciation. People here relished her "accent," the "Americanisms" in her conversation, her wit, her energy and drive that seemed to typify the young country she came from.

Having Charlie in London made her wish now that the others could join them. With the whole family nearby, she might even consider staying two or three years; by then she ought to have amassed enough money and reputation to come home for a year, able to collect at least $40,000 from "being thought so much of here." The Unitarians had practically adopted her; a Mr. Coleman, former minister at Salem, came to call almost daily. Thomas Noon Talfourd wanted to write her a play. Milman himself had praised her Bianca. She had let herself be persuaded to sit for five different painters, though she could give them only an occasional half hour. Soon she could send one of the portraits home.

She filled her letters to Susan with gossip about the London theatre and the plays she was seeing, descriptions of the scripts she could send her, excited comments about the amazing bargains she saw in the shops, Scottish woolens cut crossway for cloaks, the handsome silk stockings one could have made to order in Manchester. "Feathers are dear here, but I will be on the lookout for a cheap plume for you." Her friend Creswick, now living in Liverpool, was having a splendid stage sword made for her, crosshilted like Hamlet's, made of bright steel. Would Susan like a strand of Roman pearls? "I won't buy anything unless it is cheap," though if her plans held firm, she ought to have saved $50,000 in the three years she was considering staying. "The Americans here are as proud of me as they can be." To her mother she enclosed a note to be taken to Sully's: "give into nobody's hand but Miss Rose." Her diary notes a daily "letter to Rose, letter from Rose," however much Mary Eliza disliked the friendship: "I wish you would not mention the Sullys to me in your letters. The spirit in which you do it is most painful to me."

Charlie's own reports described the wide swath Charlotte was cutting in London. Illustrating a point in court, Talfourd had referred to Charlotte as "the second Siddons." Judging by the newspapers, Charlotte Cushman was "the greatest creature in the greatest city in the civilized world," a large compliment indeed in a city where one could witness the Queen and Prince Albert riding in glittering state to St. James Palace and watch the nobility, equipages and all, canter grandly in Hyde Park.

She was not long in receiving a summons to breakfast with the banker–poet, Samuel Rogers. At eighty-two, the author of "The Pleasures of Memory" presided over one of the choicest breakfast

tables in London where, beginning at ten, literary wit flowed as
bountifully as his fish and cutlets, brown breads and toast, coffee and
tea, and strawberries in season. Surrounded by his paintings and his
marbles, with his "pale head, white, bare, and cold as snow," Rogers
followed the proceedings with large blue eyes that could dull in sorrow one moment, flash in joyful cruelty the next, while his venomous
tongue punctuated the bright talk around him.

Charlotte was already aware of Rogers' position in intellectual
London. In the *Spirit of the Times,* his puns had been famous for
years. His friendship with Byron and Shelley was legendary. His
composure within the past year had made him universally envied:
when his bank was robbed of 40,000 pounds he had retained his
poise. "I should be ashamed of myself, if I were unable to bear a
shock like this at my age."

At Rogers' parties, usually for no more than ten, the conversation
encompassed the group; it never broke up into tedious monologues
or forced chatter. And if Rogers himself tended to be pointless in
some of his stories, his histrionics and vivid figures saved his guests,
many of whom, like Thomas Carlyle and Dickens, might have otherwise found an invitation to breakfast unthinkable.* To his friends
the Rogers personality spanned a wide gulf; Fanny Kemble found
his bitterness of tongue no more apparent than his kindliness of heart.
To him Dickens dedicated his *Old Curiosity Shop.* And soon Charlotte could write, "Breakfasted twice with Mr. Rogers in two weeks
. . . how kind he was to me . . . he is a dear old man and I like
him consumedly."

Entering his wide doorway on St. James Street overlooking the
Green Park, Charlotte had her first encounter with the value of
wealth to a person of taste. The invitation had been amusing: Would
Miss Cushman honor with her presence an old man who might be
able to introduce her to some interesting people, a few friends who
wished to meet her, over the humble fare of his board? When she
was ushered into the drawing room and presented to the cadaverous
old figure in his chair, a new chapter in her life opened.

* Dickens could write in 1870, "I have only accepted two invitations to
breakfast in my life, one from Rogers five and twenty years ago; one from
the Premier [Gladstone] for this very week" (*The Letters of Charles
Dickens* [Bloomsbury, England, 1938], *3,* 772).

That first morning Rogers regaled her with recollections extending as far back as Dr. Johnson and personal reminiscences of Mrs. Siddons in 1795. Stumping among his treasures, he referred offhandedly to the stories behind the Raphaels and Michelangelos, the Rembrandt self-portrait, the Velasquez and Tintoretto on his crimson walls. In his third-floor library he showed her letters by Johnson and Sterne, Burke and Gray, and Milton's agreement for the sale of *Paradise Lost,* a display that amazed and delighted her no less than it did Elizabeth Barrett on another occasion.

Seated at Rogers' board, Charlotte's own stories and firm opinions found a ready audience. Though Rogers enjoyed the spotlight of his table, he happily shared it with aggressive intelligence. When Bryan Waller Procter agreed with Rogers that ballet as art was hardly admirable though theatre managers were wholly justified in offering it as long as it paid, Mr. Lumley, manager of Her Majesty's Theatre, took up a spirited defense. With such stars as Fanny Ellsler and Taglioni, ballet was not only a great art form but also the popular adjunct to opera that could make opera pay.

Charlotte agreed in theory with Lumley, though if the programs he had offered lately were fair examples, ballet could be "meretricious and immodest," and the pleasure it afforded was "animal, not intellectual." Unlike high drama, it served no moral purpose and therefore was hardly worth a decent community's support.

Another guest saw no reason to praise ballet as "poetry in motion," when all it was was shapely legs. Folk dances were certainly poetry in motion, but where was the poetry in a pretty woman standing on one toe, with the other straight out in the air, "more suggestive of the acrobat than of the dancer?"

On the mornings Charlotte would be present Rogers made it a point to choose his guests from names she wanted to meet, from names that Rogers knew could help her, like Bulwer-Lytton, who had written his warm congratulations after her debut. Would Miss Cushman consider playing the poisoner in a dramatized version of his novel, *Lucretia?* From such meetings, other meetings and invitations followed.

With Rogers' rival as a breakfast host, the "very agreeable, kindly" Richard Monckton Milnes, Charlotte found a common bond. "Dickie" Milnes was heir to lands in Yorkshire from which Pilgrims had emigrated to Plymouth. A dapper little man at thirty-six —a "pretty little robin-redbreast," Carlyle called him—with long blond hair and very little chin, Milnes' major purpose was cultivat-

ing wits and talents at his home in Upper Brooke Street. Carlyle
teased him: "If Christ were again on earth Milnes would ask Him
to breakfast, and the clubs would all be talking of the good things
Christ had said." When young Henry Adams recalled him at breakfast, "behind his almost Falstaffian mask," he remembered his broad
intelligence, his relish for the contacts and collisions of society. Unlike most of the wits of London, Milnes' social position led straight
to a peerage. Few ever declined his invitations, least of all an ambitious young actress who ten years before had helped run a boardinghouse.

Milnes took a special interest in likely Americans. His long critical review in 1839 had launched Emerson seriously in England; he
counted Charles Sumner an intimate friend. Toward the United
States in general, he took an almost paternal view; while criticizing
its "genius for hand" over "genius for head," he could welcome all
signs in London that he might have underestimated it. His invitation to the American Miss Cushman followed naturally.

And Charlotte's flirtatious friend from Detroit and Buffalo, Captain Marryat, reentered her life with invitations and an introduction
to the formidable Lady Morgan, intellect and novelist, who bade
her attend a great evening party in William Street. Lady Morgan's
high humor and rouged cheeks and wig put Charlotte at ease among
the great names in English society. With a wide-eyed Charlie in
tow, she moved down a receiving line dotted with fashionable names.
Circulating, she met a man whose promise impressed her immediately, young Lieutenant Disraeli.

Charlotte soon found herself at the center of such gatherings, invited at times as a kind of lioness to attract other names. From her
own small parties at 92 New Bond Street, word spread that Charlotte Cushman was a marvelous party entertainer, especially impressive as a singer. Though she had never regained her upper notes, she
talk–sang her way through a long list of dramatic ballads. An early
friend, George W. Bell, noted the interest that centered in Charlotte when she started to sing. At some grand soiree, where "all
London" was assembled, the chatter and laughter might continue
through the singing of some distinguished amateur, but when Charlotte seated herself at the keys or assumed a dramatic stance, ready
to recite "Lord Ullin's Daughter" or sing "We Were Two Daughters of One Race," the chatter died to a silence. If it was not the
beauty of the voice, it was Charlotte's "intensity of feeling" that

riveted her audience. Her Spanish ballad, "The Avenging Child," set the crowded rooms into tumult.

In the background, Charlie noted the words of praise that were never expected to reach her ears, "but they did." At table, she set the diners laughing with her imitations of a hen being chased and caught, a cork being pulled, the cawing mistrust of a parrot, quick stories told in brogue. At a party given by Dinah Mullock, Charlotte recited Kingsley's "The Sands o' Dee" so disturbingly, with a voice like "a skipper at sea," that the prolific young novelist Margaret Oliphant was rather frightened.

Other names came calling. The young poet Eliza Cook deluged her with poems. "To Charlotte Cushman" extolled her for flinging new laurels on Shakespeare's brow. At their meeting, Charlotte recognized in Eliza an intuitional bond. Eliza's taste in dress proclaimed a determination to be herself: "staring" red plaid, sable cuffs two inches deep, hair cut short like a man's, neck encircled in frills extending to her waist. Eliza expressed herself as freely. Tilting back in her chair, planting both feet on the fender, she bluffly ordered a glass of beer.

Like Annie Brewster and Rosalie Sully, young women in England found in Charlotte a strong attraction. The magnetism that audiences applauded carried over into her social relationships with women her age who came to "kneel" at her feet. If none could define the quality, few doubted her force and self-possession, her manner that clearly announced, "I know what I'm doing." For Victorian girls such a young woman held unique interest, a kind of wish fulfillment. That she could amuse and entertain only strengthened her hold, a bond that did not always please Charlotte herself.

Two years her junior, Eliza Cook soon became a constant companion. And in that fact centered a buzz of comment that eventually reached Philadelphia. Charlotte's diary for May 10 carries the cryptic results, "Letter from Rose, breaking my heart." Rosalie's letter of May 11 brought further tears. "Oh, forgive me, dear Charlotte, and believe me when I tell you again and again that my love for you remains firm and unshaken spite of all the cruel reports that are circulated against you." Parted for years, they must drag along a wretched existence until time proved to the world Charlotte's innocence. Charlotte must remain assured that "I am as fondly yours as ever I was the 6th of July last—that pledge I still wear." Since her departure, the bracelet had never been unclasped. Her father had made a bracket for the cardinal's cage outside the north window. "In the afternoon your mother brought me a letter which explained all."

Cruel or not, the reports surrounding her friendship with Eliza Cook did little to lighten the social pressures upon her. And her work at the Princess's occupied her now more than she wanted. On three different nights she did her best to breathe life into a play James Kenney had written for her. But though the applause was considerable, despite the shower of bouquets that had rained down from the boxes, *Infatuation* had failed. "It may, perhaps, do me some little injury, but I can afford a trifle, and my next play will bring me up." On May 18, Maddox extended her run again. "The idea of acting an engagement of forty-seven nights in seven old plays," she wrote her mother, "and being called out every night, then to have one's engagement renewed for thirty nights more, is a thing that would astonish the natives on the side of the world you inhabit now, but which I hope won't hold you long."

If wanting the family with her in England had something to do with a desire to cancel the difficult rumors, it also had much to do with a flowing heart, for with her joy in having Charlie in London, she was more and more strongly convinced that the good life here had to be shared. "I have given myself *five years more,* and I think at the end of that time I will have $50,000 to retire upon; that will, if well invested, give us a comfortable home for the rest of our lives."

A Star in the Provinces

(1845)

Already, Charlotte could visualize the day when Susan herself would make a London debut. Opposite her hot-blooded Romeo, Susan's willowy Juliet would create a sensation. On that point, when several steamy June nights withered London's interest in theatre, she ran into trouble with Maddox.

Casting about for some novelty, Maddox remembered Charlotte's American success as Romeo; the sight of a woman in unlikely tights and doublet just might perk up the crowd. His note to her about it brought her up short. Without tipping her hand, the reply she sent by Charlie mentioned other roles that seemed "more appropriate." Charlie himself could make suggestions, though he must positively not bring up Meg Merrilies. The gypsy hag was too crude, surely, for the Londoners she had met at the Princess's.

The report Charlie brought back, however, confirmed an unhappy fact she had long known about this brother. Confused, Charlie had let Maddox believe somehow that his sister actually wanted to play Meg. Maddox had debated. In itself, Scott's tired old piece could hardly attract anybody, yet who could predict the stir Charlotte Cushman might cause as the hag? He had gambled on her before.

Hearing this, she could only look at her brother amazed. Charlie was clearly no man to depend on. The sooner she placed him in some clerk-type position that could accept his shortcomings, the happier it would be for both of them. He could preen himself in her light as long as he liked, but she would look beyond him for any practical help.

Still, Charlie had committed her to Meg, and this was the fact that troubled her. Like Nancy, the ragged gypsy was surely too coarse and raffish. Yet when she saw Charlie's crestfallen look, his shame at having failed her, she shrugged: "It can't be helped. I will do it as it has never been done before!"

By June 10, when she sprang into the moonlight as the tattered old hag, she had worked changes. With adequate time to prepare, she had carefully planned the costume and used all her new skill at makeup. With Sallie's help, painting her skin took a full half hour. Under the brush, her firm flesh became shriveled cheeks and projecting bones, withered neck, and sinewy arms and hands. Donning the drab rags, stuffing her own hair into the tangled gray wig and binding it all with a cloth took the rest of the hour. To the forlorn old beldam she had created in New York, she had added a blend of pathos and mystery, an element weirdly psychic.

With Meg's silent leap to the stage, London saw a towering sibyl with bony arms extended, tense, rigid in fluttering rags, coils of hair escaping the folds of a twisted kerchief. When she darted a claw at Henry Bertram, when a voice "from another world" began crooning a lullaby, Madame Vestris, who had come over from Covent Garden, felt her blood turn "cold."

Standing on tiptoe, thrusting her crooked staff over her head, her eyes flashing, her weird cries rose to a shriek. One critic saw the performance, not as acting, but as inspiration "as great as anything Rachel ever achieved." When Meg charged old Dominie Sampson to admonish Henry not to forget her, but to build up the old walls in the glen for her sake, the conviction behind her words suggested the ghostly light that would flicker over the stones.

Standing in the wings, Charlie watched the faces staring up out of the chill that Meg's dying agonies spread over them. Women unable to watch the terrible writhing covered their faces. Transfixed, awe-struck expressions followed the ragged heap's final quiverings.

When the curtain ended the play, Charlie witnessed a London triumph. The audience burst into "screeches" of applause; hats peppered the air. A few moments later when Charlotte bounded through the curtains with her own dark hair brushed free of the wig, her face washed clean of its swarthy wrinkles, a new frenzy shook the house. Afterward, Eliza Cook gave her more poems and an amusing sketch of herself as Meg, fierce-eyed, standing triumphantly erect with staff in one hand, a trumpet bedecked with an American flag in the other. She called it "Yankee Hanging Out Her Banner," a declaration that Charlotte's new victory heralded all Yankeedom's challenge to the world.

On the strength of this new ovation, Charlotte expected a sellout benefit the next week. But the muggy weather was against it, and, as Charlie reported it, Maddox had worked hard to spoil her house, to convince her the public "did not like her," lest she demand more money. Clearly the time had come to break with Maddox.

Immediately she contracted an agent, Mr. Lea of Bow Street, to book her acting dates for a tour in late summer and fall through the provinces. In the meantime, nearly exhausted from the labors she had forced on herself, she had a vacation coming, and the arrival of her family next month to anticipate. She would do some reading, make a few calls.

The feminist Anna Jameson, a friend of Fanny Kemble, the Carlyles, and the young poets Robert Browning and Elizabeth Barrett, wanted to meet her. At the visit "the most charmingly delightful woman I have ever met" put Charlotte at ease, though Mrs. Jameson's flaming red hair, fierce eyes, square mouth, and freckles at first disturbed her. Other visits followed, in spite of Mrs. Jameson's admonitions to slow down. "Do you mean that I am *too energetic?*" Charlotte asked in a note. "Alas, I wish I could conquer my restlessness," but a sort of "Jew destiny hangs over me, and I find the one word whispered into my ear at every turn, 'on!'" much as her energies flagged.

Through a letter from Mary Howitt, she met Mary Mitford, author of *Rienzi,* in which she had played at the Park. Mrs. Howitt's letter sang her virtues: Charlotte was a "glorious creature," as superior in character as in talent, and if ordinary young men did not cause a furore over her looks, the sound-hearted kind would acknowledge her power and greatness, her beautiful intellect.

The meeting with Miss Mitford among her roses and hollyhocks at her home, Three Mile Cross, near Reading put Charlotte in the presence of a silver-haired little woman with an ugly face, a Victorian lady not at all repulsed by the outpourings of her friend Elizabeth Barrett: "Love me, dearest Miss Mitford, my dear kind friend—love me, I beg of you, still and ever, only ceasing when I cease to think of you." Charlotte was enchanted with the playwright. When Miss Mitford left the room for a moment Charlotte remarked to another guest: "What a bright face it is!" a face that in spite of its plainness carried "a summer brightness." And Mary Mitford was no less enchanted with Charlotte in the letters she wrote of the visit to Elizabeth and to her friend Mrs. Partridge: "I have had a very interesting American visitor, Miss Cushman, the tragic actress—a very superior woman. They say she is an actress of great genius."

In the busy months since her London debut, none of Charlotte's joys matched that of planning the family's move. She was still the focal point of their interests, the major support of their needs, and no stronger reason kept them in Philadelphia now than had earlier kept them in Boston. By June, she had their passage to England fully arranged; they would arrive in London by mid-July.

As the time drew near she balanced her excitement with house-hunting. "I am getting quite nervous as the time draws near to expect my mother and sister (they must be here in a day or two), and quite long for them." She wanted a garden with birds for Mary Eliza, play space and trees for young Bub, ample rooms of her own for entertaining. She settled at last on a furnished cottage at 1 Garway Road in rural Bayswater, five miles from Covent Garden. She and Sallie and Eliza Cook had the garden paths swept and the house shining and decked with flowers when her mother and the others finally arrived from Liverpool, distraught from the rough ocean passage, overjoyed like herself that the separation had ended at last.

After the laughing embraces, Charlotte held each one back at arm's length. Mary Eliza had aged, but under the lace of her cap, her face held the same old Yankee firmness, her eyes the same doubts that anything could ever come right outside of Boston. In Susan she sensed a new maturity, a rounding of character that work and time had given her. And Bub was now a tall boy of seven. The lad was much too manly for such a baby name. From now on his Auntie would call him Ned.

If she sensed a coolness in her mother and Susan toward Eliza Cook, she tried to think little of it. Her mother had never grasped the charm of the gentle Rosalie; she could hardly appreciate the flamboyant Eliza. In time, the reserve might thaw, though it would not be easy explaining Eliza's eccentric dress, her outspoken manner, and vigor. In time, the family might see the change in herself, the determination to be the person she truly was in a land where intelligent women confessed more and more their irritations under society's foolish restraints. Eliza proclaimed her own independence a little too loudly perhaps, but Charlotte would not say no to her.

Once settled, she was ready for guests at the Bayswater cottage. In some nervous response to the recent excitement, the family had all been ill the first few days. Mary Eliza had gone weakly to bed; Susan came down with a cough; Charlie dragged himself each morning to his new job with an insurance office in Chancery Lane. But they had all regained their strength when Westland Marston and his wife came calling. To the English, Mary Eliza was a homely, genial example of American women, confiding at once her hardships in trying to keep house—where everything was so "strange"—on a weekly budget under "three pounds and *a half,*" an expression the Marstons found quaint.

Returning their visit, Charlotte found a person no less strange at the Marstons'. "Among our guests was a man of great erudition and worth," Marston recollected, "who had written one or two creditable dramas in verse, liked and respected in spite of his delusion that nature had meant him to be a great actor." B—— had a terrible voice, but the fact had never deterred his "elocutionary displays." When he begged Charlotte to do a scene from *Macbeth* with him, Charlotte refused. He then offered to do a scene, solo, from *Othello.* Charlotte whispered to Marston. "You're a friend of poor B——'s; . . . don't allow him to make himself absurd."

But when some of the guests encouraged him out of politeness, Charlotte would have none of it. "Mr. B——," she said. "You may think me uncivil for interfering, but please remember that acting is the work of my life, and that I seek the society of my friends for a little change. Please don't set the example of recitations." When someone suggested the recitation should be the only one of the night, B—— was delighted. "Oh, it's a shame!" cried Charlotte. She looked around at the others. "Mr. B——, I tell you the truth. You can appreciate dramatic poetry, and you can even write it, but you cannot declaim it. Nature has not fitted you for it. Do sit down, then; don't give your friends, who so much admire you, the pain of seeing you attempt what you cannot perform." Still undiscouraged, B—— bowed to Charlotte's candor.

During that same visit, Marston gave Charlotte a message from Bulwer-Lytton: he was still eager to rewrite his *Lucretia* for her if she ever cared to consider it.

Early in August, the *Athenaeum*'s music critic, Henry Chorley, brought Charlotte and Robert Browning together at a musicale.

Charlotte was only partly prepared for Browning. In spite of the awe she felt in his presence, he hardly looked masculine. As Mary Mitford had said, Elizabeth's bearded poet could have been a "girl drest in boy's clothes . . . about the height and size of a boy of twelve," with brown wavy hair to his shoulders. But Charlotte could forgive him; he had given her the words from "Paracelsus" to help her withstand her ocean ordeal.

When Charlotte finally met him, she mentioned the proofs she had just seen of Hans Christian Andersen's new novel, *Only a Fiddler*. Browning thought a few moments. "Now I think of it, *I* seem to have written something with a similar title—nay, a play, I believe, —yes, and in five acts—'Only an Actress!' " Later at home, Browning wrote Elizabeth that he had found the American Miss Cushman "clever and truthful looking."

Wending his way through the cheering provinces, William Macready had kept an eye on Charlotte's success in London. When Benjamin Webster approached him with a Haymarket offer, asking what assisting performers he would require, Macready replied, "No one," though if asked to suggest, "I should name Miss Cushman." And Edwin Forrest, swallowing his pride, told a theatre manager in Bristol that Charlotte Cushman might welcome an offer to appear there with him.

But neither actor could tempt her; she could do well enough without them. When Maddox sought Charlotte for early September in a joint appearance with Macready—"Miss Faucit I am told won't go"—she remained firmly opposed. Her country engagements would "not admit of it." To his diary Macready complained of "the woman's perfect inconsistency."

The only appearance that interested her now was the *Romeo* she soon hoped to do with Susan. Before Charlotte left London, they ran quickly through their *Romeo* lines. And she reassured Charlie once again that his mistake with Maddox had worked out well enough. After London's raves, Meg Merrilies should go well in England's lesser houses; with it she would test her real drawing power.

Acting to top houses in the provinces, she soon found that her London agent had served her ill. Interested only in his cut, Lea had

ignored all geography in arranging her tour, and, strange to the
territory herself, she wasted valuable time retracing her steps on
trains and muddy coaches through Dover and Brighton, Bath and
Swansea, Manchester, Sheffield, Hull, Glasgow and Edinburgh, and
Newcastle-on-Tyne. When the theatre "Royal" in Norwich turned
out to be a disreputable "low" house, she broke the contract and
mollified the manager with cash: playing it might damage her reputation. She fared better in Hull, where her Bianca caused tears to
flow "unbidden, not only from those of her own sex, but from eyes
altogether unused to the melting mood."

On September 22, she took her success to the Queen's Theatre in
Manchester, where conditions seemed right for a test run before
London with Susan, though some of the other actors appeared second-
rate.

"Who is your Mercutio?" she asked the manager.

"There I think we shall be all right; I have got young Wallack."

Charlotte looked at the playbill. "I don't see his name."

"No, he calls himself Mr. Lester."

"Very inexperienced, I am afraid."

The manager agreed, "But he is said to have a good deal of
promise."

After the performance, Charlotte agreed that the classically handsome Mr. Lester would bear watching. Throughout the Manchester
run, she became increasingly sure of his talent. Before she left town,
she called him to her. "Young gentleman," she said, "there is a great
future before you, if you take care and do not let your vanity run
away with you."

Lester took Charlotte's advice to heart. Her letter of recommendation to Benjamin Webster at the Haymarket got him his first acting
job in London, his first encouragement toward a notable career in
later years, when England and America knew him as Lester Wallack.

By the time Charlotte left Manchester she had sealed an important friendship with Geraldine Jewsbury, who had come crowding
toward her in the greenroom. Geraldine's recent novel *Zoe* had
shocked staider sensibilities in England; even Jane Carlyle, who had
been her good friend since 1840, had found it "too strong," and the
dour Carlyle had tossed the volume aside as "George Sandism," the
work of a school teaching "phallus worship," with Balzac and Sue
for prophets and Sand herself "for a Virgin." For a time "the ardent
little provincial" with her untidy red hair had been more ardent
than Jane Carlyle knew how to manage. "My dear," Geraldine had

165

written, "let us look at our lot boldly in the face at once; if it has been given us to love—for it is not every woman who receives that terrible gift—let us submit without vain struggling." To all of which Carlyle had snorted: "I wish she could once get it fairly into her head that neither woman nor man, nor any kind of creature in this universe, was born for the exclusive or even for the chief purpose of falling in love, or being fallen in love with."

To Geraldine, Charlotte was the complete embodiment of "protection and strength," a nature capable of the engulfing friendship Geraldine relished. And in the correspondence that soon flourished between them, Charlotte disclosed her appreciation. As a forthright champion of women's rights in England, Geraldine saw ample proof in Charlotte that female determination could triumph in a masculine world, even one presided over by a Queen determined to keep women forever bound in the chains of domesticity. If Geraldine in her novels could damn the restraints society imposed on her sex, Charlotte as the brilliant new star of the English stage could stride boldly through England, the shining example of woman's right to live as her nature ordained. Their appreciation of each others' efforts toward recognition fully balanced the passion in the friendship.

When Charlotte confessed that her ceaseless pace since arriving in England was beginning to tire her, Geraldine offered an essay of advice: "You have had enough to drive to destruction a whole regiment of *men,* let alone women." When Charlotte confessed that the social artificialities in London had depressed her at times, Geraldine could sympathize: "Living in London society does under any circumstance make one exquisitely sad." Charlotte must accept as normal her revulsion to the glare of popularity and triumph in which she had moved for the last few months. No nervous system ever born of woman "could stand it."

When Charlotte mentioned a deeper concern, her friendship with Eliza Cook, Geraldine understood fully. "Now for what you darkly allude to. I know something of that worry too, but yr. way of putting it makes me doubtful the sort of friends that are grumbled at . . . if you know them to be worthy, if they are true and faithful as well as loving, follow yr. own instincts. You need love to keep you up in yr. daily course more than other women. You are essentially true and noble-minded yourself, and second motives will never hold you. If they are worthy, cling to them. You are quite strong enough not to get entangled in any undesirable adjuncts." Society had never yet thanked anyone "for minding its clamor, rather despises them for being moved," said Geraldine. But this of course depended on circumstances. "If those they want you to give up are true and faithful and sterling, and *deserve* yr. love, then I shd. say keep to them thro' evil and good report, but don't go making a grievance for people who don't deserve it." Jealousy pervaded the lines, but Geraldine could only conclude, "Miss Cook wd. think me very good if she cd. believe that another person might love you as well as she does."

As for Charlotte's Romeo, Geraldine admitted that valid arguments might question a woman's taking the part, but in her opinion, "it was a most effective performance." London would surely acclaim the skill and insight of the new team of sisters playing the leads.

October found Charlotte in Edinburgh's Theatre Royal, no longer the wide-eyed American tourist, but a name written large on the billboards. A sixteen-year-old actor, John Coleman, spoke for Edinburgh's reaction. When the curtain went up on *Fazio,* he discovered a massive woman towering above a man of medium height, Bianca's unbecoming costume contrasting sharply with Fazio's elegant doublet and fine hose. Her head was plastered with huge coils of tow-colored, lusterless hair. Between her eyes and her defiant mouth "which opened and shut like a vice" yawned a "chasm, in the centre of which a minute pimple suggested an apology for a nose." About her "strange, weird figure" Coleman saw no trace of feminine charm; when she spoke, her voice, instead of sounding "an alarum to love," was guttural.

By the end of the first act, Coleman was thoroughly bored, but the curtain for the next act caught him before he could leave the stage box. He was still bored at the end of the second, staring back dully when Bianca's eyes fell squarely on him as she delivered her lines. But with the beginning of the third act—"wondrous glamour of the actor's art!"—from the moment Bianca came to denounce her faithless spouse, "I had eyes and ears only for the poor demented creature whose face was transformed into the mask of Medusa, and whose eyes glittered with internal fire." Bianca's frantic "There's dancing here! And I—yes, I—have been dancing, too!" left him "shivering and shuddering" until the bell heralding Fazio's death sounded the knell for his wife.

For a long moment, a silence "awful and profound" filled the hall; then the audience "arose like one man," their voices mingling in an acclamation one might hear "only once or twice" in a lifetime. "I think they must have gone mad; I know I did," wrote Coleman. "With tears streaming down my cheeks, I waved my handkerchief and shouted myself hoarse." When the actress came forth for her bow, "all nods and becks and wreathed smiles," the ungainly apparition of the first act had become a woman—"yea, a woman of rare and radiant beauty!" From that time on, Coleman "never noted the lack of comeliness in Charlotte Cushman."

Next morning, Coleman overheard a conversation in the manager's office. "The audience was so cold and apathetic," said the voice of Bianca, "that I really believe I should have 'dried up' altogether if that beardless boy in the stage box, with his insolent airs, hadn't so stung me to the quick that I made up my mind to 'go' for the puppy. For the first two acts I might as well have tried to thaw an iceberg; but in the third I hypnotised the young cub, and, when I went forward at the end, he waved his handkerchief and shrieked and shouted like a maniac!" "They were not so demonstrative to Mrs. Siddons when she made her *debut* here," Murray rejoined happily.

Coleman, hat in hand, was waiting to apologize when Charlotte left the manager's office.

"You here? An actor?"

"Not yet, madam," he replied. "But by-and-by I hope to be one."

"Hope springs eternal in the human breast!" said Charlotte.

Playing a brief supporting role in *Guy Mannering*, Coleman was waiting for his cue "when lo! there swept on like a whirlwind a great, gaunt, spectral thing," clad from head to heel in shreds and patches. Its locks were iron gray; its face, arms, and neck were like a mummy's "new risen from the sepulchre"; its eyes flamed fire. "Then came my cue, and upon the instant I was kneeling at her feet. About to rush away to do her bidding, she seized me by the throat, and with a man's strength," Meg hurled him to the ground. "Who could have thought that those withered arms had such strength in them?"

Another actor was hardly so lucky. The man playing Dandie Dinmont was much too small for the role, and at the final curtain, when *"la grande Charlotte"* tumbled into his arms, his legs gave way, and down he went on his back, "clinging valiantly to Meg as she fell on his stomach." Stifling his laughter, Coleman had never seen two more grotesque objects—she "dead above, he alive, all alive! below" struggling for air.

Safe behind the curtain, the cast exploded into laughter. They were still laughing when the curtain went up for the call. Charlotte sprang to her feet, hands clenched, teeth fixed, eyes glittering. Dandie thought she was about to strangle him. "And she culd have din it tae, laddie!" he said later.

But the roaring out front was still "so loud, so enthusiastic, and so long continued that it seemed as if the mere concussion of sound must have rent the roof from off the building." Charlotte suddenly burst into joyous laughter herself, playfully slapped Dandie's face, "and ran off to her dressing room, like a two-year-old." Coleman called her "a deuced good fellow." From her lips Shakespearean lines which "in this superfine age we have suppressed as indecorous" lilted joyously.

Among the admirers who came crowding to her door were the Edinburgh phrenologist George Combe and his wife Cecilia, daughter of Mrs. Siddons. In delighted response to their invitation, Charlotte soon found herself in their elegant home with its "glorious fires." Over tea and Madeira, if the subject was Cecilia's mother and her concept of Lady Macbeth ("fair, feminine, nay, perhaps, even fragile . . . captivating in feminine loveliness"), the Combes' flattery in launching Charlotte socially in Edinburgh interested her almost as much.

When Susan came north for another trial run of *Romeo* before London, the Combes further extended their hospitality, though some of their eagerness cooled when their staid neighbors objected strongly to Charlotte's "masculine" demeanor as Romeo, her straight limbs as "strident as those of a youth," her amorous advances toward her sister so erotic "that no man would have dared to indulge in them" publicly. In due course Combe was writing Cecilia's cousin Fanny Kemble for details about Charlotte's family, reputation, and "private virtue." "Why the deuce doesn't he look for it in her skull?" complained Fanny.

Combe's advice about Romeo brought a detailed reply from Charlotte. "I can only assure you the ideas you have been kind enough to give me are entirely *new to me*." Had Combe spoken earlier, she could have used his help. "As it is, your hints have only *plunged me into trouble,* for I find the subject, *in a new light entirely,* and myself bound under a penalty of 200 pounds to fulfill my engagement." Unable to forfeit her contract, she could "only hope for the indulgence of my friends in the mistake which, without the slightest notion of indelicacy, I have made." Combe must understand that she had only wanted to give Susan the support "I knew she required and would never get from *any gentleman* that could be got to act with her." Surely there was less indelicacy in two sisters performing the roles than in father and daughter, as Charles and Fanny Kemble had done on occasion. Combe and the offended people of Edinburgh must recall her precedent in Mrs. Kean, who acted Romeo and Ion repeatedly without bringing down any cries of "indelicacy."

Privately, however, Charlotte had to confess that more was involved than mere support for Susan. Her Romeo had created objections before; Philadelphia had whispered against it. Yet the whispers had not obscured the public's very real interest in an actress performing the role. The public had expressed itself at the box office.

The matter posed a dilemma. In every sense, she meant to be a respectable actress; her vows to Mary Eliza and herself stood as sound now as ever, but a public performer sooner or later yields to public interest if she wishes to attract paying houses. Not willingly would she offend anyone's moral sense on stage, but at the box office her Romeo was surefire. Newspaper reactions to her work so far hardly bore out her fears, but, rightly or wrongly, as an American she felt a special handicap when facing the world's best drama critics. For all her debt to James Barton and Macready, she could not claim to be the product of any of the great English acting traditions; her "want of school" worried her. To make her mark, she must tackle roles she could clearly identify with her own name. "I must act in parts where comparisons cannot be instituted or I fall . . . unless in some such out of the way thing as Romeo." And no less to the point, she could act Shakespeare's passionate youth with all the sincerity and respect any actor had ever brought to the role. The compromise ignored none of her principles.

Unfortunately, her explanation to Combe did not settle the matter. Edinburgh continued to wonder about an actress, intent on social acceptance, who would display herself so "questionably": was there more in the young actress' motives than met the eye? Charlotte herself put up no further defense, but the matter involved a complex of reasons. She would be an honest performer; she would be an honest woman. She could bring understanding to the role; playing it, she could satisfy most of her audience. As Shakespeare's star-crossed lover, she could vent a level of emotion that she recognized more and more as basic to her own nature. Romeo was more than a role.

She sent Susan back to London, rounded out her own work, then filled her last afternoon with a ride in the hills and frank talk over supper with John Coleman. In the long conversation between them, she revealed more of herself than she normally exposed to anyone. Coleman found her full of advice: "No actor should ever marry till he's forty; no actress should ever marry at all, or, if she does, she should quit the stage!"

To Coleman's complaint that he was getting nowhere as an actor, she retorted, "You don't smoke, you don't drink, have the torso of a young Hercules, a voice like a trumpet and not seventeen!" He should count himself lucky—doubly so on this fabled stage where so many English stars appeared every season, where, unlike Shakespeare's day, the heroines were now played by real girls, not by beastly, scrubby, louts of boys. Playing opposite them, "you villain," Coleman could have the "pick of creation to make love to!" Then in a rare moment of self-revelation, a shadow flickered across her heavy features as she finished her little speech. "My god," she said to Coleman, "were I a man, instead of a wretched, miserable woman with a face like an owl!"

At Glasgow's Theatre Royal on Dunlop Street, John Alexander welcomed her as the "immense" new find of the season. Charlotte respected Alexander. When Forrest had failed to attract large houses, Alexander had decreased the number of supernumeraries for his plays. Forrest had shouted, "You are an ass!" but Alexander had stood his ground: "You, Mr. Forrest, are simply a guest; and, judging from your behavior, a very disagreeable one you are."

When the playbills went up for Meg Merrilies, throngs jammed the box office. Playing one of the gypsy boys, J. H. Stoddart considered Meg's death—"all of a heap on the stage, looking more like a bundle of old rags than a human being"—the most "effectively dramatic piece of business" he had ever witnessed. The Glasgow *Dramatic Review* labeled the new star a performer "after our own heart, the most original actress we have ever seen."

En route back to London, Charlotte could agree with Sallie that the trip had boosted her stock. From these first attempts in the provinces she knew what it was, at last, to be rated a star—"more varied and alive," a Glasgow critic had cried, than Helen Faucit. Determined now to demand star treatment and a salary to match, she could return to London ready to introduce Susan as a second contender for English praise.

In the meantime, she settled herself for a few quiet weeks in the Bayswater cottage, played hide-and-seek in the hollyhocks with young Ned, bore up under Mary Eliza's steady complaints of discomforts in this alien land, and coached Susan for the night in late December when they would appear at Benjamin Webster's Haymarket Theatre in *Romeo and Juliet*—Edinburgh's whispers notwithstanding.

14

"A Very Dangerous Young Man"

(1846)

Before Charlotte had taken her final bows in Edinburgh, an undertone of further gossip had reached her. "Some of the *hospitable* people of Edinburgh took it into their heads that poor Sue was not married." By the time Charlotte had arrived in London, her memory of Scotland had become "*anything* but agreeable." Letters from the busy George Combe were waiting.

She could not lightly toss off the ugly words. Why should the Scots care about Susan's marital state, and why should she herself let the matter rankle so deeply? In facing the question, Charlotte faced a new fact about herself. As her social circle widened, these recent months in England and Scotland had added a further range to her personal values. If acting had earlier seemed quite sufficient to center a life upon, it no longer seemed so adequate.

Cheers and bouquets at her feet could not cancel a city's gossip. "What justice of friendships," Combe wrote, "would it be to hear reports circulated against you that, if unrefuted, could necessarily exclude you both from all virtuous society?" She might have ignored Edinburgh's suspicions if success in the world she now occupied had not become something more than high billing on a placard. "We have been obliged to send for marriage certificates, bills and papers, to prove our respectability," galling as the whole affair was to her pride and "mortifying" to Susan. "Thank God, we can meet the slander boldly."

The whole affair smelled of jealous intrigue, with one prominent face glowering in the shadows. Combe's letters soon divulged the fact that Edwin Forrest, now appearing in Edinburgh, had chosen this means of embarrassing her, to pay her back for "embarrassing" him at the Princess's. To the friends she and Susan had made in Edinburgh, Forrest was broadcasting a torrent of slurs about Susan's "immorality," the details of which "I forebear," wrote Combe, "to place in writing." And Helen Faucit's name, intentionally or not, figured in the ugly campaign. Theodore Martin, the man who hoped to make Helen his wife, was openly spreading reports about Susan which he said he had picked up in London, feeling it his duty "to warn" her Edinburgh friends "for their own protection."

"If you have a male relative," advised Combe, "it is his duty to call on Mr. Forrest for his proof." If not, Susan must either prosecute Forrest for defamation of character or present written proof from the persons he had named "that what he says in their names is false." Unless such efforts were made, Susan could never move in Edinburgh society.

Charlotte took some comfort in the fact that Fanny Kemble came forward, however reluctantly, to defend her in letters to Combe, though Fanny's recent arrival in England gave her reason to fear a new threat. Separated at last from Pierce Butler, Fanny had come home, determined to regain stardom in roles that Charlotte fully meant to claim for herself. "Stout, middle-aged, not particularly good-looking," as Fanny described herself now, she had lost the youthful charm that had been her greatest asset. In its place, her age and weight might fit her perfectly for Lady Macbeth and Queen Katharine.

For Charlotte, the days immediately ahead would show if any of her fears were important. Certainly the *Romeo* debut in London was vital, and both sisters bent their efforts single-mindedly toward it. Long hours of practice at the Bayswater cottage and tryouts in Southhampton busied them until the London opening on December 30.

In presenting a female Romeo, Benjamin Webster had no fear of the "moral offense" that Combe had predicted; moral offenses, if not too openly flagrant, could as surely fill theatres as empty them. Well before opening night he had taken his stand on the impression Charlotte meant to create. During rehearsals, when the Haymarket company had risen up in resentment of these "American Indians," the Misses Cushman, who insisted on doing the original Shakespeare instead of the familiar watered-down Garrick version, Charlotte explained herself to Webster. "Understand me, pray, that I am thoroughly prepared to do whatever you wish," but not necessarily to appear in this Garrick "flummery" to please a lazy company.

Webster posted his reply on the greenroom wall: any lady or gentleman who made any difficulty or raised objections to the wishes of the Cushmans was welcome to leave the cast. The matter was clear. Now that Drury Lane and Covent Garden were no longer the only licensed houses in London, Webster would overlook no opportunity to make the Haymarket London's outstanding house, its most exciting stage, having the most fashionable clientele.

When the curtain rose on Verona, the actress portraying Romeo gave no hint that she was anything other than Shakespeare's love-sick swain. Answering Benvolio's questions, Romeo's masculine vigor established the vital illusion.

"What sadness lengthen Romeo's hours?"

"Not having that which, having, makes them short."

"In love?"

"Out—"

"Of love?"

"Out of her favor where I am in love." Against Susan's delicate femininity, Charlotte was completely the athletic force pursuing her. Few Romeos in London's memory had looked young enough and passionately agile enough to be convincing, but watching this fiery young gallant, one witness was soon exclaiming that this Miss Cushman seemed "just *man* enough to be a *boy*."

The love scenes rang with a passion London had not seen for years; the impulse in Romeo met a balance in Juliet's "maiden modesty." Throughout the play, Charlotte carefully matched her actions to the words. Romeo's parrying sword thrusts with Tybalt only furthered the illusion that in this young actress London had discovered a new Romeo of consummate grace and skill. When Romeo's single lunge ended the fight, one woman was heard to whisper, "Miss Cushman is a very dangerous young man."

Watching the acting, Westland Marston saw in Charlotte a virile power greater than that of any male actor he had ever seen in the part. "The house was roused to the wildest excitement, as if by some tragic event in actual life." Another found the performance so real, Romeo so "ardently masculine" and Juliet so "tenderly feminine," that he felt the least Miss Cushman could do, once the engagement was over, was marry her sister. In another report, the play's final scenes could only be seen "through tears," a "testimony" far more telling than all the ringing applause.

175

At home, Charlotte and Susan could only wait tensely now for word from the critics. When the papers arrived, they were not disappointed. Charlotte Cushman's Romeo is "far superior to any Romeo we have ever had . . . a living, breathing, animated, ardent human being," cried the *Times*. To *Lloyd's Messenger,* "Passion spoke in every feature, and the illusion was forcible and perfect . . . She is the best actress that has appeared upon the English stage since the days of Miss O'Niel." Sheridan Knowles considered the acting "a triumph of pure genius." Let London recall Edmund Kean's third act of *Othello,* said Knowles. "Did you ever expect to see anything like it again?" In Miss Cushman's acting there was no trick. "No thought, no interest, no feeling seems to actuate her, except what might be looked for in Romeo himself were Romeo reality. . . . My heart and mind are so full of this extraordinary, most extraordinary performance, that I know not where to stop or how to go on."

Though the reviews for Susan were hardly so flattering, her efforts were "promising." "Many actresses now on our boards could play Juliet in a manner immeasurably superior," said the *Illustrated London News,* but *John Bull* welcomed her "considerable merit." Knowles fully agreed; she played Juliet "admirably"; her place on the London stage was assured. The *Illustrated* devoted a full page to a drawing of the balcony scene.

To crown their success, within a few days a note arrived from Samuel Rogers. "My dear Miss Cushman, Can you and your dear sister come to breakfast with me tomorrow morning at ¼ before 10?" And from Geraldine in Manchester came a shower of praise, echoing her torrent of comment to Jane Carlyle. Jane sniffed her reaction. "Her letters have been filled with lyrics about this woman —till I could stand it no longer—and have written her such a screed of my mind as she never got before—and which will probably terminate our correspondence—at least till the finale of her friendship with Miss Cushman."

The *Romeo* triumph helped explain Charlotte's failure to note Susan's reaction. The phrase that now recurred again and again in the press, "Miss Cushman and her beautiful sister," sounded like praise, but its reference to Susan's beauty implied that Susan possessed little else. "Miss Cushman" meant Charlotte with all her stunning powers; "her sister" was the pretty one.

"A Very Dangerous Young Man"

Due to the play's popularity Webster decided to extend it indefinitely. On January 17, "The rush to see Miss Cushman as Romeo continues; and on the nights when this gifted actress performs, every available corner is occupied." A week later, "Miss Cushman fills the house, literally to the ceiling, three times a week as 'Romeo.'" When word reached New York, the *Spirit of the Times* proudly quoted Sheridan Knowles; for Charlotte in London "the genuine heart storm was on."

Not that the play lacked detractors. Late in the month Robert Browning wrote to Elizabeth: "I went last night, out of pure shame at a broken promise, to hear Miss Cushman and her sister in 'Romeo and Juliet,' The whole play goes . . . horribly; Romeo goes whining about Verona by broad daylight. . . . Whatever is slightly touched in, indicated, to give relief to something actually insisted upon and drawn boldly . . . *here,* you have it gone over with an unremitting burnt-stick, till it stares black forever." Browning did not declare himself quite so boldly in conversation with Charlotte herself at Henry Chorley's.

When a letter arrived from George Combe the first week of February, wanting to know how the enterprise had turned out ("Was my view . . . subverted or condemned by the ultimate result?"), Charlotte could grandly reply that his judgments about London were, for the most part, dead wrong. So wrong in fact that she tackled another male role almost immediately. Her success as Ion in Talfourd's play was even greater, in *John Bull's* opinion, than Romeo. For her Viola to Susan's Olivia in *Twelfth Night,* she wore a knee-length skirt, a velvet jacket, and a sash and dagger at her waist.

In the flush of her continued success, she put a question to Westland Marston. "I want you to write me a drama, and I can tell you at once the sort of character I should like—in fine, I long to play a woman of strong ambition, who is at the same time very wily and diplomatic, and who has an opportunity of a great outburst when her plans are successful—in short, a female Richelieu."

"Captain Charlotte," Marston answered (using a nickname "her straightforwardness had caused some of us to give her"), "are not your qualities rather those of passion than of diplomacy? You can fight, perhaps, better than you can manoeuvre."

"A great soldier," Charlotte replied, "must be a diplomatist too. I feel I could act the dissembler splendidly."

177

Marston assured her that "for one of the sincerest women alive to show herself a successful hypocrite" would be a triumph of art.

"You know what I want," she said. "Think of it."

Marston would think of it, but he was sure that his other commitments would forever prevent his writing the play Charlotte wanted.

Throughout the spring, *Romeo* attracted full houses. In the February *Almanack of the Month,* Gilbert Abbott á Beckett described the scene at the Haymarket doors.

"But what's the attraction? Why thus do they rush, man?
Don't you know? 'Tis Romeo, played by Miss Cushman"

And he carried his fun a step farther, though he echoed Browning's discontent with the other actors.

"Now, as for the acting—though 'tis not complete—
It is, on the whole a most exquisite treat.
Miss Cushman and sister—the Friar, the Nurse,
Have never been better, and often been worse;
But here, approbation, I fear, must be ended;
The less that is said will the soonest be mended."

Charlotte's resemblance to Macready did not escape á Beckett's notice either.

"What figure is that which appears on the scene?
'Tis Madam Macready—Miss Cushman, I mean.
What wondrous resemblance! the walk on the toes,
The eloquent, short, intellectual nose—
The bend of the knee, the slight sneer on the lip,
The frown on the forehead, the hand on the hip;
In the chin, in the voice, 'tis the same to a tittle,
Miss Cushman is Mister Macready in little.
The lady before us might very well pass
For the gentleman, viewed the wrong way of the glass.
No fault with the striking resemblance we find,
'Tis not in the person alone, but the mind.

Mister Macready cared little, one could be sure, for the witty comparison.

THE DAILY GRAPHIC

AN ILLUSTRATED EVENING NEWSPAPER

39 & 41 PARK PLACE

VOL. X.   All the News. Four Editions Daily   NEW YORK, SATURDAY, MARCH 4, 1876.—TEN PAGES. $12 Per Year in Advance. Single Copies, Five Cents.   NO. 928.

LADY MACBETH

BIANCA IN "FAZIO"

QUEEN KATHARINE

NANCY SYKES

MEG MERRILIES.

CHARLOTTE CUSHMAN

Charlotte Cushman 1843
From an oil painting by Thomas Sully

Charlotte Cushman 1845
Drawn by Theresa Kenney the week of Charlotte's London debut

Charlotte and Susan Cushman as Romeo and Juliet

From a drawing by Margaret Gillies in *The People's Journal*
(London), July 18, 1846

A Staffordshire figurine was modeled after this drawing between 1846 and
1852, copies of which are in the Mander and Mitchenson Collection, London,
and the Folger Shakespeare Library

Charlotte Cushman as Mrs. Haller

From a lithograph by G. B. Black of the
painting by Wm. Henry Watkins

Charlotte Cushman as Meg Merrilies

From a drawing in *Theatrical Times*
(London), September 5, 1846

Charlotte Cushman 1853
From an oil painting by William Page

Charlotte Cushman about 1856
From a photograph in Thomas Ryan,
Recollections of an Old Musician
(New York, 1899)

Charlotte Cushman as Platform Reader about 1875
From a portrait engraving by Alonzo Chappel

Charlotte Cushman in the Hall of Fame
From the bronze bust by Frances Grimes

"A Very Dangerous Young Man"

With Queen Victoria's unbridled support, only P. T. Barnum's Tom Thumb outdrew Charlotte's Romeo during this spring of 1846. At the Bayswater cottage, life settled into a busy routine, now that Charlotte and Susan were both established at the Haymarket. With Susan's name defended against all Forrest's charges, with its firm appearance on the Haymarket bills, Mary Eliza might have adopted a happier outlook, but as she grew more comfortable, she found less and less joy in the life swirling about her. To Geraldine Charlotte's mother seemed a querulous, embittered old woman, resentful that Charlotte's greater fame seemed a threat to Susan. "The younger daughter Susan was the mother's favorite."

The fact explained much about Charlotte's own hunger for recognition, especially among the circle of women that continued to expand around her. And if Susan truly resented Charlotte's greater eminence, her charm gave her compensations, among them the attentions of young Gansevoort Melville, Secretary to the American Legation, who sought out the Cushmans and came to call. A gifted orator blessed with a majestic figure, flashing black eyes, and a forehead "as noble as Daniel Webster's," Melville remembered Charlotte's earliest acting in Albany, where he and his young brother Herman had eked out a living in the family's cap and fur store.

Gansevoort had watched Charlotte's climb to American fame; his meeting her now was a tribute to her English success. In recent months, he had busied himself with frequent London visits to Washington Irving, lately in from diplomatic service at the Spanish court, and with seeing Herman's *Typee* through the presses. In reply to his note of January 30, Charlotte invited him to Bayswater.

After spending most of the day correcting proofs of Herman's book, Gansevoort made his way out to the cottage. "I was welcomed by Miss Cushman and introduced to her mother, sister, brother, . . . The mother is a 'rale American,' a fine hearty old lady. The sister is pretty. . . . Miss Charlotte Cushman is a woman of plain tho' expressive and intelligent features, tall and rather full person, full of conversation and vivacity and decidedly agreeable, tho' dashed strongly with masculineness. It was 11 when I left."

Melville could hardly have missed Charlotte's "masculine" manner, garbed as she was in the strange costume she was affecting more and more. Fully determined to be herself, she made no effort to simplify the matter for the highly mannered society she chose to move in. The fact presented a paradox, a dilemma few Victorians easily understood. Why would any woman willingly make herself outlandish in a man's collar, cravat, and Wellington boots? Charlotte never explained, but the case had to do with her Boston honesty. If life on the stage was a constant pretense, life offstage would be otherwise.

The artist in her had grown since she had left Philadelphia, but the woman had grown even more. A dozen reasons could justify a person's seeking acclaim on a theatre stage, but ever since Edinburgh, she had known more and more surely that life, if she were truly to live it, would have to be clothed and transacted in her own terms—not necessarily the terms that would guarantee perpetual applause. The conviction might exact a cost, but she was prepared to pay. She was secure enough now at the heart of an admiring circle that she had little fear of rejection. It was a simple question of being true, and now was the time.

Gansevoort saw the family again at a concert. "I met many Americans, Mrs. Cushman, Miss Charlotte and Miss Susan Cushman . . . There were there also [Charles] Dickens and his wife—both coarse and vulgar in appearance, Eliza Cook short dumpy and hair most boyishly dressed. . . . I took a seat by Susan Cushman and maintained it. She was by far the prettiest person present. . . . After the concert I accompanied the Cushmans home to Bayswater —I escorting Miss Susan."

By the nineteenth Gansevoort had eyes only for Susan at a dinner given by G. P. Putnam, the publisher, for guests including Eliza Cook and Charlotte. "Mr. P. has a large and beautifully arranged collection of autographs which we inspected. Illustrated editions of Moore's Melodies, Lockhart's Spanish ballads, and The Beauties of the opera occupied Miss Susan and I for some time." Three days later, Melville made another "very agreeable" visit to Bayswater, "Miss Susan appearing . . . to great advantage. Her manners are certainly feminine, lady-like and high-bred. They go to Dublin on Saturday—to play an engagement there."

Though the little flirtation was a happy send-off for Susan, Melville's attentions only planted a wistful envy in Charlotte. Not all her powers on stage had ever brought anyone quite like the handsome Gansevoort Melville knocking at her door. She found what cheer she could in the fact that London's approval of her Romeo had stretched the run to an unprecedented thirty performances, a success that could have gone longer had she not already booked herself for six weeks in Dublin and beyond. On the strength of these latest ovations, she could demand fees dwarfing anything she had ever received in America.

For all Dublin's certainty that its taste was better than London's, the force of a Haymarket victory was not lost on the Irish. Charlotte's success in Dublin's Theatre Royal was practically assured. Her coming to Dublin added a sparkle to life on both sides of the footlights, where audiences were famous, if not notorious, for tempests always about to break loose.

Dublin liked serious acting; it had its own ways of laughing at stage pomposity or at anything else that struck it odd. Once during a performance of Knowles' *Virginius,* just as the maiden's father tenderly placed her hand in the suitor's, saying almost through tears, "My drowning voice and choking utterance upbraids my tongue that tells thee she is thine," a distant voice in the gallery shouted, "I forbid the bans!" During a *Hamlet,* when Lucianus, nephew to the Player King, stole across the stage to pour poison into the sleeping King's ear, a gallery voice sang out, "Aha! ye poisoning blackgyard! I'm watchin' you!" And from across the house another had cried, "Whisht, Tim, wid ye! or ye'll wake up the ould gintleman aslape in the cheer!" Charlotte knew to beware.

Before such could happen to her, more serious word reached her from Scotland. In the staider air of Edinburgh, catcalls and hoots from the audience were rare. All the more reason why the hisses that broke up Macready's Hamlet at the Theatre Royal the night of March 2 got headlines. "Acted Hamlet, really with particular care, energy, and discrimination," Macready assured his diary. "At the waving of the handkerchief before the play [within the play], and 'I must be idle,' a man on the right side of the stage, upper boxes, or gallery, hissed. I waved the more, and bowed derisively and contemptuously. He remained, however, very staunch to his purpose, but the audience stood by me and bore it down."

Edwin Forrest was known to be in town, and Macready's suspicions could easily believe that his jealousy had prompted him to come to the theatre, secrete himself in an upper box, and watch for a chance to embarrass his English rival. A day or so later, an eyewitness who had seen the dark eyes and bulldog jaw of the famous American reported the fact to Macready. "I feel glad," Macready noted carefully, "that it is not an Englishman—but no Englishman would have done a thing so base . . . The low-minded ruffian! That man would commit murder, if he *dared!*"

In Dublin, when a guess about Forrest's implication reached Charlotte, she was certain. She told Calcraft, the manager, "It is Forrest," a report Calcraft lost no time in sending to Macready. For better or worse, the *Spirit of the Times* gave New York a full report of the matter on May 9.

Had Forrest been in Dublin, Charlotte could have imagined a similar hiss at herself. But she received no such complaints. Her Romeo to Susan's Juliet brought the same intense cheers it had set off in London. In the banishment scene, when she fell prone to the floor, taking "the measure of an unmade grave," she waited moment after moment for the great outburst of applause to end. When quiet reigned, a fine Irish brogue cried out, "Bra-vo, Char-let!" And Charlotte added her laughter to the crowd's. The cheering continued, with one faction trying to outshout the other's favorite. A voice sang out, "Three cheers for the divil!" At that, when both parties had cried their lungs hoarse, Charlotte and company went on with the play.

No disturbance ever troubled the nights when she and Susan played Romeo and Juliet, or when she appeared alone as Meg, "the grand triumph of the night," cried the Dublin *Evening Packet*. Men held their breath while listening "to the wild language of the sybil, uttered with a passion, a power, an impestuous force that carried all before them." In her fluttering rags, with the wisps of her hair escaping, "all idea of mere scenic illusion" was forgotten.

Before she finished her Dublin run, Charlotte wrote again to George Combe. Surely by now she and her sister could rest from the knotty questions raised against them in Edinburgh. Surely, after Forrest's treatment of Macready, all Edinburgh knew how to interpret "anything he might choose to assert." His hissing Macready was proof enough that the man lacked every regard for decency.

Leaving Dublin, she took heart in the *Freeman's Journal*'s praise of her talents. "Should that gifted lady again visit our shores, and again gratify us with her truthful impersonations, we . . . will hail and welcome the advent of genius, tenfold." Her many and wonderful struggles, "as an unaided, unsupported female, to reach her present proud position," would not soon be forgotten among Dubliners.

Whenever she came among them again, she could be certain of an Irish welcome, a cordial offered to genius "in the person of a stranger and a *woman*." The Irish farewell was praise indeed, and it gave her courage as she and Susan departed again for Scotland.

Friendships and Grief in England

(1846–1847)

Though Edinburgh raised little objection now to Charlotte's Romeo—London's approval helped guarantee that—it did not so easily accept the odd clothes she sported. But the matter seemed unimportant; the Combes and their friends were willing to take her as she was. In her man's hat and coat, she delighted again in riding with John Coleman up Calton Hill. The view from its summit encompassed the distant North Sea, the Cheviot Hills ranging to the south, and the rolling green world that made up Scott's Border country. Under the clouds that seemed always to boil up over Edinburgh's skyline, she could agree with Francis Parkman that the expanse around her was one city view that could truly be called sublime.

At rehearsal, she could tuck up her skirts and her petticoats and stride around in her boots while she polished off Tybalt, despite the shocks she might detect in the Edinburgh housewives who wandered in. She could ignore the report that some man had nicknamed her "Charley de Boots," suggesting in her a desire for something indecorous. She would not bother to explain herself. Even Coleman could assume what he pleased: that she had donned her mannish clothes out of pride in her figure.

In Glasgow on May 20, Susan's Juliet was "a quiet, and in some parts a very effective portraiture," but praise for Charlotte's Romeo matched London's: her "fiery energy in bursts of passion" excelled all Glasgow had ever seen in the part.

Offstage, she directed some of her fire to money matters. Macready could mutter about "the woman's perfect inconsistency" in rejecting him, but she now asked for and got the highest salary Liverpool had ever paid any actor except Macready and Edmund Kean. She could keep her own counsel when it came to finances and the need for anyone's patronage. And Susan collected her own share of acclaim for her Marianna in *The Wife*: "a great performance—the *beau ideal* of a woman."

More interestingly for Susan, a love affair with an actor seemed to be brewing, though Geraldine's replies to Charlotte's letters about it brought dire warning. "She will get into a scrape about him if she does not take care. People cannot be so pretty and well dressed as she is, with impunity, down in the provinces." With a moustached sweetheart like this one, "Vesta herself could not stand it!" especially in Liverpool "where the proprieties bite dreadfully." Charlotte must use every possible trick to get rid of him.

Sound or not, the advice carried the seeds of a rupture between Charlotte and Susan. In an affair of the heart, no sister ever welcomed another's efforts to "protect" her. Charlotte had made it her business in Edinburgh to clear Susan's name; she assumed that it was now her proper concern to protect it. But she was not long in finding that Susan felt perfectly ready to lead her own life. Charlotte's help at her London debut had been a fine bit of family support. She could appreciate the loyalty in Charlotte that still prompted it, but she had her own life to lead, and it might or might not include Charlotte.

The moustached actor disappeared quickly, but a more eligible suitor, James Sheridan Muspratt, soon took his place. The respectable scion of a Liverpool manufacturing chemist, a founder of the British chemical industry, Sheridan plied them with invitations. Like his father, young Muspratt had a deep interest in all the arts. Dickens and Sheridan Knowles were family friends; Sheridan's name reflected the depth of the latter friendship. The Muspratts delighted in entertaining the best names in British society under their gabled roofs or at garden parties on the lawns of their country estate, Seaforth Hall. Its slopes took in a wide view of the Welsh mountains; the perfection of its lawns and gardens typified the elegance of Liverpool's wealthiest class. With its fogs and the black smoke polluting its skies, Liverpool might leave much to be desired, but flowered estates like Seaforth were "regal paradises." Meeting Sheridan Muspratt was the shining event of the Liverpool run.

Unbeknown to her, in Birmingham Charlotte unforgettably impressed a fellow actor. At rehearsal, Fred Belton had seen a very plain woman wearing a common brown dress, a black bonnet, and a paisley shawl glide toward him "snake-like," then, swooping like an eagle, pounce upon him with hurried explanations of business in the different scenes. Belton supposed she was the mother of the star—"mother professionals, as a rule, are objectionable when doing duty for their daughters." But he soon discovered his mistake; this Charlotte Cushman was no common metal. The vain creature would never dare, thought Belton, to go on as Julia; still, she had a "devilish deal of stuff about her!" Twelve o'clock at night must come at last; "that's one comfort."

When curtain time came, Belton was standing in the wings ready for his garden scene with Julia when he saw a girlish figure with delicate flowing locks, wearing a broad-brimmed garden hat, white muslin gown, and a pink sash glide to his side. Belton gazed at her, amazed. Mind and makeup had mastered face, form, figure, and voice. Throughout the play Belton was so carried away he barely remembered his cues. And one was especially important. In rehearsal, Charlotte had instructed him to answer an octave above her when she cried, "Can these nuptials be shunned with honour?" During the performance, when Belton reached his proper octave, Charlotte ascended an octave above that, "Then take me!"

The applause was "rapturous." In his excitement Belton squeezed "like grim death" until Charlotte whispered gruffly in his ear, more "like a coalheaver than a lovelorn damsel": "If you squeeze me so tight, I shan't get breath for my next speech."

Returning to London, she and Susan found that, in April, Gansevoort Melville had died suddenly. His death cast a pall over the Bayswater cottage that only grew worse in the heat of a stifling June, the sultriest month on record. Theatres could hardly stay open as crowds of people fled to the parks and the steamers on the Thames in a vain effort to escape London's "cauldron-heat." Playing to a wilting audience at the Haymarket on the twenty-fifth in *Twelfth Night,* she and Susan were doubly flattered when the boxes tossed them bouquets.

Clearly, the time had come for a holiday. As for next season's plans, Charlotte had none. To Webster she could only remark, "All novelty of my acting Romeo is rubbed off," which was partly a way of saying she was too exhausted to find excitement in acting at all. The thing to do now was pay a leisurely visit to Geraldine in Manchester and catch her breath. The rest of the summer she could afford to be idle.

Through Geraldine she at last met a woman about whom she had long been curious. "Self-invited to meet me," Jane Welsh Carlyle came at one o'clock and stayed until eight. "And such a day I have not known! Clever, witty, calm, cool, unsmiling, unsparing, a *raconteur* unparalleled, a manner *un*imitable, a behavior scrupulous, and a power invincible." Jane Carlyle might be plain, even unattractive, but she was an "unescapable woman," a combination rare and strange.

With her hair smoothed tight over her ears, accentuating her sharp nose and black eyes, Jane Carlyle's quick tongue and candor hardly made her a woman to trust; one might not like her at first, but one could not forget her. Jane's intense meeting with Charlotte and the correspondence that followed were a symptom of disturbance at Cheyne Row. Once in 1844 Jane had threatened to leave Thomas. Again the next year she had written him: "Husbands are so obtuse! . . . want always to be 'treated with the respect due to genius,' exact common sense of their poor wives rather than 'the finer sensibilities of the heart,' " and so their marriage had come to "what ye see—if not precisely to 'immortal smash' as yet, at least to within a hair's breadth of it!"

Yet Jane was no angel. She labeled herself "a brimstone of a creature," not at all the decorative hostess her lantern-jawed spouse wanted. Once when a strange man had accosted her rudely on a dark London street, Jane sniffed, "Idiot," and calmly moved on. When a visit to a house in the country bored her, she datelined her letters, "Hell." After twenty years of marriage, she could still tell a friend, "I can't bear to be thought of only as Carlyle's wife." At age forty-four, Jane Welsh Carlyle was a forthright spirit that Charlotte, at thirty, fully approved.

The chance to know Jane better in London remained a bright prospect as Charlotte took her leave and moved on to Malvern in Worcestershire for a long rest and the much-touted "water cure" of its springs. Taking the cure, she read with pleasure Mary Howitt's article about her in *The People's Journal* for July. Of all the reams about Charlotte Cushman that had appeared in the English press, Mary's article best recognized her as a person, its praise implying an attack on the "shriveled souls" of Edinburgh who had questioned her garb and her morals. "All artist-life, and that of the actor among them, requires for its full perfecting the highest powers of human nature—the resistance of temptation, self-denial, and purity of life." In time to come, these virtues would be recognized as the central strength of the greatest geniuses. "It is because we recognize in Miss Cushman an approach to our ideal of the greatly pure in art that we regard her as one of its noblest representatives." Nobly gifted, Miss Cushman "takes a noble view of her art." Her acting was not merely imitative; it was "action: the very action of nature, and therefore it is always true."

The routine at Malvern was rigorous—"I hope you had good medical sanction before you ventured yourself upon it," wrote Geraldine—but it worked. Treatment began before seven, when she stepped into warm water for a regular bath, then onto a slab for a rubbing ("It sets every nerve and pore in your skin on to the full gallop of doing their duty") and an hour's sleep flat on her stomach. After another bath and a ten-minute rub, "till you are as red as a rose," she went for a walk before breakfast.

The eager walkers and runners who passed her might have escaped from a Dickens novel. Dickens was no believer in the Malvern treatment, but he could describe those who were: "O Heaven, to meet the Cold Waterers dashing down the hills, with severe expressions on their countenances, like men doing matches and not exactly winning! Then, a young lady in a grey polka going *up* the hills regardless of legs; . . . [and] an old man who ran over a milk-child, rather than stop!—with no neckcloth, on principle; and with his mouth wide open, to catch the morning air."

After lunch came more bathing, a cold-water wash of the spine for four minutes ("making your brain feel as suddenly fine and clear as if it had been changed in a second from curds to spun glass"), then a "lamp bath" seated on a wooden chair, more scrubbing and rubbing, and a cold shower. After a sitz bath at 5:30 she had dinner and went early to bed. When Carlyle tried it, he grumbled, "I found water taken as a medicine to be the most destructive drug I ever tried." But for Charlotte, Malvern's "electric" air and its springs amid the elaborate gardens and climbing roses brought peace to the flesh, bliss to the nerves.

A jaunt up to Yorkshire with Eliza Cook rounded out the summer interim. When their host, William Forster, gave Charlotte a bolt of steel-blue alpaca from his textile mill, she had it made into identical dresses for herself and Eliza in "masculine style, tight-fitting bodice, lapelled, showing shirt front and ruffles." She regaled her hosts with the Irish stories she had picked up in Dublin, and, seated at Forster's piano, she half-sang, half-uttered her way through the collection of songs that always delighted her London guests.

Throughout her months in England, a few verbal supporters at home watched Charlotte's career take shape. To the Brooklyn *Eagle*'s editor, Walt Whitman, Charlotte Cushman was the actress of all his hopes. Totally American, the product of pioneer stock that had braved the hostile Atlantic, she fulfilled Whitman's vision of the nation's artistic potential. Standing up against all adversity, she had declared to the world her intention to become truly herself. She carried her own destiny as she saw it. To Whitman, in her success there was a message uniquely American.

A comment in the New York *News* had touched off his cries: "What an idea" placing Charlotte Cushman second to Mrs. Kean in the scale of talent in the dramatic art. "Mrs. K. is a pleasing actress; but C. C. is probably the greatest performer on the stage 'in any hemisphere.'" Next day he was still outraged: Not only was Charlotte Cushman vastly superior to Ellen Tree Kean, but it was an insult to compare her with anyone. "Charlotte Cushman is *no* 'second Siddons': she is *herself,* and that is far, far better! From what we have seen and heard . . . C. C. is ahead of any player that ever trod the stage." Fanny Kemble, Ellen Tree, Macready, Kean, Kemble— all had, or had had, their merits; their acting had afforded many a rich treat for an audience. But Miss Cushman "bears away the palm from them all."

"We don't know how others may think; but we consider it a shame," wrote Whitman, "that such a woman as Charlotte Cushman should ever have been allowed to be superseded by the fifth rate artistic? trash that comes over to us from the Old World." In his judgment, New York had seen Charlotte Cushman throw more genius into the Widow Melnotte than had any number of stars from England's tired "Theatre Royals."

Charlotte pondered such American comments. Had the time come to go home? London fame had already paid off in Britain's provinces. Who could predict how well it might pay off on American boards? She filled her letters to Rosalie with speculations. In the end, in spite of her temptation to return without anymore agonizing delay to Rosalie, she knew that remaining in England held the greater wisdom.

Macready's diary gives a clue to further matters on Charlotte's mind this fall of 1846. "Note from Miss Susan Cushman, wanting to separate from her sister, and ally herself professionally with me!" During the interview that followed, Macready endeavoured "to per-

189

suade her of the mutual folly of herself and sister separating, but urging her to conciliate and succumb rather than part."

Susan had reasons for wishing to be independent. In America, she had made a name independent of Charlotte's. She had acted a roster of parts that New York and Philadelphia had applauded. Tyrone Power had praised her "racy humor and love of fun," her clever support in his comedy pieces. The London *Sun*'s homage to her Juliet now was surely a matter to note: "the most lady-like representation of the most lady-like character that Shakespeare ever drew."

To be known in England as "Miss Cushman's sister" was hardly her idea of proper success. When the matter came to open discussion, Charlotte could not dispute the logic. Nor could she honestly encourage Susan to go her own way. Success had crowned them together; could they hope to do better apart? Why not let time make the decision? In the meantime, steady letters from James Sheridan Muspratt indicated that time might have an ally.

Back in London, Charlotte pursued all the civilized delights the city could offer. Invitations soon guided her to the nearby village of Chelsea, to the Cheyne Row house of the Carlyles, "a right old strong roomy brick house," Carlyle called it, with a heavy front door that had opened to most of the literary and artistic greats of the age.

Being Jane's guest was not easy. Actresses did not often enter her doors. Fanny Kemble, for one, was much "too green room all over" to suit Jane's taste, and while Macready came frequently, there was less interest in him as actor than in his wide-ranging conversational powers. Almost in spite of himself, Carlyle demanded the lead in any group; he had long ago set Jane straight on that point—"I must not and I cannot live in a house of which I am not head"—though in his more genial moments he confessed a sympathy for Jane. Beside him "any other woman might have gone mad."

Firmly set in his mahogany chair, his blue eyes flashing, Carlyle held court, and the visitor who hoped to utter a word soon learned he must squeeze it into one of the rare pauses in Carlyle's verbal torrents. Emerson ranked Carlyle with "immense" talkers like Samuel Johnson. "If his pistol missed fire, he would knock you down with the butt-end."

Browning had brushed against Carlyle's monologues. At tea, when the kettle boiled and Carlyle talked on and on, making no move to hand it to Jane, Browning had fetched it himself and filled the teapot for her, then stood by her table, holding the smoking kettle. "Can't you put it down?" asked Jane suddenly. Confused, Browning had popped it down on the carpet. When Jane exclaimed, horrified, Browning snatched it up quickly; a brown oval mark was burned in the new rug. At last, Carlyle stopped long enough to rescue him. "Ye should have been more explicit," he told Jane.

"No mortal in America could pretend to talk with Carlyle," said Emerson. Nor did Charlotte seriously try. The real point of her visits was the woman who quietly managed on the edge of her husband's tempests to attract no little attention to herself. When Margaret Fuller visited Jane in November, she sympathized. "She is full of grace, sweetness, and talent. Her eyes are sad and charming," but "Who can speak while her husband is there?" Leigh Hunt appreciated her; their neighbor had made her forever young and charming in "Jenny Kissed Me."

Jane held her own court in her drawing room overlooking the street. In time, friends who came to visit Carlyle often remained, as Charlotte said of herself, to worship at the feet of his wife. And unlike her thundering husband, Jane could listen as well as speak— uttering her satirical stabs in a soft Scottish voice, telling witty stories, falling into a sort of "creative silence" when she sensed another voice wished to be heard. Her upbringing had prepared her to meet a man's conversation point for point.

One of Jane's regular guests, whom Charlotte often met, was the Italian revolutionary, Giuseppe Mazzini, a slim dark man in his early forties, with a "spiritual" face, a noble forehead, and sad eyes, who talked intently of the bright days ahead when Italy would at last be unified, free of the foreign yokes it still struggled under. Carlyle dismissed his hopes as "rose water imbecilities," but Jane took his defense. "These are but opinions to Carlyle; but to Mazzini, who has given his all, and helped bring his friends to the scaffold, in pursuit of such subjects, it is a matter of life and death."

Other political figures found their way to Jane's door and into Charlotte's friendship. Louis Blanc, the French revolutionary, remembered Charlotte's Mrs. Haller from the year before but lacked enough English to tell her about it.

Away from the excitement at the Carlyles', Charlotte relaxed with her red-headed friend, Henry Chorley. An "irritable, nervous" creature at times, Chorley could be kind and affectionate to his friends, though Edward Fitzgerald was certain that when Chorley died, "the Angels must take care to keep in tune when he gets among them." Chorley could pen memorable lines. His hymn "God the Omnipotent, King Who Ordainest," written in 1842, would soon find itself in the

Anglican hymnal; one day its phrase "God give us peace in our time" would gain fame in another context. Together, he and Charlotte spent rare leisure hours rummaging through London shops or sat, inconspicuous in the shadows, observing another actor's efforts—even if doing so filled Charlotte at times with doubts about her own talent.

Watching the great French tragedienne Rachel in July filled her with wonder, even if she could not follow the language. No actress she had ever seen could delineate the darker passions—hatred, revenge, seething jealousy—with a force comparable to Rachel's. While her Jewish face lacked ordinary beauty and sweetness, it held the appeal of a wondrous sadness. If she did not melt an audience to tears, she could suggest profoundest truth, rising simply and austerely above lesser elements around her. Her magnificent voice conjured up Greek poetry and sculpture, "the spirit of antiquity made manifest in the flesh," the vision Praxiteles captured in marble. As Phedre, Browning called her "exquisite." After she had taken the poison, exhaustion and paralysis slowly enveloped her; sadly, coldly, calmly, she submitted to Fate. Her force and terrible naturalness almost suffocated her audience.

Transfixed in the presence of such grandeur, such genius, Charlotte could only think of her own efforts as mere posturing, mere sketches compared to Rachel's "unapproachable art." Leaving the theatre, the enchantment left her. Doubts of her talent engulfed her. "Despair took possession of me, and a mad impulse to end life and effort together."

Talk at the Carlyles' during the autumn of 1846 centered on Browning's Wimpole Street coup. Speaking of Barrett's tyranny over his daughter Elizabeth, Anna Jameson herself may have planted the seed of action. "Can nothing be done to rescue her from this?" she had asked Robert. Browning's taking the reins and rescuing Elizabeth, marrying her, and, after Mrs. Jameson joined them in Paris, taking her to the restorative climate of Italy had brought a happy glow to the Cheyne Row regulars. Elizabeth reported the "delightful" letter that had come from Carlyle; not for years had a marriage occurred in his circle in which he so heartily "rejoiced."

When Charlotte and Susan took *Romeo and Juliet* on tour in September, the London *Theatrical Times* cheered them forward with words that rang "the miraculous success" Charlotte had made in England. "Mentally and physically in the present day, we have no English performer able to compete with her."

In late December the tour took them again to Liverpool. For New

Year's, Sheridan Muspratt invited them to Seaforth Hall for a fancy dress ball. Beginning at nine, a line of carriages began rolling slowly up to the Hall's wide doors and, in the light of tall flares, disgorging their passengers. By ten, more than 180 guests had gathered in rooms lit with wax candles and decorated, amid the statuary and paintings, with Christmas greens and mistletoe. Costumes followed the wildest whims; some of the guests, like Charlotte, even came prepared to change several times.

In the Liverpool *Journal's* account, Charlotte's name and a description of her garb headed the list. As Claude Melnotte, her "gallant bearing attracted much notice and many jests." Later, she appeared costumed for two other roles, while "the beautiful Miss Susan Cushman" came dressed as a French marchioness, "her dress being of the most recherché kind." Another prominent guest, Geraldine Jewsbury, came as a Spanish Lady, and various Muspratt women were Turks, Greeks, Cracovians, and flower girls. Several "old English gentlemen" sported buckled shoes, powdered wigs, and cocked hats.

During the dancing, "an obstinate bachelor of our acquaintance," remarked the *Journal,* "declared he never felt himself in so much 'danger' before." If the obstinate bachelor was Sheridan Muspratt, his defenses were down before the evening was over. If his engagement to Susan was not accomplished that night, it was formally sealed soon after.

During her run at the Adelphi, Charlotte Cushman could give the swains of Liverpool food for thought, said the *Mercury.* As the love-impassioned Claude Melnotte, she made "love-making, as practiced by the other sex, appear a very stale, flat, and unprofitable affair." As for Susan's Pauline, the pride with which she surveyed her prince, her burst of rage, scorn, and despair on discovering his terrible trick was given "with beautiful effect."

Before leaving Liverpool, Charlotte enjoyed a reunion that eleven years before would have seemed like the wildest dream. Mary Ann Wood had come out of retirement to sing at a concert, and Charlotte's meeting with her at the concert hall rekindled their old friendship and gave her a long-awaited opportunity to say thank you for the early confidence and advice to keep "practicing *steadily,*" those distant years in Boston. And she took a fiendish delight in rejecting another offer from Macready, who had expressed "a very great desire" to have her play with him at the Princess's.

But in the midst of her joys, a letter from Philadelphia brought the news that Rosalie Sully was dead. At twenty-five, her friend of all friends was suddenly gone and with her had vanished her dearest dream. Without Rosalie's delight at her success, without Rosalie's smile to welcome her home, what good was victory? Rereading the terrible words, she withdrew into long silence. Locked in grief, she recalled the day Augustus' death had "sent the waters" over her soul. But by now, Charlotte had proved to herself that she could master her tears. The lesson learned in Albany must rescue her now.

She threw herself into another six weeks of work in Dublin, then into a tour of Limerick, Cork, Glasgow, Edinburgh, Perth, Dundee, Leeds, Newcastle-upon-Tyne, Sheffield, Hull, Birmingham, and Manchester. When she closed in Liverpool, she and Susan rested a week at Seaforth Hall. Then she persuaded Susan to tear herself away from Sheridan and go with her to Paris. But back in England, she dropped her guard and let herself be heartsick at last. Collapsed at Malvern, she would bide her time until reason or faith should tell her to think about acting again.

16

"The Greatest Melodramatic Actress in the World"

(1847–1848)

When rumors of her collapse reached Philadelphia in June, the *Pennsylvanian* spread the word that Charlotte Cushman, "the greatest female performer in this, and probably any other country," was prostrated: she had barely been saved from the grave. The *Spirit* trumpeted the alarm that Charlotte was "sick in England and may retire forever."

A month earlier Chorley had taken her to task about her health. He might not realize all the reasons for her sudden despair, but living as she had of late "on the railroad," he could still advise her not to move "hand or foot or eyelash" until the doctors gave her the word. At Malvern, she must gather her energies again, devise a simpler course for her life, and not even consider returning to London until fully able.

Speaking practically, London had little to offer just now. Even Fanny Kemble's fabled name was attracting only the meagerest houses. About Fanny's Juliet, Chorley could only say that it left him "cold, and surprised and sorrowful." What money people were willing to spend was going to opera—Mendelssohn's new *Elijah* was a sensation—and to Jenny Lind, the new Swedish soprano at Covent Garden. Even Rachel, in competition with the ingenuous singer, was finding the going difficult.

Chorley's advice made sense. Away from a London that had lost all its appeal, Charlotte could relax, in spite of the *Theatrical Times'* oddly expressed good wishes (for all her "ill-built" appearance and

195

the fact that "in point of sex" Miss Cushman "is almost amphibious," the *Times* hoped that her health would soon mend, that "she may attain a century") and in spite of Chorley's assurance that she would soon be well enough to star in the play he had written for her.

As far back as February her excitement about Chorley's *Duchess Eleanour* had circulated all the way to Florence. "I warmly wish that Mr. Chorley may succeed with his play," Elizabeth Barrett Browning had written to Mary Mitford, "but how can Miss Cushman promise a hundred nights for an untried work?"

But attractive or not, promising or not, she knew at last that London was after all her headquarters. By late summer, her energies partly revived, her spirits refreshed by the icy waters at Malvern, the time had come to put herself back in harness. She could shed no more tears for lost joy.

When an offer came from Maddox—at Macready's urging—to share his October bill with Macready, she could read it in a new light. Appearing at last in London with the tyrannical force that led her to it was a step she had delayed long enough. After three years, with her name established in all the right places, could Macready's rampaging ego trouble her? More importantly, could she sidestep the release it offered her from her grief?

In a speech concluding his 1847 season, Maddox thanked his patrons, then reminisced for a moment about his house: "I think we can certainly call this a legitimate theatre"; Fanny Kemble's recent work and Macready's Shakespeare had brought new prestige to the Princess's "and is not the talented Miss Cushman—whom I first had the honor of introducing to a British public—'legitimate,' too?" That lady, Maddox happily announced, would soon appear with the great Macready on "the opening of our next campaign."

Charlotte made her way back to London, buried her regrets, established firm ties with a Unitarian Church, and took new quarters for herself—the family would remain in Bayswater—close to her work at 1 Baker Street, a more proper abode for the social role she now planned to play with a vengeance. It would, she hoped, fill an emptiness. When a struggling artist "sighed for success" within her hearing, her response—"Buy it, as I am doing!"—shed light on the wider role she intended to play. Hardly concerned any longer about success on a London stage, her move to Portnam Square made clear her plans for social arrival.

She chose her location well. Portnam Square was an emerald expanse typical of urban London. Shaded by great trees, its broad walks evoked her girlhood under the elms of Boston Common. Brownstone houses of three and four storys surrounded the park, their brass-studded doors opening to London's more elegant names. Her neighbors, the Sanders, were already worth half a million.

In her tall rooms, hospitality could counteract loneliness. Singing at her piano, plying her guests with the wines and meats she now could afford, she rekindled the excitement she had relished at old Samuel Rogers' breakfast board. People who answered her invitations, the American minister, the Monckton Milneses, the Putnams, Ruskin, the Carlyles—the many names she had met through Mary Howitt and Chorley—people who came to meet the actress left knowing the woman.

For Charlotte as actress, October 4 brought a chapter full circle. In honesty she could confess a debt to Macready: without him she might never have faced the wisdom of coming to England. But now Macready's patronage offered her nothing. Appearing with him at the Princess's was a box office trick, an answer to the public's curiosity to see them act in one piece. "The noted resemblance of Miss Cushman's manner, voice,—and shall we add countenance?—to that of Mr. Macready caused the combination to be anticipated as something amusing," said the *Spectator*. Still, if life must continue, she must complement her social labors with work that could stretch her mind. Acting with Macready made valuable demands. Against the light of his art, she could display her own special brilliance.

On stage, Macready got more than he bargained for. "Acted Macbeth as well as I could," his diary noted. "Called for; led on Miss Cushman, who thanked me for the civility." It was the least she could do after almost demolishing him.

The *Sunday Times* gave the full story: the performance started pretty evenly, but it was soon obvious that Charlotte had determined not to lose a single point in her game. Throwing all her energies into the part, she quickly disconcerted Macready; "the 'old lion' soon felt his laurels withering on his brow." If the *Sunday Times* knew acting, Miss Cushman's earnestness, her "fiery eloquence" completely eclipsed "the measured emotions and frigid mannerisms" of the great tragedian. After Duncan's murder, said another paper, she "literally dragged him off the stage.'

However much the experience had harried Macready ("an anonymous letter telling me the Sunday Times and Dispatch said I was decreasing in vigour—my kind, constant, and true friends!") Charlotte had made herself clear. If Macready failed to regret his shabby treatment of her in Boston, he could thank a poor memory. "There is a certain sudden earnestness about Miss Cushman, a hasty style of darting at a point, which is quite her own, and which is really the secret of her success," said the *Spectator*. Writing to John Povey, she could report that her opening night of Macbeth was "grand"—in spite of the miserable illness she had had for the last seven months, "but I am better and hope by great care to get on." Even Macready's friend Forster praised her in *Othello*: "such a quiet picture of what we conceive the real Emilia to have been that it is quite delightful to witness it."

Charlotte could play these old parts with her eyes shut, making them almost sleep-walking scenes throughout, but she tasted a new stimulant on October 13 when she first played Henry VIII's Queen Katharine to Macready's Cardinal Wolsey. In spite of her doubts about appearing in London in parts that invited comparisons, she took the risk as Queen Katharine and won. Living memories recalled Mrs. Siddons' special "feel" for the role and Samuel Johnson's enthusiasm for it: when Johnson asked her which of Shakespeare's characters most pleased her, Sarah had replied "Katharine," because it was the most "natural," the most lifelike, and Johnson agreed. "And whenever you perform it, I will once more hobble out to the theatre myself."

Despite its stigma as Shakespeare's "weakest" play, the play whose cannons had fired the blaze that leveled the Globe in 1613, Charlotte saw in the Spanish Katharine's pitiable downfall a matchless chance to wield her power over an audience. An overflow house followed spellbound as her Katharine slowly realized that doom was upon her, that for reasons having nothing to do with justice or honor or fault in herself Henry had allowed Anne Bullen's prettier face ("O Beauty, till now I never knew thee!") to preempt her. Against the malice of Macready's Wolsey, Charlotte's Katharine became the play's one sympathetic character, the epitome of noble woman insulted and betrayed, creating even Anne's sympathy: "So good a lady that no tongue could ever pronounce dishonor of her . . . To give her the avaunt! It is a pity Would move a monster."

Afterward, observers disagreed about Charlotte's "style." Some saw in it Mrs. Siddons' classic grandeur; others, missing the grand manner "required" by the lines, rejected Charlotte's humanity in an "almost statuesque" role. She had given Katharine "physical attributes," made her a plain woman and a queen "to the world."

But for eyes left weeping at Katharine's death, the question of "style" was meaningless. Chorley saw women "wiping their eyes on apricot-colored bonnet-strings." Charlotte had built toward that effect throughout the whole play. Reactions to various performances echoed the force Charlotte achieved in this first portrayal. At her entrance, dressed in flowing crimson, Katharine made clear her respect for Henry and her scorn for Cardinal Wolsey.

Kneeling at Henry's feet, her words trembled as she confronted his doubts at the legitimacy of their marriage. As Heaven was her witness, Katharine had been a true and humble wife, subject always to his "countenance," glad or sorry with it.

> Sir, call to mind
> That I have been your wife, in this obedience,
> Upward of twenty years, and have been blest
> With many children by you. If in the course
> And process of this time you can report,
> And prove it too, against mine honor aught,
> My bond to wedlock, or my love and duty,
> Against your sacred person, in God's name,
> Turn me away, and let the foul'st contempt
> Shut door upon me, and so give me up
> To the sharp'st kind of justice. . . .

Until then, she begged him to spare her "till I may be by my friends in Spain advised, whose counsel I will implore."

When Wolsey assured her her interests were fully represented by "these reverend fathers" here assembled, Katharine turned in fury to him, struggling to hold back her tears. Then she looked away, pointed back toward him, and cried with a withering scorn, "Lord Cardinal, to *you* I speak!" expressing in her words and the accompanying gesture "lofty womanhood's superb contempt" for all "duplicity and meanness."

Leaving the court, when Henry had her recalled, "Katharine Queen of England, come into the court," and her attendant said, "Madam, you are called back," Katharine comported herself with "the air of a lioness." Head erect, her massive figure towering, her eyes "glowed" with anger as she waved him forward: "What need you note it? . . . Pray you, pass on."

199

But slowly breaking under her sorrows, she had donned the black velvet of grief by the time Wolsey and Cardinal Campeuis came to her apartment to give her "counsel."

"Ye tell me what ye wish for both—my ruin. . . .

Would I had never trod this English earth
Or felt the flatteries that grow upon it!
Ye have angels' faces, but Heaven knows your hearts.
What will become of me now, wretched lady!
I am the most unhappy woman living.

Near the play's end, hopelessly ill, Katharine's querulous "sick" tone became profoundly moving. Her halting "Reach a chair, So; now, methinks, I feel a little ease," broke with groans, then with a comfortable grunt of relief. When she learned of Wolsey's death, she elicited further sympathy. "So may he rest. His faults lie gently on him!"

Katharine's flashing indignation at a messenger's rudeness—"You are a saucy fellow. Deserve we no more reverence?"—her queenly anger clearing for a moment her voice and lifting her body, heightened the effect of her rapid decline. An "unearthly beauty and sweetness" in her acting touched one listener's heart "below the source of tears."

Dying, Charlotte caused Katharine's voice to thicken. Reaffirming her love for Henry, she commended "to his goodness the model of our chaste loves," his young daughter Mary. Then her cries became pathetic. Let Henry have pity upon "my wretched women, that so long Have followed both my fortunes faithfully," and upon her serving men; "they are the poorest (But poverty could never draw 'em from me)." Then she made a last request, delivered with the slow clutch of death on her throat. "When I am dead, good wench, Let me be used with honor. Strew me over, with maiden flowers, that all the world may know I was a chaste wife to my grave. . . . Although unqueened, yet like a queen, and daughter to a king, inter me. I can no more."

Acting the part, she had astonished even Macready; her final scene had set off a storm at the Princess's. But leaving the cheering theatre, she could feel only a deep dejection that echoed partly from Katharine's long dying, partly from a personal grief that still lay too near the surface. It had felt good to be busy again, but could the play do her real good or she any good to the part? Could she continue to act a grief too nearly like her own?

Macready muttered his hostility next day. "Looked at paper in which I read a notice of last night's performance, that seemed to me most insulting and detracting—but *what* are my critics?" But for Charlotte, the London *Times* was ecstatic: "The broken up attitude of that ghastly figure in the chair, the benignant smile that seems ever ready to vanish away in death, the flush of banished pride at the unmannerly entrance of the messenger . . . the look of approaching beatitude in sleep, when she is cheered by a celestial vision, are so many nuances all truthful to the last degree. . . . The whole scene is a refined specimen of histrionic poetry." No ordinary intellect, declared the *Times,* could dive so deeply into the play's meaning and find such expression for it as did Charlotte Cushman as Queen Katharine.

A note from Chorley gave her further assurance: "It has given me a higher idea of your powers than any I have yet seen you act." The conception, "the queenliness" of the playing—all of it pleased him, but "most of all I was delighted to hear how your level voice, when not forced, tells, and tells thoroughly. . . . I am truly glad for your own sake you played the part."

Chorley's words carried an implication. Far from incapacitating her as an artist, her sorrow at Rosalie's passing had been translated into new insight, new power to convey the deeper truths. Though the *Times* praised an intellect that could delve into meanings, pure emotion enabled her to comprehend and express what she found. The wages of suffering were art.

Another good to come from this run with Macready would be an added weight to her purse—when and if she ever braved a return to America. After Forrest's attack on Macready in Edinburgh, she doubted that any English star would soon attempt an American tour—especially in the light of the testimonial dinner Edwin's American friends had recently tendered him. Writing to John Povey at the Park, she imagined that, without foreign stars, America might soon be thrown on her own resources—"which will be much better for you, I am sure." Despite her success in England, she could report scant vigor in the British theatre. Here, translations from the

French and two- or three-act pieces were axes at the root of a dying tree. "Bye and bye *when* we have in the States a drama of our own and which we ought to have . . . there will be none in England." A Whitman editorial could hardly have phrased it better. Povey must copy and publish "where they will do me good" the clippings she enclosed of her recent notices—against the day when she would return home, "gallop through the country as fast as I can, and make as much money" as possible.

This run at the Princess's brought a happy reunion with John Gibbs Gilbert, her childhood friend whose early success had fanned her own ambition. Matured into a tall, reserved gentleman, already one of America's favorite comedians, Gilbert was "getting on very finely here," she reported to Povey, "fast making himself an immense favorite." But the joy in renewing a friendship was tempered by an outbreak of anger backstage. However much he wished to keep a paying actress like Charlotte happy, Maddox offended the sensitive Susan. When rumor held Macready responsible for Maddox' taking Susan out of the *Hamlet* cast, Macready coolly declared his ignorance and unconcern: "it was of no consequence to me what either individuals or a multitude thought of me." But Charlotte herself thought plenty, especially about the wily Maddox, and she found the necessary words: he and his whole theatre might "go to hell."

Macready fired off a word of advice. He hoped Charlotte had not yet made a decision on the subject of her letter to Maddox. "I should like to speak to you upon it, thinking, that the opinion or counsel of a cooler one might enable you at heart to form a more deliberate judgment."

Whatever Maddox' justification, Charlotte's blood told her to void immediately her contract with the Princess's: she could afford to fly in the face of any such man as Maddox. But she throttled her anger and felt happier when Susan garnered high praise on her own the middle of November. As Juliet, this younger Miss Cushman "sometimes rises to the verge of the sublime," cried the *Theatrical Times.* Though she was no Helen Faucit, she was "a remarkably pretty woman . . . a very pleasing actress." For once, praise for Susan even outshone Charlotte. As Romeo, the elder Miss Cushman's "Americanisms" sometimes offended the ear, though as the peculiar Meg Merrilies, even her faults were beauties; she "is the greatest melodramatic actress in the world." Bearing these facts in mind, Maddox might watch his manners.

True to her hopes, Charlotte's social whirl swept her up dizzily, and along with her, Geraldine Jewsbury. Geraldine's fame had opened almost every door in Victorian London simply because, as Jane Carlyle put it, "she had put her cleverness into a *book,* above all a book accused of immorality." When Rogers and Monckton Milnes both pursued Geraldine for breakfast, Jane sniffed, "Upon my honour I believe if a *Lady* had been tried for murder . . . she would have a better chance of 'getting' on in society here than one of whom nothing had been *talked.*"

Invitations poured in. The wife of the new American minister to the Court of St. James, Mrs. George Bancroft, noted her delight in meeting both Charlotte and Susan at dinner. "They are of Old Colony descent (from Elder Cushman), and have very much of the New England character, culture, and good sense." Over Chorley's artichoke hearts and champagne Charlotte and Susan—"hot from the Princess's"—impressed an American guest, Mrs. Brookfield: the younger "has considerable prettiness. The elder one, *the* one, talked without reserve about acting."

Bathed in the light of such gatherings, fully aware of her own attraction, Charlotte broke out the sense of humor she seldom revealed on stage. She delighted in mimicking Maddox. At dinner, she could use her darkest tones on a waiter, looking him deep in the eyes and asking, "Is your name Sam?" recalling the same comic sense in Mrs. Siddons, who could say to a cloth salesman in her most tragic voice, "Will it wash?"

As Charlotte busied herself more and more in London society, things were changing at the Bayswater cottage. Susan was sending Ned off to school in Yorkshire and making plans for a wedding in June, "unless something unforeseen occurs to Dr. Muspratt." When Charlotte finished her run at the Princess's, Susan struggled alone against Maddox. When she blamed "indisposition" for missing a rehearsal, Maddox again struck off her name and substituted another actress. The occasion was the London debut on January 5, 1848, of another American hopeful, Anna Cora Mowatt, in *The Hunchback.*

Though Susan missed several other rehearsals, she reported for the last one ready to play Helen, demanding to know why the character had been reassigned. While Anna watched, embarrassed, an angry scene ensued, so filled with fireworks that "a casual spectator might have supposed they were rehearsing some tempestuous passages of a melodrama"—until Maddox ordered the stage cleared and rehearsal continued. Forced to retire from the scene, Susan turned back a moment and offered an apologetic hand to Mrs. Mowatt. In due course the *Sun* could report that "America has within the last three years given us Miss Cushman, the greatest tragedian at present on the stage, Mrs. Mowatt, the most interesting young tragedian, the most lady-like of genteel comedians."

In Susan's unladylike outburst, Charlotte read the signs clearly. With pleasure and silent envy, she could not question Susan and Sheridan Muspratt's impatience. To a solitary heart, the life ahead for the lovers seemed far more richly impelling, more real than all her social rounds, her efforts to fill the tomorrows facing her.

Time to Go West

(1849)

🌹 The years that had seen the former choirgirl at Emerson's
church become a top star had seen its former minister achieve
a success no less dramatic. Freed of his pulpit irritations, Ralph
Waldo Emerson had risen to national eminence as a lecturer. Of
late, his popularity had prompted his making a second tour of Britain,
where his quiet manner but highly charged ideas drew throngs of
young men to him. Arthur Clough commented that for many of his
followers Emerson completed the vision of life that Carlyle had only
promised.

For the Carlyles, the intense Mr. Emerson made a difficult guest
at Cheyne Row, "face to face and (over-) soul to (over-) soul!"
For two days, Jane lived on the "manna" of his speech, but able to
bear no more she escaped to her bedroom *"to bathe my head in cold
water."* To Jane, Emerson was a man with two faces, the one,
"young, refined, almost beautiful, radiant with—what shall I say?
'virtue its own reward!'" the other, decidedly old, "hatchet-like,
crotchety, inconclusive—like the incarnation of one of his poems."
Beaten at his own game, the volcanic Carlyle himself shouted his
relief when Emerson finally departed. "I was torn to pieces, talking
with him, for his sad Yankee rule seemed to be, that talk should go
on incessantly except when sleep interrupted it."

In Manchester, Charlotte invited Emerson to call. Talking to
him, it surprised her to find that, for all she owed him as a source
of her early courage, his thoughts and poetry now had little to say
to her. She could sense no passion in his lines, no parallel at all between his unconventional views and the goals she had set for herself; she could place little faith in his doubts about "consistency,"

his disdain for public opinion. Transcendentalism now seemed the notion of naïve young men, whereas maturity had led her, a person dependent upon the crowd, to a certain respect for the crowd's values, however much her dress offstage might seem to say different.

Emerson wrote home his pleasure in the Manchester talk with Charlotte; "an agreeable visit it was," he told Lidian, though the pleasure surely centered more in recalling their years on Hanover Street than in any intellectual excitement they still shared. For Charlotte, the visit measured the long strides she had taken since she first climbed the steps into the choir behind Emerson's pulpit. Views she now held would have astonished her fifteen years earlier. To the question, "My dear Miss Cushman, do you read Emerson?" she could now reply, "No."

"Is it possible you do not admire Emerson?"

"Quite possible." She did not discount, however, the value she placed on the blue-lined souvenir Emerson left in her hands, a signed holograph of his poem, "Rubies."

Practicalities interested her far more than Emerson's generalities. She kept a close eye on the effects Fanny Kemble was creating, especially in "her" roles, Lady Macbeth and Queen Katharine. If she felt herself threatened, she could hardly regret Macready's disgust with Fanny as Lady Macbeth. "I have never seen any one so bad, so unnatural, so affected, so conceited" and, he added prophetically, so "*disagreeable,* but her pride will have yet a deeper fall." Nor could she grieve sincerely over Geraldine's description of Fanny's Julia: "she looked dreadfully thin and worn and was much agitated when she came on . . . much too roug'd (to look well)." About March, when Fanny decided to concentrate on platform readings from Shakespeare, Charlotte could not hide her satisfaction; she had no interest in that art herself. When Fanny's new popularity enabled her to buy the small house she had wanted in Lenox, Massachusetts, and leave England, Charlotte shed no tears.

A further highpoint of the spring came March 22, when Susan married Sheridan Muspratt amid high ceremony and Mary Eliza's happy tears in Liverpool. At least one daughter was scrubbed clean of the theatre's doubtful greasepaint, able at last to assume a proper role, secure in a home of her own. When the marriage brought hearty approval from Sheridan's London friends, Alfred Tennyson and Charles Dickens, no one was surprised. Muspratt had taken a beauteous bride. To the elevated circle Susan now entered, the theatre's loss seemed far less momentous than Liverpool's gain of a new social ornament. For Charlotte, the wedding occasioned a quiet pride, though it lost her a dependable Juliet.

But there were compensations. Proceeding to Manchester, she relished the flattery when a talented hopeful, Sara Coxin, sought her advice. When Sara swore her determination to be a great actress, Charlotte applauded. She filled her letters to Sara throughout succeeding months with trade secrets. Sara must never despise honest labor. "How many there are who have a *horror of my profession!* Yet I dearly love the very hard work, the very drudgery of it, which has made me what I am." She must stand her ground with managers. "Value yourself with managers and they will prize you more. Never oblige them, they easily forget favors. Do always what you engage and *no more!*"

Throughout the months preceding the wedding, Charlotte had pondered the question of replacing Susan. If her Romeo had lost its novelty to London, she knew the provinces still clamored for it. Wisdom said keep it ready, but where could she find a dependable Juliet?

In Clifton Hampden, when a tall young woman of twenty-eight knocked on her door, she found her answer. Would Miss Cushman accept an eager pupil? In Matilda Hays, Charlotte immediately recognized a superabundance of feminine charm. With training she might become a perfect Juliet—far more apt and attractive than any stock actress she could expect to meet in her travels. An agreement was reached between them. Having no ties, Matilda could accompany her on the tour; if she followed Charlotte's coaching, she could appear with her in the fall.

The eager pupil became at last an intimate, a spirit as freely capable of friendship as Rosalie Sully. The bond that ripened between them almost eclipsed Charlotte's forthcoming appearance in July with Macready in a command performance before Queen Victoria.

July 10 would celebrate Macready's departure for another American tour, a step that worried his friends deeply. Dickens confessed that *Martin Chuzzlewit* and *American Notes* had roiled the waters between the United States and England, that his having inscribed one of his popular novels to Macready might pose his friend problems: "I wish to heaven I could undedicate *Nickleby* until you come home again."

Nor did Macready find much assurance in the hostile articles he read in "that detestable heap of filth," the New York *Herald,* hinting at possible war between the United States and England, or the rumors he heard in April about Charlotte. "Received an insinuation that Miss Cushman was endeavouring to do me mischief in America!" If Macready could fear Charlotte's mischief, he could hardly expect her gratitude for earlier "favors." On June 29 he received her note "very cavalierly consenting to act Queen Katharine, if her expenses were paid." After dinner at the home of Charles Dickens, where the guests included Susan and Sheridan Muspratt, Macready ripped off a reply to Charlotte, "willingly" dispensing such aid.

For Charlotte, the command to play for the Queen came late, in a sense, in all her British triumphs. She might have wondered if Victoria's unconcern smacked of England's general disdain toward things American if *Punch* had not twitted Victoria and Albert openly for years for their disinterest in London theatre. And this performance "bespoken" at Drury Lane had taken contriving. A vast circle of Macready's friends had petitioned him to appear in the Queen's presence "in one of the characters of the national drama" to which he had rendered special service. London's social and literary greats had signed it: Bulwer-Lytton, Browning, Monckton Milnes, Carlyle, Hallam, Tennyson, Count Dorsay, Cobden, Charles Kemble, and the like. John Braham, London's beloved tenor, would come out of retirement to sing "God Save the Queen."

Victoria herself did not record her reactions to *Henry VIII,* but on Charlotte and Macready permanent scars remained. Snorts and groans from the pit and the galleries repeatedly interrupted the early scenes, totally disregarding the brilliance scattered throughout the house, the presence of the royal family—the Queen and Albert, the Queen Dowager, the Duchess of Kent, the Duchess of Cambridge —seated amid flowers in their velvet box. Macready had anticipated some noise, after his criticism a few weeks before of an audience's rudeness to a visiting French company. Fearing retaliation, he had felt relieved when Dickens, who had arranged the benefit, stationed plainclothesmen in the pit lest a disturbance occur.

When commotion broke out, he begged the Queen's permission to address the crowded house, "understanding they were incommoded for want of room," to ask them please to receive their money and leave. Not until the noise subsided could the play continue, with Charlotte spelling out, against Macready's arrogant Wolsey, the bitter defeat and slow death of a woman and a queen not at all like the imperious young monarch peering down stiffly at her through her jeweled glass.

After the play, a reception in the greenroom for the friends who had petitioned Macready's performance and a formal presentation to the Queen and her Prince Consort rounded out, rather hollowly, an evening that might have been an artistic triumph, royalty's recognition of queenly acting talent. Instead, perhaps because the occasion had gotten off to such an unruly start, Victoria and Albert stiffly expressed their thanks and departed to deep curtseys and polite applause—recalling not at all the high drama Macready had known in 1839 after his Claude Melnotte, when Victoria had bade him approach, smiled her thanks ("I have been very much pleased"), and permitted him to light her way out of the theatre, backing before, with candles held over head. After *Henry VIII* Macready did the gentlemanly thing for once and published a card expressing his gratitude to Charlotte and the actors who had suffered the ordeal with him.

When Charlotte received word that Captain Marryat had died at age fifty-six, the remembered compliment of his old flirtation in Detroit caused her to smile. The friendship with Marryat had never grown deep, but she could thank him for his early sponsorship in London.

Throughout the spring and summer, she happily shared a portion of Geraldine's fame. Geraldine had made her the prototype for the main character in her new novel, *The Half Sisters,* a defense of women's rights to love freely, once women proved themselves capable of something more than "simple wifehood." "We are touching on better days when women will have a genuine normal life of their own to lead," cried Geraldine, "no longer feeling their destiny *manqué* if they remain single." Assertive women like Charlotte Cushman, Jane Carlyle, and herself owed the world no apology: the three, said Geraldine, were actually indications of a development of womanhood, as yet not fully recognized, "of certain higher qualities and possibilities that lie in women." Whatever eccentricities people might see in their ilk were mere "consequences of imperfect formation, immature growth."

Though Jane Carlyle protested the book's dedication to herself, decrying it "unfit for circulation in families," Charlotte as the character embodying the novel's main theme accepted the flattery.

She accepted a crested invitation from the Duke of Devonshire to visit his Yorkshire estate near Skipton, to join him for dinner and conversation at his hunting lodge, for long carriage rides past the hedgerows crisscrossing his fields. In the quiet house he turned over to them, she and Matilda spent long hours, "anxious and full of labour," preparing for Matilda's October debut. To mark his pleasure in their visit, the Duke presented Charlotte with a cameo ring and a carved set of chessmen.

Despite her obvious "nerves," Matilda's debut with Charlotte in Bristol on October 16 came off well enough; Matilda's "great nature and force of expression" promised even happier nights ahead. When a London paper declared its certainty that Matilda's fine figure and expressive face would realize her "utmost" hopes, perhaps even "eminence," Charlotte acknowledged a bounding satisfaction; in the long series of engagements that now could follow, who could predict the range of this new friendship?

The friendship ripened into deep attachment. To the dismay of some—Elizabeth Barrett Browning, for instance—she and Matilda soon arranged a bond of permanent affection. As Elizabeth saw it the bond was a "female marriage." "She and Miss Hays have made vows of celibacy and of eternal attachment to each other—they live together, dress alike." Wherever Charlotte would go, Matilda would follow. When Elizabeth later remarked to a friend that she found the arrangement strange, the friend assured her, "Oh, it is by no means uncommon." Even Boston had "Boston marriages."

Uncommon or not, Charlotte found within the arrangement a pattern for life that had struggled in the back of her mind ever since her friendships with Charles Spalding and Charley Wiggin in Boston. If it could scarcely offer the intimate rewards of marriage, it supplied a release at last from loneliness. Charlotte's photographs reflected her confidence in the new personal role she had chosen. Posed in a wide bow tie and stiff white shirt buttoned from collar to waist, she heightened the "masculinity" of her manner by the forthright, tailored air of her clothes. When Mary Eliza and the family raised eyebrows, Charlotte stood her ground. Everyone had his own life to lead. Within her code of values, the bond with Matilda made perfect sense and would prevail.

After New Year's, Dublin cheered the new team in *The Lady of Lyons*. To Charlotte's Claude Melnotte, Matilda was the ideal Pauline. For Miss Hays "we do predict . . . a lofty position," wrote the *Theatrical Times* in January 1849. Throughout the remaining months of the season, as Charlotte came more and more to relish the new friendship, she and Matilda carried their careers to new acclaim in the provinces. Hull could hardly find words for Meg Merrilies. "It was perfection."

Aided in her work, companioned in her sympathies, she could bring herself in the spring of 1849 to face again a difficult question. She had succeeded on every British stage that mattered; she could probably repeat her successes endlessly. But with victory behind her, had the time come now to confront new challenges, to attempt further triumphs at home? With Matilda, she could brave at last a return to Philadelphia and the empty chair she would find at Sully's. When she met an able young actor in Liverpool, C. W. Couldock, eager to tour with her in America, perfectly willing as Macbeth and Fazio to pattern his business on hers, she faced the compelling evidence. The time to go home had arrived.

Before she completed her plans, disturbing word reached London the middle of May—Macready's tour through the States had met violence. Throughout the months of the tour, Forrest had busied himself in efforts to embarrass his English rival, broadcasting reports that Macready had created all manner of rudeness against him in England in 1845, that the British press had attacked him repeatedly, had blamed him solely and unfairly for a hiss in Edinburgh that was only one of many that had rained down on Macready. Consequently, when hisses and tossed pennies and a rotten egg greeted Macready in Philadelphia on October 20, the actor had waited until the noise abated, then assured the crowd that he had never shown hostility toward the popular American, even though Forrest had hissed him publicly in Edinburgh, behavior which no American, surely, would condone between artists. Though the booing continued, somebody's shouted "Nine cheers for Macready!" set off a comforting round that had petered out in a few feeble cheers for "Ned Forrest."

To this, Forrest replied with a card in the Philadelphia *Public Ledger* calling Macready "a superannuated driveller" who had connived on the night of Forrest's first appearance in London with Charlotte Cushman to "hiss me, and did hiss me, with the purpose of driving me from the stage," all of this months before the affair in Edinburgh.

By the time Macready had completed his swing through the South and had arrived in New York, he had become in many American eyes more than an actor, more than a reminder of excellence investing the British stage. He had left New Orleans filled with hatred "for this odious country," where only a helpless minority understood anything about taste, high feeling, or gentlemanly spirit. A drunken ruffian in Cincinnati had hurled half a dead sheep at him. Macready had made new friends, his acting had brought him more than 20,000 pounds, but around him clustered a seething hostility toward England. By May 1849, Forrest's own name had become a battle cry; Macready's, the focal point for many Americans determined to heap on him all their resentment of England, her arrogance, her difficulties over Oregon.

Macready's opening as Macbeth at the new Astor Place Opera House in New York on May 7 foreshadowed events to come. As if to draw the ugly affair to a head, Forrest had engaged to play the same part the same night at another house. A faction of his supporters, organized as a party to attend Macready's performance, set up an abusive cry when he appeared, showered the stage with rotten eggs, asafetida, groans, screams, and catcalls ("Off! Off!") and displayed a banner, "You have ever proved a liar!" A rain of apples, lemons, bits of wood, and potatoes accompanied further shouts, "Down with the English hog!" A chair from the gallery crashed down on stage; another fell into the orchestra. More followed.

Macready would have dropped his engagement then, had not a group of New Yorkers—among them Herman Melville and Washington Irving—sent him a long note next day, deploring the riot and "praying him to remain." When Macready agreed reluctantly to reappear on May 10, Forrest again posted the same play for the same night and did nothing to stop his fans from issuing notices, organizing meetings, and attempting to buy out the house. Though the Astor Place manager, James H. Hackett, tried to block them, a few still managed to get in.

The performance had hardly begun before the toughs set up a

howl—"Get off the stage! Clear out, God damn your English soul!
Hoo! Hiss-s-s-s! Three cheers for Ned Forrest!"—and began hurling
missiles onto the stage. When police ejected the ringleaders, pandemonium broke loose outside, where 20,000 people had congregated.
Fighting the police, picking up loose paving stones in the street, they
battered the theatre's doors and broke windows, one rioter shouting,
"Burn the damn den of the aristocracy!" At this point, the Seventh
Regiment and a cavalry troop marched in to take over. In the wild
scene that followed, horses panicked, and the New York City Sheriff
ordered a volley of shot to be fired over the rioters' heads. Misun-
derstanding the order to fire over the heads, the soldiers blasted
straight into the crowd. When order was at last established, Macready had escaped in disguise into the darkness of Eighth Street, a
theatre stood almost wrecked, a city square had been almost denuded
of paving stones, an unknown number of men had been injured, and
some twenty people lay dead.

Reporting the news, the London *Times* opined that England,
proudly, was not so viciously nationalistic; it was gratifying to know
that England had applauded Charlotte Cushman to the very echoes,
when it might have jeered her for the hotheaded land she came from.
And the *Illustrated London News* complimented its readers for
separating art and politics, for recognizing the fact that "genius" in
Charlotte Cushman was "genius, just as mediocrity in the case of
Mr. Forrest" was nothing more. Dickens wrote his sentiments to
Sheridan Muspratt: "Forrest I take to be a raving madman."

When the dust finally settled and Macready had sailed for home
("I thank His goodness that I am safe and unharmed"), Charlotte
was left with some open questions. Could she safely brandish the
triumph she had achieved on the British stage in the face of such
anti-British feelings? Would the frenzied mind of the public abuse
her as Macready's protégée? And what about Forrest? What mischief could she expect from him, knowing how deep his resentment
of her extended? Could she predict at all the reception she might
encounter?

In the end, she knew that running a risk was the only way to an
answer. Through Mary Eliza's tears, she tried to explain the factors
involved, emphasizing the economics. Surely, if America accepted her
at all, it would value her English fame and weight her pockets accordingly. Reassuring Sallie that the summer seas must surely be
calmer than the waves they had crossed five years before, she set her
course toward home.

213

A friend and critic shored up her courage for the expected ordeal ahead. Westland Marston looked at her departure as an artistic completion: "She came from America an actress of promise; she returned there one of the leading actresses of her time."

"Hurray for Our Charlotte"

(1849)

Her first day out of Liverpool, Charlotte could feel her spirits lifting. Her campaign in England had paid off in every respect save one—Rosalie Sully had not shared her victory. Now, pondering her fears about the reception ahead, she took comfort in the fact that her thirty-three years had seen her slay many dragons. For herself, she had proved the power of work as an antidote to sorrow, the force of courage as a formidable weapon.

On September 1, when she first sighted New York fear and grief and elation poured through her. Docking, she saw immediately that New York had gone on growing. Moving in her open carriage through scurrying crowds and jangling teams, she saw only vigor and drive lighting these American faces, a youthful urgency she suddenly realized she had missed in Europe. In her room, when Sallie brought her the papers, "California!" and "Gold!" leaped out from the pages. Only whisper the word "gold," cried the *Weekly Yankee,* "and its worshippers fall down on their knees." Tell where it could be found, "and millions rush to the spot faster than they would go to heaven."

In a sense, her coming home now was part of that gold rush, no less than the pell-mell dash of wagons and horses—over the plains and Rockies toward Sutter's Mill. She had made herself clear to John Povey: she had come home "to make as much money as possible."

To plan her campaign, she would first touch home base in Boston. In New York she must face whatever troubles the Forrest–Macready affair might foment, but here she could rally her forces and greet the friends, celebrity seekers, and editors who streamed to her door. The stream was the privilege—or penalty—of stardom. Who could predict what it meant about the public reaction she could expect on stage?

She had a clue one evening when she and Matilda went to the Howard Athenaeum, where Hackett was playing Falstaff. To avoid the crush, they had waited until the play was into its second scene before taking their seats. The minute she entered, a buzz began filtering over the audience. In spite of her wish to hide, out of courtesy to her old friend, somebody sent up a cry: "Three cheers for Charlotte Cushman!" When the cheers died down, another cried, "Charlotte Cushman, the Siddons of America!" And then, most heart-warming of all, "Hurray for Our Charlotte!" Nodding to Hackett, who had stopped the play, she turned and smiled to the audience. Honor might be hard to achieve in one's home town, but returning to it proved much about the success one had captured abroad.

At home, she savored the fruits of her victory, renewing old friendships, proud and humble one day when Charley Wiggin came up to press her hand, then tilted his head and smiled ruefully as he backed through the door. When the new force in Boston publishing, James T. Fields, wrote to beg one of her poems, she could only send a formal regret: "Of late years her numerous engagements have prevented her from paying the attention she could have wished to composition, so that an original poem, worthy of consideration, is, she regrets to say altogether beyond her."

Yet Fields was hardly a man to drop the matter. An editorial talent at thirty-two who would attract to his fold the likes of Longfellow, Lowell, Whittier, Holmes, Thoreau, Emerson, Harriet Beecher Stowe, Tennyson, Thackeray and Dickens would not be deterred by a stiffly correct refusal. His plea brought a visit. In her rustling skirts, the woman whom Fields saw sweep into his shop at the corner of Washington Street and School was certainly no beauty. Successful people often entered his doors, but this woman had an air, a quality.

Charlotte was sorry she could give him no poem, but she could use a goodly supply of his books. When Fields escorted her through the green curtains into his cluttered office, the talk that followed laid the keel of a friendship. The bright young man with the molded chin whiskers and the great flowing tie smiled his thanks, then dispatched a clerk with the long list of titles she needed.

Back at the Revere House, she relaxed at night with the books, after she had spent her days with her mind stuck firm to the New York days ahead. Fearful at heart, she gave no hint of the matter in the business letters that flowed from her pen. For her work in New York and beyond, she must have the same terms as those given to Macready and Forrest: half the box office each night. She could act no more than five nights a week. W. H. Chippendale could claim, as her agent, one percent of her profits. If Chip found serious objection in the New York managers or anywhere else, "I had rather not act, other means being open."

The stand was a gamble, but she would not undersell herself or the market worth of her English name too soon. With her best, managers would get their money's worth. And with C. W. Couldock arriving soon from England, she could offer an added attraction "without extra expense to the management." She saw no need to mention Couldock's fiery temper. The important thing was that he held most of his fire for the stage.

Before she left Boston, the papers reported in full late developments in the Pierce Butler household. After persecutions and bitter restraints upon Fanny's freedom to see her children, Pierce had sued for divorce on grounds of desertion. On September 22, Fanny Butler became Fanny Kemble again, supporting herself with her tireless, sharp pen and the platform readings from Shakespeare that moved the New York *Times* to report, "No play can be as well rendered throughout as Mrs. Kemble reads it; we are bored by no miserable creatures in subordinate parts."

With Couldock's support Charlotte could be sure that her own casts would include few "miserable creatures in subordinate parts!" In that respect, her hopes for Matilda Hays had not quite worked out. Moving from town to town where she could never predict the skill she might find in local actors, Matilda's steady support on stage had been a blessing, but during the late months in England, Charlotte had seen a disheartening change come over the girl. In the strife to master new roles, the routine that Charlotte had thrived on for years, Matilda's zeal and conviction had quavered. Over tea one tearful afternoon, she and Matilda had reluctantly faced a difficult fact that was obvious to both of them. A stage career for Matilda was out of the question. But when it occurred to them that the change

217

suggested a separation, Charlotte immediately offered a plan. From now on, Matilda would accompany her as confidante and companion. Matilda could earn her keep, as it were, by supplying a sense of home for Charlotte. Charlotte smiled in relief when Matilda put out her hand and agreed.

With her heart at ease, Charlotte could direct her attention to other matters. When a hopeful new playwright, George Henry Boker, sent her his *Anne Boleyn,* she promised to read it carefully, to consider bringing it out herself if she were right for it.

In Boker centered a question about the profession she had chosen to work in. She expected her own labors to pay in good solid cash, but she could attempt a second mission during this uncertain return. In her absence Walt Whitman had pursued his favorite topic about the role the drama must play in his vision of mature America. The nation's stage could be the "mouthpiece of freedom, refinement, liberal philanthropy, beautiful love for all our brethren, polished manners and an elevated good taste." In it, men could observe the follies of "unbridled passions"; wives and husbands, the follies of "contentious tempers."

Charlotte would lead no crusade, but with Brooklyn's young editor she could envision a future when Americans might value their actors and playwrights as they now did their novelists and poets. And her own talents, whether or not she performed in an American play, might be one means toward that new recognition.

In New York, approaching the new Broadway Theatre, where she had chosen to launch her campaign, Charlotte saw a magnificent structure at the corner of Pearl and Worth streets. Inside, its brilliant gas lights had lately enhanced the stunning debut of Lester Wallack, the young English talent Charlotte had encouraged. On its immense stage, between the festoons of its crimson curtains, Charlotte would soon know if New York had buried its memories of the Astor Place Riot, if it had forgotten whatever connection it might have seen between herself and the hated Macready. On October 8, she would open in Kotzebue's surefire old play, *The Stranger.*

Mrs. Haller in Kotzebue's dark tale of marriage had served her well with the English in 1845; it offered her ample chance now to show the Americans the genius London had recognized. Mrs. Siddons herself had long favored the role. In it, a superior actress could display the whole spectrum of human goodness, despair, and inner suffering.

When the heavy curtains swept open, in the sudden hush there might have been hisses and outcries against her links with Macready. Instead, whistles and cheers and a standing ovation exploded around her. To the 4,500 faces she nodded quickly, relaxed her pose slightly, then bent her thoughts to business. Within seconds, a happy, grateful American star must change in the crowd's eyes to a ravaged picture of heartbreak.

At the start of the play, the Baroness Waldbourg is a contented wife, the proud mother of two beautiful children, but a conniving friend convinces her that the Baron has long been unfaithful. Grief-stricken, she runs away with him; he seduces her, but learning the truth, she leaves him. Totally broken, she assumes the name Mrs. Haller and accepts a position as housekeeper to a Countess. When a kindly Stranger proves to be her husband, her shock is so great she faints. Discovering the tragedy between them, the Countess brings them together. The Baron forgives his wife, but Mrs. Haller cannot forgive herself. Their children dash in, the boy to his mother, the girl to her father. Mrs. Haller cries out her grief and dies.

The role had a fascination; the tears need hardly be faked. When Couldock's forgiving Stranger made her reclaim her jewels, Charlotte kept her eyes to the ground, afraid to look up. When she took the gems at last in her hands, she let her eyes rise slowly to his, then gasped wildly, shuddered, and poured out her shame in a flood of tears. When the children ran toward their parents, overjoyed at their reconciliation, Charlotte knelt silently weeping. As the curtains closed slowly, she tottered, swayed heavily, then fell senseless in a terrible heap of dying remorse.

No one could doubt the audience's sympathy for the stricken lives on stage. Watching Charlotte's death, women cried openly. When Charlotte, her calm self again, broke through the curtains for the first of her bows, bouquets at her feet and weeping faces greeted her. Nowhere in the tiers or boxes could she see any sign of the glowering eyes or resentful brows of Edwin Forrest.

The *Spirit Of The Times,* her old champion, found Charlotte "a little stouter in figure" but polished by time and experience abroad, though "she always was very clever," one of America's "intellectual jewels." *Albion* celebrated her return "in every sense of the word a complete triumph." Echoing Boston, the *Weekly Yankee* hailed the conquering heroine, "emphatically *Our Charlotte.*"

Careful critics recognized in this "new" Charlotte Cushman a precision with words that matched Forrest's; in her reading, meanings now came "as clear, as transparent" as if the thoughts themselves were "transferred through the senses." Her "points," deliberately built moments of great intensity, burst, when they came, like great star showers. Her petrified motion seemed more thrilling than the action itself, as if in her sudden rigidity, she stood enthralled by some tumult of vast perceptions.

Reading such praise, Charlotte could acknowledge a double pride: Americans could appreciate now this virtuosity she had developed abroad; they had critics at last who could evaluate her properly. As for Couldock, if the *Spirit* could not label him "a theatrical gem of the purest character," it could salute him a thorough gentleman and scholar.

In the run that extended through the twenty-seventh of October and the return she played in December, Charlotte acted all the roles that now stood as her trademarks: Lady Macbeth, Rosalind, Julia, Queen Katharine, Beatrice, Mrs. Simpson, Juliana (in *The Honeymoon*), and Meg. Nightly, the Broadway stood packed to the rafters.

To questions about why she moved "so much" on stage, Charlotte tipped her cap to Mrs. Siddons. A beauty like Siddons could afford to stand still and be looked at, but she herself could not dare the scrutiny. To let her own lack be noticed would dissipate "half her influence." It was Charlotte's undying sense of ugliness that accounted for part of her style.

Now she could play Meg for all its chills and shudders. In her rags, beauty would have handicapped her. At her dressing room mirror, applying the ugly brown stains, her fingers felt a new, instinctive power. When a painter asked her how she knew where shadows and lines belonged, she replied, "I don't *know,* I only feel *where* they ought to come."

Much as she herself preferred Lady Macbeth and Katharine, she soon accepted the fact that her American public rated her Meg her "greatest." "With an outlandish dress and a trick or two, I can bring much more money to the theatre than when I give the public my heart's blood in my finest characters." From now on, her old gypsy fortune-teller would be her fortune-maker.

In December, when the *Spirit* chided her for bringing home some of Macready's tricks—his posture, his drawling out words in "a most unnatural tone"—she could counter the barb with the smile the *Weekly Yankee* had given her a few weeks before. In a story headlined "Cush-mania," one breathless man had rushed so hard to see her Meg Merrilies he had trampled a group of children.

A cartoon, "Cushmania, Before and After," caused her more smiles. "Before" showed her, the American player, struggling to wake up her audience by threatening to stab herself. In "After," she stood grandly aloof, the English success, while a theatre manager implored her on bended knee to accept a money bag marked $1,000. Such was the reward of a London reputation.

If she had overheard it, the talk in one elegant New York household would have gratified her even more. Hearing his parents discuss Charlotte Cushman's brilliance, the seven-year-old Henry James "languished" while his parents dressed for the Broadway Theatre, then lay awake until they returned to hear them relive her vivid splendor as Queen Katharine.

By late fall, Charlotte had all the proof that her return had been wise. In the complications that success had brought her, she knew she must have the help of a full-time business manager and agent. William Corbyn would handle the welter of correspondence, the negotiations and contracts and travel details that her acting tour, after New York, entailed. Now, with Matilda and Sallie to tend to the homefires and Corbyn to badger the managers and railway conductors, she could relax a bit and relish her triumph.

Through her hotel windows in Philadelphia, when she saw a ragged heap below singing piteously for money, she opened her purse and sent Sallie down with the money.

"I never hear a woman sing like that but I think I might have been doing it myself."

A Queen's Progress

(1849–1850)

Charlotte moved down to Philadelphia lulled, it turned out, falsely. If she expected a brass band and welcome home speeches at the Walnut, she overlooked the important fact that the city of brotherly love was the hometown of Edwin Forrest. Stormy applause greeted her entrance, October 29, in *The Stranger,* but an angry press outshouted it next day. Nobody could accuse Forrest directly, but when one paper screamed "anti-American" at her for bringing along the English Couldock to support her, when another paper jeered that England had taught her nothing but Macready's mannerisms, when still another cried that she had come back a wretched "attitudinizer," Charlotte recognized the telltale signs of Forrest's work with the press.

She might have grieved at the bitter hostility if every night eager crowds had failed to jam Walnut Street and overflow round the corner. To reach the stage door she and Sallie forced their way through a crush of people begging for autographs or grimly determined to touch her. On November 8 when the Governor came to see her as Meg, the box office turned away hundreds. Still, if the papers could not ruin her with the Philadelphia public, they cheerfully supported her rough reception backstage. Against herself and Couldock, Charlotte found the Walnut company ranked almost solidly. Her "lofty manner" annoyed them, wrote one reporter; by "her supercilious and ridiculous airs" she meant to show, he supposed, that "her aristocratical associations" in England had forever set her apart from "her poor sisterhood" at home.

Charlotte could waste no thoughts on her "sisterhood." Fanny Kemble and William Macready could grandly disdain the greenroom lest they rub shoulders with mediocrity, but she understood well enough the sullen looks she saw in these lesser faces. An envy all too human had sent them running to the Philadelphia papers. In this light, she could discount the papers' demands that the once "sensible Yankee girl" become herself again. Whether or not she had really brought home a taste for "the ribbon and the star," she had assuredly not come home to apologize for English success. She would cheerfully occupy whatever pedestal existed for talent. If jealousy now accused her of "airs," she would be the star that better critics than these had recognized. If envy accused her now of managing people necessary to her, she would mind the main chance like any good Yankee when opportunity opened.

When her run concluded in late November with the largest receipts ever taken in Philadelphia—neither Forrest nor Macready nor Kean had ever outdrawn her—she could rest content with her victory, secure in the knowledge that whatever fiasco Forrest had planned had come to nothing. Before she left Philadelphia, she took time out to invest in some local real estate. Money put into property now might ease the road ahead if a fickle public ever changed its affections.

Heading for Boston, Charlotte counted her blessings. Couldock had a high temper, but he filled his role well; he did not upstage her. With Matilda at her side, marshaling visitors that daily flocked through her rooms, she could bask in a sense of home and permanence, no matter what the hotel. In Sallie, she had found a maid who could deal with the upsets that always went with travel, late arrivals, lost luggage, damaged stage props, the numberless little reversals that complicated her life. Once on stage when she forgot a speech, she moved to the side where Sallie fed her the lines. In the best New England sense, Sallie had "faculty." In tribute, her last day in Philadelphia she bought a house for Sallie's mother and laid the deed for it in Sallie's hand.

In Boston she would court no risk of failure—either on stage or in the drawing rooms of Boston's best houses. Though the National Theatre was now run by her old childhood friend William Pelby, she rejected it because its location was "unattractive." She also rejected Thorne's Howard Athenaeum because it could not match her terms. When the Boston Theatre raised the price of its tickets to meet her demands, she agreed to play there.

For this, Boston's best critic upbraided her soundly "Acorn" blamed her "ruinous" prices for the fact that her opening as Mrs.

Haller was not jammed. It was a fault of the whole star system, said "Acorn," that a star was able to bleed a town white before moving on, leaving the earnest local company struggling to stay alive. Charlotte saw the weak points in the system; she herself had suffered in her early days at the Park when the regular company played to forlorn-looking, thinly scattered audiences, while the very next week crowds "crushed each other to get a sight of some flippant, well-puffed star." The difference now was the value she could give the crowd's dollar. No flippant pretender, she was now fully aware of her worth as an artist. But she was no longer strictly an artist. Only foolishness ever prompted a businesswoman to sell her wares too cheaply.

Boston paid well for her acting, though "Acorn" raised loud cries against her "Macreadyism," her greater "art and less nature," her rolling eyes and screwing round of the mouth as Lady Macbeth, her Rosalind that was "ungraceful in the extreme."

Against such cries, a lesser talent might have come to doubt her own gifts. Her rough American honesty, her "naturalness" had repelled some London critics. Now, her English "artistry" offended the louder critics in Philadelphia and Boston. The matter finally became clear when she learned that James "Acorn" Oakes and Edwin Forrest had long felt a tender regard for each other. She tossed off the criticism as "friendship" inspired.

Other voices proved friendlier the evening she and Matilda answered Longfellow's summons to dinner at Craigie House. Charlotte accepted the compliment gracefully. From his eminence at Harvard, Longfellow's fame as a poet had become international two years before with his *Evangeline, A Tale of Arcadie*. To be asked to his dignified yellow house in Cambridge was to share a little of Longfellow's own social, intellectual, and artistic grandeur. In a party that included the James Russell Lowells and Frederika Bremer, Charlotte feasted on canvasback ducks, quails, Roman punch, and three American wines. In a sense, the hospitality noted the risen status of the stage in Boston that was partly the fruit of Charlotte's efforts. To Longfellow, she stood now a cultural fact to be recognized, though in private he confessed, regarding her style, "I like less acting better."

For the first time back in America, Charlotte felt the excitement she had known in the vivid conversations at Jane Carlyle's table. In Lowell, whose Yankee *Biglow Papers* were spreading his own fame worldwide, she saw a person a little like herself, another nod to Emerson's challenge to stand forthrightly American before the world. In Miss Bremer, the queer little Swedish novelist in lace cap and ribbons who had come to America to study its women, Charlotte greeted a kindred spirit, a determined champion for greater female recognition. Frederika made mental notes for the report of the meeting she would later publish, praising Charlotte as an "honest, earnest, and powerful soul." If the American actress looked "almost better in private than on the stage," Frederika could credit her "frank, blue eye, the strong intelligent forehead," and the strong opinions she voiced over Longfellow's interesting wine.

Charlotte's return to Boston brought her further rewards when the red-haired Julia Ward Howe, who would reap later fame as a poet of battle hymns, bade her and Couldock to dinner—"Compliments to the Wild British. Bid him surely come." Charlotte saw in the small shapeless Julia a wit that could range all over Greek drama, women's rights, her husband's memories of Byron at war in Turkey.

When Theodore Parker, the Congregationalist minister, called on her backstage, he brought her a copy of Robert Cushman's sermon, "The Sin and Danger of Self Love," in tribute to the success she had achieved beyond Robert's wildest visions. In her conversation with Parker, she recognized the humane zeal behind his *Letter Touching the Matter of Slavery* that had recently bombarded America.

Tributes and invitations were one thing, but more fun just now was reading her box office sheets each day. Getting one's price began with knowing one's worth. She had not been joking when she had frankly labeled this American return a determined campaign to make money. In that sense, the "sensible Yankee girl" had indeed come home.

The flurry of letters she mailed from Boston specified the fees she demanded ahead. Corbyn could handle the bookings, but she herself would negotiate fees. Planning another run in New York, she briefly considered combining her talents with those of a popular ingenue, Jean Davenport. Couldock she could depend on, but nowhere in America had she found an adequate Juliet or a Celia for *As You Like It*. She would pay a fixed income each night to a young actress of talent who could support her creditably. Jean ought to consider "the good it would do her to act with me" before the "peculiar class of people" she could attract.

Her last few nights in Boston, she saw no reason to scotch the rumor that these might be her last appearances. In the theatre, a star's "farewell" exuded a box office magic. To be honest about it, whether she truly meant to retire now or not, the more money she made on this tour, the brighter shone the dream beyond it, the day when she might pursue a different ambition happily free of the upheavals and discomforts of acting.

Looking south, she realized that Theodore Parker's concern over slavery touched Sallie. Arranging her New Orleans engagement for February 1850, Corbyn must determine exactly the troubles she and Sallie might suffer. Did Ludlow and Smith, the managers at the St. Charles, understand that Sallie, a free colored servant girl, must be shown every courtesy? They must "write me clearly on this point directing me how to ensure the girl's safety from arrest or stoppage." In addition, their accommodations must be in a private house, away from the crowds that would dog Charlotte's steps at a hotel.

She would make the best of the crude trains and slow boats. If pioneers just now could brave a savage continent in the clumsiest covered wagons, she would not complain that American trains were hardly the speedy facilities she had enjoyed in England, though riding west through Pennsylvania and Ohio, she knew that Dickens had not wholly exaggerated his "agonies" on American trains, roaring pell-mell down the middle of dusty streets, hissing, screeching, scattering sparks over oblivious pigs and screaming horses and children. Inside the shabby hot cars, men sat crowded in seats back to back, smoking and spitting, making travel almost intolerable for fastidious people. At the numerous places where they had been forced to change trains, rude trainmen had thrust their heads into the car to cry, "Come out to the baggage car and tend to your plunder!"

Beyond Cincinnati Charlotte and her party fared better, relaxing as best they could aboard the puffing steamboat that threatened any moment to explode. Charlotte tried not to think about the human suffering that helped smooth her passage south. By the light of pine torches at night she watched the sweating black faces "wooding up," easing their work at times with dolorous song. By day she and Sallie caught fearful glimpses of light-skinned mulattoes below decks, sitting listless and dumb in fetters meant to foil their escape.

In the years since Charlotte had first known New Orleans, flames had taken the splendid St. Charles and the fortunes of James H. Caldwell, but Noah Ludlow and Sol Smith had rebuilt it. It was to this "clean, bright, and beautiful" theatre that Charlotte directed her steps. Rumbling along in her carriage, she glimpsed an occasional familiar shop front, an iron tracery decorating a window, but what caught her eye now were the playbills plastering her route. "Our Charlotte" Cushman had returned to the city that had first recognized in a frightened beginner the attributes of a star.

The Heart's Conviction and
Early Retirement

(1850–1852)

"Genius!" cried the *Picayune*. "Extraordinary vocal power!" cried the *Bee,* recanting its old sting about Charlotte's voice. Reading the words to Sallie, Charlotte found a happy reminder of the favor these New Orleans people had done her so many years before. Their goodwill now was a heartening send-off for the run she was beginning.

Throughout the run, whether she played the tattered gypsy, the spirited Rosalind, or Lady Macbeth, Charlotte set off frenzied applause. Even in *The Stranger,* a play which the *Picayune* man dismissed as "sickly" and sentimental, she seemed able to do no wrong. Her sufferings as Mrs. Haller were stunningly real. Rarely had an actress played in New Orleans who could manage her voice so superbly, said the *Picayune*. "Rich and melodious by nature," its inflections enabled her to utter every variation of feeling, "so that each pulsation, every throb of the heart, is reflected." It was her "sobs and sighs, and groans, rather than the text of the play-wright, which elicited the applause of the audience by touching their sympathies."

Backstage, affairs were no less happy. Charlotte's early ties with Macready might have handicapped her with Ludlow and Smith, who still bore scars from his blasts against them in 1844 for ignoring the business outlined in his promptbooks. To Macready's shouts of "Stupid!" Ludlow had stomped off to his office: Mr. Macready could say anything else "in writing!" But Charlotte was too much a professional to explode in a fury when the St. Charles people needed coaching. Like Macready, she had sent her acting copies ahead with her instructions penciled in carefully, but she knew the value of tact when rough spots still showed up in rehearsals. The St. Charles people were craftsmen, unlike the sorry lot at the Walnut.

Charlotte's tact and hard work paid off. Her twenty-seven nights in New Orleans were the longest run ever known in the city; she had played to greater receipts than even Macready. Couldock himself had pleased New Orleans: As the Stranger he had performed "remarkably well." Writing Henry Chorley the news, Charlotte figured she ought soon to be able to return to England at least thirty thousand pounds richer, ready to live the best life her brilliant American success could afford. Already she yearned for the elegance of Mayfair, the conversation, poise, and grace of her Portnam Square rooms.

Playing Mobile and Savannah, the rawness and laziness she saw everywhere in the South irked her. She and Matilda tried vainly to find any bookshop that carried Longfellow, when in every village in England they could have bought him easily. Jogging along the roads through the plantations, she tried not to see the slave gangs. At distances, half-hidden in the clumps of great oaks that framed them, she glimpsed the white-columned, baronial homes of the planters, proud riders in white panamas and black string ties she passed on the roads. The ragged small towns passed in a blur of pigs running loose, of unpainted wooden houses and sagging fences, of Negro children swarming about their mothers in red bandannas. When April found her in Charleston, the town's "flattest month of the year," she gritted her teeth, then refused to play to half-empty houses for a "not over-courteous" manager and determined to push on north.

By the time she had weathered the bouncing stagecoaches and stuffy trains to Washington, she was thoroughly homesick for England and happy to find proof again that some parts of the country, at least, were civilized. Driving along Washington's muddy, catalpa-lined streets, she could imagine the city that might one day enhance the banks of the Potomac. Already a square stub of marble promised the day when a soaring white shaft would honor the nation's first president. Already the gaunt iron ribs of a dome were rising over Capitol Hill. But as yet Washington's 50,000 people had only sketched the broad outlines of a city.

At the Adelphi Theatre, on May 1, she set off the usual cheers as Meg Merrilies. Next night, gripping her daggers, her Lady Macbeth electrified the audience; her tone, the expression of her face, her manner were "peculiarly fine."

But for the money, Philadelphia interested her more, a fact made plain in the card the manager of the Arch Street Theatre published a day or so before she arrived. "The enormous expense attending Miss Cushman's engagement" required him, said E. S. Connor, to ask a favor: would his box holders please use their own boxes and not fill up the front seats which he could otherwise sell? To avoid raising prices, even though he had hired "first-rate, celebrated auxiliaries" for Miss Cushman's run, he must suspend his "free list" entirely.

However much she cost Connor, "satisfactory" was Charlotte's own word for the flood of dollars she pocketed in Philadelphia. Now she could face her month at the Astor Place Opera House in New York more calmly, if not fully sure she was wise to appear with an English actor where blood had flowed in protest over English talents "dominating" the American stage.

Standing tense in the wings at the Astor Place the night of May 13, Charlotte dreaded the reception she and Couldock might soon meet. Remembering the furious cries and hisses that had boiled up here last May when Macready came on stage was all too fearfully easy. Tonight, who could predict what trouble might be brewing? Sallie had taken a peek through the curtains and come back smiling: There were no angry banners in sight, no ominous bundles that might spell rotten eggs and vegetables. Still, no one could know anything until the curtains parted and she and Couldock appeared.

The ordeal was over in a few minutes. When Charlotte bounded on stage, the applause was courteous enough; the crowd sat hushed and enthralled while her Romeo poured out his rising passion. If Couldock's Mercutio offended anyone's flaming patriotism, apparently Charlotte's triumph in London, her victory over the English on their own ground, was enough to allay the fires. A year had been long enough for tempers to cool. On June 1 the *Prompter* labeled the whole engagement "brilliant." To Charlotte's old standby, the *Spirit of the Times,* her Rosalind was "swashing," "martial," the best Rosalind one could imagine. "We are delighted to have our countrywoman acknowledged as the best actress in her line in the land."

From the Astor Place she moved on to Niblo's Garden, expecting to act the remainder of June, but when frantic word came from Susan, she canceled her contract and took the first ship to Liverpool. Susan's baby daughter, Ida, was on the point of death from some unexplained illness. She stayed three weeks with Susan and Sheridan, offering what comfort she could. When the baby began to recover, she took full advantage of the time to become reacquainted with young Ned, now twelve and strangely unhappy and sullen in Sheridan Muspratt's house. Charlotte tried to plumb the cause of Ned's trouble, but nothing came clear.

She acted two nights in Liverpool, then sailed for home. The September night she arrived back in New York she acted again at Niblo's, a fact which proved to one paper that the Atlantic was, after all, becoming little more than a bridge. To welcome her back, a sellout crowd jammed the Garden, "compelling the curious to perch on chairtops for a view of the stage."

In September, she moved on to Boston to fill a round at the Howard Athenaeum and relax between times at the new Tremont House, with its lavish decor, its baths, and its unique indoor water closets. Amid comforts like none she had enjoyed since England, Charlotte welcomed a new round of visits from the bright lights of Boston. When Longfellow called and found her away at rehearsal, he stayed on to chat with Matilda about her George Sand translations. "You ought to go to England," Matilda told him. "You are much more known and honored there than in this country." As a proof, Matilda cited their vain search for any of his books in a Southern store.

On a day free of rehearsals, Charlotte and Matilda accepted Emerson's summons to Concord to meet John Greenleaf Whittier —to bemoan together the evils of slavery, to reminisce with Emerson over their distant days at Second Church, to recall their bright friends, the Carlyles. Another day they called on Longfellow at Craigie House. A "very agreeable" visit it was, the poet told his journal. She happily arranged theatre tickets for Mrs. Horace Mann, Nathaniel Hawthorne's sister-in-law. She could only get places rather high up, but since it was a matinee, "there will be only nice people all over the house," she wrote Mary, "so you will not be incommoded in that respect."

Between all the socializing and work, Charlotte filled her time with business, detailed letters about the terms under which she would act, conferences with E. A. Marshall, who wanted to book her for New York and Philadelphia. But Marshall's proposal to share the profits with her after box office takes of $200 in New York and $100 in Philadelphia was "out of the question."

"You shall either give me half after $100 or a clear half of five nights and I will act for nothing on the sixth, or you shall give me $250 per night, and this is the best I can possibly do!"

Marshall's reply was clear. "I don't think I can afford it, but I will think of it. I had rather give a certainty, but it is too much."

She could take her time with Marshall. "You can think of it and let me know this week. It is immaterial to me whether I act in NY or not this fall."

With or without Marshall, she could avoid returning to New York just now. P. T. Barnum's protégée, Jenny Lind, had arrived from Sweden on September 7 and had touched off a popular storm. Seated behind Barnum in an open carriage, nearly smothered in flowers, the fabulous, golden-haired Jenny had moved grandly up Canal Street. Near-riots had broken out at the box office the day her tickets were placed on sale; for her first American concert, Castle Garden packed in over 6,000 people at $5 per head.

Looking beyond New York, Charlotte wondered how Jenny Lind's national tour might affect her own drawing power—how much appetite America still had for a native daughter's acting when it could feed on Jenny's glorious, bird-like singing. It might help to arm herself with another novelty. What about playing Romeo one night and switching the next to Juliet? If Fanny Kemble was not too old and fat to do Juliet, "I am sure I am not," she wrote William Fredericks. "I think a good deal of interest and curiosity might be excited."

She mentioned the idea to a crowd of friends in her rooms, among them Hawthorne, Charles Sumner, and Longfellow's brother-in-law, Tom Appleton, but when nobody took her seriously, she let the matter drop. The talk turned instead to Appleton's witty comments on the Brownings and to Hawthorne's new book, *The Scarlet Letter,* and the wide sale it was enjoying. The talk turned too to the delights Bostonians were finding in winter treks to warm, sunny Rome. More and more sober consciences were persuading themselves that one ought, if one could, to get away from the useless pains of blizzards and snow.

Busy again in Philadelphia, Charlotte soon wished she had pushed through her plan to play Juliet. The night of November 8 saw a performance at the Walnut, cried one paper, that Philadelphia would long remember with "shame and disgust." Why Marshall let the play go on, why she herself did not ring down the curtain, Charlotte could not later imagine, for by the end of the first act it was clear to players and audience alike that Fanny Wallack (Lester Wallack's aunt), the night's delicate Juliet, was gloriously drunk. By the end of act three, Fanny's hiccuping and giggling had made the play a shambles. A minute or so before the curtain, she stopped still, made one great sweep of her outstretched arms, then fell flat on her face, tangled and kicking in her draperies. The crowd burst into yells and laughter, and stagehands carried her off, her swollen red face shrieking. Watching it all, Charlotte stood dumb and helpless. Her own Juliet might have been a little unfeminine, but it could hardly have been so tasteless.

Surely, nothing worse could befall the tour she now began with a run in Pittsburgh and a river circuit through Cincinnati and Louisville to New Orleans. Despite Fanny Wallack, her crowded houses in Philadelphia had averaged $500 per night. Yet her disgust at Fanny brought home the fact, all too clearly, that there was no real guarantee against such things in the profession she had chosen. She wrote W. S. Fredericks, her friend from her days as manager at the Walnut, that she was thinking of quitting the stage for good. What advice could he give her about making a formal farewell some months hence?

On this new sally into the hinterland she would miss having Couldock's support. By now, the actor had achieved a certain fame, and he frankly confessed that he no longer wished to play second fiddle. Charlotte was not wholly sorry. Playing opposite Couldock of late, she had thoroughly tired of his temper. On stage he still served her well, but backstage and during rehearsals, his explosions shot off more and more fire. In Philadelphia she knew she no longer wished to tour with an actor who could fly into rages at another's simple mistakes. When a Salanio in *The Merchant of Venice* muffed some lines, Couldock ordered him to his dressing room.

"You played Salanio last night?"

"Yes, sir."

"And your name is, er . . . ?"

"Ogden, sir," the actor replied, nervously.

"Ah, yes, Ogden. Well, how long have you been at it, Ogden?"

"About three years," he answered, feeling easier.

"Three years, huh! Well, will you let me give you a bit of advice,

Ogden." Suddenly, Couldock's voice rose to a fury. "You take some money . . . and you go to a hardware store. And you buy a good sharp hatchet and then I want you to take it home and chop your damn fool head off!"

With that, Couldock made a furious leap at the actor and fell to clouting him over the head. The scene was worthy of an Edwin Forrest.

Thinking about Couldock took Charlotte back to her timorous first days in England and the progress the years had brought. She could rate her professional life "satisfactory." She had learned to value herself with managers; her skill in the game was making her comfortably rich. Yet, one phase of her life was far from easy. In many ways, Matilda was a disappointment. Her "nerves" often made her difficult; she often complained that nobody understood her. About that Charlotte could be sympathetic. She could imagine how burdensome life must be to a person whose hunger for fame had simply outrun her talents. She didn't know what could or should be done about Matilda, but her quiet vexation with her perhaps explained the grief Charlotte encountered in Cincinnati. Rehearsing long hours with shoddy acting companies, she had long ago learned to clench her teeth and suffer in silence, but nothing had prepared her for Conrad Clarke, a young stock actor at the National, who soon impressed her as the "cleverest young man I have seen." Clarke's Orlando packed a fire and a steely grace that astonished her.

Before long, her astonishment turned to something deeper. Playing opposite Clarke, bandying Shakespeare's tender words with this red-lipped young man, Charlotte sensed in herself a growing uneasiness. Were her sleeplessness and her boredom with Matilda signs that deep inside her a woman's heart lay sleeping, in unguessed readiness for some vibrant man's animal charm? In spite of all she had told herself about any actress' need to keep her heart free, had the time come to abandon that lonely conviction?

Talking earnestly backstage with Clarke, letting him escort her back to her hotel, Charlotte felt herself succumb more and more to his charm. He had grown up a Quaker, he told her, the proper son of Philadelphians who had opposed with pleas and head shakings his wish to become an actor, but the fire inside him had made him do what he must. To all this Charlotte nodded her understanding. Day after day, when Clarke knocked on her door, she sent Sallie away on some idle errand, then sat curled and quiet on her sofa while Clarke told her his dreams and plans. The talks became the highpoint of her day. Looking forward to them, she could imagine the time when, to this beautiful young man sprawled in his chair, his boots propped on her footstool, she might bare more of her heart than she had to any other man.

To Sallie and Matilda she said nothing. And they said nothing to her. If the company noticed the softening in Charlotte's manner, they gave no sign. Yet a stock actress guessed her feelings one night in the wings when, talking to Charlotte, she suddenly asked, "What of all things in this world, Miss Cushman, would you rather be?"

A few steps off, Clarke stood bantering the pretty actress whom the company all called "the poodle dog" for the way she wore her hair. Glancing at Clarke, Charlotte sighed: "I would rather be a pretty woman than anything else in this wide, wide world." Then hearing her cue, she rushed on stage to shriek and moan as the ragged Meg Merrilies.

A night or so before the Cincinnati engagement ended, Charlotte decided she might have been hasty in planning a complete retirement. Once back in England, she might go on acting at times—but only as the spirit moved her. To have a dependable talent opposite her, she might take along Conrad Clarke. He already knew how much she admired his talent, how deep her interest in him extended. When she ventured the matter to Clarke, his "Yes!" made her almost foolishly happy. Any plan so obviously good for her career could hardly be bad for her heart.

Through intuition and the evidence she had seen on stage of Clarke's acting ability, Charlotte knew all she wanted to know about him; nobody had told her anything. Yet she learned the rest soon enough. Between scenes one night, she was just entering her dressing room, when she heard a woman's voice say quietly, "You are Charlotte Cushman, the great actress?"

When Charlotte turned, she found a strange huddled figure holding a child in her arms. The woman looked at her, then tearfully poured out a torrent of words: "Haven't you got enough men to admire you without coming between husband and wife? And robbing me of my husband?" Charlotte looked her full in the face. "Who is your husband?" "Conrad Clarke, the father of this child," she answered.

Charlotte stared at her, unbelieving. There was no reply she could give the woman. She grasped the doorjamb. Fame had opened broader ranges of joy and richer rewards than she had ever envisioned, but suddenly, it tasted hateful and sour. She asked the woman to wait until she could finish the play.

At its curtain, she sent Sallie to bring Clarke to her. When he knocked, she opened the door. She said nothing to him, but—battling the tears that stood ready to flow—she swept a hand toward the woman and child. The shock, then the anger that flashed in Clarke's face told her all she needed. When he began angrily berating the woman for coming, when he turned to Charlotte, stuttering in his rage, she faced him, seeing him now caught in his trick. He had, of course, made her no commitments; there had been no real avowals of anything. Yet the hours he had spent with her, laying open his dreams, had seemed so much more than an actor's ambition, so truly a proof of regard that tears seemed the only possible comment. But she held her pose. As coldly as if she were waving Cardinal Wolsey aside, she dismissed the wretched Clarke and his family. Only after she heard the door close did she let herself slump in her chair, turn to her glass to face the bleak crumpled reflection.

As quickly as possible, Charlotte turned her back on Cincinnati, richer by $5,000 for her eighteen nights' work—and wiser. Writing Fred from Louisville, her tone told more than her words. "My labours are much more fatiguing than they were last year, for I have to teach every new Macbeth, and Wolsey, etc. etc., and I go into the theatre at 10 o'clock, remaining until 3, teaching people how to act, and at night they are just as bad as though I had not taught them." The routine allowed her no time for rest: "I am almost worn out with it." She blamed Clarke for nothing.

Humiliated, angry only at her stupidity, she recalled words she had not said to herself since Rosalie's death, words about actors throttling their personal feelings to have energy left for their roles. She could muster no interest beyond the definite farewell she determined anew to make soon, to put an end once and for all to the tricks and pretenses that acting made her prey to. An announced formal farewell could do her pocket no harm—and more importantly, it could free her forever from all further risks to her heart.

To add to her pain, she knew by the time she left Cincinnati that her booking agent, Corbyn, had given her wrong travel schedules and bungled acting dates farther down river—all because, she concluded, she had paid him beforehand. The fact merely confirmed what she had long suspected. No man could really be trusted. Of all the men she had ever known, which one had ever had brains—or feelings?

Reports from Philadelphia brought her a vengeful joy. Edwin Forrest's sins were finding him out at last. His wife, Catherine, was spreading the ugly story that after the Astor Place Riot, Forrest had actually sent money to Boston to foment further trouble for Macready. Hearing other terrible facts his wife was divulging about him daily, Charlotte felt only more certain than ever that marriage could never make sense for a player. She told herself that marriage to Conrad Clarke—even if he had been the man she had thought he was— would have proved a disaster.

Acting Mrs. Haller one night farther down river, she knew again how desperately she wanted to quit acting. The blundering manager, unable to find two white children to appear in the play's last scene, and without telling her anything, met the emergency by sending on two little Negroes. She almost dropped her lines when she saw them, but since the audience seemed willing to accept the matter, she played on. But at the moment when the children were led up to the elaborate cage-like arbor—there to wait out of sight until the meeting between Mrs. Haller and the Stranger—first one terrified child, then the other, cried, "Me won't be put in de calaboose! Me won't be put in de calaboose!"

When nothing could stop their cries and yells and the audience broke up laughing, the green curtain had to come down prematurely and the play hobbled along without them. Charlotte determined then that any time she ever played Mrs. Haller again her contract would specify white children, or else.

When a painful hoarseness waylaid her in Louisville, she suffered again all the pangs that knowing Clarke had brought her. Days later, miserable with a bilious colic, she faced again the big question. With a purse full of money, what madness could prompt her to keep on acting? Why shouldn't she take her fame and comfortable gains and retire—with the easy conscience that her hard work had long since justified?

"I wish I could get a few bottles of Mrs. Haydon's gin," she wrote Fred. Perhaps he could forward a case to New Orleans by one of the California steamers. Her aching throat was a real problem now; the gin might help her relax.

Thoughout her run in New Orleans late in January 1851, her throat continued to trouble her. At times, her voice left her completely. Until just before curtain time, she could only speak in whispers; some nights the curtain was rising before she could talk at all. With this added worry, surely it was pointless to keep on. Besides, she knew the full truth now about acting, the tricks and shams, the dingy paraphernalia that made up what the public called "theatrical splendour." Much as she had once objected, Macready and Fanny Kemble were right; sooner or later, any sane person must doubt the "properness" of theatre. Contemplating the clean, dispassionate life she meant to live in London, she could feel no sense of mission, no pride in being a working woman. Whatever ambition had fired her once had gone out.

The crowds she drew in New Orleans brought her no lift. Though she was the "great card of the season," only fair houses turned out to see her. Her fear of Jenny Lind's following her west had proved right. Too many people were saving their money until Jenny could arrive in town, almost on her heels. The press' reaction to her own work, its lack of sympathy and complete unconcern for her troublesome throat, only deepened her gloom. One paper scoffed at her "violence, her startling attitudes and grimaces, her screaming tones." It would have only troubled her more to know that one woman, Charlotte's last night, had to be carried out and put to bed, Meg Merrilies had worked so hard on her nerves.

Yet gloomy or not, Charlotte would not let herself be mistreated. When P. T. Barnum wrote ahead to St. Louis, wanting to book a hall for a Jenny Lind concert—the hall that was already booked for Charlotte—she made her stand crystal clear. "I shall not object to giving up the nights required by Mr. Barnum . . . upon consideration of being paid two hundred and fifty dollars ($250) per night for so doing, which is the positive worth of those nights to me."

Reading a London paper, Charlotte found that a famous farewell to the stage had just taken place, at the very time her own thoughts about retiring stood uppermost. For all the irritations he had caused her, she read with envy the news that Macready had at last relinquished his crown. On February 26, 1851, he had played his last Macbeth, happy at fifty-eight to be free of all the vexations that acting had brought him. Macready had stayed in character to the last. Making his final exit from the Drury Lane stage, he had admonished his servant to hold the curtain close about him, lest he be annoyed by the good-byes of "those actors."

The Heart's Conviction and Early Retirement

When Charlotte read some weeks later a note of her current high status in England, she felt sure her own proper time had arrived. "In kindling and uniting the heart of a whole audience—in transmitting a stream of fire through a thousand brains at once, till they vibrate to her own, Miss Cushman has no superior," said *Tallis's Dramatic* magazine. The American actress outdistanced all English rivalry and "challenged even Rachel." If such was her reputation, what better time could she find to retire—once she had given proper notice? She would begin now to let the impression circulate that any who wished to see the great Charlotte Cushman on stage should not let the opportunity pass.

She kept that thought fresh throughout the season of 1851 and into the next, though she refused to let her plan work any effect on the quality she presented on stage. In Nashville, she might have let herself fluff through an accident. Instead, something of the old fire in her capitalized on it. Reading Macbeth's letter, she had only spoken the words, "Glamis thou art, and Cawdor, and shalt be What thou art promised," when she tangled a heel in her train and fell, sprawling. In fearful silence, the audience watched her cover the fall, not quite sure it had been an accident. She raised herself slowly, set one hand firmly on the boards, and gazed at the letter in her other hand. Then slowly she rose to a kneeling position and continued speaking. At her words, "Hie thee hither," she leaped to her feet, fully in character, to finish the speech with all the force it required. The crowd burst into cheers.

Covering the fall had felt good. Momentarily, an old excitement flowed through her, the art required in playing a part without losing herself in it. Falling, she had sensed immediately that Lady Macbeth would have been far more interested in the letter's dread words than in any foolish loss of balance. As Lady Macbeth, she had merely continued building the role.

Later, playing Meg, she could laugh when her terrible force left the actor playing Dirk Hatterick overpowered and dumb. "Well, sir, go on with the dialogue," she said finally to rouse him. When the actor apologized after the curtain—"The wonderful power of your acting completely upset me. I was no longer Dirk Hatterick, but a powerless thrall in your possession"—she accepted the compliment. "But please don't let me make you forget your business."

Nor did she suggest in New York in June the thoughts that now occupied her. At Castle Garden, she took the rehearsal for *Guy Mannering* into her own hands when the conductor failed to maintain the timing. After asking him twice to stop playing his violin and beat out the time with his stick, she at last walked down to the footlights, reached over and took the offending instrument, then marched up and down, calling the tempo and beating the time with her heels.

On July 30 in Chicago her Mrs. Haller left the *Journal* convinced that something much deeper than pretense had figured in Charlotte's acting. Her Meg overwhelmed the paper's young critic. What he had meant to analyze, he found himself responding to emotionally, his mission forgotten in "the wild and loving, the imperious and reed-like Meg Merrilies." The actress had attained the heights of art by concealing her art completely.

After another brief run in New York at John Brougham's Lyceum Theatre, playing La Tisbe in Smith's *Actress of Padua,* Charlotte directed her tired steps back to Boston. Planning her Boston appearances, she meant no arrogance when she wrote J. B. Wright, the National Theatre manager: "I really have not the courage to act with novices." Nor did she overlook in this Boston run another chance to make money. She hoped Wright would approve her opening as Bianca in *Fazio.* "I can do more for you and myself, with it than anything else, provided it is announced as the character of which I made my first great success in London, and now acted for the first time in Boston since my return from Europe."

Heading for Boston, she stopped long enough in Albany to confront an old grief. In the years since Augustus' death, she and Mary Eliza had never decided about a final burial place for the body; the casket had remained in careful storage. She determined now to send it to Boston for burial beside Elkanah. That done, she faced another family problem. Ever since her quick trip to Liverpool, she had felt a growing sympathy for Susan's boy Ned. Whether Sheridan was too strict a disciplinarian, whether the stepfather resented the boy, hostility smoldered between them. Reading Susan's worried letters, she had hit on a plan. Carefully, tactfully, she broached it: Would Susan let her adopt Ned?

In retirement, she could give the boy a solid homelife. With all her new money, she could buy him whatever he needed. With all her free time, she could lavish on him every attention. She could free him, once and for all, from whatever feelings he had about not being wanted. When Susan wrote her consent, Charlotte joyously took the bold step. Under the laws of New York, his birthplace, Ned became Edwin Charles Cushman, her legally adopted son. As soon as she returned to England, Ned could join her and, under her lead, grow up—if her plans worked out—along the lines his nature and her good sense and experience dictated. Signing the papers, she felt in her heart a new joy; she saw her future take on a new brightness. Until now she had not dared confess to herself or anyone else the emptiness in her life that this child of her own could fill.

Arriving in Boston, she took Longfellow the Spanish moss she had brought him from Louisiana, then rushed off to rehearsals. She missed his return call, but the poet stayed on for a talk with Matilda, noting the sadness he saw now in Matilda's face, "some bitterness, as of disappointment," he guessed. Another day she missed Julia Ward Howe, but business and her plans for Ned and England were far more interesting than mere social rounds.

In her rare leisure, Charlotte fell to planning the kind of retirement she wanted. She would take her lead from old Samuel Rogers and fill her house with the wittiest people, the best talk and books and art she could afford. On acting days, she still gave her best to the play, though as Romeo one afternoon, she almost had to give more. With Sarah Anderton as Juliet, she had just finished one of her tenderest speeches when somebody's crude sneeze, clearly a cat-call, broke the mood. Immediately, Charlotte stopped the scene, glared out into the dark hall toward a flurry of smothered laughter, then laid a protective arm about Juliet's shoulders and led the lady to safety. Then, still in character, she returned to face the offender across the footlights. Facing the crowd, Charlotte peered again toward the sneezer. Then she commanded, "Some man must put that person out, or I shall be obliged to do it myself!" Immediately the crowd rose, cheering, while men lifted the struggling culprit over their heads and carried him out of the hall. When the uproar subsided, Romeo shepherded Juliet back onto the stage and continued the play.

Partly to enliven these later days before she retired forever, Charlotte took on another new role. If she felt comfortable as Romeo, why not try Hamlet? First in Boston, then on November 24 in New York, she came on stage to brood through the long hours Hamlet needed to make up his mind. The public gave mixed reactions. Some said, "bizarre," a "mongrel performance." Others accepted the illusion readily enough, though the real good that came from the effort was the fact that it helped speed up her time.

In Boston, no one had watched her with more excitement than a twenty-year-old girl who came in each afternoon from Watertown.

Harriet Hosmer left the theatre ecstatic. "You have no idea how splendid Hamlet was. I used to think Lady Macbeth the finest thing that could be done, but Queen Katharine shook my foundations and Hamlet overturned it! It was grand."

When a friend brought the girl backstage, Charlotte set her down for a talk. Something about Harriet was immediately captivating: her laugh, her quick humor, the spirited way she tossed her head and combed back her short, brown curls with her fingers, as boys did, the way she sketched in the air something she was trying to say. When Harriet declared she meant to become a sculptor, Charlotte listened earnestly. After the visit, the girl wrote a friend in St. Louis: "Isn't it strange how we meet people in this world and become attached to them in so short a time?"

Before long Charlotte knew Harriet's full story: her mother, two brothers, and a sister had died of tuberculosis. Her father, hoping to toughen her, had taught her to ride and swim and ice-skate as well as a boy. Attending school in Lenox she had become a favorite of the town's famous resident, Fanny Kemble. A schoolmate from St. Louis, the daughter of Wayman Crow, had helped her gain admission to the St. Louis Medical School to study human anatomy—in hopes that she might one day carve figures in marble. Back home in Watertown, Harriet had busied herself ever since, modeling small figures in clay, dreaming of the day when wider doors might open.

Looking at Harriet's clay squirrels and birds and cherubs, sensing that this was no ordinary talent, Charlotte determined to help the spirited girl. In the chance, she saw a beautiful recompense for the early favors she herself had received. Perhaps when she came back to Boston, she told Harriet, she could suggest a plan. Bidding Charlotte good-bye, Harriet felt "as if I had lost my best friend."

The interest Charlotte took in Harriet helped her through a rough time with Ned. Once his adoption was final, she wrote the boy that she would help him obtain whatever education he wanted. She had hoped he would choose some school in London near her, but the boy told her his heart was set on the United States Navy. Would Auntie help him get an appointment to the Naval Academy? After an engagement in Philadelphia, disappointed but reconciled to the fact that this adopted son had no real intention of ever living with her, she moved on to Washington to see New York Senator William H. Seward, who might help her swing Ned's appointment.

By the time she left Washington the middle of January 1852, she had the matter secure, and in Senator Seward she had found a new friend. Something in her had immediately sensed a kindred spirit in this witty, garrulous man with the long beaked nose and side whiskers. If she returned to Washington in the spring, she assured him she would gladly accept Mrs. Seward's invitation to visit them at their house on Lafayette Square, near the White House.

With Ned's affairs settled, Charlotte could bring her days in America to a close. She had come home to reap as much money as possible, and by mid-spring she was almost content. She had put some of her earnings in Philadelphia real estate; she had arranged with New York investors about putting more of her money to work. After farewells in Boston, New York, and Philadelphia she could return to England, confident that she had made her time in the States pay.

When she mentioned a New York farewell in March to John Brougham, he objected to her high terms. Edwin Forrest and his wife had been fighting each other for months in a highly publicized divorce trial. At its end Forrest stood a proved adulterer. Catherine, the injured victim, quickly returned to the stage to capitalize on the ugly publicity. Sympathetic crowds packed her theatre, and Brougham doubted just now how much any other actress could draw. In reply, Charlotte curtly refused either to lower her terms or to work with anyone who dared suggest that alongside Catherine Sinclair "any *after* affair would fall far short." None too heartily, Charlotte hoped that Brougham might "secure a more attractive feature than you seem to consider, yours very truly, Charlotte Cushman."

The urge to cut herself free of all such tasteless connections merely spurred her determination to get on with her plan. In Boston the first week in March she took sweet satisfaction in reading the playbills the National Theatre had plastered about: "Farewell engagement of Miss Charlotte Cushman! The highly gifted American artiste . . . being positively her farewell engagement in Boston prior to her final retirement from the Stage."

So it was official. Urgent regrets on every hand might attempt to dissuade her, but her mind was made up. The pattern her life would follow and the places she would live it were now nobody's business but hers. She had not dismissed Boston's drawing room talks about the endless delights of sunny Rome. When a Boston doctor assured her that her chronic hoarseness would improve only if she sought a milder climate, she saw her way open. She would return to London— free forever from the blistering heat that every household in America seemed to worship—renew her English friendships, then in the late fall wend her way south to Italy.

Looking ahead toward Rome, she answered a recent letter from Mazzini, the Italian patriot she had met at Jane Carlyle's. Mazzini had heard of her plan to come to Rome. Would Miss Cushman kindly contribute some money, however little, to further his campaign for Italian unification? She sent him the money, then drove out to Watertown. Would the good Dr. Hosmer let Harriet go with her to Rome to study with some famous sculptor? Surrounded by Rome's treasure of marbles and classic ruins, inspired by the city's "artistic air," who could guess what success Harriet might achieve? When the Wayman Crows in St. Louis pledged their financial help to Harriet, Charlotte's plans were complete. She and Matilda, with Harriet in tow, would make their first big venture into the life of the idle rich.

In Washington to visit the Sewards, she mentioned her plans to the popular journalist Sara Jane Clarke, who wrote under the pseudonym "Grace Greenwood," and soon she had added the red-haired Grace to the party of "jolly female bachelors" she would lead on Rome. Another idea struck her: decorating her London walls with portraits, she ought to feature the Americans who best accounted for the heights American culture was reaching. When Grace wrote Hawthorne about it, he sent a graceful reply: "I wish my reputation, such as it is, had come earlier, so that my face might have been in request while it had the grace of youth. . . . However, after the impression of her own face, which Miss Cushman has indelibly stamped on my remembrance, she has a right to do just what she pleases with mine. I am gratified that she wishes it." When Longfellow also agreed to sit for a portrait, Charlotte wrote him gratefully. Should he ever visit England again, he would find himself proudly displayed "among my Penates."

She told Philadelphia a brief good-bye in early May to a flood of bouquets, despite some objections that as Lady Macbeth she had painted "the thoughts and words too closely," pulled too explicitly at her breasts when speaking the line, "I have given suck, and know How tender 'tis to love the babe that milks me."

Her farewell to New York must serve as her national good-bye. For the last time in America, she would play her round of characters, pack up her promptbooks and costumes, and make her exit. Partly to round out these fruitful two years at home, she persuaded Couldock to leave his tour long enough to support her. Before she left for the theatre the night of May 15, 1852, she penned her feelings: "Tonight is my last of labours. I am more glad, heartily glad, than I can tell you, for I am weary beyond description."

New York could remember her as Meg Merrilies. The press next day echoed the applause. "Her dying scene, can we ever forget that?" For a moment, the *Spirit of the Times* could doubt the meaning of her good-bye, "which, it is said, is the last she will play in this city prior to her return to England, in which country she will take her farewell of the stage and retire forever from the profession." Reading the doubt, Charlotte savored again the rich taste of the word. Parting was such sweet sorrow.

With Ned safely arrived from England, tall now and fine-featured like his mother, Charlotte took him to Annapolis, proud that he wanted her to help him enroll, sad next day that the proud young man in his new midshipman's cap and stiff collar could dismiss her with such a brisk, manly good-bye. To cover the hurt, she turned her thoughts toward people who needed her help. Before she sailed from New York on July 16, 1852, she finished her plans for Harriet Hosmer. Hattie and her father would join her in Paris in the fall; then with Matilda and Grace Greenwood they would make their way toward the mecca of all serious artists, Rome.

Now, aboard the steamship *Asia,* Charlotte waved her last to the crowd on the dock. In her pocket she carried ample dollars for the years stretching ahead. Stowed below were her new portraits of Charles Sumner, Longfellow, and Hawthorne, and the large present of books Hawthorne had sent down from Boston. Only when a sudden blast from the whistle rang up the plank did another emotion flow through her. She confessed it to no one, not even Sallie, but was her "farewell" sounding a note too final? A week short of thirty-six, could she be sure she would never regret this "irrevocable" good-bye?

Dolce Far Niente in Rome

(1852–1853)

Charlotte promenaded the deck each morning, nodding to the other passengers, pleased at their silence when they recognized her. The woman they saw was tall and matronly now, her bonnet set square on brown hair pulled tight at the sides of an angular face and tucked under at the point of the ears. Sweeping past in her white pleated blouse and black skirts, she exuded impatience.

Arrived in Liverpool, Charlotte sent Matilda on to London, then relaxed at Susan and Sheridan's new country house, Rose Hill Hall, to savor afresh the splendor of English wealth, the grace of deer parks and gardens, the disdain in Susan's elegant friends for the faceless army of lackeys and maids that kept them comfortable. Wherever she moved in the Muspratt circle, the perfection of English service struck her anew. Not even Sallie, for all her loyalty and skill, had ever been so humbly obliging, but then Sallie had long since become much more than the usual maid. Her strong opinions might surprise Charlotte at times, especially her frank distaste for the fawning attention that swirled around fame, but between them had grown a working relationship that far exceeded the ordinary ties between mistress and servant. Charlotte never discounted the solidarity that hard-headed Sallie lent to her life. When she signed herself "Charlotte" in the occasional notes she slipped in Sallie's mirror, when Sallie failed to call her "Miss" Charlotte, neither one misunderstood.

Grace Greenwood was already in London. Charlotte wrote her, giving her detailed suggestions about places to go, people to see—had Grace met old Sam Rogers or Chorley?—plays and concerts she would surely find worth writing about. It was good she had met George Eliot and that George had found her "beautiful." Now she must see Madame Grisi. "So grand an actress, to my mind, has not lived on the lyric stage and, with the exception of Rachel, I don't believe so fine an actress ever lived."

Resting at Rose Hill, Charlotte made out her schedule for the October trip to Rome and read through the clippings that Susan had saved for her during her years in America. Just last month *Sharpe's London Journal* had compared her to Rachel. "That earnest and steady glance they both possess hushes at once to silence every trivial thought; then the deep tones, conveying a meaning in each syllable, arouse the elevated instincts of our nature; an awe . . . fills our soul." The American Cushman and the French Rachel had sprung from different backgrounds, but "in vain the Atlantic divides and the countries differ; genius knows no limits and but one language—that of truth and inspiration."

At any time, the words would have seemed pleasing enough, but now they carried a special flavor. What could be nicer than reading such praise in a national paper at the close of a hard-fought career? "Europe has not tired of Rachel, and both America and Europe are always ready to welcome Miss Cushman—but when years and years are gone by, they will still be remembered—because the impression, on seeing both, is like an event of one's life . . . their genius will live forever."

About that, could she be sure? Were memories so trustworthy?

In August, she and Sallie moved to the Isle of Wight—"the Eden of England," Anna Mowatt had called it, for its mellow soft air, the exquisite play of light and shadows on its flowered lanes and stone cottages. Every morning she directed her carriage up a road along the high cliffs or wandered the quiet streets of Yarmouth village on New Port, past the high gates of Osborne House, where Victoria and Albert now elected to spend much of their days. At sundown, she strolled up the slopes of white daisies that spattered the High Down to taste the clean wind from the sea. This was the life that wealth and leisure made possible. Could she ever believe, after this, that work and hot effort on stage had been better?

By early September she was settled again in London, convinced anew that no better place existed to enjoy the fruit of her labors. She had leisure now to ponder the good life and the English manner of living it. Within days, she bought a spirited saddle horse of her own and, against Sallie's protests, rode out sidesaddle each morning to take the high jumps in Hyde Park or with friends out to Surrey for a brisk morning's dash over the walls and rose-covered hedges.

She wasted no time trying to persuade Mary Eliza or Charlie to join her in some sort of family circle. Comfortable in an old gray dust cap and shawl, Mary Eliza would never adjust to London's "strange ways." The new marble-topped furniture Charlotte bought for her cottage in Brixton she liked well enough, though she gave no sign that she cared one way or the other. It was impossible to fathom this woman, though seeing the age and infirmity that had quickly settled on her, one might have made guesses. Not for years had she voiced any thoughts about herself, but the steady light in her eyes when her troubles weighed heaviest had long since faded. For all her tears late at night during Charlotte's girlhood, her mother had thrived on worry. Charlotte's money had removed all her burdens, but it had left her peevish and empty-handed. Living with Charlie, she was content to grow old, cooking his simple meals, brushing his coat each morning, scolding him weakly when he forgot his umbrella. Like his mother, Charlie had relaxed long ago in routine. Though his insurance job in Chancery Lane offered no challenge, it presented no fears either. If he still took pride in his famous sister, his early excitement in it had cooled.

All of which Charlotte took as a mandate to lead her own life. Doing it, she would look to the glitter of English high life, and to no one did she feel any cause to explain. At evening parties, she took careful note of the high fashions on the women about her, the diamond chains in their hair, the décolletage that would have shocked New York or Boston, the homage English society showered upon its titled names. Old Sam Rogers had aged perceptibly. He now passed his life in his chair, lifted in and out of his carriage, wheeled to his table, still the indefatigable host, but even sharper of tongue, more prone to rage if attention strayed from his end of the conversation. Moving near the center of this gay London, Charlotte was not even aware, until one day when Sallie pointed it out, that she had lost all her hoarseness.

The time to head south came in October, when Charlotte left with Matilda and Grace to spend en route a fortnight with a good dressmaker in Paris. Matilda's months in England had brought the color back in her cheeks, but Grace added the real verve to the journey.

Dolce Far Niente in Rome

Grace remembered well enough that she was the great granddaughter of Jonathan Edwards, but she refused to let her Puritan heritage stand in her way as a writer. At twenty-nine she was a handsome woman with expressive large eyes, a head piled high with curls, and a curiosity that kept her constantly on the lookout for subjects for popular articles. In 1850 her *Greenwood Leaves* had been a best seller, and her trip through Europe now was meant to pay off in more chatty articles for the American press. Hawthorne liked her, though reading the pieces she had already sent home from England, he tossed her off as a "scribbling female"—partly because Grace took such foolish delight in attracting attention.

At a private reading Charles Kemble gave in London, Grace became so moved that she almost brought down the house. At the end of one piece, she applauded so wildly that she fell into hysterics, then swooned dead away. Kemble looked up from his book. "Ma'am, this won't do," he said sternly. When Grace remained dead on the floor, Kemble repeated, "Ma'am, we are too much used to this sort of thing!" When Grace still gave no response, Kemble cried, "Ma'am, you expose yourself!" At that, Grace bounded up horror-stricken, adjusting her skirts. Hearing the story later, Hawthorne wondered how "she survived it."

With a temperament like that, Grace would not be one to depend on, but she would make a vivid traveler. And more important, she had ideas. Her determination to see Negro slavery abolished had become almost a crusade, and she was equally certain that American housewives deserved greater freedom. "Would I vote if I could?" cried Grace, when asked about woman suffrage. "Yea, verily, at divers times and in divers places . . . casting my vote right and left and from morn to dewy eve."

At the Gare du Nord in Paris, when Harriet Hosmer and her father arrived, Charlotte's first sight of the laughing figure bounding down off the boat train was reassurance enough. She would make this journey pay off for young talent. Back in Watertown, cried Hattie, Lydia Maria Child had wanted to know: "Do you think you can be contented in a foreign land?" To which Hattie had answered, "I can be happy *any* where, with good health and a bit of marble." And now, in Europe at last, she felt like crying for joy.

At her dressmaker's, Charlotte stood for her last fittings on the black and lavender moiré dresses she would need in Rome; then she gathered up Harriet and the others for a quick look at the Paris sights and took them all to call on the Brownings at their apartment overlooking the Champs Élysées, one of the noble thoroughfares the master plan for Paris was opening up.

Robert himself opened the door, his face half-hidden in a beard that had turned white since Charlotte last saw him. Talking excitedly, he escorted them all across to the sunny corner where his wife reclined on a sofa, then stood hovering about, interjecting quick comments. Grasping Elizabeth's small hand, Charlotte felt she might have been holding the tiny foot of a bird. At this first meeting with the famous poetess, she stood stiff and humble, remembering Tom Appleton's description of her: "a little concentrated nightingale, living in a bower of curls." In the presence of this smiling, "fairy-like creature," Charlotte felt suddenly huge and almost monstrously energetic.

While Elizabeth and Matilda talked warmly of George Sand, Charlotte noted a strange sensation in herself. Robert's tiny wife spoke with such keen sensibility, her lilting phrases were so exquisite and covered such a broad range that in her presence Charlotte felt suddenly tongue-tied. For once in her life, she was shy and self-conscious. It was a new discomfort, and she did not fully grasp the quiet doubt it planted in the midst of all the excitement outside.

The day was one of high culmination for France. Since 1848 when a new Napoleon had become President of France, the country had seen its leader's dreams of personal grandeur steadily grow. Today, October 16, 1852, Louis Napoleon was making his triumphal entry into Paris, preliminary to being crowned Emperor. Watching the parade from the Brownings' high balcony, Charlotte drank in the spectacle. The great scene seemed worthy of a classic dramatist, though at times Charlotte, as a good democrat, heard herself muttering about the folly of any country's taking so drastic a political step. But when Louis Napoleon himself came into view, escorted by a great company of mounted riders, their plumed helmets flashing in the sun, she cried out her admiration: "That's fine, I must say!" She was struck as much for the staging as for the little man's courage. Bareheaded and decked in his medals, Louis rode alone in the center of the procession, ten paces at least from his nearest guard. His delicate tact in riding alone set off great waves of cheers which he acknowledged by bowing to right and to left.

When Elizabeth exclaimed, "For the drama of history we must look to France . . . for the 'points' which thrill you to the bone," Charlotte agreed heartily. Never at home had she brushed so close to national drama, and the feeling now only deepened her joy in deciding to settle permanently in a part of the world where tradition and ceremony flowed so rich in the blood.

Standing beside Elizabeth, Charlotte found the Brownings' small son almost as interesting as the spectacle below. He stood peering down, solemn and quiet, hands gripping the balcony rail. Dressed in a velvet jacket and white drawers edged with embroidery, Pen Browning would have been laughed at in rugged, red-blooded America, but his pale little face and long golden ringlets gave him an almost ethereal charm like his mother's. "He is my Florentine boy," said Elizabeth, fingering his curls, "because he was born in Italy, where the sun is always golden."

Hearing those words, Charlotte hungered to press on for Rome. With the Brownings, she had seen for herself the blissful marriage that was making them legendary, and leaving them, she made them promise to contact her when they came down to Italy. During the visit, Elizabeth had formed an impression of Charlotte that was no less definite. "Never was a woman in the world less like an actress," she wrote her sister. "I can't conceive how such a woman would look on a stage, or speak, or gesticulate—she has just the look of a sensible woman, not at all young." The emotional bond between the actress and Miss Hays seemed odd, but "Miss Cushman has an unimpeachable character, and is as much distinguished for her general intelligence as for her professional aptitude—a little more, perhaps."

Speeding along toward Marseilles, Charlotte felt the old thrill of adventure well up inside. This trip was like none she had taken before; her ends now had nothing to do with fame or fortune. In a matter of hours, the train had left Avignon far behind, and she rushed out to her hotel balcony in Marseilles for a first glimpse of the Mediterranean. In the sun the waves rolled heavily, like blue oil flecked white. Next day, the trip took them along the Riviera's flower-decked cliffs to the fishing village of Nice and then, via the Grand Corniche road that inched up over the hills—with a view clear out to Corsica—to Genoa for an overnight stop and a change to a ship bound for Civita Vecchia. On November 12, Charlotte's "party of jolly bachelors" finished their long jolting ride in a diligence over the hilly Italian roads. Glued to her window when the team stopped to rest, Charlotte glimpsed far head and below the city of Rome.

Through the crush of carriages and pedestrians crowding the streets, her diligence rolled past the Spanish Embassy at the foot of a staircase leading up through stalls massed with flowers. At its top, against the Pincian Hill, a towered pink church seemed plastered against the sky. From Number 28 on the Corso, where the English writer and sculptor, Shakspere Wood, had arranged rooms for them, Charlotte caught her first view of the city throbbing below. She knew immediately she had chosen well. To be rich was to be blessed with choices, and she felt no doubt that she had found the best of all possible uses for the riches success had brought. In all the swirl of color and warmth passing beneath her, standing half a world away from Boston, Charlotte felt that coming to Rome was a matter of finding one's home at last.

Immediately, invitations from the other *forestieri* in town came flooding to Charlotte's door, people newly arrived from England and America who each winter made a little island in Rome where English speech expressed all the delights that art and leisure and entertaining afforded them. Of Rome, the visitors asked little, except to be left alone to entertain each other at lavish dinners and gatherings at salons, with long afternoon horseback rides on the open Campagna, the broad plain outside the walls with its vine-covered ruins, tumbling streams, and the always changing tints and shadows that played over its olive slopes and vineyards. From the moment Charlotte sipped her first taste of red wine at a marble-topped table in a *caffe,* she knew she had escaped all the dark skies, whether Victorian and Puritan. The word for life here was *dolce far niente,* sweet idleness. No wonder a thousand painters and sculptors had already laid out their chisels and set up their easels in Rome. In their velvet jackets and rumpled trousers, they seemed more intent on songs and conversations in the smoke-filled caffes than on sales.

Charlotte wondered at the change that had come already to her own precise sense of time. So much life had passed here in this city, so much force had thundered across Rome's seven hills that her American sense of history, with roots that went back less than a century, felt itself being wrenched into something less certain and sharp. Life here was to live, not to shape and constrict into some proper concept, some political notion. Wherever she turned, she saw freedom and grace; even the poverty in the backstreets, the hunger in faces cowering in the shadows seemed picturesque and alive. Rome's fountains said it perfectly. Long ago the city had piped the clear-flowing waters of its hinterland straight into its heart, where its gushing fountains made perpetual music and set a perpetual mood. It was a rare day that did not see some procession, state coaches of crimson and gold and the *Guardia Nobile* with their white cloaks and glittering helmets en route to some church or St. Peter's. Out on the Campagna, even the poorest peasants seemed unable to strike an ungraceful pose, whether leaning on their hay rakes or standing silent and shrouded in ragged blankets, silhouetted against the sunset.

In forestieri society, the leadership changed periodically, but just now the American sculptor, William Wetmore Story, was its head. In him lay intertwined all the motives that brought art and wealth together in Rome. His studio was a mecca for newcomers and visitors; few came to Rome without some intention of taking home a piece of sculpture or painting—whether an antique fragment or a newly cut piece of carrara. But Story was more than a working artist. The son of Justice Joseph Story, founder of Harvard's law school, he attracted visitors as much for his flawless social name as for his artistry. To aspire to some place in the circle which he dominated was, for most, a clear matter of finding favor with Story personally.

Charlotte found no reason to court Story's favor. She had made her own circle in London; she had never needed anyone's social wing, nor would she incur any debts now. Within days, Story knocked at her door. The man Sallie admitted was a slight, nervous figure, swarthy, with deep-set eyes, yet graced with a wit that sparkled. Charlotte greeted him as a fellow Bostonian, letting the conversation go as he wished. Story had come to make Miss Hosmer an offer. His sculptor friend, the English John Gibson, might be able to help her. Charlotte hesitated, then called in Hattie and her father. When Story saw the daguerreotypes of Hattie's pieces in Watertown, he poured out compliments. Gibson must meet this American girl.

It piqued Charlotte slightly that matters were being so quickly taken out of her hands, but Gibson was, by every report, Rome's finest sculptor. He had been the pupil of Canova himself. In due course Story was back with Gibson's ecstatic word: "Send the young lady to me, whatever I can teach her she shall learn!" When the meeting with Gibson came off at his studio in the Via Fontanella, the little man in dusty smock led them through a garden of orange trees, past a gurgling fountain, to a back room lighted by a high arched window. Smiling, Gibson told Hattie in a little ceremony that he

253

was giving her Canova's own studio. She could begin work whenever she liked; together they could plot a routine.

So, Hattie was settled, and though Charlotte felt glad about it, she was taken aback that Hattie quickly set her own pace in Rome, with or without her. The mothering instinct had come to nothing again, and for all her wish to shepherd and protect and batter down doors, she found in Harriet little real need. The girl would live at the Corso apartment, but she would spend all her days with Gibson, observing his skills, sketching his models, copying Roman and Greek drapery; Charlotte was left to fill her own days as she pleased. Grace was off for "color material," Matilda sat quietly reading or handed around the cups at the tea table, but Charlotte herself could not sit idle. She read all the books and plays that time had never allowed her before. She wrote the long letters she had promised, signing them with her great, swirling signature. She spent whole mornings idly shopping—buying some ivory miniature or bronze that struck her fancy, some tiny gold charm to add to her heavy watch chain—or passing slowly through the endless rooms of paintings and marbles and jeweled treasures in the Vatican galleries.

Each afternoon at one, she pulled on her black riding habit and bowler, ordered a horse brought around, then set off sidesaddle for the Campagna. The rides filled most of her afternoons. Toward four, she slowed her horse to a trot, then picked her way slowly up a pine-tufted hill to gaze out over the scene below. To the far south loomed the rounded blue Alban Hills, away to the east lay Tivoli's white bluffs and fountains, and a little nearer, the muted pink ruins and broken arches of Hadrian's Villa. Over it all, arched the incredible sapphire sky that seemed such a blessing after Boston and rainy England.

Sitting quietly, Charlotte asked herself why such radiant beauty and freedom were not enough. Was leisure a thing one must learn to manage? Did retirement, like a career, demand special talents? In this warm land where life had pulsated for so many centuries, why did she suddenly feel cold and unhappy? Finding no answers, she chided herself for discounting her blessings, then remounted and charged off to Rome.

Evenings she filled with endless dinners. Over somebody's port or madeira, she indulged all her zest for conversation. Rome's political swirls and rumbles were good for an hour, and the Crimea could fill another. Word came to her ears almost nightly that one day—just when no one could say—old Pio Nono, the squat old Pope hiding behind his high Vatican windows, must give up his temporal hold on Rome. But witty talk and long, perfect dinners were hardly enough to fill the emptiness she sensed more and more keenly. She did not forget that work and the pressure of schedules had irked her, but now, suddenly free of all pressures, she was blessed with too many choices, no discomforts, and no sense of purpose at all.

Whenever somebody begged her, she sang at some gathering: Fanny Kemble's sister, Adelaide, was a famed Roman hostess now and had sought her out. She recited the speeches that had spelled her high moments on stage and smiled at the tears she could still cause, delivering some somber ballad. She took an eager delight in leading visitors to the many studios where the artists were all too happy to lay down their tools and talk for an hour. She was even thrilled, one day, when an Italian sculptor begged her to pose. "Ah, Signora," he cried, enraptured at her form, "If you will only cover your face and let me carve your figure, I will make you the most magnificent goddess of beauty the world has ever seen."

But with time on her hands, Charlotte let herself become too much concerned with things she could not control. There was something incorrigible in Hattie. Between long stints at her modeling table, she had taken to horseback rides with a vengeance, even riding alone at night through the dark streets. When the chargé d'affaires in the American consulate offered to protect her on such excursions, Hattie thanked him, then made him the same offer. When her solo rides brought criticism from Romans and Americans alike, Hattie tossed back her curls and cried she was free to do as she pleased—until the Roman police intervened.

Grace Greenwood fared better, though Charlotte found herself no more necessary in Grace's plan. The good journalist, Grace chose to remain in the background observing, determined to dig out the facts about Rome's coming political upheavals—though this was difficult to do, since certain parties had learned that the American Miss Cushman had forwarded money to Mazzini and, as a friend of Miss Cushman, she was suspect herself.

About her status among the Italians, Charlotte cared not at all. Closer home, she might have fretted about Story's opinions if she had not already marked him off as a fool for taking such a womanish delight in his social holds on the forestieri. Charlotte boldly ignored his remarks about her and her "emancipated females" at 28 Corso. It was no secret that Story found her singing ridiculous. "The Cushman sings savage ballads," he wrote Lowell, "in a hoarse, manny voice, and requests people recitatively to forget her not. I'm sure I shall not."

Partly to busy herself, she began a crusade on behalf of the female artists in Rome, especially Hattie. Doing so, she ran square into Story. Hattie had not bothered to thank him for his help, and now the sculptor felt a positive dislike for the girl. "She is doing very well and shows a capital spirit," he wrote Lowell in Boston. "But it is one thing to copy and another to create. She may or may not have inventive powers as an artist. If she have, will not she be the first woman who ever had?"

To prove Story wrong, Charlotte now made it a point to lead her visitors to studios where various women like Hattie were trying to prove their "inventive powers." For a time, the crusade amply channeled her energies. When wealthy Americans asked her advice about places to visit, she took them to Hattie's studio to watch the vigorous girl in the velvet beret pound away like any man with her mallet and chisel, to stroll among the Romanesque figures she had placed on sale. Whether Hattie cared much or not, Charlotte found defending her a pastime made doubly sweet because it gave her a chance to oppose the arrogant Story.

One male artist, however, impressed her differently. By early 1853, Charlotte had heard much praise for William Page, an American portraitist who had been a pupil of Samuel Morse. Admiring his work in America, Emerson said his figures seemed so real they would "bleed." Now in Rome, Page was creating a tremendous following. With such a talent at hand, and an American talent at that, Charlotte determined to commission a portrait. At daily sittings for Page, she developed a growing interest in this burningly talented—if sorely troubled—painter. In Page, she found perfect proof of her old admonition: artists and happy marriage seldom go hand in hand. Watching the man fret and erase, then suddenly dash down something inspired, she came to enjoy his wide-ranging talk, his instructions about altering the pose to something more like herself than a model. Lowell had written a poem about the ordeal of sitting to William Page. "He wishes me to look (d'ye see?) as 'twere profoundly thinking, that he may paint me, not as if I were a bale of cloth or a log of wood, but rather as a poet and an author; So, while he shifts from chair to chair, considering my attitude, I take my pen (at his request) and thus display my gratitude."

After weeks of sittings, Page delivered the finished picture. This was certainly no prettified likeness from a Thomas Sully. Page had painted her life-size and real, a heavy-jawed, unsmiling woman clearly aged thirty-six, wearing a dark everyday jacket, a studded white shirt and striped bow tie, her hair brushed down smooth to the sides. The face looked pleasant enough, she supposed, though Page had scarcely bothered to suggest any grace or feminine charm. Yet for all its honesty, she liked it, and in her eyes it only took on added merit when it soon became celebrated.

When Charlotte held open house to show off her Page portrait, even Story liked it—as art. "The finest portrait I think I ever saw," he wrote Lowell. When the Brownings, newly arrived from Paris, dropped by, they were ecstatic. Robert had never seen "such modern art, certainly," and Elizabeth called it "something wonderful—soul and body together." Writing Mrs. Jameson, Elizabeth was not surprised at the furor it was creating. "Did Titian ever produce anything like it?" the other American painters in Rome were asking.

Happy with her picture, Charlotte and her "emancipated females" pursued other interests this easy spring of 1853. Grace would remember the time as "the golden year" of her life, days she filled making notes for articles and visiting the Vatican sculpture galleries. "The Apollo (Belvedere) I should like to see every day of my life . . . to lift a curtain, and gaze on that transcendent image of life and light . . . the energy and joy of existence with which it so abounds." Hattie was almost lyrically happy working at Gibson's elbow. "I would not live anywhere else but in Rome, if you would give me the Gates of Paradise and all the Apostles thrown in." America was a glorious country, "but this is a better place for an artist."

In most respects, Charlotte felt the same. But it was not many weeks into the spring before she knew that part of her own disquiet stemmed from something she saw in Matilda. More and more, Matilda had withdrawn into a quiet shell, obviously at odds with the bounding energy around her. Charlotte could understand most of the feeling. It was an obvious fact to them all that, among them, Matilda was the weakest talent, the vaguest personality, the one least likely to achieve anything. The defeat was sad to watch, but Charlotte saw nothing positive to do about it. As the days passed, with Matilda perpetually glum and sour, Charlotte grew more and more troubled.

257

As winter warmed into spring and dinner parties gave way to picnics on the Campagna, Charlotte only felt more unhappy. She led
her group to Naples for Holy Week and declared, with the others,
that Sorrento was surely one of the loveliest places on earth; "a
young festive queen, rose-crowned," Grace called it, "gently caressed
and sung to by the capricious sea." But returning to Rome, Charlotte
knew she had problems. Was Matilda's unhappiness a vengeful dislike of Charlotte's other friends?

In a female ménage, some ill will had been inevitable perhaps, yet
pondering the matter, Charlotte recognized in herself a feeling she
had not expected in paradise. In her heart, she knew she was utterly
bored. Did that explain Matilda's sad eyes? Perhaps—but before long
Charlotte realized something more disturbing. Her resentment flar-
ing, she asked herself how Matilda and the willful Hattie could have
dared to form an attachment between themselves that included no
place for her. How could they so lightly dismiss her friendship?
Worse still, how could they so coldly discount the generosity she had
brought them in open hands?

Hurt, feeling sore and unwanted, she realized one night that she
could not live like this. Her idle hands hungered again for a work-
shop. Inactivity in all this silly, tinseled boredom with nothing to
occupy her mind but injured pride was folly. In her suffering, her old
hoarseness suddenly gripped her. For days she wandered aimless and
wretched about the apartment, grieving that nobody seemed to care,
whispering when she must, sitting morose by the window, too dismayed to make any plans. She knew she must leave Rome, yet to do
so would force a showdown with Matilda and forfeit, perhaps, a bond
she had long valued. Between a husband and wife, a marriage contract made many things easier, but between herself and Matilda what
ties still held? Without explaining, she simply announced one night
that she had decided to return to the stage. If Matilda was ready to
leave, Sallie could pack in a few hours. If the announcement surprised
Matilda, nothing in her face betrayed her. She nodded quickly to
Sallie.

En route north, they stopped in Florence a day or so to visit the
Brownings. The bouquet Charlotte sent to Casa Guidi, their airy
apartment facing the Pitti Palace, brought a quick reply from Elizabeth. "You are too good. Your flowers are miracles of beauty. Can
you come on Wednesday and will you? And if in the meanwhile you
will accept us tonight as we are with nobody to help make the fire
burn—then will you come tonight too?"

Seeing Elizabeth again, her small figure drooped in a large antique chair, her curls spilling out from under her lace cap, seeing Robert darting about as always, his talk a veritable shower of pictures and vivid stories, Charlotte felt suddenly happy again. Rome was far behind her and London lay just ahead. She mentioned the fact that she was still interested in Chorley's play *Duchess Eleanour* and might bring it out in London sometime. Later, Elizabeth turned the talk to spiritualism and her firm belief that friendly spirits were abroad in the land: their dear novelist friend, Isabella Blagden, had had all sorts of proof from the spirits; several had moved her hand to write "messages." Charlotte listened attentively, though with little more conviction than the doubt she saw in Robert's face.

Later, Isa Blagden, an exotic little woman with blue-black hair and jet eyes, invited them out to her villa high on a hill overlooking the Arno. Here Charlotte found the entire Florentine colony of English and Americans assembled to do her honor. Bulwer-Lytton and Frances Trollope and her son Anthony stood talking beside one window, and Hiram Powers, the American sculptor, and his beautiful daughters stood grouped around Isa herself. When Isa persuaded a tall English girl to sing for them, Charlotte accepted a gold chair by the fireplace, filled this warm afternoon with flowers. After the girl had finished, someone begged Charlotte to sing. It had been weeks since she had trusted her voice, and she hesitated a moment. But soon she turned to the girl: "Since you have sung so exquisitely to please me, I will sing horribly to please you." Then laughing, she seated herself at the keys and half-talked her way through "The Sands o' Dee."

But pleasures like these were too gentle now to interest her. Discussing Chorley's play with Elizabeth had merely convinced her the more that happiness was action. Charlotte knew that returning to work, she was in a sense returning to life. On July 5, 1853, she was back in London.

She stopped a while with Mary Eliza and Charlie in Brixton, then moved on with Sallie to Malvern. Tired from the journey across Europe, Matilda had chosen to remain in London, and Charlotte gave scant thought to the matter until one morning a stiff little note arrived from her friend. Matilda had decided to go back to Rome—to Hattie, of course. In Charlotte, a grief welled up that was more loneliness than sadness. The foolish Matilda could do as she pleased. No vow held her, once she wanted to leave. Soon another letter brought a stab to Charlotte's heart. Word from Philadelphia reported that Conrad Clarke was reaping success at the Arch Street Theatre. He and his wife were valued members of the regular stock company. So much for the griefs of the heart.

However close the rupture with Matilda came to breaking "my heart, if not my head"—as she later wrote Grace—she knew by the time she left Malvern for London that "there was something higher and grander" than grief. Squaring her shoulders, she knew again that work, her "old religion of labour," could "sunder the rock meant to crush me."

Work and Idleness

(1853–1857)

Charlotte lost no time in contracting with J. B. Buckstone for a January run at the Haymarket. To put herself back in harness as quickly as possible, she hurried out to Liverpool in early December to fill an engagement—and relish again the sound of the heavy curtains sweeping open, the sudden hush that fell over the audience, then the great burst of applause as she came on stage.

Playing all her old roles was like putting on familiar old clothes. Acting was life; she had been foolish ever to doubt it. At her invitation, various Muspratts came backstage to watch her make up. Sheridan's brother Edmund hardly believed her skill in makeup, a skill that turned healthy cheeks and strong arms into those of a gaunt, disheveled, old gypsy. From out front, her singing and acting achieved such naturalness that Edmund scarcely remembered her as "the Charlotte Cushman so familiar to us off the stage."

In the hurry that went with all this return to action, Charlotte failed to read carefully a letter that came from her business agent, Louis Harlan, in Philadelphia. Back in October, Harlan had sent her a check for $3,000 and the promise of more when he sold some of her Philadelphia land. Now, Harlan wrote, if the agreement between them was still satisfactory, she must sign the enclosed power of attorney and return it immediately; he could then manage her affairs even more profitably. At the moment, fascinated with her work, Charlotte lightly skimmed the document's wording, then quickly scrawled her name to the bottom of the page. Unaware of its implications, she mailed it—then rushed off to rehearsal.

She spent Christmas with the Muspratts at Rose Hill. Since 1849 Susan and Sheridan had become the parents of two other daughters, and to Charlotte's joy, Susan had named one of them Rosalie. Playing with Ida, Rosalie, and Mabel, Charlotte counted again her blessings, then made it a point to renew an old American acquaintance. Nathaniel Hawthorne had recently become the United States Consul in Liverpool, and at his office the day after Christmas she thanked him for consenting to pose for the portrait, then told him she hoped soon to call on his wife at their quarters in Rock Park across the Mersey. Immediately, Hawthorne insisted she come for dinner on the twenty-ninth and remain overnight.

Hawthorne's stuccoed house stood near the top of a winding wet street, its dooryard filled with dripping shrubbery. At the door, Sophia Hawthorne and the three small children greeted her, their wide eyes shining, awed at the presence that loomed above them. Sophia quickly warmed to her—to her "very untheatrical" manner and bearing, as Sophia described her later, so dignified "that I should never suspect her to be an actress."

Over dinner, if Hawthorne complained of the irksome chores his job as Consul demanded, if he grumblingly called Liverpool a "black hole," he spent most of his time questioning Charlotte about Rome and gently chiding her about her apparent intent to stay single. Rather saucily, Charlotte invited him to realize that the state of her heart was nobody else's business, but she promised to consider again the "fate matrimonial" he recommended. As for Rome, it was paradise compared to the gloomy wet skies and malodorous fog that Liverpool suffered in winter. Recalling her rides out on the sunny Campagna, gathering great bunches of spring anemones and violets, Charlotte realized suddenly that her memories of Rome were becoming almost happy. After dinner, Charlotte let the Hawthorne children —Una, Julian, and Rose—climb up in her lap to finger the tiny gold charms she wore on her chain—the little enameled palette, the easel holding a tinted landscape, the tragic and comic masks, the tiny dagger, the small opera glass, the little gold harp with strings—then regaled them with stories about how she had gotten them from friends in Florence and Rome and New Orleans and London.

Next morning, Charlotte seated herself at Una's piano and sang one of Lockart's Spanish ballads so well that she made Sophia's blood "tingle." On the seven-year-old Julian she registered her greatest impact, not so much for the entrancing stories she told him and his sisters as for what he called later "her hearty good-will in bending her great and gracious self" to an urchin who leaned "rapt" against her knees.

"I had never seen a theatre, and did not know what an actress was, but I loved her."

Late in the day, Julian watched their visitor disappear slowly down the steep street as his father escorted her to the Liverpool ferry. Years later, he would recall the "love madness" that Charlotte had enkindled in him that day. As a grown man, looking at her photograph, he would counter the charge that Charlotte Cushman was a homely woman: "Well, of course a photograph never does one justice." Her nose wasn't classic perhaps. But the power and splendor in her face "took captive your soul."

And seeing Charlotte safely aboard, Hawthorne himself began planning the letter he would write George Ticknor in Boston about "the night Miss Cushman dined and spent the night with me (that is, in my house)."

When she opened in London in January 1854, Charlotte felt a double joy that she had never foolishly told England good-bye. Shrewdly, she appeared now, after an absence of five years, in the old vehicle that had first caused London to welcome her into its arms. Bianca in *Fazio* served her splendidly. The *Illustrated London News* greeted her with the fervid words she was used to: "We welcome most heartily this reappearance of Miss Cushman, with powers evidently not diminished, but, as its strikes us, increased." If some critics praised her "power of will," her "intense strength," while lamenting her "lack of womanliness," Charlotte told herself that it was her womanly heart that had prompted her return to acting at all. And for all her "lack of womanliness" Buckstone extended her contracted twelve nights to the forty the public demanded.

Acting three nights a week—sometimes as Meg, sometimes as Romeo, sometimes as Queen Katharine—at a fee that made Buckstone wince, she had regained by the end of the run her strong sense of purpose. The top critics had crowned her Katharine the best "I had ever done in the way of artistic excellence." In that role at least, she had been everything "womanly, queenly, pathetic, and gentle." The *Times* found her Meg elevated by genius "into the highest rank of tragedy"; another paper had seen "what the unassisted resources of acting may achieve with the mere idea of a fine part." In Miss Cushman's acting, said its critic, human tenderness blended with an "Eastern picturesqueness of gesture." She made the refined sentiment beneath Meg's heavy feebleness and clumsy old age "wonderfully startling."

Acting again, reading the critics, Charlotte felt quietly happy, in spite of the fickle Matilda. As if to fill that emptiness, she found herself the toast of a circle that now included, not merely fashionable people, but clever artists and scholars. Composers, singers, and creative intellects flocked to the Tuesday receptions with which she filled her beautiful rooms at 4 Earl Terrace in Kensington. Greeting them at her door, it gratified her to hear that her coming again to the London stage brightened the gloom that had settled upon them in February over the approach of war in the Crimea. After one especially brilliant *Macbeth,* the Duke of Devonshire presented her with a gold and onyx dagger to use whenever she played in London.

Later, when Matilda returned to London, contrite and sorrowful, Charlotte received her coldly; then reading the questioning fear in Matilda's eyes, she held out her hands. Strength could forgive a weakling. Now that she had found again her own purpose, Charlotte felt only compassion for anyone who found life such a constant loss. Matilda had come back—"never again perhaps to be what she once was to me, but still, perhaps, better for us both that I am not so dependent upon her."

Matured and wiser, paying calls with Matilda, finding Matilda waiting up for her on the nights she came home tired from acting, Charlotte felt easy again. Now she could devote her leftover energies to riding or driving her elegant new phaeton along the curving ways in Hyde Park.

And she remembered her promise to Henry Chorley. When the timid little playwright screwed up his courage again and asked her to bring out his *Duchess Eleanour,* the eagerness in his deep-set eyes, the gentleness in his small hands, challenged her sympathy. Rereading the play, she found the story of medieval intrigue impressive enough, and its central character, driven by mental torture to the brink of suicide, offered strong possibilities. Rehearsals and Browning's recent letter to Chorley saying he "confidently" expected to see it succeed deepened her hopes. But after playing it only two nights in early March, she and Chorley knew that *Duchess Eleanour* had failed. The *Times* critic blamed its muddy development of character, though Miss Cushman, he said, had played "finely." Reading the verdict, Charlotte was left with a puzzling thought. No role she had ever "created" had struck fire.

From time to time word reached her of Hattie Hosmer's growing success in Rome, a matter of friendship as much as art. On a recent trip south, the Brownings had taken a shine to Hattie; Elizabeth called her "a great pet of mine and of Robert's," in spite of the eccentric life this perfectly "emancipated female" led, dining alone at the cafes "precisely as a young man would." It pleased Charlotte to hear that another friend had impressed Browning. Writing John Forster ("Do you know,—you must,—Miss Cushman?"), Browning insisted that he call on the actress to see her pictures by William Page—"as noble a fellow as his works show him."

In May, Charlotte left London for a run through Birmingham and Sheffield as far north as Yorkshire, where in sudden disgust with the local talent, she let herself assume for a moment the haughty air of a London star. When she learned at rehearsal that an actor barely out of his teens would play Henry VIII to her Katharine, she stopped the business immediately: "What! This youth, this slip of a man play Henry the Eighth!"

When the manager explained that this actor was the only man available, Charlotte went along with the plan only after she made it clear that such a Henry doomed the play to laughable failure. But during the performance, when Henry proved himself more than adequate, even skilled in some scenes, she regretted that she had been hostile toward him. Next morning she stopped the rehearsal, then looked across to the young man. "Mr. Hamilton," she called. "I was guilty of a great rudeness to you yesterday, and more than that I was as unjust as I was impolite. You held your tongue like a gentleman. I should not feel easy in conscience if I did not make my apology to you in as open a manner as possible."

In June, sad word from Liverpool rekindled other dark memories. Susan had hoped to join her in Paris for a round of classical French theatre and dress fittings, but when Ida died suddenly, Charlotte cut short her Paris holiday and rushed to Liverpool. She added her tears to the family's, then helpless and filled again with the wave of grief that Augustus' death had left her, she went back to London and poured out her sympathy in long letters. "I grieve from my heart, dear Sue, for all your sadness and depression; but can you not think that God's will is best . . . that the taking away of this lovely child was for some good and wise purpose, though through our earthly eyes we cannot recognize it?"

In 1837, she would have read such words with shudders of disbelief, yet now she could look back at that distant April, calm in the knowledge that out of Augustus' death and later ones she had created a life and an art. If Susan suffered Ida's death to be "a means of bringing you nearer to God and heaven, you will find in time that it will prove a tender rather than harrowing sorrow, and you will be indeed saying, 'Thy will be done.'"

One happy note had brightened the dark days with Susan. A Liverpool friend who had recently visited Ned in Annapolis had found him a stunningly handsome young man, completely happy in his studies. Reading Ned's recent letters to Susan, leafing through the pictures in Susan's fat albums, Charlotte regretted again that she could not be vitally involved in Ned's life—that however much she filled her days with good work and silly females and the praise of strangers, she could not replace a hunger for family.

In the fall, after filling commitments in Dublin and the provinces, she engulfed herself again in London's social whirl. When she visited Brighton, the guest of the Duke of Devonshire, she read for his large assembly the whole of *Henry VIII* and became excited with the idea that someday, if she ever thoroughly tired of playing with local actors, she might follow Fanny Kemble's lead and make a career on the reading platform. But just now, a greater interest concerned the home she wanted in London. To be an active hostess again, however much she privately confessed that society's heart was hollow, she needed a proper house.

The four-story Georgian structure she finally bought in Mayfair stood at 1 Bolton Row, on the corner of Piccadilly across from the Green Park. The house was convenient to the theatres where she would be working, as well as to the homes and clubs of people she expected to entertain. On its high paneled walls, she could already envision the paintings she would bring from Rome, among them the Page portrait, his "Venus," and his copy of Raphael's "Madonna of the Chair." From her high windows overlooking the park, she could imagine herself in some wild stretch of the Adirondacks—except that these trees were so neatly grand and aloof, with fat lambs frolicking over the velvet grass. In the distance the Gothic towers of Parliament and Westminster Abbey were proof enough that this was really the heart of London. Once she finished hiring a staff to supplement Sallie, she set herself to writing her invitations.

With Sallie to see to her needs, with an English butler—a haughty sort named Wilmot—to direct the household, she could fake worry about the cost of it all, though part of the fun of this life was the knowledge that she could afford it. "I am as tired as I should be if I had—nothing to do," she wrote a friend. "I have made up the house-bills each week in *ten minutes,* but have no money left to pay them with, my fortune is exhausted, all my trinkets up the spout, and I expect every day to be arrested for debt. . . . Wilmot finds me 'the easiest, but the most forgetfullest of missusses.' I go out and forget to order the dinner, and am followed to the carriage door for 'Horders, please, mem.' "

She tore herself away from the joy of equipping her house long enough to play another brief run through the provinces. In Sunderland, she gave a quick acting lesson to a talent that was clearly not run-of-the-mill. Rehearsing *Guy Mannering,* she was struck by Bertram, played by a young man named Henry Irving, and she passed on to him a trick she had learned from Macready. Irving must learn to let his thoughts show plainly before he put them into words. After the performance, she gave him further advice. His handing Meg a purse filled with broken crockery was all wrong. True, it would clink like gold when she flung it in disgust to the ground, but the scene could be played with deeper meaning. "Instead of giving me that purse, don't you think it would be much more natural if you had taken a number of coins from your pocket and had given me the smallest? This is the way one gives alms to a beggar and it would have added greatly to the realism of the scene." When Henry Irving later became the acknowledged heir to Macready's crown in England, he paid full tribute to the early lead he had gotten from Charlotte Cushman.

At Buckstone's behest, in December 1855, Charlotte played another run at the Haymarket as Queen Katharine and Romeo, "always an event on which to congratulate the playgoer," said the *Illustrated London News,* but other critics were less complimentary. Douglas Jerrold in *Lloyd's* cried that if Charlotte's Romeo was "full of flame, it is the flame of phosphor—it shines but it does not burn. We could as soon warm our hands at a painted fire." A visiting German was impressed even less. In town to conduct the London Philharmonic, Richard Wagner liked the play's setting and costumes, but Romeo himself seemed a "curious illusion." After the first act he told his companion how surprised he was at "their giving the part of Romeo to an old man, whose age must be at least sixty, and who seemed anxious to retrieve his long-lost youth by laboriously adopting a sickly-sweet, feminine air." When his companion checked the names in the cast, he cried, *"Donnerwetter,* it's a woman!"

If Charlotte ever learned Wagner's reaction, she recalled one of her early reasons for doing Romeo in London when no able actor looked young enough for the part. Reading Jerrold, she asked herself now, at age thirty-eight, if pretending to be young Romeo was not crowding her luck a little. Yet time had given her a point to stand on when she pondered such questions. She had no wish or intention to look ridiculous, but if crowds could applaud her Romeo, she would take her cues from the crowd.

Charlotte's life in London now was more than working to please critics. For all her pleasure in the crowd's applause, she lived now for other sounds, just as happy. The thud of the brass knocker on her door, the swish of the door opening to admit old friends and callers on reception afternoons, the bright conversation that took its lead from some idea she injected—such sounds filled her needs no less surely. To each of her guests she tried to leave the impression that he was special, that however much others might question his statements, she herself was charmed by such fresh information. If children were present, she leveled her talk to them without ever cutting herself off from the adult debate around her.

One of her keenest delights, as she had expected, was showing her art collection, especially the Page portrait, then standing back and savoring her visitors' comments. "Your picture of me is more admired," she wrote Page, "than I can describe to you." His technique of painting flesh tints as a transparent overcoating delighted every person who looked at it. Even John Ruskin wanted to see it. Unfortunately, old Sam Rogers was too senile now to invite to her own breakfast table. Recently, when Jane Carlyle had been especially bright at his table, he had turned tired, rheumy eyes to another guest and cried, "Who is *she?*" Charlotte could have basked in old Sam's comments about her Venus picture, a work which James Russell Lowell told Page "all the galleries in Europe would contend for if it were by Titian."

When her Page pictures began to turn dark, she blamed the heavy coal smoke in the air. "Unless you build a gallery in London you never get a decent light in which to hang a picture," she wrote Page reassuringly, "and unless they are taken down and washed every month they will get dark." To make certain they received gentle treatment, she reserved that task for herself. Yet she had been warned that Page had odd ideas about toning his pictures, that mixing his paint he used too much boiled oil, and that his pictures must grow black in time. Some Lowell had seen had reached "a mulatto stage . . . which, considering the prejudice of color, is a pity." Happily, Charlotte could see no such permanent trouble in her own pictures. She was on a trip to the Lake District when she heard that the Hawthornes planned to visit London, but she wrote that she hoped they would come again later when she could show them her "little store of art."

Thinking about her treasures, she confessed in a letter to Page from Malvern that she might come back to Rome now that she and Matilda had put their troubles behind them. "I am in so much better state mental and physical than I was while there that I long to see what the effect would be upon me to see it under happier influences." It might be sometime within the next year, if she did not make a trip to America—perhaps even California.

In May 1856, Charlotte was in Paris, shopping, when Ned arrived in France as part of a graduation cruise from the Navy. Pleased by his gentlemanly grace in his Navy whites and his fresh reports from America, she realized suddenly that she wanted desperately to make a trip home. Besides, word from Philadelphia was none too comforting. Earnings from her Philadelphia property were down, and when Ned suggested that Harlan might be cheating her, she berated herself for ever signing the paper that gave him power of attorney. Might it not be smart to go to America to check on the matter? While there, she might test her name again at the box office.

Seeing Adelaide Ristori acting in Paris only confirmed her intentions. For weeks, the fabled Venetian actress had rocked Paris with her efforts to challenge France's beloved Rachel, first as Phedre, then as Medea. With her stately figure, shining chestnut hair, and luminous eyes, Ristori had a natural power and warmth as an actress that seemed to melt all the rules. Alexander Dumas, the elder, had knelt at her feet and kissed her skirt after one performance, and after seeing Ristori's Medea, Charlotte was no less ecstatic. At the breakfast table in her hotel the next morning, Charlotte declared firmly that Ristori clearly outshone all competition: "Rachel is a great artist and is almost faultless, but Rachel is a machine; Ristori is a woman." Before she left Paris, Charlotte called on the grand Italian and, through an interpreter, showered her with all the praise one artist could give another.

When Ristori came later to London to repeat her triumph, Charlotte honored her at a lavish dinner at 1 Bolton Row, where everything—menu, costumes, the special waiters she had hired—was Italian. The table was decorated with the Italian tricolors, and Charlotte wore a white dress that combined the red, white, and green in its ribbons. Even the cook, eager to glimpse the legendary Ristori, disguised himself as a waiter long enough to come in and place a dish grandly before her.

Much as Charlotte worried about her American income this autumn of 1856, entertaining the Italian actress made her hunger again for another winter under Rome's "summer skies." She told herself now that the old irritations in Rome had been partly her own fault. Returning there, she could invest her time more wisely—and ignore whatever seemed a direct slap at her heart. By late November she and Matilda had completed their plans, and she penned a quick note to T. H. Carrick about the miniature he had recently made of her. "My friends all think it pale—but when it was painted I was overhurried and you were very unwell." In spite of her face's shortcomings, surely a painter could help that somber countenance to a little more color and charm. Leaving Wilmot in charge of 1 Bolton Row, she and Matilda took the train for Dover.

In Rome, she found Hattie delighted to see her, not at all abashed that Matilda had come along. Seeing Hattie again, Charlotte was still not sure what to make of this impudent little American who dressed and behaved like nobody else. The Prince of Wales had recently bought one of Hattie's statues, a sprightly Puck like the one she had made for Charlotte, and now she kept her stonecutters busy turning out copies for $1,000 a piece. The Brownings were back in town, and Elizabeth was delighted when Charlotte agreed to read her new poem, "Aurora Leigh," at a gathering of *forestieri*. In her rented quarters, Charlotte quickly established her own routine: she was always "at home" on Saturday evenings.

If the return to Rome had been partly to test Matilda, the question answered itself soon enough. One morning Matilda appeared at Charlotte's bedroom door, her bags all packed, to announce that she was returning to London. A friend, Bessie Parkes, had offered her a writing job on a new magazine, *The English Woman's Journal*. Hearing the news, Charlotte could muster no grief. The friendship that had made them occupants under one roof for nearly ten years had come at last to mean little. Each of them said the right things. They smiled and embraced, yet both knew that this was the final parting.

Thus, without the delicate Miss Hays, life was easier; friendships were Charlotte's free choice again. Later, when word of George Eliot's reaction to Matilda reached her, she offered no argument. For the new journal, Bessie Parkes had "talent and real ardor for all goodness, but," said the novelist, "I fear Miss Hays has been chosen on the charitable grounds that she had nothing else to do in the world."

As the winter unfolded, Rome's skies stayed sunny. Hattie would never grow up, yet watching the girl's fame and popularity spread, Charlotte took pride in the fact that she herself had matured enough to expect no credit. Almost daily, Hattie bounded around at mid-afternoon to persuade her to come for a ride on the Campagna or on Saturday mornings to join the English hunt she had organized. Such interludes with Hattie were hardly the stones of a friendship, but then it was good to know that neither heart was involved. And once in a while, Hattie even managed to seem grateful. Charlotte Cushman "is like a mother to me," she wrote Wayman Crow, her benefactor in St. Louis, and "spoils me utterly. How good and thoughtful she is." Consequently, Charlotte's affections were uncommitted when a would-be sculptress arrived from New York. Emma Stebbins had studied art in various American studios, but she had only lately concluded, at forty-one, that if an American woman hoped for any success in the arts, she must first make a name for herself in Rome, where the best teachers and the best markets centered. In Emma, Charlotte recognized the talent and character that could win out. When Gibson declared his belief in her talent, when Paul Akers, the American sculptor, accepted her in his studio, Charlotte found herself ready to champion Miss Stebbins' career. Within weeks, she and Emma were friends.

With energy to back up her gifts, Emma was soon skilled enough to accept commissions from the touring Americans whom Charlotte steered to her door. Emma was no timid violet, no Matilda Hays shrinking into the shade. Yet she had a feminine gentleness, a sweetness Charlotte had longed to find in a friend. The friendship that grew between them was a bond between two aggressive talents, creative minds and sensibilities that fully knew the scope of their powers. By the time they returned from an Easter excursion to Naples, Charlotte and Emma knew they would plan their lives together. They donned black bowler hats for their daily rides in the Borghese, for picnics of red wine and cheese under the pines; often at night they went with other Americans to view the sculptures in the Vatican Museum by flickering torchlight, a trick that made the antique carvings come luminously alive.

When Charlotte learned for certain that Louis Harlan was an out-and-out fraud, that he had falsified the records of interest due her on some $70,000, she asked Emma Stebbins to make the trip to America with her. It would be embarrassing, perhaps, to go back to America and take back her farewell under the pressure of financial losses, but this blissful winter in Rome had clarified her ambitions. Rome had attractions now that London, for all its intellect, could not match. Rome was where Emma, the sculptress, needed to be. Yet, with the approach of summer and the brick-oven heat Rome exuded from June through September, it was fully clear that they must get away. When Emma agreed to go with her, Charlotte determined at last to make another onslaught on the American stage.

Packing, Charlotte pondered the advice Hattie had given her. Why not rid herself of the wily Harlan and take on a business counsel who could be trusted? Wayman Crow was a flourishing businessman in St. Louis, an investor with his thumb on the money pulse of the country. As Hattie's benefactor, Charlotte could expect a ready welcome from Crow. Hattie dashed off a quick note for Charlotte to take to St. Louis.

Against the day when she and Emma returned, Charlotte scouted all the available apartments in Rome. The location she contracted at last, a tall apartment at 38 Via Gregoriana, had one of Rome's noblest views at the head of the Spanish Steps above the Piazza di Spagna, near the beautiful pink church of Trinita dei Monti. From its windows, Rome stretched clear and sparkling way past the soaring dome of St. Peter's. It would be a perfect winter home.

Heading for America, Charlotte touched base with Mary Eliza and Susan; then with Emma beside her at the rail, she sailed from Liverpool. W. H. Chippendale wanted to manage her forthcoming tour. She might act one month in New York; she might act two; it was too early to tell. As for Chip's wish to book her for California and Australia, that could only be done after many details came clear. "I must have a large sum in both places to induce me to lose so much time and take so much risk," she had written him.

Yet about one possible risk, Chip's letters had reassured her. Nobody in America had really believed that she meant her "farewell" to be permanent. With audiences eager to see her again, it would be foolish to stand on a word. Women changed their minds every day. With the elaborate plans she now had for Rome, it was good to know that she still had access to big money.

Artist and Businesswoman

(1857–1858)

If Charlotte came home in September 1857 primarily to refill her pockets, she chose an unlikely time. Since her "irrevocable" farewell five years before, American business had gone wild. The country had overextended itself in industry and land speculation; it suddenly found itself now, with the end of the Crimean War and the resulting slump in foreign markets, in deep depression. Charlotte's own hopes for a lavish life ahead found little encouragement as she and Sallie observed from their carriage the changes that New York had undergone. The city had obviously gone on growing; new five-story buildings now towered where empty lots and family houses had stood before. But boarded-up shop fronts stared at them now; in the shadowed doorways tattered figures sat huddled, raising empty hands to the glum faces passing by.

But W. E. Burton ushered them jovially into his office at his New Theatre on Broadway, tossing off Charlotte's worried questions. True, recent months had been the darkest season in memory; the dozen theatres in New York were indeed suffering difficult times, but a glittering name like hers on a marquee could still create excitement; hands would gladly dig deep to see Charlotte Cushman. Besides, greenrooms all over New York had guessed her secret; her timing was perfect. She had kept herself out of the limelight just long enough to enhance her appeal now as some foreign exotic.

Charlotte might have countered Burton's interesting theory with a simpler story, but if her "timing" paid off, for whatever reason, she could hardly complain. Stardom was, of course, only partially talent. It was no less a pose, a pose that required a star to maintain a certain distance. No star could remain long in the public view lest it come to see her at last as an ordinary mortal. The proof would be in the box office, beginning September 28 with *Fazio*.

At her hotel, Charlotte had hardly taken off her bonnet and cloak when callers came knocking. It was good to be back in New York, but in the sudden crush of visitors, Charlotte wondered if she could possibly work. When James Murdoch called, protesting that actors ought to despise the custom, Charlotte cried at him: "You astonish me! Look there," she said, pointing to her bulging calling card stand. "I have all those to return, though I have been busy at it ever since my arrival. One cannot be too careful of popular interest," especially if popular interest meant cheering crowds at Burton's.

For her opening gun in this new American campaign, Charlotte had chosen her play carefully. Many eyes would be seeing her now for the first time. Upon them she must register all her range and power, almost as if this were a fresh debut. She was not long into Bianca's woes and sufferings when she knew she had triumphed again. The *Tribune* next morning delivered the proper verdict. "She is all she ever was, and more. Time has not touched her with a feather of his gray wing." She had gained weight, to be sure, but in the process Miss Cushman had returned to the American stage "less metallic in her passions . . . more tender, more delicate."

The sellout houses fully confirmed her hopes. No outcry complained that she had rescinded her word "farewell." Instead, nightly crowds jammed Broadway, lamenting that all the seats, even standing room, were gone long before curtain time. During the month-long engagement she played her old standbys: Lady Teazle, Mrs. Haller, Lady Gay, Rosalind, La Tisbe, Queen Katharine, Meg ("She was born for the part," cried the *Spirit,* "and having performed it, her destiny is fulfilled")—even Romeo. The *Evening Post* doubted that anything had "ever been seen on the stage more perfectly successful" than Meg Merrilies. For her Rosalind, the *Spirit* pulled out its rarest adjectives: "What fine and novel coloring, what new meaning by emphasis alone." Watching the frenzied ovations Charlotte drew night after night, Burton extended her contract for most of November.

Engulfed in the cheers, Charlotte concluded that as an artist she could not let herself off so easy. To test her powers in a role wholly new to her, she would play Cardinal Wolsey in *Henry VIII* on November 13. Burton approved the idea, partly because he, along with Wagner, saw that age and poundage had unfitted Charlotte at last for her old heart's love, Romeo. Playing "the scarlet sin"

presented difficulties, but she welcomed them now, in spite of the
noisy evidence each night that she could go on acting forever the old
titanic characters that had cemented her fame.

To carry conviction, her Wolsey must match, in bearing and impact, the other male roles, especially in the high-tension scenes when
the wily Cardinal knows at last that he has lost Henry's favor and
must counter the attacks of Surrey and Suffolk without the royal
grace to support him—maintaining all the while the lofty, compelling
state of Shakespeare's brilliant "high Cardinal." She must forget all
her innate sympathies. As Katharine's demon assailant, her Wolsey
must show not the slightest compassion.

Audience sympathy inevitably went to the suffering Queen, yet
Charlotte's Wolsey attracted more than a little compassion. Dis-
credited at last, replaced by other men in Henry's affection, Wolsey
could only croak his regrets and advice: "Go, get thee from me,
Cromwell. I am a poor fall'n man, unworthy now To be thy lord
and master. Seek the King. That sun, I pray, may never set! . . .
Some little memory of me will stir him—I know his noble nature—
not to let Thy hopeful service perish too."

Later, even Katharine could feel a sympathy for any Cardinal who
could cry out, "Cromwell, Cromwell! Had I but served my God
with half the zeal I served my King, he would not in mine age Have
left me naked to mine enemies."

The cheers that exploded over the words confirmed Charlotte's
own satisfaction in the role. No living actor, one critic declared,
could equal the power this actress had injected into the Cardinal's
fall. "She made old playgoers recall the times of Cooke, Kean, and
Macready." Later perfomances sustained the verdict. Charlotte Cushman's Cardinal was "one of those intellectual triumphs which indi-
cates the actor's power to depict thought as well as passion." In her
deep rich tones, sometimes whispered, sometimes shouted, New York
had never known a grander Wolsey.

November had seen the worst box offices in New York history.
To stay open at all, theatres had dropped their prices to almost nothing. One night when more than 15,000 people in all New York had
bought theatre seats, the average cost was twenty-seven cents. Yet
Charlotte closed her seven-week run with bursting pockets, firmly
certain that western cities would now pose no problem. She wrote
full instructions ahead: "I think Macbeth a bad *first night* play because Lady M is not on in the last scene, and much of the effect of

my drawing, I think, depends upon the first night." For it, "Fazio
. . . is better."

While Emma Stebbins stayed in New York with her sisters, Charlotte took to the circuit through Troy, Albany, Buffalo, and down
to Philadelphia. For a send-off, the New York *Express* praised her
for championing American status abroad: "Just now, when our race
horses are distancing competitors, and our yachts have won leading
honors in England, we have a little pride in pointing to the stage
also, and claiming American prominence there. England has no actress like Charlotte Cushman." Unique in her art, she typified the
success that seemed particularly American. "With her, position has
been won, step by step, against disadvantages and early disappoint-
ments that would have crushed an ordinary woman." In her victory,
her countrymen took pride.

Another proud name in the American theatre soon came to Charlotte's notice. Young Edwin Booth had just begun a career that
might destine him for the top of the ladder. The son of erascible,
unpredictable, old Junius Brutus had so impressed Julia Ward Howe
one April evening in Boston, playing Richelieu, that she turned to
her husband and cried, "This is the real thing!" A night or so later,
Booth's dreamy, poetic Hamlet convinced her anew that a great new
star had risen. When Booth's manager came to ask Julia to write a
play for him, she joyously agreed, and when the austerely beautiful
young actor himself came calling, Julia found him so "modest, intelligent, and above all genuine" that she began planning her drama
immediately. In her plans, some miracle must entice Charlotte Cushman into the cast.

When Julia wrote Charlotte that her play would follow the
Phaedre–Hippolytus story, Charlotte took an interest. Throughout
the fall of 1857, Charlotte filled her letters to the "Dearest and best
of Giulias" with advice and suggestions. Julia must pattern her chorus
after *Antigone*. "You know—during pauses in the acted drama while
the action seems to rest, the chorus play their parts on each side of
the lower (or audience part of the) stage, the strophe, antestrophe,
and general chorus. This I want done."

Julia fired off a delighted reply. "Well, dear, your letter quite changes the world for me. That you should appear in a play of mine is already in itself a success, and what you do cannot fail." Her words, said Julia, sprang from a double joy. In the triumph Charlotte Cushman had achieved as a woman, "I feel much better about womankind."

"Can you not send me a fair copy," Charlotte answered, "such as one would act or read from?" the better to visualize the staging. Alongside Edwin Booth's young fire, Charlotte imagined herself as the Phaedre, burning with passion for the foolish Hippolytus who scorned his stepmother's advances. For playwright and actors alike, the play could be an American triumph. "If woman can accomplish it," Charlotte assured Julia, the play would be produced in Boston no later than next January.

Unfortunately, one woman's excitement could not accomplish what another female, more strategically placed, could. Reading the script, E. L. Davenport easily imagined the play's success at his Howard Athenaeum in Boston, in spite of its "dark" subject, but when his wife disliked the small part in it for her and threatened to make trouble, Davenport returned Julia's play.

Bitter and disappointed, Julia Ward Howe determined never to write again for the stage; the risks for American playwrights were far too great in this strangely uncultured country. And Charlotte stood helpless and angry, while the fire that had surged in her died. If reports about young Booth were even half true, America could have seen a genius create a role to challenge anything ever done by the boorish Edwin Forrest. Deflated herself, she could only scoff now at Davenport's stupid weakness. Writing Julia, Charlotte affected no foolish modesty. "My dear," she cried, "if Edwin Booth and I had done nothing more than stand upon the stage and say 'good evening' to each other, the house would have been filled." It was lamentable proof of America's naïveté that just now no other manager would risk bringing out a "dark" American play.

To get on with the business at hand, Charlotte braved a six-day train ride in mid-January 1858 through the snows of Ohio, Indiana, and Illinois. She played to full houses at James McVicker's new theatre in Chicago and afterward assured a reporter that she might visit California during the spring.

Charlotte then moved down to St. Louis for a two-week run at Wood's Theatre where, between stints, she could meet Wayman Crow, Hattie's friend and adviser. At her opening as Romeo, the grace of the bird-like Juliet almost overpowered her. Mary Devlin's limpid talent outshone all the skill Charlotte had ever seen in a Juliet. The girl's face was not truly beautiful, but it glowed with a delicate charm which the dark ringlets at each side of her face only enhanced. This girl might rise to the heights if properly trained and encouraged. Watching out front, Wayman Crow's daughter thrilled enviously during the balcony scene when Romeo returned again and again, hungering for another embrace, finally pressing one of Juliet's curls to his lips.

Next morning, when Charlotte entered Wayman Crow's book-lined office, she confronted a commanding figure, a strong face set with animated blue eyes that radiated character and judgment. In the talk that followed, hearing Crow spell out the pros and cons of various investments, she concluded that this man—unlike most others she had known—had a canny brain that could serve her well. Remembering her bitter losses with Harlan, she would not give Crow control of her property, but he could advise her through letters about the wisest means of keeping her money at work. Crow echoed her heartily; railroads, mines, and city real estate were sure to pay off in time. In the country's present ills, she must expect no miracles from her new investment counselor—but in this great America, crises could not last forever.

When the business conference ended, Crow ushered in his nineteen-year-old daughter Emma, a spirited, dark-haired beauty that reminded Charlotte of Hattie, though Emma was all ruffles and lace—not at all the type to care about making a name in a man's world. When the Crows invited Charlotte out to their lavish house overlooking the Mississippi, her friendship with the family deepened as, day after day, Crow sent his carriage for her. Nights when she played Meg Merrilies, she took Emma Crow backstage to watch her put on her makeup, though the time was no social occasion and the girl sat quiet and unnoticed in a corner. Watching Charlotte, Emma Crow sat disbelieving as the woman she happily claimed now as a friend transformed herself into some grand unknown character. After Queen Katharine's dying scene, she rushed back each night to make sure the death had only been acting. When she found Charlotte in her dressing room, her healthy self still, she fell laughing into Charlotte's arms.

Together, Charlotte and Emma Crow went for carriage rides along the teeming river where steamboats took on or disgorged their cargoes, past wagon yards filled with stamping mules and ox-teams and leather-faced men whipping wagon trains into line for their long westward roll through Indian country. Already, rumor had it that by September regular stagecoaches, pulled at top speed, would shrink the 2700 miles between St. Louis and San Francisco to a mere twenty-six days. Thinking about that trip, Charlotte figured she might someday brave it herself, might even take along this bundle of gaiety beside her—the perils of the trip notwithstanding.

At Wood's Theatre, Charlotte made another lasting impression. When she told the prompter she needed a boy to carry her heavy basket of stage jewelry each evening to and from the theatre, the prompter pointed to J. B. Pond, a lad who lived on the seven dollars a week he made as callboy. "I must have somebody that I can rely upon who will walk faithfully by my side," she said. She would pay a dollar a night.

Throughout her run, Jimmy Pond carried her basket faithfully. On her last Saturday, when the boy failed to report, she found him backstage in the shadows, curled up ill on a pile of drapes. She spoke to him a few minutes, then slipped a twenty-dollar gold piece into his hand.

Next day, when the Crows bade her good-bye at the gangplank of the *Baltic,* the steamboat to New Orleans, Charlotte kissed her fingers to the girl waving tearfully down below and vowed in her heart that letters must somehow maintain this friendship. Downstream, Charlotte mailed back letters that struggled to express her feelings for Emma Crow. "Who but the dearest 'little love' in the world" would have put up the delicious lunch that "comforted me marvelous much on my tedious journey to Cairo?" she wrote, or "sent me such a pretty, nice, sweet, loving, clever note as the 'dear little love' I have inspired in my old age?"

At her writing desk in the lounge of the *Baltic,* Charlotte remembered again the parting scene in St. Louis. "I have to thank you, dear, for all of these and do thank you and love you very much for them and more than these for the bright tears you gave me." Time, of course, would make the girl wonder that she ever declared so fervent a love for an old woman. "However I will trust you . . . my sweet little love, and believe that you will ever be true and devoted."

In New Orleans, Charlotte played Romeo with a fresh verve and passion "eminently characteristic of the great poet's creation," as the

Picayune said, mirroring the new affection that had blossomed in St. Louis. "Time has dealt very kindly with our accomplished tragedienne, and we do not remember ever seeing her look better." After her happy days up river, New Orleans at carnival time offered Charlotte the perfect match for her own high spirits. To rehearsals, she brought a new zest. When a scene in *The Actress of Padua* required her and the walking lady to kneel reverently at a shrine, Charlotte coached Catherine Reignolds for more than an hour in order to achieve the right tone. When her terrible Meg made Catherine forget her lines and stand speechless, she glared down amused at the girl, then reached out, lifted her firmly, and set her down where she belonged.

Charlotte's fourteen nights netted her $5,310, an incredible take in the light of the country's depression. Her delight increased even more her last evening when a white-haired, bent old man in a black silk coat came to her dressing room. R. D. Shepherd, her old benefactor in Boston, had come to tell her that he had just witnessed the fruit of his early hopes. In the midst of her delighted cries Charlotte grasped Shepherd's hand and promised to sit for a portrait as soon as she got back to Rome. Giving Shepherd a marble bust for his library was the least she could do to repay him.

Moving north aboard a series of bouncing coaches, Charlotte bore up under the dust and the splashing mud and the late spring snows by planning the times ahead. Shrewdly placed, all this new money ought to support her plans for England and Rome. Soon she could say another quick farewell to Boston and New York. Meanwhile, she proved in Nashville again what a trouper does in an emergency. Once before, she had covered her shock on stage when she snagged a heel in her train and fell to the floor. Now, when she held her candle too close and her veil burst into flame, she continued her speech, all the while ripping off the veil and quickly stamping out the fire with her foot.

Writing St. Louis, Charlotte poured out her hopes that Emma Crow could visit the new apartment in Rome next winter. With the letter she enclosed a bracelet made from her own brown hair twined in gold. When the other Emma of her heart, Miss Stebbins, joined her in May in Washington, Charlotte counted her blessings complete; she had cast loneliness and grief behind her.

She and Emma declined Senator Seward's invitation to stay in his home on Lafayette Square, but she filled her afternoon visits with him conjecturing about states' rights and foreign policy, then sat attentive while Seward, his long Roman nose bobbing up and down, punctuating the air with his big cigar, spelled out his dreams for a great America that would one day include all of Canada and Mexico. "The improvability of our race is without limit." She laughed at his quick anecdotes, all the while realizing just how closely she and Seward thought alike, even paralleled each other in temperament. She and Emma rode with him one afternoon up Capitol Hill to see the slow progress the builders were making on the tall dome.

Leaving Washington, Charlotte chuckled at the note Seward had enclosed with her new passport. Charlotte must complete the form it contained and return it for filing in the State Department. Seward imagined the satisfaction "it must give you to have an opportunity to describe yourself, your face, complexion, glossy hair, chin . . . and lastly your age," but the record would be useful in history, and in the meantime, "if you shall get the country into any (scrapes) while you are abroad, we shall have the satisfaction of knowing just what the subject of controversy is, an advantage which belligerent states seldom enjoy."

After Providence, Charlotte was ready to tell Boston another good-bye. At Elizabeth Peabody's bookshop on West Street, she invited a crowd of old literary friends to the theatre, then smiled on stage when she saw the eccentric Miss Peabody, clad in an outlandish tall hat and black shawl, peering at her from one of the boxes. Elizabeth sat raptly watching Charlotte's Katharine blend slowly "the infirmities of dying with the majesty of her spirit." "In the very death," she said later, Charlotte "went out of the body almost visibly."

The playbills had advertised this two-week run as Boston's last chance to bid a proper Godspeed to "the greatest living actress." But watching Charlotte's acting, Edwin Forrest's good friend "Acorn" lamented that it "startles and thrills" but it "does not please." Full of Macready mannerisms, Miss Cushman's Lady Macbeth was too much a bully: Macbeth would have hurled such a shrew out of his castle. But "Acorn" admitted that whatever differences might exist in the minds of critics, Charlotte Cushman was "a woman of extraordinary intellectual strength and power."

That power registered deep on young Louisa May Alcott. "Saw

Charlotte Cushman," she told her diary, "and had a stage struck fit." Louisa never became the actress she dreamed that night of being, but as a novelist she later used the excitement she had felt when she made the actress, Miss Cameron, in *Jo's Boys,* a near-translation of Charlotte. "Miss Cameron had lost her lover years ago," she wrote in 1886, "and since had lived only for art." When Josie confesses her dreams to Miss Cameron ("I don't expect to be a Mrs. Siddons or a Miss Cameron, much as I long to be"), the actress replies: "It would be pleasant to me to know that when I quit the stage I leave behind me a well-trained, faithful, gifted comrade to more than fill my place, and carry on what I have much at heart,—the purification of the stage."

To Charlotte's last nights in Boston, another girl who would make her literary mark reacted strongly. "The other day, upon returning from Boston," Kate Field wrote in her journal, "after having become excited over Miss Cushman, I shut myself up and wrote some verses to her," in reply to which "I received a cunning little note from Charlotte Cushman. She says she will write again. Oh, if I could only have a European correspondence with her, how delightful it would be *for me.*"

But the most astonishing visitor Charlotte received was the shambling, tousled figure who came hat in hand to her door at intermission. Mr. Topliff, her father's cutthroat old partner, was destitute: could Charlotte lend him some money? She stood silent, letting the amazing request sink in. Her eyes blazing, she glared at Topliff, while he shuffled his feet, abashed and downcast. Her first thought was to hurl the wizened old crook out the door. But she recognized in the scene a beautiful justice. Still unspeaking, she untied her purse, took out some large coins, and thrust them into his hand. He could not miss the scorn in her gesture, the canny revulsion in her eyes. But he could not guess her motive. Topliff's name had always stood for all her earliest pains and struggles, but she recognized now a peculiar debt she owed him.

That night, standing on stage among the farewell bouquets the ushers laid at her feet, Charlotte delivered the curtain speech that echoed her feelings about Topliff. "On the 8th of April, 1835, then eighteen years of age . . . I launched my tiny craft upon the sea of public opinion, in a course of alternate storms and calms, which has known no retrogression, but which has ever been onward." Boston's approval, among the earliest breezes, had always filled her sails, but "I have met many land rats, and water rats (pirates, I mean)

283

cruisers under false colors, mermen and mermaids, rocks, shoals, and quick-sands." But with hope at the prow and a steadfast will at the helm, "I have, after twenty-three years' voyage, come into the port of friends' esteem, with the colors of independence nailed to the masthead." Saying the words, she knew now that without Topliff's bitter part in Elkanah's failure, she might never have found her role.

New York gave her a send-off as warm as Boston's. On July 6, answering the roaring applause out front, she pushed through the curtains at Niblo's Garden to make a grand, sweeping bow, then announced her intention to retire forever, unless "fortune should prove adverse" once again. Memories might have questioned the meaning of Charlotte's word "farewell." They had believed her once; could they believe her now? The *Times* next day took her seriously. Charlotte Cushman had cut off her American career "unnecessarily." A law ought "to prevent her doing so."

For Charlotte, the word was sincere as always. In 1852, she had cut her ties honestly; acting involved too many sordid contacts. Now, she was tired. With Emma Stebbins wanting to get back to work, she could return now to the rich life in Europe with a fortune safely invested. So far as anyone could predict, on this midsummer eve of 1858, she need never go back on her word.

At Home in Rome

(1858–1860)

At forty-two, Charlotte felt she had chiseled her celebrated name and her characters deep enough on the public platform. She pictured herself now on an easier private stage, her homes in England and Rome, where she could slip into whatever role whim and affection dictated. With Emma Stebbins happily content at her side, there could be no doubt, surely, that she could find in Rome outlets enough for her energies.

Ten days later, at tea in Susan's leafy garden, Charlotte heard all the news about Ned, that he had left the American Navy to join the East India Merchant Marine, that during a recent cruise to Calcutta he had fallen prey to cholera but miraculously was mending. Ned's pictures showed a beautiful young man with piercing eyes, fluted nostrils and sensitive chin, a black mustache and side whiskers. Charlotte had her own opinion about the foolish life Ned had chosen when he could so easily join her in Rome and move among cultivated people, where she could open for him such interesting doors—and, incidentally, where she could help mold his character.

Regretting that she could do so little about this willful adopted son, she moved on to Malvern, to spend six easy weeks while the baths, the strolls, and the long letters she wrote Emma Crow relaxed her from her labors. In London, she stopped long enough to check with Wilmot at 1 Bolton Row, store her costumes safely away, pay a few courtesy calls, accept a few invitations, and forward a string of good pearls to Mary Devlin in St. Louis. Then she booked tickets for Rome.

Out at her mother's small house in Brixton, she sensed a hostility in Mary Eliza, if not in Charlie. Patiently, she explained again the routine she would follow in Rome, and just how Emma Stebbins figured in it. Yet in Mary Eliza's pursed mouth, she read nothing but disapproval. There seemed no way to make her mother understand the depth of the bond that constituted her life with Emma or the pleasure she found with her other "aristocratic friends," as Charlie called them. She reminded herself at last that she was beholden to nobody, Mary Eliza's old ways and old creeds notwithstanding.

After Paris and Strasbourg, she and Emma took a rumbling diligence for the hairpin ride over Mont Cenis, with its flowered meadows and waterfalls, then down into Italy around Lake Como for the train to Florence, where she found Isa Blagden and Elizabeth Barrett Browning still wildly excited over spirit writing. But Charlotte was more interested in her talks with James Jackson Jarves about the antiques he could help her acquire for her Rome apartment. Soon, she pushed on south through Tuscany until one late afternoon, from a pine-tufted outlook, she sighted again the purple hills, the silver river, and the gold and umber cluster of Rome.

When her carriage rolled up the Via Gregoriana and stopped at Number 38, Charlotte was home. Her bronze doorway stood recessed under a beveled arch; overhead jutted four tiers of balconies. To her right up the short street, she saw the salmon towers of the Trinita dei Monti church that fronted the Spanish Steps. Farther on opened the wide promenade of the Pincian Hill with its scarlet gardens, its flocks of rooks, and its dark jagged pines.

Inside, she and Emma Stebbins rejoiced again at their luck. The marble rooms would make a comfortable home, yet they were adequate too for the Saturday evenings Charlotte planned. Her back windows opened out over multicolored houses and churches, the winding Tiber, and farther on the Pantheon, Hadrian's Tomb, and St. Peter's—and beyond it all, the plains and rolling green hills of the Campagna. In her back garden she found acanthus, tumbling geraniums, and orange trees, and fragments of Roman sculpture embedded in the walls; in a far corner, a vertical shaft of a well opened, far below, into a cavern where serving women from the neighborhood came to fill their buckets.

In the busy days that followed, making the rounds of the antique shops and studios, gathering statuary, more paintings, and rare Italian cabinets and carved chairs, Charlotte rejoiced again in the wealth that work had brought her. Here in Rome, she could afford a life that would have cost her double the price at home. Under one roof, there was ample space here for Hattie Hosmer—who had already accepted Charlotte's invitation and moved in—for Emma Stebbins, and for herself in the second-floor suite with its sunny front windows and an alcove for her writing desk. Below, Sallie had her own quarters.

During Charlotte's absence, Hattie had set for herself a schedule that would have toppled a lesser vigor. After nightly parties, she joined a table of bearded sculptors in the smoky Caffe Greco to talk shop and hotly defend the merits of women as artists; then about one o'clock she bounded home unescorted for a few quick hours of sleep. At seven she leaped out of bed, tore off to work amid her clay figures, her great marble blocks, and charcoal sketches until late afternoon, when she galloped off for a pounding ride on the Campagna. By night, Hattie was ready for more parties. When the Hawthornes came down from Liverpool, overjoyed to be free at last of the Consulate and the Mersey's glowering skies, they found her perched atop a scaffold, her black velvet cap and short skirt matching perfectly her puckish greeting, the rapid strokes of her hands shaping the clay. Her obvious delight in her work captivated all the family, though Hawthorne hoped privately that this good Watertown girl would someday adopt a more sober style.

Charlotte fully agreed with Hawthorne. Having the girl here in the apartment, she had thought she might quell Hattie's energies a little, bring her to form, as it were, yet there seemed little she could do with Hattie, except shake her head and recall the days when she herself, in boots and cravat, had dismayed a proper England. Hattie led her own life and welcomed advice from no one. At a late dinner party one evening, when a monocled Englishman offered to escort her home, Hattie convulsed the table: "No gentleman goes home with me at night in Rome."

For Charlotte, Emma Stebbins was more to her style. When Emma took a studio nearby in the Via Sistina, Charlotte joined her for a lunch of cheese, prosciutto, and fruit each day at one; then while Emma finished off her work for the day, Charlotte sat in the cool window and wrote long, endearing letters to Emma Crow, describing her lazy routine: "I have lived a life of labour, and now that I have achieved a position and a fortune to support it I feel that I am only right to enjoy what is thrown in my way."

After lunch they returned to the apartment to change into black skirts and hats for an afternoon ride. On days when they planned to take the high jumps on the Campagna, Charlotte rode her Italian horse, Othello, who seemed to understand on instinct the sudden precipices that made a Campagna ride so exhilarating. "Unsurpassed days," Emma called them, "days of glory and beauty." Home for an early dinner, they were ready for guests by eight, or after an evening alone—teaching Bushie, the new Scotch terrier, to "play the piano" or "sing"—they were in bed by eleven.

Sallie and her Italian maids had the apartment ready for Charlotte's first big party in January 1859. Moving gaily among the palms and flowers, the cages of twittering birds, her guests saw the antique cabinets Jarves had sent down from Florence, their handles like battered shields, the gilded monogram locks on their doors. Women who wandered into Charlotte's bedroom saw the portrait of Jane Carlyle on her wall. Downstairs hung her paintings by William Page, her Sully portrait, and, in her bookcases, her autographed copy of *The Scarlet Letter*.

Ensuing months saw her Saturday evenings become social events for Rome's *forestieri*, occasions for welcoming newcomers from London or Boston or New York, where sculptors like Randolph Rogers, Story, Gibson, Paul Akers, and Louise Lander, painters like Page, poets like the Brownings, novelists like Hawthorne, Harriet Beecher Stowe, and the Trollopes, and musicians like Adelaide Sartoris matched wits with cardinals and Vatican people, with Dickie Milnes —now Lord Houghton—and American tycoons like William B. Ogden and Emma Stebbins' rich brother, Henry. Writers argued ideas they would later expand in print. If Dickie was right that conversation is the "happy counterplay of witty minds," politics and science and business vied with art and high humor around Charlotte's candlelit table.

Here, Page defended his "rediscovery" of Titian's pigmentation and fumed that the Paris Exhibition had just rejected his "Venus Rising from the Sea"—"a wonder of light and colour and space and breathable air," Mrs. Browning called it—on grounds of its nudity.

With Hattie cheering him on, Gibson argued that modern sculptors in their pursuit of "the ideal" should follow the Greeks in painting in eye color and in staining their marble pale gold—perhaps with tobacco juice—to bring out its warmth. To which Hawthorne muttered from his corner, "Were he to send a Cupid to America, he need not trouble himself to stain it beforehand."

The small, wiry Story doubted that honest sculptors ever turned their clay models over to stonecutters. Mallet and chisel were a sculptor's own proper tools: "If I want a line different—a blow, and there it is." To this, Hattie quickly rejoined. Story himself had said more than once that Michelangelo had wasted precious hours roughing off chips when his genius might better have turned to new visions. Her studio workmen saved her days, dutifully copying leaves, turning drapery folds, while she worked up new ideas in clay. Randolph Rogers agreed with Hattie. At the moment, there were seven Nydias in his studio, each in some state of completion by a cutter armed with caliper and chisels.

Hawthorne developed ideas about a sculptor's responsibility, which he soon broadcast in *The Marble Faun*. Since marble did not decay, since it ensured immortality to whatever was carved in it, the worthy sculptor had an almost religious obligation to commit no idea to it "save such as may repay the marble for its faithful care." Slumped on a sofa, puffing his black cigar, Hawthorne pondered American women like Louise Lander and Hattie, young women thousands of miles from home, going fearlessly about, pursuing their own artistic fulfillment.

White-haired Frances Trollope, down from her villa in Florence, set off gales of laughter with her jabs about how the "nudo" in antique sculpture so scandalized visiting Americans. It reminded her of her visit, thirty years back, to the sculpture gallery in the Pennsylvania Academy, where a female attendant had whispered, "Now, ma'am, now: this is the time for you—nobody can see you—make haste." When Fanny stared at her surprised, the woman explained: "The ladies like to go into that room by themselves, when there be no gentlemen watching them."

Morality aside, Hawthorne wondered if all nudity in art was justified. Man was no longer a naked animal. "His clothes are as natural to him as his skin, and sculptors have no more right to undress him than to flay him." Yet he readily confessed that the romantic sense of eternity in Rome played tricks with one's wish to be literal. In America, struggle as one might, it was difficult to write a romance "where there is no shadow, no antiquity, no mystery, no picturesque and gloomy wrong, nor anything but a commonplace prosperity" in broad daylight—which was just the reason, was it not, why they had all come to Rome?

Hiram Powers regaled them further with his stories about the average American's disbelief that good art should cost money. "Two thousand dollars! My stars!" he quoted one of them. "Why I bought one t'other day for two hundred dollars, and it ain't plaster neither, for I drew my jack-knife right across her nose, and it never made a scratch."

Hopping about, Browning injected a special excitement into the talk, but he so rarely pursued one topic for long that following his ideas was often maddening. Why did he so seldom, Charlotte wondered, center his thoughts on spiritual matters? There was something truly objectionable about a poetic sensibility that focused so short. "He says some splendid things," she later wrote Emma Crow, "but most of his finest is spoiled by materialism—or rather man-ism."

Secure in the fame that *Uncle Tom's Cabin* had brought her, Harriet Stowe put up her feet on Charlotte's fender. In that position, she could "talk till all is blue," she cried gaily. When the question of women's rights came up, Harriet poured out a sermon as fiery as any her brother Henry Ward had ever preached in Brooklyn: "Did anybody ever think that Mrs. Siddons and Mrs. Kemble and Ristori had better have applied themselves sedulously to keeping house, because they were women?" To that, Hattie cried amen. A woman's talents were not hers for nothing. Every woman had the god-given duty to educate herself for any profession that interested her and to practice it for her own good. She should be free to set her own course, work toward her own goals. Most women, of course, would always choose a partner to fight their battles for them, but the gifted few would always prefer to make their own way in the world. "What fun it would be to come back to this earth after . . . a hundred years or so and see what has been going on in flesh while we have been going on in spirit."

Clapping her hands in agreement, Charlotte bade them recall something Lydia Maria Child had said years ago. Someday, men and women would think of themselves as equal members in a domestic team, would perceive that "there is no separation or discord in their mutual duties." They would be one: "the treble and bass of the same harmonious tune."

In the spring, when a starry-eyed Kate Field arrived from Boston with her aunt, Charlotte welcomed them the evening her guests were Levasseur from the Palais Royal Theatre in Paris and former President Pierce—who was "very polite" but not a man "of much fun." Yet since talk in Charlotte's salon was free to take any turn, darker notes inevitably crept in. Living in Rome was not wholly bliss. Rome's legal system was maddening. At carnival, young Julian Hawthorne stood amazed that the crowd took no notice when a woman, disliking a young man's flirting remarks, whipped out a dagger and ripped him open. And for reasons no American could comprehend, when trouble broke out among these passionate screaming Romans, the first to complain in court was automatically declared innocent. In this Papal country, no Protestant church existed —though it was hoped that sometime in the future permisison might be obtained for worship somewhere outside the walls.

Furthermore, no one went safely abroad at night—Hattie's loud cries to the contrary—unless he went armed and carried his own wax tapers. Servants were always a problem. Charlotte's cook, Augusto, was a *chef par excellence,* yet she had had him little more than a month before she realized that he carried on a constant graft in the kitchen, extracting his own percent of supplies. All over Rome, petty thievery flourished. If one let himself notice, the streets were appallingly dirty—"malarious and fleay," Hattie cried gaily—and its people were wholly immodest and as uninhibited as children. Shaking their heads, Charlotte and her guests agreed that life here was interesting. They had not come to Rome to change it.

Real unpleasantness was rare the winter of 1859. Yet into the sweetness and light that enlivened Charlotte's gatherings a grievous fear intervened. With her guests, Charlotte felt a growing concern for the big American question of slavery that the papers from New York and London daily featured. Kate Field had heard it voiced strongly in Florence.

"Last Monday slavery was attacked," said Kate, "and I, an American, in the mingling of Italian, French, and English" had to protect her country. "Foreigners cannot understand the 'peculiar institution,' and that it is no child's play to free 4,000,000 blacks. The English, the very creatures who forced it upon us, are most bitter against us."

American papers never let their readers forget that states' rights and union and Negro slavery were questions that would not wait unanswered forever. *Uncle Tom's Cabin* and John Brown's recent wild scheme at Harper's Ferry foretold tragedy. In the dread thought, Charlotte recalled the worry she had seen in Seward's eyes whenever such questions arose, the human misery chained below decks as she sailed the Mississippi. War must not come; elections next year would provide the answer.

A closer war troubled her now. Already, gunfire could be heard almost within range of Rome. Napoleon III and Victor Emmanuel, King of Sardinia, had lately agreed to destroy Italy's insufferable inconvenience as a divided nation. When battles at Magenta and Solferino destroyed Austria's hold on north Italy, Napoleon turned his attention to the Rhine, leaving Victor Emmanuel free to encourage insurrections in Sicily that could eventually unify all of Italy.

When Garibaldi's efforts in Sicily and Naples succeeded, only Rome itself—still loyal to Pius IX—remained independent. Now, with the Pope's hold on Rome gradually weakening, who could predict what changes an altered Vatican status might bring the *forestieri*?

At ease among her treasures, Charlotte found the question almost rhetorical. Had they not all seen old Pio Nono make his usual appearances in St. Peter's? Had they not seen the tears of the faithful thousands massed in Piazza San Pietro to see the beloved old Pope appear on his balcony to smile and raise his arms in blessing? The end of the church's political hold on Rome seemed too far away to be real.

Charlotte tried not to waste her thoughts on worry. At her table, when the question arose about which was the greater art—poetry or fiction? painting or sculpture? she laid down her fork and delivered the conviction her life had taught her: "When God conceived the world, that was poetry. When he formed it, that was sculpture. He colored it and that was painting. Then, as his crowning work, he peopled it with living beings, and that was grand, divine, eternal drama."

Not so, cried Adelaide Sartoris. Music was still supreme. Later in the evening, when Adelaide told them that Fanny Kemble had recently made a brilliant success in New York reading *The Tempest,* the report proved, said Charlotte, just how right she had been about acting. Yet, if the group wanted proof that music was worthy enough, Charlotte would gladly oblige by singing. Enjoying her joke, she took her seat at the piano and sang one of her comic ballads—"Father Molloy."

Writing Elizabeth Peabody later, Charlotte was grateful that Boston propriety had found in her art a proper Godliness. "No one knows better than myself, after all my association with artists of sculpture or painting, how truly *my* art comprehends all the others and surpasses them." Such was a "truth more or less powerful as one is more or less truly gifted by the good God."

Sparring ideas with her guests, Charlotte wondered how Susan could bear gloomy Liverpool. Or for that matter, how anyone could live in America without the vigorous wit that swirled so delightfully here. If America had no monuments, no art traditions, the least she could do in Rome was offer a stage where the drama of art could be played, where even women could argue their deepest convictions— and American and English money could meet artists who needed customers.

Since American tourists seemed to believe that a Roman picture or statue was better than one created anywhere else, she gladly fostered the notion by arranging visits where sales could be made. Whether thinking about Page or Emma or Hattie, or American financiers like William B. Ogden—whose railroads were pushing westward toward California—she made the system profitable for both sides.

"Dear Mr. Story," she wrote, "Will you come quite socially to take a cup of tea with us on Saturday evening?" to meet a few Americans, "strangers to you, but worth cultivating (?) in the *studio* way."

Already she knew that without her for a salesman, Emma Stebbins would be lost. Emma had force as an artist, but her shyness had become a private joke between them. To Emma, every path was crowded with lions, and she wasted much time thinking how to avoid them. But with Charlotte nearby, arguing that most lions were imaginary, Emma agreed that she might be right—for any one particular lion. Together, they happily composed a team—if not quite the treble and bass of the harmony Lydia Child described.

For herself, Charlotte could socialize or not as she pleased. Out on the Campagna she galloped through meadows and past ruins that challenged her to clamber through them. When she rode to the hounds with Hattie, she sometimes came in the winner, then sank into a camp chair under a striped marquee for a picnic of ham and hard rolls. On days when she lacked "spirit" for the Campagna, she summoned Penini Browning, who kept his pony in her stable, to ride with her in woods closer home. At nine, Pen was still so pretty in his curls and velvet that she wished, with Hawthorne, that his father might somehow make him more robust and earthly, give him "a thicker scabbard to sheathe his spirit in."

When Ned wrote from England that he had come back, fully recovered from cholera, she flooded him with letters to join her. Surely, the sea life had little to match the place she could offer him here. When Ned arrived, Charlotte knew at once that, at twenty-one, he lacked nothing as far as looks were concerned. It remained to be seen if he had the intellect to profit from all the advantages. On a picnic at Hadrian's Villa, with Emma and Hattie and Kate Field, she assured Ned that Rome was where he ought to be. But Ned, it developed, had merely come down to Rome to see Auntie—and to say he really preferred, just now, a life at sea.

Ned was packing to ship for Australia and Charlotte was down with a fever when a telegram brought word that Susan was ill, that Charlotte and Ned must come. Ned rushed north immediately, and Charlotte followed as soon as she could raise her head. On the twenty-fourth of April she took the new train to the coast, made connections for Marseilles, and arrived at Susan's bedside five days later.

Struggling for breath, Susan hung during the next three weeks between coma, sudden chills, and hysterical laughter. On the ninth of May, Charlotte asked the doctor when he expected a change. His reply dismayed the family: "She is going very fast." In dumb surprise, Charlotte could only cry out in anguish. "You don't mean to say she is dying?"

She recoiled in shock at the answer. Since Susan's marriage, Charlotte's far-flung career and travels had diverted her thoughts away from the domestic routine that had more and more occupied Susan. But now, at Susan's death, she plunged into bitter sorrow. Writing Emma Crow, she could not describe her sadness, except to say that only Sheridan's and Mary Eliza's surpassed it, she supposed. Heartbroken, Ned and the two small sisters, Rosalie and Mabel, cried piteously when she tried to read them a Liverpool paper's words about the good the Cushmans had brought the city. "When the gifted lady who bears that name took first rank in the first class of her profession, her sister, Miss Susan Cushman, shone like a vision on the same boards with her." To the public's regret, Susan had left the stage, but "the high qualities which fascinated the audience blessed a happy home." Death had laid its hands on a lady outstandingly "dignified" and "accomplished."

Charlotte bought a special carriage for herself and Mary Eliza and Ned to ride in the black procession that wound its way to the Liverpool Necropolis the afternoon of May 13—then sent it to London, a symbol like the blood stained jacket, for safe-keeping. To ease Ned out of his grief, Charlotte arranged a job for him on a Liverpool vessel supplying coal to the French Mediterranean Fleet. He could spend his liberties with her in Rome. She remained with Sheridan's grieving family until late in August, hoping that he would let her take the motherless girls to rear. But the man and his haughty mother stood firmly opposed and became hostile when she insisted.

Back in Rome, Charlotte struggled to find an interest to fill the gap Susan's death had created. Hattie's antics amused her: fox-hunting, Hattie had fallen at least thirty times, not for bad riding but for daring. Emma's growing excitement with her own work was pleasant to see: making the portrait bust for Shepherd was her big fascination at the moment. And Charlotte was left to fill her time pleasantly, with daily rides or talks with the Brownings at their apartment in the Via del Tritone. But down deep, her zest had vanished. "I feel myself more indifferent to life, and death has less terror for me than it ever had before," she wrote Emma Crow in October. Couldn't Emma persuade her father to let her come to Rome for the winter? Charlotte rejoiced when Wayman Crow consented. The girl would arrive around Christmas.

By the time Ned's job expired, he had made a big decision. If Auntie still wanted him, he would live in Rome. Overjoyed at his words, Charlotte was happier than she had ever been since her London victory in 1845. Now, she could help Ned forget the years when as a troubled boy he shuttled between his grandmother in Brixton, his mother in Liverpool, and boarding school in Yorkshire—feeling unwanted and having no sense of permanence. Wherever Auntie was was home. The back bedroom upstairs would be his. In the stable, he must take his pick of the horses. Would he like to take dancing and fencing lessons? Together, they must see to his clothes.

Theodore Parker's coming to Rome for his health gave Charlotte another interest. Racked with tuberculosis, worn from his long career as a champion of Negroes, Parker sat huddled and weak in his rooms, convinced that Civil War must soon ravage America. Almost daily, Charlotte helped the feeble old man downstairs to drive in the sun with her. "Many thanks for all your favors," Parker wrote in his quavering hand, "the drive the other day, the old-fashioned chicken pie this day." The great loaf of Indian corn bread she had brought was "like a song of Zion sung in a strange land among the willows. It carries me back to dear old Boston once more."

Sallie set the work routine in the household, but lacking Italian neither she nor Charlotte herself could do more than throw up their hands when shrieks and skirmishes broke out in the kitchen. "Running a household of hens," Charlotte wrote Kate Field, who had gone on to Florence, "is difficult and requires molto pazienza which, alas, I have not, by birth or education." Down in the stable, she never knew what new disorder she might find. And Ned was, strangely, no help; he had taken her at her word, it seemed, and spent most of his days away on some horseback escapade. "My spirit has fainted as often as fifty times a day, and a revolver the only thing to be desired, for my servants first, and then myself."

In late afternoons, whenever she stood with Ned at the back windows watching the sun disappear behind St. Peter's, Charlotte pondered again the political stresses rumbling inside its halls—and the future for them all, here. "Italy for the Italians is the word and will be the deed," she wrote Kate. It would not surprise her to hear that the Pope had called in his bishops and set off a revolution all over Europe. But be that as it may, "We shall again see Rome the Capital of Italy." The French troops camped in the Borghese Gardens would sooner or later see to that.

Life took a new turn in December with the arrival of Emma Crow. Ned was no poet, no scholar, but he needed no special gifts to sense the romantic charm that Rome offered the young. Inviting Emma Crow to Rome with Ned in the house, Charlotte got more than she bargained for. However simple her motives—about Ned and about bringing Emma to visit—two problems quickly became clear. For all her convictions about the goodness of work, she could hardly argue that Ned must labor, when money so obviously was not the question. In her house, where Ned's every wish was met by an adoring aunt or a servant, only folly would have tried to persuade a young blade that he must shoulder his load, especially when Auntie had already made her big dreams for him so clear. With her means, she wanted Ned's soul to grow. "He need never become like the crude, sweating 'western men I have known.' "

Though maternal love planted the sentiment, it could not harvest ambition and character. In her own youth, Charlotte had plotted her course out of deep need and pursued it. But Ned's problem was not so simple. Along with his sea bag of souvenirs, Ned had brought to her house all the charm and vague skills of a ne'er-do-well. If Auntie wanted his soul to grow, he was willing. At the time, Charlotte did not notice that he said nothing at all about being grateful.

The other problem centered in Emma Crow. Much as Charlotte adored Ned, and much as her heart turned over each time she met Emma's happy eyes, it was not her purpose, certainly, to play Cupid between them. Loving them both, she wanted the love of both fully returned, undivided. She had not imagined that Emma and Ned might fall for each other. A gnawing doubt disturbed her: was Emma's marriage to Ned what *she* wanted? Could she honestly recommend this harum-scarum young man as a husband? She was hardly mother enough, she supposed, to resent a little whatever girl caught Ned's fancy, yet what was Emma Crow to *her* that the thought so troubled her sleep? When she sensed the icy hostility that flashed at times between Emma Stebbins and Emma Crow, she only despaired more. The visit that had seemed so inspired ended early in February with Emma Crow's waving a tearful good-bye, mainly to Ned—and Charlotte's staring hurt and uncertain at the disappearing train.

Charlotte broached her worries to James and Annie Fields when they arrived from Boston for Carnival, 1860. The eminent American publisher and his young wife ought to have a comforting thought or so for a troubled old maid—and mother. The Fieldses did not fully guess her concern—why worry about a healthy young man's falling in love?—but their coming did bring diversion. Driving them up and around the Pincian for the sunset, to Pamfili Doria to gather anemones, welcoming them for late breakfasts at 38 Via Gregoriana, Charlotte made the most of their visit. "A most clear hearted, clear headed woman," Annie said about Charlotte in her diary, in vast imperception of her friend's real condition just now.

Meeting Ned, watching Charlotte blindly spoil him, Annie Fields could not miss the resemblance between this prince living in Charlotte's house and the golden boy she met at the Brownings. When Pen complained one morning that riding every day in the Pincian bored him, Annie suggested he ride somewhere else. "Oh, no!" Pen shook his head. "My pony and I have to go there. We are one of the sights of Rome, you know!" What could Miss Cushman expect of the decorative youth she was training to be just like him?

Leaving for England, the Fieldses made a suggestion meant to help Charlotte find a solution to her problem. Could an actress of her vast talents ever be happy offstage? In her diary on March 1, Annie wrote, "We have persuaded her I think, to go to California to play a short 3 months or so and take the money which is waiting her there." The middle of March when Ned stood at Charlotte's side to welcome the Brownings to dinner ("a feast of reason and a flow of soul and champagne," she wrote Emma Crow), when he escorted her and Emma Stebbins to Harriet Stowe's gala party, Charlotte's thoughts were really turning on the Fieldses' suggestion.

She took her time deciding. By late spring, she had made up her mind about nothing. Rolling along in her carriage on the Pincian one afternoon, she spied a familiar figure in lavender silk. She swept down out of her carriage and rushed across the Promenade, hands thrust out, pouring out a volley of words, to greet Adelaide Ristori. When the great Italian recognized her, she dropped her lace parasol and ran forward, exclaiming, "Brava! Brava!"

Charlotte still had only a few Italian expressions, but in their broken talk, understanding neither her own wild phrases nor Adelaide's ecstatic replies, Charlotte recognized deep in herself a heavy chagrin. Ristori had never made any foolish decision to retire. Seated beside Adelaide on the marble bench, seeing the vital brilliance in her magnificent eyes, Charlotte read a point for herself clearly.

Days later, when a surprising note arrived from Fanny Kemble, who had come to visit the Sartorises, Charlotte doubled her efforts toward making some decision. Fanny, it seemed, was ready at last to forgive the friendly interest that once had looked like meddling; she recalled now that packed among her stage effects in Lenox, she had a very elegant crown: "You must permit me to send it to you," said Fanny's note, "as some small return for those far more beautiful things [Charlotte's flowers] with which in the early days of my acquaintance with you you adorned my room." In the meantime, could she send her a few ornaments, "a small token of my former obligations to you?"

So, Fanny was friendly again. If Charlotte's genial reply took Fanny "back to the old old days when you . . . compassionately tried to smooth away some of my thorns," Charlotte felt again, writing it, the old urge to ride out and conquer that had long ago galvanized her ambitions.

A letter from Mary Devlin wanting advice only whetted her craving for action. Edwin Booth and a Boston lawyer were both begging her to marry them. What should she do? Charlotte had not met Booth, but knowing actors and the perils involved in marriage to them and knowing the erratic strain in Booth's family, she recommended the lawyer.

Nearly two years ago, gathering up her farewell flowers, Charlotte had not imagined that sweet idleness might again sour. But now, when Hattie left suddenly for Watertown at news that her father was dying, Charlotte broached a bold plan to Emma and Ned. Now that Emma had had her year's work and had finished the bust for Shepherd, now that her bronze "Angel of the Waters" was ready for Central Park and her beautiful "Lotus-Eaters" was finished, couldn't they all go back to America, where Charlotte could take up again her own work? When Ned suddenly took an interest, and Emma tipped her head slowly and smiled, Charlotte blessed the bond her four years with Emma had welded.

To Ned's letter to Emma Crow, she scrawled a postscript that more than displayed her feelings. If Ned was restless and miserable "unless he is writing to you and good for nothing to himself or anybody else," Charlotte could not "bear a letter to go off to you without one word from me, for I know how disappointed I should be if a letter arrived without some word from you." So, although Ned had probably told everything already, "I must send you one line to tell you that you live fondly in my thoughts' deepest places, that I long for you, want you, as perhaps you do me, that no human being exercises so peculiar a power as you do over me and that I am not whole without you! Does that make you happy, darling?"

Alarums of War and Mr. Seward

(1860–1861)

For Charlotte, the "good" life was never more hard to define than in the fall of 1860. The old creed that work and duty and the glorification of God spelled the real meaning of man's time on earth weighed heavily in Charlotte's uncertainties as she grew older and richer. The leisure that her wealth made possible had brought confusion.

Letters she wrote during her last days in Rome informed her American friends that circumstances were "forcing" her back to the stage ("I shall be in Boston again sometime in December *professionally*—I am ashamed to say"), that her style of life in Rome had proved unduly expensive, that her dreams and ambitions for her son Ned, who planned to marry soon, had created new drains on her pocket.

Deep down, Charlotte knew there were better reasons to return to battle. The good life was a mixture of pressures. Too much leisure, too much work—along neither road had she found fulfillment. More important, without some concept of duty to depend upon as a guide, whether that duty was to an audience or to another person or to her own talent, she felt too much a wanderer through a trackless wood. It was incidental that hard work paid off in money, incidental too that Ned's plans would prove expensive.

Only Emma Stebbins saw the inconsistency in Charlotte's concern about Ned: her notion that working for Ned would necessarily make him happy. Emma might have enlightened her: Ned could see to his own needs perfectly well; requiring him to do his own work might even encourage his "soul to grow." But the matter was delicate, and where Ned was concerned Emma had already learned that silence was golden.

Charlotte's returning to America involved another feeling, one that came from reading the headlines. If the Gulf States pulled out of the Union and if war exploded as a result, she wanted to be in America when it happened. Frivolous expatriate life was all well enough when affairs at home ran smoothly, but now, living in dream-like ease across the Atlantic when people at home were nobly confronting the bitterest worries, her conscience troubled her. Whisking Emma Stebbins and Ned through London, she mentioned her "shakey" finances to Jane Carlyle. She explained to Charlie—now married and none too happily—and Mary Eliza that the expenses involved in Ned's wedding plans made her trip to America mandatory. Yet throughout the stormy crossing, she found ease in knowing that going home now was "right."

She did not, however, let that sober conviction spoil the greetings that welcomed her home. If the two years away had indeed heightened her glamour, if the Boston papers now wanted to call her "legendary," she accepted the role indicated. If his respect for her mind prompted Bronson Alcott to invite her out to Concord to hear one of his famous "conversations," this time with Whittier, Charlotte held herself perfectly still and grandly intense while Bronson's daughter, Louisa May, and most of the crowd sat admiring her. If the Fieldses asked her to breakfast mainly to urge her to follow her fame to California, Charlotte accepted their compliment. Yet recent word from Wayman Crow in St. Louis painted such a dark picture of the journey by Butterfield stage through savage Indian country that the thought rather frightened her now.

For the present she chose an easier course. To get ready for New York, Charlotte took a farmhouse in Newport for two weeks, well away from the resort's noisy, fashionable life. Strolling with Emma among the wild pink roses along Newport's low cliffs, she watched the blue waves surge up the white beaches and break in foam on the rocks.

When she reached New York, she smiled when the *Times* told its readers what had "really" prompted Miss Cushman's second return. She had never left them for good; "the impulse of genius" had goaded her back to the stage, the nervous thirst that genius always feels for battle. Miss Cushman had fooled nobody, and it was a pleasure now, as always, to welcome back to her proper station "so

great an honor in every sense to the National Stage as 'Our Charlotte.' "

Returning to work in October 1860, Charlotte quickly discovered
that the easy years in Rome had left her little energy for long engagements. She welcomed the worshipful droves that crushed to
her door, the invitations that piled in white drifts on her table;
when Sallie complained, "You can never bear to be quiet, you always want company," she confessed to the charge. Afternoons in
bed on performance days were one answer. The roaring applause that
greeted her again and the old thrill she felt playing her part were the
other. Sweeping proudly off the stage at the end of the play, her
head held high while the applause poured over her, Charlotte was
overjoyed to see in Emma's smiling face her full understanding, her
awareness that Charlotte's return to the stage, however much it was
costing her in time lost from her chisels and mallets in Rome, was
justified.

It was gratifying too to read about herself again in the papers.
The *Times* cried its old pleasure in seeing her "die"—her Katharine
did it so "superbly"—though seeing Miss Cushman come grandly
to the footlights at the end of the play to smile and gather up the
bouquets pleased its man just as much. Two thousand disappointed
fans had to be turned away at the box office the first night she played
Meg. She had hesitated to resurrect her sordid old Nancy, but even
that wretched character set off an ovation. When the Prince of Wales,
then visiting America, saw her perform—"quite without ceremony
. . . as he had not been invited"—he sent her an ebony box to
express his pleasure.

So, it was good to be working again, good to know that she was
still appreciated in the roles that always gave her pleasure. A later
age might wonder that each time she "returned" to the stage, indeed, each time she reappeared in a town, her audiences demanded
nothing different. When somebody questioned her about her own fa-
vorites, Charlotte gave a straightforward answer. Her characters
were equally dear: "I try to make them all best, and leave my public
to judge which I can like best."

But why would crowds pay again and again to see the old plays,
pieces that had lost all novelty, whose very plots were tritely familiar.
As Charlotte well knew, the answer lay in virtuosity. Someday, the
play itself might be the thing and its actors only incidental, but to
the eager crowds that jammed Charlotte's performances in 1860, the
play was secondary—when an actress who compounded genius and

fame and legend gave life again, with ringing words and slashing gestures, to towering protagonists. Her dying queens might create sympathy, her gypsy Meg might horrify, but eyes watching her now admired her artistry, her points achieved as skillfully as arias in opera.

At the end of her forty-eight nights at the Winter Garden, Charlotte counted her final take, appreciating the newspapers' amazement that her income for the run, if figured proportionally, more than doubled the salary paid the President of the United States. She could sympathize with James Buchanan, and not merely because a woman outearned him. Like any actor, she had scars to prove that the actor's lot was not easy, but she would not willingly face one-tenth of a President's woes. Out of friendship, she rejoiced that Seward had lost the Republican Party's nomination for the Presidency. In the talk at the Alcotts, one guest had been a Mr. Stuart, "conductor" of the Underground Railroad of "this charming free country," as Louisa had put it. Hearing his comments, Charlotte had felt her own fears about coming months heighten.

Riding through New York's banner-hung streets, watching the noisy campaign parades below her hotel window, Charlotte pondered with Emma the outcome of the approaching election. However loudly the banners shouted economic promises, their loudest undercurrent was slavery. Lincoln had made no speeches, issued no statements that Southerners could misrepresent. Yet turmoil lay crouched in the shadows. On election day, November 6, she wrote Wayman Crow for advice about a new issue of insurance bonds: "I note what you say about withholding any further investments until we see whether my 'Republican Friends' as you are pleased to call them 'bring about a dissolution of the Union.' " Yet Lincoln's administration, if elected, would surely be the most "reputable, conservative, and protective we have ever had." Reading her papers in Rome, she had already reached that conviction.

And however much she abhorred slavery, if Southern passions were to threaten the Union forever, then "better, infinitely better that it should at once be dissolved," amicably if possible, "but if not—not!" About that, Seward was right. However despicable the Negroes' plight, did the North have to shoulder the burden of setting them free and risk splitting the nation in the process? The blacks were God's poor, Seward had said more than once, as they always had been. They must find their own proper level. Actually, what danger could spring from an amicable separation of the States, if it came to that? Under the law, bad marriages could be dissolved. "Better be respected and apart, from the integrity which may exist in each," she wrote Wayman Crow, than be despised by the world because there is no respect for Union.

About her investments, did Mr. Crow agree with Fields that Boston real estate would always be safe? Was $17,000 too much to pay for a fine house and lot on the water side of Beacon, with an open view of the river? "You see how I bother you. Spinsters are notoriously troublesome if they get a foot hold."

Lately, Wayman Crow had said, fairly enough, that he would consent to Emma's marrying Ned only if Ned held a job. Charlotte wondered if Seward as Lincoln's incoming Secretary of State might help, possibly with an appointment for Ned as American Consul in Rome? For Ned and Emma, she could see two long-range openings ahead. She could furnish 1 Bolton Row to their taste—assuming that Ned went to work at something in London. Or better still, she could set them up in a fourth floor apartment at 38 Via Gregoriana—especially if Seward granted Ned the Consulate—and they could all live together, she and her beloved Emma Crow and Ned, as one family. In the meantime, if Fields could locate Ned a temporary position in Boston, she would be eternally grateful: "Heaven knows how earnestly I desire him to succeed." Could Jamie advise him about friends and lodging? Ned might listen to a man when he only ignored "old Auntie's notions."

When Wayman Crow gave his consent to the marriage after Lincoln's inauguration, if there was no war, Charlotte was relieved: "Ned has been one of my large anxieties and to feel myself so much helped with regard to him is a great blessing." Emma Crow could be Ned's salvation.

No less important, his marriage to Emma could fulfill one of Charlotte's richest dreams. Much as she loved Ned, or tried to, there had been little doubt from the start about her affection for Wayman Crow's daughter. Even now the matter was not wholly clear, but in the back of her mind she had always envisioned the time when young Emma could occupy a permanent place in her life. If Emma's marrying Ned could achieve that place, so be it. All parties could gain in the process, though Charlotte did everything now that honesty demanded to let Emma Crow see that Ned was a bundle of immaturities, a selfish adolescent who might never grow up. Saying that, her conscience was clear. Having heard it, Emma Crow could make up her own mind.

With the match more or less settled, Charlotte took her triumph to Boston in early December. At the Fieldses' dinner—"I was enchanted with Lowell, as I always am and have been"—word circulated that a statue of the late Horace Mann was to be made for the State House lawn. Considering American women's shabby chances in the arts, Charlotte saw immediately that the commission could be a real plum for Emma Stebbins. When she learned that Elizabeth Peabody and her sister, Mrs. Horace Mann, would choose the sculptor, Charlotte sent them free tickets to all her plays. Elizabeth took keen delight in the performances: "I do not know but I thought Rosalind the most marvelous of all." Charlotte's wit and grace and makeup made her "seem but twenty-eight."

Later in the month, in Philadelphia, Charlotte had her first chance to act with the slender, poetic Edwin Booth. She had relished the thought of this meeting, but at rehearsals she quickly revised her opinions about this celebrated young star with the flowing black locks, the deep brooding eyes, and noble profile. Booth must surely know that Macbeth was no delicate Hamlet, no insipid refined intellectual. He was more nearly "the grandfather of all the Bowery villains." Booth nodded in agreement, but in the performance he made Macbeth a "mere willow." She could only flash her disgust and urge and scold him on to murder, while Booth stifled a wish to cry out, "Why don't you kill him? You're a great deal bigger than I am."

Watching both stars, a famed observer muttered, "Ridiculous!" Resenting the rising star he saw in young Booth, still bitterly convinced that Charlotte Cushman had ruined him in England in 1845, Edwin Forrest sat glowering and snorting when Booth entered, gazing moodily at the ground. "What's the damn fool doing? He looks like a super hunting for a sixpence." In the sleep-walking scene, when Charlotte solemnly moaned that "All the perfumes of Arabia will not sweeten this little hand," Forrest laughed his scorn. "*Little* hand! Why it's as big as a codfish!"

Interpretations aside, the meeting with Booth occasioned a happy reunion backstage. Gaily ignoring Charlotte's advice, Mary Devlin had married Booth in July, and because her husband wished it, she had renounced her career. The young wife who rushed into Charlotte's arms after the first night's curtain expressed no regrets about

305

it. Whatever Edwin wished he would have. But listening to Mary eagerly spell out her plans, Charlotte kept her sad thoughts to herself. To bury a talent like this because of a husband's ego! Only cruelty in a man could extract such a promise from a wife so gifted.

While Charlotte was still in Philadelphia, Fields mailed her an advance copy of the February *Atlantic* containing an article Paul Akers had written about William Page. "America's finest contemporary portraitist," the sculptor called him. But reading the piece, Charlotte found that it actually glorified her. In a certain portrait, said Akers, Page had depicted the "fearful tumultuousness of a Lady Macbeth, the passionate tenderness of a Romeo, the Gothic grandeur of a Scotch sorceress." The artist had recorded a face "rendered impressive by the grandest repose—a repose that pervades the room and the soul." Seeing it, one felt himself in the presence of a woman who had "borne on through and above all obstacles of discouragement and temptation."

Charlotte immediately wrote Annie. "What he says of me is wondrous." For once, her face had been given some credit; a critic had looked beyond her "ugliness." Yet strangely enough, Akers had not identified her. "Do you think," she asked Annie, "that an Editor's note might put my name at the bottom of the page?" The occasion seemed to deserve, somehow, a bit more detail.

While she was still in Philadelphia, Charlotte's doubts about Booth prompted her to tackle Hamlet again. If Mrs. Siddons had risked playing the Dane, why shouldn't *she?* On January 28, 1861, she inched herself into Booth's tight costumes and put herself through Hamlet's paces, feeling swept up by the dazzling poetry, the virile heart that most actors overlooked in the role. Next day she wrote Emma Crow: "I acted the part so much better than anything else I have done here that I am really amazed at myself."

Unfortunately, Philadelphia disagreed. A vigorous, well-fleshed woman in her forties playing the Prince was too much—especially for Booth and Forrest, though a few days later in Washington, when a delegation of Congressmen petitioned her to play it for them, the elegant silk playbill carried Charlotte's delighted answer: "I am happy to meet your wishes."

Talking with Seward, Charlotte found the Washington air boiling with trouble ahead. Seven states had already left the Union. In his debates with Douglas, Lincoln had made clear his moderate views on the presence of "slavery amongst us and the difficulties of getting rid of it in any satisfactory way." He hoped, he said, that his incoming administration could arrest its spread, but he had no intention of leading the country to war. In Seward's parlor, Charlotte heard all the controversy expressed and debated, noted the worried faces that came and went through his doors—while Seward himself insisted that if war came, it would not last sixty days.

Yet Charlotte recognized clearly Seward's valiant efforts to hide his fears, especially from Fanny, the shy, plain-faced daughter whom he obviously adored. When Seward turned his attention to other visitors, Charlotte tried to befriend the awkward Fanny—especially when the girl confessed how "stale" and "unprofitable" she felt alongside her brother Frederick, a young man of singular intellect and beauty. Charlotte could sympathize with any plain girl, especially one who had no mental gifts either, who suffered among all the vivid personalities who came and went in her father's house. To reassure Fanny, Charlotte proposed that they maintain a correspondence. The day she left for New York, Charlotte gave her a small gold ring to seal the friendship.

She tried to bury her own fears in work. Back at the Winter Garden in late February 1861, dragging herself "through blood" as Nancy, she "horrified" the *Times,* though it wondered if any Bill Sykes could kill a woman so muscular. Any man would have a tough job defeating "so powerful a will and so strong an arm." Yet however much she despised the role, Charlotte found in it an outlet for her own pent-up emotions, as the time for Lincoln's inauguration approached.

On March 4, on the steps of the Capitol, Lincoln took his stand. "Physically speaking, we cannot separate. We cannot remove our respective sections from each other, nor build an impassable wall between them." On his inauguration Bible the new President swore to maintain the Union—peaceably if possible. In that thought Charlotte felt her own hopes renewed. Two days later she wrote Seward. Some free moment when the new Secretary of State was not too "worn down by cares," would he consider appointing Ned Cushman the next American Consul in Rome? Married, the young man ought to be highly effective.

In Boston the middle of March, Charlotte borrowed Edwin Booth's costume again to play Hamlet. But she played to poor houses. Too many fears had been loosed when Maine's regiment marched down State Street, singing "John Brown's Body," ready for war if Lincoln issued the call. Yet for Charlotte, family matters were more important just now. Lincoln was already President and war had not come. Wayman Crow would honor his promise to Ned.

On March 21, Charlotte joined Booth in New York to play *Macbeth* at the Academy of Music, still convinced that his Macbeth was a flimsy, pale thing. Then, three days later, she took the train to St. Louis for Ned and Emma Crow's wedding. Before the flower-banked altar, she watched them recite their vows, then turn as man and wife to smile their happiness at her—while she sat dreaming grand schemes. Her wedding present to them was a house in Boston at 70 Pinckney Street, quite near the Fieldses. The checks she now gave them would furnish it. She had thought she might give Emma a special gift, a purse containing a thousand dollars in gold, but she decided against it lest Ned feel some resentment.

The wedding had come in good time. On April 13, when newsboys ran through the streets shouting that General Beauregard had fired on Fort Sumter, Charlotte knew that all hope for peace had withered. Now Lincoln would have to use force. With guns trained against the Union, she could only declare, with Lincoln, that war, however tragic, must come. On April 27, 1861, Charlotte ended her benefit for war volunteers at the Howard Athenaeum by singing Holmes' new stanza for *The Star Spangled Banner*.

> When our Land is illumined with Liberty's smile,
> If a foe from within strike a blow at her glory,
> Down, down with the traitor that dares to defile
> The flag of her stars and the page of her story!
> By the millions unchanged, when our birthright was gained,
> We will keep her bright blazon forever unstained!
> And the star-spangled banner in triumph shall wave
> While the land of the free is the home of the brave.

But far-off war was too big and too terrible to ponder. Better channel her thoughts to battles she might win closer to home. As long as Ned's work kept him and Emma in Boston, she would see to their social position. With the young Cushmans settled in their new home, Charlotte detailed a guest list for their first big reception in May. Among all the proper Bostonians, "Why not call on the Booths at the Tremont and ask them; it will give others pleasure to see them. . . . You can tell Mary Booth that I told you to call and ask her." Ned must go in person to invite the Fieldses; they had been more than kind to present them to Emerson and Holmes and Mrs. Stowe. "Have tea handed round and cake and wine," she instructed Emma. Ned must buy some greenhouse flowers "with *stems.*"

Advising "her children," Charlotte made no effort to throttle her delight in seeing them properly installed in a Boston that she herself, against all odds, had had to work to enter. Jamie Fields' note to her, a few days after the reception, only deepened her satisfaction. On behalf of Ticknor and Fields, Publishers, could Charlotte lend him $5,000? "You know how well our house stands, and I need not to say to you anything more about," except that with authors like Hawthorne and Scott and Holmes, "our list is second to none in this country, and we mean to keep it, in spite of Harpers or anybody." Charlotte's loan would help guarantee the firm's supremacy in American publishing.

Charlotte promised Fields to do whatever she could. As for his intention to proceed normally in spite of Fort Sumter, she heartily concurred. "We shall be all right next fall." The North's "flood of men and money" had taken the South by surprise; already the moral effect was showing.

"With all the bad blood let out of the land," she wrote wishfully in another letter, "we shall be better, stronger, happier than ever before. . . . The blocks had to be cemented in Blood, and better that we should do it than leave it to our children."

Under the terrible clouds, Charlotte felt an almost physical lift to her spirits one morning when Emma Stebbins rushed in with the mail. Hearing her delighted cries, watching her dance around in a circle, then hungrily reread her letter, Charlotte caught Emma's sudden passion to get back to Rome and pick up her tools. Emma had received the Horace Mann commission. In that, Charlotte saw her own future turn. She had had her year's work; she had honored her patriotic urge to come home. Now, Emma's needs were crying their valid demands.

Since the commission said nothing about money—was it that Emma was only a woman?—Charlotte wrote a quick note to Jamie. Couldn't Fields persuade Charles Sumner to stump the state on behalf of funds for the project? If Jamie got "somebody clever" to write a eulogy of Mann, she could deliver it herself at a benefit. "In this way *women* will raise the statue."

For while the country was so fearfully preoccupied with slavery, it might give some thought to its downtrodden women. Thinking about that, Charlotte would go back to Rome out of duty to women in general. In June, when Thomas Wentworth Higginson met her in Boston, he recognized the fire that had taken hold of her. After producing her, Higginson wrote, America could win pardon for "a million half-alive women."

Against the chaos of war, distant Rome seemed now an incredible paradise where, despite its Popes and Garibaldis, frivolity could flourish almost shockingly. Yet visualizing her return, Charlotte found comfort in knowing that idleness was no longer the object. She had joined a campaign. More privately, she faced her heart's commitment. Acting these past months in America, she had been apart too much from Emma Stebbins. Where Emma went now, she would follow.

She would not, however, leave America without another comforting word from Seward. The man she knew as a true kindred spirit understood well enough about duty: his sense of it kept him living in Washington, aiding an awkward, untried new President, when he might have lived in a happier, more cultivated place like Rome. Talking with Seward, it was good to recall that warfare and politics actually related to nobler concerns. John Adams had said it in 1780— that his duty required him to study politics and war now, that his sons might later study mathematics and commerce and agriculture, so that their children in turn might study painting and statuary, music and poetry. In the long range, if she could not shoulder a gun and fight at the front, she could go home to Rome, the art capital of the world, and do her bit beside Emma for the world of the future, when war would be obsolete.

With Seward, she rode out the afternoon of July 1 to Arlington Heights to see the raw entrenchments and military camps springing up in a circle around Washington. Fifty thousand volunteers were already stationed in white tents in and about the city, and in the humidity the dust from marching feet, galloping cavalry, and rumbling wagons hung like a pall. To Seward she mentioned that Algernon Chase's son, Lewis, hoped to obtain an appointment to the Military Academy. Would Seward help? The Secretary's reply took her a little aback, but by the time they had returned to Lafayette Square, she gratefully accepted his offer. He would help her place her request where it would do the most good.

Together, they walked across the Square, through the iron gates, and entered the guarded white portals of the building where lamps burned throughout the night. Charlotte had seen the President on his rides about Washington, tall and sober in his dusty black suit and black stovepipe hat, his cavalry guard riding beside him with drawn sabres held upright. But only when Seward ushered her into Lincoln's second-floor office at the White House did the new President become real.

The lanky figure that rose slowly to greet her was not prepossessing. There was an obvious backwoods clumsiness about the man, a deep lack of polish. But Charlotte quickly sensed in Lincoln a warmth and sentiment that made her forget everything else. Standing beside the flag in front of his marble fireplace, tilting back in his black leather chair, Lincoln drawled his eager references to the theatre, especially Shakespeare, to plays he had seen recently when he had slipped unannounced into a box. Regrettably, he said, he had not yet seen Miss Cushman herself on stage, especially since *Macbeth* was his favorite play. Smiling, pointing a bony finger at her, Lincoln hoped she would not retire—and mean it—before he could see her Lady Macbeth.

Charlotte thanked him. She had only slowly discovered, she confessed—and that by bitter experience—that a workhorse was nervous without his harness, that an actor was lost with nothing to do. She saw a gentle envy play momentarily across Lincoln's face, yet something in his somber manner, his character, and quick wit made her suddenly happier about this new president.

Passing again through the gates, she still felt mixed emotions, she told Seward, about this brooding man who had gravely shaken her hand, yet a quality in him set him apart somehow from all other men she had known. Only the next week in Boston did she remember the point of her White House visit. "I was so completely taken up with him and his humour," she wrote Seward, "that I forgot my mission and came away."

Bidding Ned and Emma Crow good-bye in Boston, Charlotte explained again just how truly Emma Stebbins' needs encompassed her own. "I love her very much," she wrote them later; "she is the finest nature I have ever been thrown in contact with, the very truest and dearest of human beings and I want you both to love her." Life was involvement, whether one wished it or not. Their own marriage surely had convinced them of that.

Two events just now dramatized that matter all too well. Elizabeth Barrett Browning died in Florence on June 30, leaving Robert so desolate that Isa Blagden wondered if he could survive. Then scarcely more than a week later, paralyzing word went out from the Longfellows in Cambridge. Frances Longfellow was sealing up packets of her daughters' curls when her dress caught fire from the candle; she died the next day. "How can I live any longer!" Longfellow had cried.

Looking toward Rome, Charlotte answered her own heart's dictates. Seeing the light that sprang into Emma's eyes when a note arrived from Hawthorne wishing her much happiness abroad and "trusting that your native land will receive many memorials from your hand as beautiful (if possible) as the Lotus-Eaters," she was ready to face her duty. On the seventeenth of July, 1861, she and Emma headed home.

26

A Woman's Power in the Xational Struggle

(1861–1863)

 "The news brought by the last steamer has made me so sad and so heartsick," Charlotte wrote Emma Crow from London, "that I hardly know how to talk or write about it." Yet the tragic defeat at Bull Run must somehow be seen as proof of God's goodness. The recruiting would surely go better now, and in the flush of success the South would be less careful next time. The Devil helped his own at first. "Let those laugh who win."

In Paris an invitation from Rosa Bonheur, the painter, summoned Charlotte and Emma to her turreted studio near Fontainebleau. Talking with Rosa, watching the zest the mannish little woman brought to her work among the animals she used as models, Charlotte discovered a fear that made her suddenly dread the long days ahead. How would she feel, totally bereft of her own art? Over a lunch of bread and wine, grapes and pears, while they talked of their admiration for each other's work, Charlotte felt her fears deepen. She knew sadly what she was sacrificing for Emma.

Back in Rome, while Emma threw herself heart and soul into work, Charlotte filled her time writing long letters back to America. Her weekly reports to Emma Crow became full essays. In tightly packed onionskin pages, writing from left to right and then crosswise from top to bottom to save postage, she ranged over all the topics that challenged her mind.

About Ned's irresponsibilities, she was frank. "Ned is affectionate, dear, and a good disposition, but he thinks more of his pleasures than his duties." His mother and grandmother had spoiled him, and though it might take years, his wife must exert every effort to set him straight. About money, Ned was a careless child. If he ever considered "going out" without her, Emma must put her foot down. "It is not right or proper, and if begun so early, will grow upon him." When business took him away from Boston a few days, Charlotte sympathized fully with Emma. "Oh, dear, if I were only a man that I could have been born to care for a woman."

She was philosophical: "The wish to be better, the strong desire to live higher, purer lives, the determination to be worthy in spite of lets and hindrances, the small conquest over self today, shall lead to the larger tomorrow, until we get nearer to our true mosaic of life —the one spot which we have been destined to fill worthily, highly, perfectly, without flaw, if we would follow the Creator's law for us."

She was candid about herself and the family: she knew that Ned and Mary Eliza resented her household in Rome, especially her friendship with Emma Stebbins. Emma paid her own bills, but even if the truth were otherwise, she would owe Charlotte nothing, because together they had found so much happiness. "If I were to swear this before a magistrate neither my mother nor Ned would believe it." But let them think what they would. "I have always done the utmost of my duty by them and ever shall."

She tried to express her religion: she had joined the other Protestants in Rome recently in petitioning the Vatican to allow them to build a church inside the walls, but creeds were merely creeds after all, "and whether propounded by Jesus, or any other of *woman born,* they are simply scaffoldings which surround the temple, and by which different thinkers mount to their distinct and separate entrances." She could find God in any church. Any good and earnest man who led a pure life, who worked for the good of others, who led her to think higher and better things herself "is my saviour." Nobody could doubt a First Cause, and "whether we call it God, or nature, or *law of the universe,* it amounts to the same thing." For herself, "I believe in all things good coming from God, in all forms, in all ways; my faith is firm in him and his love. I believe in instincts marvelously." Sin was only weakness, "which entails upon us evils which we have to combat." Hence, man must strive to lead a "life of unselfishness, a life of devotion to—well—doing everything a human being can do for the largest good of all."

In her new leisure, Charlotte took up her correspondence with

Jane Carlyle. Coming through London, she had enjoyed again the
flattery of Jane's interest. At Cheyne Row she had listened to Jane
and Thomas' "wondrous" talk, admired again their wide-ranging
minds, and been amused again at Thomas' bluster. When she learned
from a London friend the middle of December that terrible headaches
had made Jane unable to write, Charlotte saw again why Carlyle
and his sharp-tongued wife were so often at odds. Thomas had tip-
toed one morning into Jane's darkened room to ask if he might order
some mint jelly for her. From deep in her pillows, Jane had whispered "Yes," but she wanted some changes in it. He took his instructions carefully, had them repeated twice, "looking all the time
with his old Norseman face and figure grandly unfit for the task,"
but he was so anxious and tender and childlike in being taught what
he had to do that in a quarter of an hour, the maid came in to say
that Master had turned back, still not sure of his mission. "Would
Mrs. Carlyle tell it him again?"

To Jane, Charlotte offered her sympathy: "How shall I tell
you, dear, that I have been sad to death over your illness. . . . What
comfort can I bring you, who have no power even at this distance to
bring you healing of any kind?" From conversations with various
Englishmen in Rome, she was stirred to her soul at England's "evi-
dent sympathy" for the American South and unspeakably angered at
the notion that slavery was a natural inheritance into which a large
portion of the human race would always fall, regardless of how
strongly compassion tried to free them. Pray God that England
would not make excuses for interfering in a matter that was strictly
America's business. But should hostility break out with England, "I
shall choose *my* English for fighting with," wrote Charlotte, "and
you shall be first. I could be content to be whipped by you and kiss
your hands."

Recovered by late January 1862, Jane replied gratefully: "My
dear! my dear! I want to put my arms around your neck and give
you oh such a good kiss. . . . I should like to lay my head on your
shoulder and take a good cry. That is how nature prompts me to
acknowledge your dear letter . . . rather than with any written
sentences that my poor nearly extinct brain can gobble together in
these hard times." But since the gods would not "annihilate time and
space to make two lovers happy," she must write without further
delay, lest she appear both fickle and ungrateful "when, God bless
you, I am as far as possible from being either and as unwilling as
possible that such an idea should be entertained of me *by you!*"

315

To Emma Crow Charlotte wrote a confession: "I am in such despair when I get such letters, for my head at the best of times is not equal to these great women and here in Rome I never seem to have any solid foundation of ability either to write or to talk."

With Seward she felt more comfortable. "You will be too busy for me to intrude upon you long, and I will only tell you how anxiously I have watched your movements from the distance, and how hard it is to be patient, as you are and must be, with all the miles between me and the great events which are taking place at home." Every hour seemed to make matters less clear. "Sometimes I am faint and sick at heart as the clouds of injustice and wickedness rise up on the side to obscure my true vision." Seward must "believe that I write to you in all affectionate interest and that I am anxious for and about you, although my faith in you is so strong." The dangers surrounding him daily did not frighten her, for he was strong enough to meet them, "but a word from or about you would give comfort to the heart of your faithful friend."

Still, she wrote Seward, with Emma's needing her in Rome "I am fain to think that my place is here, where I can help those of my own sex to work better than I can at home." Indeed, if Seward could ever turn his thoughts away from problems, did he think Miss Stebbins might be given an order to make some statue for the Capitol when it was finally complete? "It would be a good encouragement to our *women workers!*"

When an ecstatic letter from Emma Crow brought word that she and Ned were expecting a baby in the fall, Charlotte was immediately full of motherly advice. "How I shall pray God that it may be a healthy and dear little thing to bless and comfort you." To make it so, Emma must regulate her mind "during the whole time you are bearing it by a *sense of duty* and respect for your obligation and don't suffer yourself to be made nervous or angry or fretful. . . . Give it peace to grow and develop well."

About names, they might think of Allerton for a boy—it would honor the wife of the first Cushman to set foot on Plymouth Rock —and for a girl, well, Charlotte would be lovely, but perhaps Emma would prefer giving it her mother's name. About rearing the child, they must avoid tossing it about. Its feeding must be kept to a schedule. From the start, they must surround the baby with beauty, even to hiring a pretty nurse. And please, however appalling the thought, if anything should happen to Emma, couldn't everybody be told now that Aunt Charlotte would take the baby to rear?

In May, when word came that Emma had lost the baby, Charlotte's sympathy came from memories. In her girlhood, she wrote, she had been "called upon to bear the very hardest thing that can come to a woman," and while Emma might doubt that disappointment in love could equal a mother's grief in losing a child, the abortive romance in Albany had seemed no less devastating at the time. But grief had passed; loss had brought compensations. It had helped her—she could say now—to see clearly her real purpose. Otherwise, "I should have been casting about for the 'counterpart,' and not given my entire *self* to my work." Properly enough, most women looked to one end in life, marriage, an end no doubt best for the largest number, but it "would not have been wisest and best for *my* work, and so for God's." Sooner or later, a way must open for her and Ned and Emma Crow to live together, either in America or Europe—or wherever God's will determined.

In the meantime, she must center her efforts doubly hard on helping Emma Stebbins' Horace Mann project. The bronzist in Munich was demanding $1,500 in advance, another $1,000 when the casting was finished, and the remainder when the statue was delivered at Rotterdam for shipment. Writing Fields, Charlotte urged him to get the money together as soon as possible, hopefully a large enough sum to include something for Emma. And incidentally, Fields must pass on to Lowell how much she admired his *Biglow Papers*. About America's current problems, "there is more said in those papers than has been said by any writer or speaker yet," especially in such lines as these:

> The hardest question ain't the black man's right,
> The trouble is to 'mancipate the white;
> One's chained in body an' can be sot free,
> But t'other's chained in soul to an idee:
> It's a long job, but we shall worry thru it;
> Ef bagnets fail, the spellin'-book must du it.

Riding idly on the Campagna, Charlotte forced herself to notice the beauties of another spring, yet day after day, she moaned inside whenever she thought of the positive things she could have been doing in America. Parties were hardly the answer, though she continued to give them and accept invitations to other people's empty affairs.

Nor were feelings among the "three old maids of the Gregoriana" quite what they should be. Though she kept herself hard at work on a colossal statue of Zenobia, Hattie had been snippish and jealous ever since Emma Stebbins returned from America bearing the news that she had been given the Mann commission. More than once Charlotte had had to speak to Hattie about her selfishness. After all, Hattie lived at 38 Via Gregoriana rent free and had few complaints coming. In Rome, the other disappointed American sculptors were even more jealous.

Charlotte found herself in the eye of the storm. Long ago she had sensed Story's resentment, and she was even more certain of the scorn she saw in Randolph Rogers' eyes. Her determination to battle with them now might have seemed like personal ill will or busy work to ease her boredom, if it had not centered in her favorite crusade. More than once at a social gathering, while the crowd was wiping its tears after one of her songs, she saw Rogers half smirking in the shadows. Warfare between them opened when at other gatherings Rogers offered to sing the same songs. No one could doubt his skill as a mimic, and he brought off roars of laughter parodying Charlotte's voice and gestures. When he finished, he sat smiling, then turned in wicked delight to watch Charlotte force herself to applaud.

According to the American Consul, this explained why Charlotte's anger soon included all of Rogers' friends. In that group was the Consul himself, William J. Stillman, against whom Charlotte began pulling strings with Seward. She had known Stillman years before when he reported theatre news for the New York *Evening Post*; she had entertained for him when he first came to Rome following an intimate friendship with John Ruskin. Her wrath, said Stillman, really began in a question about American passports.

At the outbreak of war, the State Department had ordered its consuls to cancel all passports and issue new ones only to those Americans who pledged allegiance to the United States government in Washington. When Charlotte arrived back in Rome, she refused to surrender her passport. Instead, she wrote Seward, complaining of Stillman's "rudeness." When Seward backed up his consul, from that day, said Stillman, war with Miss Cushman was "open and malignant."

A Woman's Power in the National Struggle

For Charlotte, the sheer incompetence and boorishness of the American consul were grounds enough to plead with Seward to have him replaced. Even William Story would be better than Stillman, though Ned Cushman might qualify best of all, especially with her at his elbow. When Stillman recognized this, he only increased his campaign against her. Complicating things almost too much was the delicate personal condition Charlotte now confided to Emma Crow. Could Emma send her some bottles of "Dr. Kennedy's" medicine for women who had reached that difficult period when "nature is presumed to take revenge" upon them for "unemployed faculties?" Women ought to be very careful at such times, "and I have tried to be this winter, but I am afraid I have given my poor nerves more to attend to than they can well bear."

The thing to do was get away from the cross fires in Rome—its summers were unbearably hot anyway—especially when Wayman Crow offered to send Emma over to England for August. In London with Hattie and Emma Stebbins, Charlotte made herself clear to Ned's wife about her devotion to Miss Stebbins. "I know that you would never deprive me of a happiness and my life with Aunt Emma," especially since "she is so dependent upon me that she could die without me and I know it."

Visiting the Carlyles, Charlotte poured out to Jane her grievances that the people around her allowed her own heart so little freedom. When Sheridan Muspratt surprisingly agreed to let Susan's daughters come up for a visit, she was overjoyed but so pressed with details that her nerves threatened to break. Hoping for another visit with Jane, she could only write her a quick note: "God knows whether I shall accomplish it, for while these children are with me, I do not seem to belong to myself or be mistress of my time or actions." She simply had no time to look up Browning, who was miffed when she failed to call.

Leisure in England was scarcely more pleasant than leisure in Rome. England's "smugness" and scorn for the American North bothered Charlotte more than ever. By the time she had seen the Carlyles once more—"having heard some of his wonderful sledge-hammer arguments against the way they are doing things in America" —and stood in Paris for dress fittings, she was back in Rome writing Fields. "Send, send, oh send the *Atlantic Monthly*. My soul aches for it."

In her frustration, she confessed her troubles to Fields: "I hear you are making your fortune. Alas, why am I not? If Emma had only been content to stop in America this year, I would have made mine too, but she would not, and I sit here and grieve." She was still suffering losses because of Harlan's mistakes in Philadelphia. Many years ago she had made up her mind that it would be "a mistake to trust any of your sex," she told Fields. "Hence my spinsterhood. Why was I ever so weak as to trust my property to one of them?"

By Christmas, her hands had broken out in a flaming rash which her doctor said might be helped by applications of starch but could only be cured at a sulphur spa. But Charlotte knew that action, better than any medicine, was what she needed. Word of the glorious triumph at Vicksburg in January 1863 cheered her. The Mississippi was in Northern hands at last, but no matter how grievous the loss of life for both sides, the war must not end before slavery was eradicated once and for all. The news that Emma Crow was pregnant again raised her spirits even more.

A break in Charlotte's empty routine came in a letter from Henry W. Bellows, director of the American Sanitary Commission, the country's civilian effort to assure its fighting men that American homes and hearths still cared about them. Volunteer women all over the Union were knitting sweaters, folding bandages, serving as nurses—yet the Commission itself needed funds. Would Miss Cushman come home to act in benefits in the major cities?

When Emma Stebbins insisted that she could happily spend most of the time with Isa in Florence, Charlotte saw her way clear to answer. By June 6, she and Sallie were on the high seas. To limit her temptations to make a full acting tour, she had packed costumes for only two roles, Lady Macbeth and Meg. At Queenstown, Ireland, she and the other Union passengers sent up a thunderous cheer at news that General McClellan had just fought an overwhelming victory at Antietam. During the voyage, hostility threatened to erupt with the many Rebel sympathizers on board, and in New York when the pilot boats hove in sight, a skirmish broke out as each group, eager to hear the news first, struggled to possess the gangway.

"What news?" a voice sang out as the pilot made his way up the plank. Charlotte and the crowd closed in around him. "Lee has passed the Potomac with 25,000 men and is marching on Washington, if not already there!"

Hands that held hats ready to toss in the air dropped slowly. Heavy, outraged silence fell over the Northern group when the Confederate sympathizers began cheering. When she could stand it no

longer, Charlotte stamped her foot on the deck: "I don't believe it!"
Her anger broke the tension. A voice called out, "Three cheers for
Charlotte Cushman!" The cheers lasted until she had made her way
down the plank and into Emma Crow's arms.

At her hotel, Charlotte dashed off a note to Seward. "I am again
upon 'my native heath' and among my first wants is to see and hear
from you that you are well, *doing and being!*" Since Lee had by-
passed Washington and moved on north, she purposed making "an
invasion—or 'raid' (to speak in the vernacular of the day) upon you
in Washington." Her niece, Mrs. Ned Cushman, would come with
her. In spite of his thousand cares, could Seward drop her a note?
"The sight of your hand writing will be good for 'sair e'en.' " Seward
replied immediately. "You and your niece will find rooms in apple
pie order at my house. I have not thought it necessary to look further."

The Washington she entered in late June 1863 had changed
sadly in the past two years. The hills were spread with hospital bar-
racks and tattered gray tents housing thousands of wounded. Huge
four-horse wagons were common sights rumbling up Fourteenth
Street to one of the hospitals. Ambulatory patients trudged aimlessly
up the main streets in long, sad processions. From time to time,
cavalry troops galloped by or picked their way through the great
droves of cattle that milled through the dust, their drovers on horseback cracking their whips and shouting. Except for the misery it
all represented, the scene might have been a painting by Rosa Bonheur.

Charlotte's first look at Seward hardly cheered her. Sleepless nights
had taken their toll of Mr. Lincoln's Secretary. But in breakfast
conversations with him, in late afternoon talks after he had trudged
wearily home, she saw the deep lines in his face relax at some wit-
ticism, some insight from her that helped relieve his tensions. Seward
was at heart a poet, she recognized again, and she lightened his cares
by describing the brilliant beauty she had left behind on the Campagna.

More than once Seward asked her advice about some matter of state.
When Lincoln himself turned in at the gate, his face drawn with
worry, to sprawl a few moments for talk with his Secretary, Seward
insisted that Charlotte remain in the room. Sallie had stopped in

Philadelphia to visit her mother, but on June 29, Sallie's wire to Seward amused him so much he showed it to Lincoln. "The Rebels are expected here. What shall Sallie do?"

Watching the President, Charlotte saw his face break in a smile, then relapse again in sadness, as if a lamp inside had suddenly gone out.

Charlotte's talks with Seward ranged over more than the war. Should she transfer her investments to the other side of the Atlantic to hedge herself if worse days were coming? Could Seward give her any hope that Ned might qualify for a consular opening, if and when one occurred in Rome? The unmistakable pessimism in Seward's words left her wondering. Had he been serious when time and again he had shaken his head and sadly commented, "If the future of the country shall continue until then"?

Seward acknowledged her bread-and-butter note in brighter spirits. After Gettysburg, General Lee had pulled back his campaign and now the clouds seemed to be lifting. "I can't but think how much more agreeable your visit here would have been for yourself if it had come now when the bright sunshine of victory is shining upon us," but perhaps it was just as well that she had seen some of the trials that went with guarding a nation in civil war. He hoped she would come again in September.

When Seward sent her two volumes of his published correspondence, Charlotte wrote her gratitude. "No living man in our country could have written these letters but yourself or steered the barque of state so skillfully through the perils at home and abroad." Many felt this who did not speak "their thinkings," and many of Seward's grateful friends might never reach him except through good wishes and prayers, yet "Your children's children will find the fruits of your labours and be glad."

But talks and letters with Seward were, after all, not her prime reason for coming home. After two weeks at Newport enjoying the sea air and walks along the low cliffs, weeks that confirmed her growing conviction that if she ever came home to live it would be here, she was ready to work for the Sanitary. On September 12, 1863, she played Lady Macbeth at the Academy of Music in Philadelphia opposite Edwin Booth, still irked at the man's preposterous delicacy in the part, but filled now with sympathy for the grief in his eyes. Mary Devlin Booth— "the tiniest woman ever called wife," as Annie Fields had labeled her—had died in February, leaving him and their daughter Edwina in despair. Yet she did not recant what she had once written Emma Crow: *"Edwin Booth is not a gentlemen* and to my mind has no more gentlemanly instincts, which would make him hesitate to hurt a woman or give her pain, than Mr. Edwin Forrest." Mary Booth's husband was living proof how short the country was of gentlemen, "men who would never descend into being 'Masters' merely for the sake of . . . showing their power over a weak woman."

Next week, Charlotte was in Boston for more good talk with the Fieldses. At dinner, Annie saw through some of Charlotte's interest in this acting trip. "She can't endure to give up the stage," Annie remarked in her diary. "She is a woman who lives for effects." Yet watching her Boston benefit on September 25, Annie was smitten again with Charlotte's Lady Macbeth. "Her reading of the letter when she first appears is one of her finest points." And though she found no hint of beauty in the devilish part, it was "delightful to hear the wondrous poetry of the play intelligently and clearly rendered." The sleep-walking scene was fine—"that deep-drawn breath of sleep is thrilling."

A few days before her Washington, D.C., benefit, when John P. Usher, the Secretary of the Interior, escorted her through the new Capitol rotunda, Charlotte took the occasion to put in a word for Emma Stebbins. Had Usher thought of adding a Columbus statue to the sculpture collection already begun there?

For the benefit on October 17, Charlotte could have used either of Washington's two theatres, Leonard Grover's lavish new National on Pennsylvania Avenue or John Ford's older house on Tenth near F Street. Both managers begged her, but she selected the National because of its Shakespeare company—and because rumor held that Ford, willy-nilly, catered to Rebel sympathizers.

Grover spared no cost in presenting the star whom his ads hailed "the most gifted actress of the present age." He brought in J. W. Wallack, Jr., for Macbeth and E. L. Davenport for Macduff. The night's program was printed in red ink on a lacy sheaf of white satin edged in ribbon. At her entrance, Charlotte found the theatre jammed. To her left, in the President's flag-draped box, she saw Lincoln sitting grave and stiff in his chair. With him sat his wife, his young son Tad, and his private secretary, William Stoddard. In the box to her right, she saw Seward, Fanny, Emma Crow, and the Frederick Sewards, all cheering. Every part of the house was crowded with dignitaries.

Watching Charlotte's Lady Macbeth glower and swoop and wander in her sleep, Emma Crow sensed the joy of a veteran newly returned to battle. Offstage, Auntie might be the strong shoulder, the wisdom and brains that she and Ned both envied sometimes and feared a little, but between her and the statuesque presence on stage, Emma saw no connection. Auntie's power on stage was mainly a matter of voice. With it she could cast any spell, move any crowd to feel whatever she wished. There was no trick about it; its perfect tone came, said Emma, "from a perfect heart," from a throat "like the Arc de Triomphe." One never missed a whisper, however far back he might be sitting.

At the end of the play, when Charlotte came through the curtains for her bow, a smiling Lincoln and his family stood cheering, and the women in Seward's box tossed her an elegant bouquet. The night had brought the Sanitary Fund over $2,000.

Two nights later the Baltimore proceeds were lower (due to the manager's negligence, Charlotte discovered), but receipts at the sold-out New York benefit on October 22 more than made up—even though mismanagement had allowed scalpers in Wall Street to sell many tickets for $20. With Edwin Booth, Charlotte took the ovation that erupted at the final curtain. Next day, the *Tribune* hailed the event "brilliant, the greatest theatrical success of the year." The *Spirit of the Times* was not surprised that the box office had cleared nearly $3,000. For its own taste, said the *Spirit, Macbeth* was too bloody and dark, but this had been an unforgettable performance by America's two reigning stars.

In New York, Charlotte let herself be persuaded to play one other performance. On October 28, she played Lady Macbeth to John Wilkes Booth's Macbeth at the Booklyn Academy of Music on behalf of the American Dramatic Fund.* As a child John Wilkes had taken delight in dressing up "as Charlotte Cushman as Meg Merrilies" and sending the Negroes on his father's farm shrieking. Now, as a man, he demanded complete realism on stage: often his sword thrust and fisticuffs left scars and bruises—in return for which he often got the same. He frankly admitted that after playing Richard

---

* I find no proof for the report that John Wilkes Booth carried to his death a scar on his neck put there, as he solemnly declared, when Charlottle Cushman's vigorous acting with him in 1863 tore open a recent surgical incision.

II, he generally slept bandaged in steak and oysters. One night when a sword caught him square on the forehead and sent the blood gushing over his eyes, the actor playing Richmond had cried, "Good God!" But Booth had muttered genially, "That's all right, old man! Never mind me—only come on hard, for God's sake, and save the fight!"

Soon after the New York benefit, Jamie Fields invited Charlotte to help dedicate the great new organ in Boston's Music Hall. Annie herself had written an ode, anonymously, which Charlotte would deliver on November 2 as a prelude to an elaborate concert played by six different organists. Clad in black silk, Charlotte read Annie's lines eulogizing Boston, the founding fathers, and the young men now dying in battle.

To celebrate, the Fieldses gave a supper afterward for Charlotte, the Oliver Wendell Holmeses, William B. Ogden, and Mrs. Howe.

With that, Charlotte's mission home was complete. Sailing for Rome, she could rest content that her five nights' work had brought the Sanitary more than $8,000, the most striking example America had yet seen, said Henry Bellows in a grateful newspaper card, of "woman's power and will to do her full part in the national struggle." When a huge album of watercolors and oils reached her in Rome on December 22, Charlotte felt doubly rewarded. Artists in the five benefit cities had taken their own means of adding their thanks to the country's.

A Hunger for Home

(1864–1865)

Coming through London in December, 1863 Charlotte found furious letters from Hattie. The *London Art Journal* was daring to charge that her colossal Zenobia, which she had just sold for $4,000, was actually by one of her workmen. To satisfy Hattie, Charlotte stopped long enough to start legal proceedings against the paper. At Brixton, she found Mary Eliza sadly declined. Her face had lost its color; her eyes could do little more now than stare piteously when she was not sleeping. For days, Charlotte fretted about her duty. At last, seeing no change in her mother, knowing no way to predict what might happen, she moved on south, fearing that at every stop a wire might recall her to the bedside.

Arriving in Rome, she tried to imagine the import of her final talks with Seward. The Secretary had promised nothing, but he saw no reason why Ned might not qualify one day for the Consulate. Toward that end, Charlotte set to work redecorating the fourth floor apartment and the rooms that Hattie had suddenly vacated, without a word of thanks for the five years' free shelter, to move to her own new flat in the Palazzo Barberini.

Hattie's move was hardly surprising. About that, Charlotte had her own opinions, a feeling Browning voiced perfectly sometime later. "Hatty is just old Hatty—less interesting, as is the way with all such pretty things after a time: the 'not-niceness' of her conduct is the old story." Yet much as she resented Hattie's ingratitude, it was good to know that the *London Art Journal* had retracted its charge. The *Athenaeum* had even printed a letter from Story: the celebrated Zenobia was truly "the product of Miss Hosmer's own mind and her own hands." Without Hattie, Charlotte now hoped more strongly than ever that the young Cushmans might one day join her.

"A whole week has passed, and again I am at my writing-table," she wrote Emma Crow in January 1864, "talking by 'word of pen' to my darlings over the sea. . . . How are they? What are they doing, thinking, feeling? Do they love me best in the world? Do they want me as I want them?" She could answer for one, and they for two, "and so all is well; and my conclusion is that we are very happy people, and having only one large cause for disquiet, namely, separation."

One cold afternoon she ordered her coachman, Giuseppi, to drive her and Emma Crow's sister and brother-in-law up around the Pincio. When one of the horses began dancing a bit, Giuseppi struck him with a whip, the horse kicked and Giuseppi struck him again so hard the frightened gray team tore off up the Pincio. Rounding a corner, the barouche side-swiped a carriage, then crashed into a tree. Charlotte and her guests picked themselves up, unhurt but speechless.

But most days passed uneventfully. With Emma at work on further commissions, Charlotte filled her time reading—"On Sunday I did not go to church, but stayed at home to read the three cantos of Longfellow's 'Dante' in the January number of the 'Atlantic.' How beautiful they are!"—or writing letters of pithy advice to the young Cushmans: "Show me a man's intimates, and I will tell you what that man is. . . . I bless my mother for one element in my nature, or rather my grandmother, ambition. I cannot endure the society of people who are beneath me in character or ability. I hate to have satellites of an inferior calibre."

Between times, she flooded the mails with letters about her investments, particularly stock she had bought in Ogden's new Chicago and Northwestern railroad. Nights she filled as she pleased with the usual round of parties.

Without really meaning to, Charlotte continued to leave the impression with the male sculptors in Rome that she meant to wreck them. Privately, she called them "chiselers," but when Story accused her of saying his statues were really the work of his cutters, she stood firm. "*I have said no such thing!* I know that all sculptors require assistances from even human tools; all sculptors, I believe, have them, and *if* I say this of *you,* I say it of all!"

But Story would not be mollified. "Miss Cushman is mouthing it as usual," he wrote Charles Eliot Norton, "and has her little satellites revolving around her." About that, Charlotte confessed how she really felt to Kate Field. Story was an "independent humbug who took other people's ideas for himself."

Writing Fanny Seward, Charlotte found plenty to praise in other men. "Have you seen Whittier? . . . He is a true soul, with a pure poet's heart." She was equally sure of Tennyson. "Last night I was reading for some young friends from England the 'Guinevere' Idyll of Tennyson and the 'Lady of Shalott'; and every time I read him I am more and more impressed with the beauty of his rhythm. . . . 'The Lady of Shalott,' read in a *measure* slowly, is like a gently flowing river, 'as it goes down to Camelot.' "

In June 1864, Charlotte felt grimmer realities intervening, especially when Rome began seething in its normal summer heat. A new onslaught of rash spread over her hands, and her doctors insisted again that only waters at a spa like Harrogate, England, could cure it. Mary Eliza was still failing, and Emma Crow was pregnant again, after three miscarriages. Fearing a fourth, Charlotte prevailed upon Ned to let Emma come over for the final months so the baby could be born in the cool of an English summer, where Auntie could smooth away the details.

With her mother and Emma Crow and Emma Stebbins, Charlotte lazed away July and August on Harrogate's high tableland. Then, as time neared for Emma Crow's baby, she took a house near Manchester "until the event be over."

Once tiny Wayman Crow Cushman had been safely launched in the world, and mother and child had returned to America, Charlotte filled her letters with advice about rearing him. "A mother who devotes herself to her child, in watching its culture and keeping it from baleful influences, is educating and cultivating herself at the same time. *No artist's work* is so high, so noble, so grand, so enduring, so important for all time, as the making of *character* in a child. . . . No statue, no painting, no acting can reach it." About the baby's character, "we shall see if we cannot make a *clever* man of him, and then it will not matter much who was his aunt."

On March 4, 1865, Charlotte wrote home from Rome her satisfaction in the day's events in Washington. How grand Abraham Lincoln must feel that "by the sheer force of honesty, integrity, and patience," he had overcome faction to such an extent that he was today, "by the *convictions* of the whole people," placed again in the Presidential chair. Upon his shoulders rested the hopes of republican institutions for all future time. "God help him to keep true and faithful!"

The seeds she had nurtured carefully with Seward bore fruit in February 1865, when the State Department announced that, with Stillman's resignation, Edwin Charles Cushman had been appointed U.S. Consul in Rome. Now, with the apartment ready for Ned and Emma and baby Wayman, "Big Mama" as she now signed her joyous letters to them—could throw open her doors and welcome her family home. Yet when they arrived in April, Charlotte felt a sudden misgiving. Did Ned really have the character and judgment necessary for the job? She would not let him, of course, make serious mistakes. And when she saw Emma Crow and the baby, "the very loveliest child, white and pink, with the largest loveliest blue eyes you ever saw," she believed that Ned had cause enough to make good. To make him feel properly responsible, she suggested that he pay a token rent for his quarters.

With the sudden new rhythm of life that entered her marble apartment, with the flurry of maids who rushed upstairs whenever the baby whimpered, Charlotte could not imagine greater happiness. Yet even more was in store for her when, on April 11, news flashed down the telegraph wires from London that Robert E. Lee had surrendered at Appomattox. "Today my pride, my faith, my love of country is blessed and satisfied!" America had achieved new glory. "My heart swells and my eyes brim over as I think today of her might, her majesty . . . her inability to recognize bondage."

Four and a half years ago she had caught Seward's conviction that no matter how high the cost, the Union must be maintained and slavery abolished. Today, she could rejoice with the crowd of other Americans who massed in front of the Consulate at 28 Piazza di Spagna and then swooped up the Spanish Steps to 38 Via Gregoriana, singing and rejoicing. America was at last "one sole, undivided—not common, but *un*common—country, great, glorious, free."

And then almost immediately came the sad word that Seward had been severely injured in a carriage accident on April 5, his jaw broken on both sides. And finally, most heartrending of all, came the news that no American in Rome—or anywhere else—could believe. "Assassination is not an American practice or habit," Seward had written early in the war. But an event at Ford's Theatre the night of April 14, 1865, proved that it would never again be considered impossible.

Writing Emma Crow, who was in London, Charlotte could not believe the fearful news that reached Rome on April 27. "It is too theatrical a thing to be done by an American." The thought of what America had lost "makes my heart ache with terror for the results . . . I am unable to do anything else but sit and clasp my hands in dread and fear." When later reports named Lincoln's assassin, she believed it easily: John Wilkes Booth, "the madman . . . the perfectly reckless daredevil." How appalling for Edwin Booth and his family. "Poor little Mary! She has escaped much torture and suffering." Poor little Edwina, this dreadful crime would "attach itself to her and all the family forever and forever!" And poor Edwin himself. "I cannot see how he can ever hold up his head again, or present himself to a public."

Coupled with that horror came the almost overpowering news that Seward, helpless in his bed, had been murderously attacked at nearly the same moment by one of Booth's conspirators. Lewis Payne had appeared at his door and identified himself as a messenger from the doctor. When Frederick Seward reached for the package, Payne insisted he must give Seward the medicine himself. When Frederick refused to let him enter the bedroom, Payne struck him with the muzzle of his heavy pistol, leaving him bleeding and unconscious, then rushed upon the Secretary with a knife and slashed his face. Seward's male nurse repulsed him then or he would have cut Seward's throat. Screaming in the corner, Anna and Fanny saw it all.

"All the Americans here meet, look at each other, and burst into tears," Charlotte wrote Fanny. "Your father's life is prayed for as never man's was before." If he was able to hear it, would Fanny try to convey to him "through your loving words what I would say but cannot."

By August, Charlotte tried to look at the nation's tragedy in some sort of historical frame. "At last then—having great national crimes to register—we have a history!" she wrote Kate Field. "At last, we are of the 'Great Peoples.' Strange that it must be ever so. The baptism of blood for each great truth to have a name!" But the nation had survived; a new President, for all his hot temper and sympathy for the South, had taken hold. Seward had left his bed in May—his head covered with a close-fitting cap, his jaws still fastened with wire—and taken up his duties alongside Andrew Johnson, though his own life continued to center in grief. Unable to bear up any longer under the horrors recent months had brought, his wife died suddenly in June; after that, Fanny fell into serious decline.

A Hunger for Home

In Rome, a happier note was the report that Emma's toga-clad bronze of Horace Mann had arrived in Boston and would be unveiled on July 4, a companion piece to a bronze Daniel Webster. Emma debated about going home for the ceremony, but with the statue out of her hands, she felt "like a soft-shelled crab—at the mercy of everything." She decided to stay safe in Rome, where the only imperfect note was Ned's family's apparent unwillingness to understand Miss Stebbins' place in Auntie's life. But about that, Charlotte wasted little concern now. Emma Stebbins was as "true, noble, self-sacrificing" as ever—and much in need of moral support when the verdicts came back from Boston. The *Transcript* and the *Advertiser* both found Emma's Horace Mann a "mass of bad drapery," and William Story's wife called it "the very worst thing I ever saw."

With "this old man of the sea" off Emma's shoulders, Charlotte was determined now to see that Emma got every penny due her for it. The friend of her heart deserved it; a woman had been deprived of her rights. In England for another cool summer, she found her mother seriously fallen off; Mary Eliza was now a querulous, fault-finding old woman complaining at every discomfort and blaming all her troubles on Charlotte's "unconcern." Charlotte tried to read the complaints as senility's innocent mutterings; she admonished herself not to fret about matters she could not change. Instead, she threw herself anew into correspondence with Seward.

The sight of Seward's handwriting, however shaky and almost painfully difficult to read, brought her a cheer she had not felt in months. To most of his friends, Seward must write through an amanuensis now, but Charlotte, he declared, was of "different metal." "How much I do miss your good bright thinking," he wote in September. "How many high questions of state and delicate questions of manners I have to treat of every day in which I could interest you and profit by your experience and sagacity." Her "faithful and affectionate friend" ended his letter with a pregnant question: "When may we expect you home to stay?"

At the time, Charlotte managed no ready answer. Of her forty-nine years, she had lived more than fourteen abroad. Yet hearing the word "home" filled her now with yearning. The hunger made no real sense, she told herself; her heart really centered in the lives that circulated around hers in Italy and England. But in the days stretching ahead she could not discount a growing urge to return to her roots. Had the war and assassination and Seward's brush with death

331

brought her close, in a new way, to a sense of her own mortality?

Charlotte was too good a Victorian to miss her time's concern for "death's dark angel." When life was action, she could push the dark thoughts to the back of her mind, but heading for England, she had found a new heaviness stealing into her letters, a subtle awareness that she herself was merely one of God's billion creatures who knows that he has passed his crest and entered a downhill road. She might have persuaded Emma Stebbins to push on with her through Liverpool and to the first ship to New York, if doing so would not have forced her to try to explain more than she herself understood.

Vague Foreboding

(1865–1869)

🌹 Charlotte never put stock in hunches. She had listened while Isa and Elizabeth Browning talked spiritualism, but she had kept herself uninvolved with realms outside of the practical. In letters to American friends she could follow one paragraph about her religious "uneasiness" with "Let me know something of Delaware and Hudson and Penn Coal Company property. . . . If anything very capitally good comes in your way as an investment, think of this 'old maid' over the water and put in for her as well as yourself." But her low spirits the fall of 1865 foretold matters more sober.

When Charlotte came through Florence in late October, Isa found her looking older and thinner. "I do not think she is happy," Isa wrote Kate Field. Nor by January 1866 had she shaken off her deep discouragement: "I feel suddenly and unnaturally old. . . . I am a broken winded hunter and have no longer any spring in me."

Much as she had once thought that Ned's family would add blissful joy to her life, she found now—through no real fault of theirs—that her beautiful rooms were merely another source of depression. "At home every evening; if anybody strolls in we are glad to see them, give them a cup of tea, and then stupidly talk about—anything —nothing—until 10 o'clock when we all prepare for bed, in fact the contrast between this house this year and last year could not be believed in, unless seen."

Charlotte's vague sadness became sudden shock when news about Jane Carlyle reached her from London in April 1866. Jane had gone riding in a brougham in Kensington Gardens with her dog on her lap. Near Victoria Gate, she had stopped to let the dog out for a run alongside, but a brougham coming from the opposite direction knocked him over. Frantically, Jane leaped out, but finding that only a paw had been bruised, she picked up the dog, resumed her seat in the brougham, and signaled her coachman to drive on. After a circuit or two of the Park, the coachman asked if the dog was all right. When Jane gave no reply, he stopped and asked a passing lady to look in upon Mrs. Carlyle. The woman saw Jane slumped back in her cushions, her hands limp in her lap. When she failed to answer the woman, the coachman jumped down from his box, threw open the door, and found Mrs. Carlyle dead.

And then, within a few weeks, Charlie wired from London that Mary Eliza had taken a bad turn and that Charlotte must come immediately. Troop movements in Italy had commandeered every conveyance north, and Charlotte could leave Rome only after frustrating delays. In Paris, she received the death message. She only reached Liverpool in time to follow her mother's casket to the grave beside Susan's.

Moving Mary Eliza's furniture from Brixton to 1 Bolton Row, Charlotte grieved that she had known her mother so little in the years that had followed her swift rise to eminence. Suddenly, she was overcome with remorse and a deep sense of loss; however little her family appreciated her, she was losing them, one by one. When Charlie confessed his own sense of emptiness and lack of purpose now that his mother no longer required him in England, Charlotte pushed aside her grief and began writing letters to various men in America. Could William Ogden find Charlie a place in his company that required "patient and methodical attention more than intense genius?" Could Seward give him some routine job in the State Department? "He will not let me support him and be idle, which I would gladly have him be," but the loss "I have lately met with in my poor dear mother makes me so anxious about other members of my family that I am willing to risk the chance of a refusal from you rather than not ask for that which might keep one of them longer with me."

In London, she had no heart now for social routine. Writing Fanny in July, Charlotte reported that she had perhaps insulted Mrs. Charles Francis Adams, wife of the Ambassador, only one of the many people "to whom I have been unable to perform my social duties."

A nagging discomfort she had suffered for months added to her depression. In August, doctors in London finally convinced her she needed an operation, simple but painful, and "not a thing to be

334

talked of in a public way." Recuperating from it, she was cheered to find in Fanny's letters word that Seward was puttering again among his flowers and birds. "I think one thing that keeps his heart younger than many a boy's," wrote Fanny, "is his ardent and appreciative love of all that is beautiful in nature." And Frederick's wounds were also slowly mending.

In late summer, Charlotte begged Fanny to come to Rome next winter and idle her days however she wished, since she herself would be bound in mourning. But a grief-stricken letter from Seward in late November brought word that Fanny had died in October, and Charlotte held back her tears to write her old friend. "What terrible sacrifices have you, my good, noble, and soul-tried friend, been called upon to lay on the altar of *your country*." She regretted now more than ever that she had not gotten to America the past summer. "It would have been a great joy to me then and a great consolation to me now! . . . Ah, my friend. Truly, 'God's ways are not as our ways.' "

With Emma back from a trip to New York and Ned and his family returned from Boston, Charlotte threw herself into the whirl that had once made life in Rome exciting, but now, even with Julia Ward Howe in town, she mustered little elation beyond furthering Emma Stebbins' career. "Don't forget Miss Stebbins's 'Bacchus' or 'Italian Autumn,'" she wrote a recent American visitor. "I would like you so much to have it that if price is an object, I think she would be willing to take 400 scudi for it . . . I am sure you will find satisfaction in having something from Miss Stebbins."

When the half-Negro, half-Chippewa girl, Edmonia Lewis, arrived from Boston, Charlotte took her up as a personal project. At twenty-two, Edmonia had already impressed Longfellow and William Lloyd Garrison with her determination to become a sculptress, and Charlotte lost no time in bringing attention to this "poor little soul, who has more than anybody else to fight." The first statue she completed in Rome indicated fully the line her work would follow.

An ideal figure of Hagar illustrated, said Edmonia, her strong sympathy "for all women who have struggled and suffered." Her "Hiawatha's Wooing" impressed Charlotte so deeply that she and a group of other Americans bought it and presented it to the Boston

335

YMCA, as proof that "a race which hitherto in every age and country has been looked upon with disfavor" was capable "of producing work worthy of the admiration of cultivated people."

In hopes that high wit and music might restore her spirits, Charlotte reestablished her evenings at 38 Via Gregoriana, often welcoming 175 people. She turned her thoughts to another project, one that had interested her ever since she read Annie's ode at the dedication of the new organ in Boston. A Danish sculptor in Rome, Wilhelm Mathieu, needed encouragement, and she commissioned him to make casts of his heroic busts of Palestrina, Mozart, and Beethoven for the Music Hall as her gift to the city of Boston. She took new interest in the family when Emma Crow gave birth on June 2, 1867, to another son, especially when Ned gave him two names dear to her heart. The boy would be Allerton Seward, with the Secretary of State readily agreeing to be the baby's godfather. "Find a good Christian of any church to be my proxy." Charlotte happily nicknamed him Nino.

To escape Rome's summer heat, Charlotte and Emma settled in Bude, a village in Cornwall, which reminded her of Newport. They sat for hours among the rocks and watched the waves come dashing and booming up against them "in a wilderness of milky foam, which beats again and again on the rocks until it is caught by the wind and blown about in flakes like sea-birds." After Sallie had brought down their lunch, she and Emma settled their heads upon a convenient rock and read or dozed in the sun, fully content until the spirit moved them "to clamber about and explore."

But the holiday was only preparation for the kind of foolishness Charlotte had long feared in Ned. Back in Rome in late October, she faced the fact again that having Ned with her the past two years had done little to reassure her about his judgment. As Consul, Ned was mostly his own boss and from that stemmed his freedom to make mistakes. He was familiar with American law forbidding citizens from participating in foreign wars; more than once he had refused to sanction offers from young American Catholics eager to fight for the Pope. Yet Ned's own love of adventure, plus perhaps some taste for drama he had inherited, outweighed his diplomatic detachment. Only days before Charlotte returned from England, with Garibaldi's forces standing within four miles of Rome, Ned had decided to move out—as an observer—with a column of Papal troops. He marched with them four days, even joining in one skirmish and suffering a slight wound.

Vague Foreboding

When the report got back to Rome, indignation rode high against this American's personal involvement. Richard Rothwell, an English artist, fired off a furious letter to Seward, charging that Cushman had done service "in mortal conflict against the Italians whose inability of soul has aroused them to seek a Nationality," that he had returned to Rome boasting of the wound he had received, which "unfortunately," said Rothwell, "was not 'wide as a church door' but enough to mark his infamy and cast a stigma on the proud republic of America."

Seward wrote Ned immediately, requesting a full explanation. Ned denied the charges brought by "an old man of eccentric habit and very little reputation as an artist"; he did assert that with the commanding general's permission he had accompanied a column as a spectator, in order to obtain reliable information for Washington, and that during a skirmish the officer he stood beside had fallen injured and he had picked up a gun and fired in self-defense. Later, wounded slightly himself, he had gone to a hospital but had used his time there to help tend the wounded of both sides.

Seward's reply was firm. "No interest of the United States could be served by such a proceeding"; no reasonable motive could be assigned for it, except interest or, more, curiosity—neither of which was consistent with consular character. The reprimand from Seward, however much it embarrassed Charlotte and tended to cool Ned's ardor for action was far from enough to satisfy the Italian patriot Mazzini. "My American friends and I want him dismissed." But when Ned denied again that he had been guilty of any improper act, Seward accepted the explanation.

Improper or not, the matter was "Ned's folly" as far as Charlotte was concerned, and she made herself clear on that point to Seward. His "last dispatch to my nephew," more like a father's letter "than his folly or overzeal merited," had had its effect. "I do not think you will be troubled on his account again, in such a way! I was in England—or it would not have happened at all. It grieved me much more than I can tell you, but when I learned of it, it was too late to do other than make the best of it, but it has been a lesson well learned."

Yet for all Ned's escapades, for all her yearnings sometimes for the old days when she had only herself and Sallie and a hotel room to worry about, Charlotte found Ned's children a steady delight. "Wayman is strong but delicate looking, as fair as any girl and too pretty for a boy. Allerton is a remarkable child in his way with a

337

wonderful intelligence for seven months." Her pain about Ned eased a little when Algernon Swinburne thought well enough of Ned's explanation to Seward to send her the manuscript of a poem. Swinburne's "A Watch in the Night" was "splendid," she wrote Jamie Fields.

Elizabeth Peabody's coming to Rome in February 1868 sustained Charlotte through the long moments of depression she managed to hide. She kept the talk moving so swiftly, and on such a high plane, that Elizabeth confessed later that amid all the glories Rome offered, her talks with Charlotte Cushman had helped her arrive at new "mental maturity." The evenings Charlotte arranged in compliment to Elizabeth—on one occasion she read "The Halt Before Rome" to Lord Houghton (Dickie Milnes), and Bayard Taylor—seemed to Elizabeth like "golden hours" bursting with Charlotte's "grandly moral, delightfully human nature." In the group, a new face counted himself a "Cushmanite." Dr. James Simpson from Edinburgh noted the determined effort Charlotte made to fill her rooms with gaiety.

If someone had made Charlotte confess it, a suspicion lurked in the back of her mind that something was dreadfully wrong. In late May, when Oliver Wendell Holmes sent her the manuscript of his poem "H.W.L.," paying tribute to Longfellow, when the Boston *Transcript* printed a biographical sketch of her, Charlotte saw in these reminders of her position at home cause to wonder if a return to America might help shake off her gloom. She could tell her friends it was a business trip; she could admit to herself that it was a chance for another comforting talk with Seward. By June 21, she and Emma were at sea, enjoying random talks with old Commodore Vanderbilt, who prevailed upon her, once they had landed in New York, to let him show her around his Staten Island estate.

Too tired to think about acting, she had packed no costumes. Nor would she go in for public readings. Of late, Charles Dickens had all but preempted that stellar position in America. Last December, Dickens had created near-frenzy. By 8 A.M. the day of his Boston debut the ticket office queue had stretched nearly half a mile, and his farewell in New York in April had left a sweet taste in all America's mouth. Time had wrought happy changes, Dickens confessed, in the nation he had once so completely reviled. Leaving it, he could report changes moral and physical; changes in the amount of land subdued and cultivated; in the rise of vast new cities; in older cities grown almost beyond recognition; changes in "the graces and amenities of life." Nor, said Dickens, was he "so arrogant as to suppose that in five and twenty years there have been no changes in me."

Not even Fanny Kemble could compare with Dickens on the platform, Annie Fields told her diary after Fanny's Boston reading in January—though Annie was prejudiced, perhaps, in Dickens' favor after the splendid dinners she and Jamie had enjoyed with him in Boston. Writing Annie, Charlotte made herself clear about public readings. "I hate to read except to six people, and I won't read to a public if I can possibly help it." She had not come home to work.

In Washington, Charlotte found Seward waiting for her at the station, looking better than he had for years. At dinner and later in conversation, she was cheered to find that after his terrible sufferings, he had regained his old clarity and humor. Next day, Seward refused to suffer the heat in town; with Frederick and his wife they picnicked on Cabin John Creek, comfortable enough under the trees in spite of the 102° temperature. Another day Seward took her across to the White House, where she was "very agreeably disappointed" to find President Johnson better in every way than reports she had heard about him, not at all the bumpkin or the malicious fool his enemies considered him. He had a sort of pathos in his voice and manner. "Perhaps it is only to ladies he is so, though even men have remarked it."

In August, Charlotte accepted another invitation from Seward, this time to his home in Auburn. She arrived in the midst of an immense reception he was giving for a delegation from China and the "strong-minded women," Susan B. Anthony and Elizabeth Cady Stanton. In October, she made a trip to St. Louis to see the Crows and discuss the trusteeship she wanted arranged for her estate, in case she should die before Ned learned responsibility enough to handle it.

Back in New York, she pondered a thought that had occurred during her last talk with Seward. Her old friend would not stay active in politics forever. When he retired—or a new administration replaced him—Ned's job in Rome would be reassigned. Writing Emma Crow, she knew that the young Cushmans must make their own decisions, that they would probably settle somewhere in America, but "Oh dear, I cannot think of it without feeling sick at the bare idea. How shall I ever manage to live without *my* children and their children? I want all the comforts I can have and what comfort can I have away from them?"

In any event, she was sure now they would never make a home in London, and that relieved her of keeping 1 Bolton Row any longer. If they chose New York, they would find it the place to make money, though there was nowhere "on this side of the Atlantic to spend it." Still, where one lived while he made it "does not much matter; besides you can have very good society, if you please, in New York and that not among fast people either."

In Boston for the grand opening of the new Selwyn Theatre, Charlotte found herself as much the center of attention as the actors on stage. In the private box the managers had provided, she sat silently appalled at the acting—"Oh, my child. . . . Every human being on his own hook, no whole, no harmony"—but the house itself was splendid, the dresses beautiful. The droves of people who came up to speak to her found her "young and handsome"—words she knew were not true, but it was "pleasant to find people thinking much of you and caring." John Gilbert, looking "splendidly," brought up his new wife, Sarah.

She and Emma rounded out their visit with two weeks at Addison Childs' home in Swampscott and another quick trip down to Newport to reaffirm the charm she always found there. "Newport is to me the most charming climate on our side of the water, the sea fogs soften the skin, take out all the wrinkles and let you grow. . . . When I come home to live, as I hope to do one of these days, I shall hope to have my home in Newport."

In New York just before sailing, she called on Collis P. Huntington, one of the country's new railroad tycoons, to discuss a long-range plan for investing in one of the new lines projecting toward San Francisco. Then, on board the *Scotia,* she counted the days until she could rejoin the children, hopefully in time for Emma Crow's next baby.

The new Cushman who arrived in late November, scarcely more than a few days after Charlotte returned to 38 Via Gregoriana, was another boy, Edwin Charles—whom she and the maids promptly nicknamed Carlino. With little Wayman and Nino, Charlotte revived a custom from her own childhood, when each night at bedtime she sent them into gales of laughter with the barnyard noises she remembered hearing at Grandmother Babbit's knee. Only now she made the boys believe the sounds came from somewhere else in the room. She sat smiling and silent when they suddenly turned back to look at her, then wheeled again to look for the pigs and dogs and ducks hiding somewhere, surely, under the tables and chairs.

At Hattie's dinner for Longfellow and George W. Childs, owner of the Philadelphia *Public Ledger,* Charlotte confronted again an old question. "Miss Cushman," asked Childs, "why don't you return to America" to resume an active career? Thousands of Americans were of theatre age who had never seen her. Charlotte's reply was studied. "Why, Mr. Childs, I really can't live there as I am now living. I am able to keep my horse and carriage and I have a very charming home." With Italian prices so much in her favor, how could she afford such luxury in America? Childs was unconvinced. "I think you make a mistake by not coming."

Over tea with Longfellow in January 1869, Charlotte pondered the question—while the poet sought her advice. Did Miss Cushman find in his *New England Tragedies* any possible value for the stage? Answering him candidly, she felt her old hunger for action rekindle, yet what reason could ever make her leave the family behind? Or take Emma Stebbins away from her studio? If a return to work meant London, she might once have suggested that Rosalie and Mabel needed their Auntie handy, but with a new wife, Sheridan Muspratt valued her interest in Susan's daughters even less than before. Once, she might have said that her mother needed her closer to Brixton, if three years ago she had not buried that reason alongside Susan in Liverpool. One sudden event, however, turned in her favor in April 1869, when a letter from Seward brought word that he had resigned as Secretary of State, content that he had fulfilled his duty to the country, that the constitution was safe and union assured. After that, Ned and Emma Crow would soon be leaving.

Dressing the morning of May 9, Charlotte's vague fears and doubts became icy terror when she discovered a small lump in her left breast. Horrified, she rushed to her mirror. She raised her arm vigorously up and down over her head. There was no pain, no other visible sign of trouble. Yet a lump was there, unmistakably. Suddenly cold and trembling, she fell into a chair—while terrible memories of Grandmother Babbit's death from cancer flooded over her.

For days, she tried to hide her panic. But she could not hide her long face and silence, her sleepless nights and quick tears. When she could no longer fend off Emma's repeated questions, she knew she must tell the truth. Was this the sign she had been expecting; was now the time to pull up her stakes and go home?

Uncertain, she fled to her doctors. They advised a trip to Krankenheil in Bavaria—the waters might help. Instead, she and Emma went to Paris to seek more definite opinion. The Paris doctors ordered a quiet summer at Malvern with fresh air and exercise and careful diet; she must "amuse herself, and forget her trouble if possible." Whatever the malady, it was too incipient to diagnose. Writing Elizabeth Peabody from Malvern, Charlotte confessed that no worry had ever clutched her like this. She would see a London doctor in three weeks: "My heart sinks within me—with dread and fear."

London confirmed the worst. Sir James Paget, surgeon-extraordinary to Queen Victoria, told her there was no cure except "cutting it out," and the sooner the better. Not satisfied, Charlotte consulted another doctor, who gave her a lotion to try for six weeks: the symptoms should be more definite by then. "I have been keeping the breast covered with a compress of lead water ever since," she wrote Elizabeth Peabody. The lump, instead of decreasing, was "very much larger than it was when I first discovered it." "I am so homesick this summer for my own beloved land," she wrote Jamie Fields. Would next summer be "half so sweet and lovely?"

If there was any virtue in trouble, it lay in the deepening devotion Charlotte saw daily in Emma's eyes, the fear and suffering that Emma's face reflected. With Emma here and Ned leaving Rome in the fall, Charlotte was certain that she must—at least until she knew her own future—leave Italy. She would rent out the apartment; the place was too expensive to lock up. Now, biding her time while the lotion proved fruitless, fearing the word that must come with a return to London, she tried to rivet her mind to happier matters. "If I get over this fear which haunts me, perhaps when I come home, I will work a little," she wrote Miss Peabody.

She wrote long letters to Algernon Chase in Baltimore, full of questions about a new dye for cloth. Did it look like a bright investment? Once back in America, Ned would need some business to curb his "frivolity."

When Isa Blagden learned of her trouble, she wrote tender advice from Florence. "What you want is not external torture but internal replenishment of blood." Proper diet was the thing: "port wine, milk, glycerine taken internally, raw eggs, succulent meat, and the sedative of a kiss" every time Charlotte needed encouragement. To prove her affection, Isa hoped Charlotte had seen her article in *All The Year Round* last fall. Adelaide Ristori was a good wife and mother, but, Isa had written, "Charlotte Cushman is especially the friend of women, the one woman whose hand has always been held out to support the feebler, poorer ones of her own sex."

In London, Charlotte faced again the dread fact with Paget. Edinburgh was the place for the operation; the surgeon, Sir James Simpson, whom she had entertained in Rome. In an operating theatre, Simpson was performing wonders with a new anesthetic. The Queen herself had sung the praises of "blessed chloroform" ever since Simpson had used it on her in childbirth.

Bidding Emma Crow and the children good-bye in Malvern, Charlotte bit her lips to stave off crying. If they needed money, they must draw on her London account. Sallie and Emma would write them daily; their remaining in Malvern was better for all, since nobody knew how long she must wait in Edinburgh for the operation. Beyond that, no matter how hard she looked, time was clouded.

The Blessings of Labor

(1870–1871)

On August 17, 1869, she and Emma and Sallie worriedly checked in at the Clarendon Hotel. Next morning, Sir James' verdict was clear: the operation would take place on August 26. To pass the difficult time, Charlotte invited to her rooms the many people who, years ago, had shown her kindness. Every night she forced herself to be the wit of the gathering in spite of the pain and Emma's melancholy looks. Then the night of August 25, suddenly tired, she let her guests go early. "Don't come here tomorrow," she said. "I do not think I shall be very well for a day or two."

Outside Simpson's operating theatre, Charlie waited with Emma and Sallie, pacing, while the surgeons removed Charlotte's left breast. When she could be moved back to her hotel, they rotated as nurses, though Sallie alone managed the dressings. Charlotte had taken the operation bravely. "With God's help, she will be lifted up again," Emma wrote the family at Malvern. Ned had gone on to America, but as soon as Charlotte could raise herself up a little, she wrote with a trembling pencil, "My dear boy. I shall pull through this dark valley, as I have through many others. God bless you. Your loving Auntie."

Finding her pulse and color better one morning, Sir James assured her she was on the road to recovery. Weakly, Charlotte managed to ask, "Do you really think so, Sir James?" The dour Scotsman replied, "If I did na, I would na say so."

Within a few days, she dictated longer letters for Emma Crow. "I resist all the opiates until suffering makes me fly to them for relief," but since all was in the hands of the good God, "We will trust in Him." Two weeks later, her pale face smiling, she could receive company. Sallie trundled her into the bright sitting room. After her long pain, seeing the sunlit squares on the carpet and the brilliant green of Calton Hill in the distance made her cry suddenly, but she greeted her guests calmly, admitting only that "I have not been very well, lately."

A month later she left Edinburgh and headed for Rome, hungry for familiar surroundings, her books, her paintings, the family, in spite of Sir James' mutterings that she had lived "too long in the atmosphere of buried Caesars," that her blood needed more bracing air. She had hardly arrived before she realized that political strife was changing Rome forever, that the timeless place Rome had been under old Pio Nono would soon be like any other capital, telling time by clocks instead of slow-moving shadows on its ruins.

Writing Seward in March, she confessed that Rome had already lost much of its charm. She would come home this summer to seek a more healthful climate. If she found herself better for the change, "I shall make up my mind where to pitch my tent" and so "end my days." She would pretend nothing with Seward. "Perhaps I have not many to look forward to, for I fear my evening! But I shall at least be among those who love me, and whom I love." She would come home, she wrote him in May, to pick up her staff and "go on to the end. Let it be sooner or later."

She argued against Emma's wish to come with her: Emma's work was far from finished in Rome; her career had no reason to stop now. Yet Emma countered that reasons and needs were not all Charlotte's; the heart was a better guide. By late summer, their decision was clear. Charlotte would go home to work—for as long as time allowed her. Emma would follow.

Leaving 38 Via Gregoriana in May, Charlotte looked back at the doors that had opened to so many bright minds, so many famous faces. Its rooms had echoed to laughter, to her own songs, to incomparable conversation. In eleven years, its walls had become a gallery of the best paintings Rome's brushes could offer. Its corners and sills held Hattie's Puck, like the one that had so pleased the Prince of Wales, Emma's portrait bust like the one she had given Shepherd, Story's bronze Beethoven, and many others. Her carved antique cabinets held her weapons collection, including a sword made by the armorer of Charles II, dated 1692.* On a table lay the dag-

---

* If the *Spirit of the Times* for July 14, 1838 is correct, her collection also included "the knife found with Col. [James] Bowie's baggage in the Alamo."

ger the Duke of Devonshire had given her after *Macbeth* in London, the ebony box from the Prince of Wales. A glass case held all her promptbooks. She had wanted to have her Jarves collection of furniture shipped to the United States, but she had thought better of it when wiser heads had shaken in fear that the priceless pieces were too old to stand the jolts and jarring of travel.

Rounding the corner into the Via Sistina, Charlotte looked back through her carriage window to the waving hands and handkerchiefs in front of her house. Emma Crow and Ned stood waving, each with a child in arms, "sweet plagues and trying comforts" though they had been sometimes. It had been difficult to plan this departure. No one could say what uncertainties lay ahead.

By the time she and Emma left Paris, the canaries she had brought from Italy had nested. Something about the birds struck the hearts of both women as they clutched the arms of their chairs during the choppy crossing. To protect the birds from the noise and vibration, Charlotte wrapped a shawl around the cage, leaving only a small opening at the top. She clutched the cage close, at a sudden swell or the heartless bang of a porthole cover.

Leaving Rome, she had discovered new lumps under her arm. Sir James Paget's grave face, after his examination, told her what she already knew. A second operation must follow. To Charlotte's grief, Sir James Simpson had recently died in Edinburgh; the operation must be done in London.

Charlotte covered her feelings. If the first operation had failed, who could promise success with a second? But she said nothing to deepen the fear in Emma's eyes. On July 24, Sir James cauterized the new points of trouble, and Emma sent the report down to Rome: "There is nothing for it however but endurance, and I help her endure."

Recovering, Charlotte found little courage in learning that William Macready was so crippled now that he could not hold a pen in his hand, that he spent his days dozing in senile sleep or staring at emptiness. Her gloom deepened when headlines carried the word that Charles Dickens and Thackeray had died suddenly. "How sad it is to think that the world is darker for us and for all humanity than it was last Thursday."

When she and Emma went down to Hastings for the sea air, Westland Marston came to see her one day and watched her face light up as Charlotte told him about seeing Tommaso Salvini as Othello a few days before she left Rome. "So infectious was her love for what is beautiful and great in art," wrote Marston, that her description of Salvini's acting made him almost come alive in the room.

The morning of October 22, 1870, Charlotte took her last look at Liverpool's grim harbor and the green hills of England beyond. Time had come full circle. Sitting weakly and heavy on deck of the *Scotia,* she looked back—knowing she would never again see England. Ned's family would follow in a few weeks and proceed straight to St. Louis, where Ned would work for Emma Crow's father. In *The Marble Faun,* Hawthorne had put his finger on the feeling that now rushed through her. She would never forget her excitement in Rome each time she had checked her horse at some overlook and gazed out over the sweep of history that lay frozen below in the stones. But like Hawthorne, she had discovered a truth that only lately she had been able to see. "The years, after all, have a kind of emptiness when we spend too many of them on a foreign shore." Prudent people never forgot their roots, the nourishment in their native air. "It is wise therefore to come back betimes, or never."

Unquestionably, now was the time. On November 3, sighting New York rising tall now and freshly American, Charlotte knew something else. Illness had brought a new certainty. "Unless I would be eaten by my own corroding anxiety, I must *do* something which would so completely take me out of myself that I should forget all my own troubles." She would go back to the old profession "which I did wrong ever to leave." Long years of rest had brought only fatigue.

Charlotte felt her wisdom in coming home fully confirmed when the news flashed across the Atlantic by cable that the Italians had finally marched into Rome and held Pio Nono prisoner in the Vatican. In a plebiscite on October 2, only 1,500 people in all of Rome had voted against annexation. Hattie had joined the black-robed throng that had massed in St. Peter's to defend the Holy Father, and, as she wrote later, they had all sobbed at the sight of the doddering old Pontiff, weeping among his cardinals.

Charlotte would be slow about choosing a place to settle. Before she left England she had made one point clear to Emma Crow. Never again would she personally consider a house as any real home. She had outgrown the need for permanent headquarters; in the time she had left, wherever the children were happy would be home enough for her. Letters from Thomas Wentworth Higginson and Helen Hunt revived her interest in Newport. After Rome, any northern city would prove difficult in winter, though coming home and settling anywhere meant facing that obvious fact. She would have liked to talk it over with Seward, but in his new leisure he had left on a round-the-world cruise in August.

By January 1871, Boston was clamoring for her to return to the stage. One manager tossed aside her objections that she had brought no costumes with her by offering to supply whatever she needed and pay her seven hundred dollars a night. The offer made her smile a little. In the early days, when she had been full of energy and need, she had sometimes played in Boston for less than five dollars. Now when she had almost no energy and no money needs whatever, her cup ran over.

Charlotte and Emma spent the early weeks of 1871 at Newport proving, in spite of reports, that its winters could be as bitter as anywhere else. Yet having people like Helen Hunt and Julia Ward Howe and the Higginsons in town made it more cheerful, especially Higginson's booming enthusiasm for the place in any season. Newport was loveliest, he declared, when the north wind dappled the hills and drove the sailboats around Point Judith under heavy swirls of snow.

At Helen Hunt's, Charlotte delighted the room with her talk about George Sand and her comments about why acting was often easier in England. English audiences applauded better; they came to the theatre to be amused. When someone asked what plans she had about acting again, she parried the question. Jamie Fields had recently stepped down from his editor's desk at the *Atlantic Monthly,* and that seemed right for Jamie. "I think the sense is in knowing when to retire!" she wrote Annie.

For herself, she had happy proof that she could undo her own bad timing. Three different cities were imploring her to act or read or lecture for twice the money she had ever been offered before. Now that the public had forgiven him for being John Wilkes' brother, Edwin Booth had his own theatre in New York and was begging her to act Queen Katharine for him in the fall—at better terms than anyone else could pay.

Did she dare risk all the excitement and fatigue? "I don't like to be tempted," she wrote Emma Crow. But writing it, Charlotte knew that the time had come to face both the fact of her illness and her need to get busy. The old pains in her arm were burning again. She must check soon with a doctor in New York who had invented a treatment using electricity. Whatever the new symptoms meant, she must get into costume.

In March, at William B. Ogden's Hudson River estate, Villa Boscobel, she was troubled about facing another operation. As President of the Union Pacific Railroad, Ogden had stood at Promontory Point in Utah in 1869 to see his rails join those moving eastward from San Francisco to complete the continent's first cross-country span. In Ogden's candor, she found her answer.

"It might help, but it might not, and I will simply not take the risk that its pain and trouble might not be justified." Looking at fact, she felt better "for having made up my mind to stand pat."

By late April, Charlotte was clear about Newport. She would rent a house for the summer, persuade Emma Crow to bring the boys from St. Louis, and they would decide together about the place as a permanent home. When she visited the Fieldses in Boston, she had gotten back most of her old fighting strength. "Her full brain was brimming over," Annie wrote in her diary; "she does not overestimate herself, that woman, which is part of her greatness." Charlotte's fight with death had seemed, said Annie, to strengthen her affection for life. "She grows wiser and nobler."

By mid-July, she had made two decisions. Newport's humidity bothered her, but here was the place to settle for whatever time she had left. Seeing Emma Crow's delight in the flowers, the carriage rides along Bellevue Avenue and Ocean Drive, the little boys splashing at Bailey's Beach, she wrote a check for $9,000 to buy the corner at Rhode Island Avenue and Catherine Street. Richard Morris Hunt would design the house to be done by next summer. The gabled and turreted "cottage" Hunt envisioned was clear folly, but folly, somehow, was what she wanted now.

About acting sometime in the fall, her doctors had said "I *may act,*" she wrote Edwin Booth, "and if I find it is too much for me, I must give up! But you know I have indomitable energy and I shall try to take care and not overdo myself." She would play a six-week run beginning in late September, and Booth must meet all her terms. It only sweetened her pleasure to hear that Edwin Forrest was "hanging by his eyelids" about beginning a New York run himself until Charlotte announced her plans.

She hoped Booth could get Couldock for Wolsey: he was "so better than any of these later comers over the water." And for Macbeth, E. L. Davenport would be splendid. She refused, she said, to play opposite inferior actors, for "neither Queen Katharine or Lady Macbeth can carry the play on their individual shoulders." She wrote Charlie in London to forward her costumes from storage,

hopefully to arrive in time for Sallie to make any necessary altera-
tions. Also, Booth needed her promptbooks for rehearsing the other
actors.

If she got through this run at Booth's, the money from it plus
earnings she hoped to make later in the season in other cities would
bring her the $50,000 the Newport house would cost—though if
necessary she could sell some of her stock. For her six weeks with
Booth, she must have $18,000. "I am not ignorant of the value of
my return to the stage as a *finality*."

"Finality," Charlotte realized, sounded a new note in her thinking. Earlier times, "farewell" and "retirement" had labeled whatever choice her greater happiness dictated. But with the choice apparently out of her hands, she would not lightly use them. When
she learned that a Washington doctor had treated cancer with an
extract of tropical bark, she wrote him for full particulars, in spite
of the government report against it. After all, London scientists
had once declared that no steamship unassisted by sails could get
across the Atlantic. "If you can give me any help or hope, I pray
you to do so."

The bargain Charlotte squeezed out of Booth underscored the real
meaning she found in this return to the stage. If living demanded
breathing, then it was no less true that life for her was acting. All
else was mere exposition now, and she would waste no more time
doubting it. When she met Booth and his new wife, Mary McVicker,
she remembered again how much she had always disliked him, and
now he had a wife who seemed utterly mad. "Oh, dear, oh, dear,
what tinkering work acting must be nowadays," she wrote Emma
Crow, "when such people as either of them can make money."

In response to the great wave of applause that welcomed her entrance on September 25, 1871, at Booth's Theatre, Charlotte felt
all her pain and feebleness leave her. Tonight, as new energy surged
through her, Charlotte knew how passionately she had always needed
an audience. She could no more toss acting aside than she could
squander the few precious days she had left.

"To Dare and Do and Be"

(1871–1874)

After opening as Queen Katharine at Booth's, Charlotte tried to ignore all matters outside the facts as she saw them. If doing so narrowed her life in one sense, it helped her make the most of her time. The opening's special meaning became clear at the end of Act I, when cheers recalled her again and again to the footlights. In the wings, she threw up both arms joyously—insensitive now to all pain—and cried out: "How have I lived without this through all these years!" At last, she was clear about acting's place in her life. She understood now that commitment reached much deeper than fame, or interest, or money, or critical praise. Charlotte had always said that her art was supreme, that her calling was full and enveloping. But words were inadequate now, and the difference centered in something that she, as a limited mortal, had only lately discovered. Lying in bed all afternoon to gather her strength for the night's work, gulping the comforting, whiskey-soaked biscuit Sallie made her eat between acts, she fended off the worried cries of her friends.

Seward's note on October 8 said he could not imagine the motive that had prompted her to return to acting, her making "an effort so prodigious and so incongruous" with her health. Was it in her case, as it was in his, asked Seward, "that the more sickness and infirmity attempt to chain you down, the more determination you summon to resist the fetters?" Emma never stopped complaining that Charlotte's making herself act night after night was foolish and wicked: her public had no possible claim on her; the money could never justify all the pain. And Sallie was even less understanding. Why did Charlotte insist on working herself to death?

The phrasing was interesting, but it had little relevance now.

Fully involved, she would act until death overcame her. When the *Times* welcomed her back, a gray-haired veteran with gaunt cheeks now but "an artist whose powers, ripe as they are, still show so much of 'progress' and so little of 'decay,'" when the *Tribune*'s William Winter said her Queen Katharine cast "a radiant light" and in tribute placed a lock of her hair in a tortoise shell box along with one of Mrs. Siddons', when the New York *Standard* said that such applause as that greeting her entrance was "heard but seldom in a generation"—she saw that her point was not lost. If suffering had enriched her art, she could accept it.

In younger actresses, a quieter, more natural style was emerging, but the critics, of whom New York now had several equipped to evaluate her, found her unique and incomparable. To John Rankin Towse, her "artful pauses" were always followed by "swift, bold, and perfect executions"—each of her actions inspired by "an unfaltering intelligence." John D. Stockton found in her style a "perfect balance of her passion and intellect," the "charm of reserved power."

Charlotte was too deeply immersed in the nightly excitement at Booth's to give real thought to newer talents coming along, to Adah Isaacs Menken, Fanny Davenport, Clara Morris, or to their differing styles. She had built her art out of materials nature had given her. Since beauty was not among them, she had centered her craft on the vigor, the broad gestures, the ringing tones that best matched her figure and stature. Opposite a Booth or a Lawrence Barrett, she could complain about playing with such "little men," but she would not trim down her interpretations.

Opposite Booth on October 19, when she played Lady Macbeth for the benefit of thousands left homeless in a devastating fire that had leveled much of Chicago, she drank in the applause, knowing that she had never played with greater conviction. She was "incarnate power," wrote Winter: "towering above Macbeth and pointing beyond him to the coming Duncan who 'must be provided for,' hers was a talent reduced not at all by age or illness."

Seward understood fully enough now her urge to keep on working. Back home, he wrote her encouragement. "Pray write to me at Auburn and tell me what will be the most convenient time and way for us to come together, review the events and incidents which have occurred in the interval since we parted, and contrive how we may come to live nearer to each other hereafter."

Though her body cried out in pain after the curtain each night and she had to let Sallie massage and bathe her left side with hot compresses, when she strode onto the stage for rehearsal in the morning, the company saw a woman, fully refreshed, determinedly ready for business. Working, she resorted to no impassioned outbursts. When the page to Queen Katharine muffed his approach to her throne, she quietly stepped down and showed him how to give the part the proper dignity and grace. But she stopped the rehearsal when the Dominie Sampson introduced new tricks in *Guy Mannering*. After thirty-two years of practice as Meg, she would tolerate no tampering."If you have any new business or any gags to introduce in this scene, please reserve them until I have left the stage."

By the time her forty-two nights had ended, she and Booth were richer by $57,000. Managers throughout the country besieged her, but she was too tired to consider anything long range—her throat was too raw, and she was too shrewd a businesswoman to leap at their bidding. "My being careless whether they take me or not is a great thing, for of course they all want me the more," she wrote Emma Crow. When a letter arrived from Isa congratulating her on the "great things you are doing," saying she and Mrs. Browning had always been women "of genius," Charlotte smiled. Pondering her own success, she could pity Edwin Forrest, who had played to near-empty houses back in February, an infirm, embittered, rejected old man.

By late November, Charlotte was eager to tackle Boston, especially now that a public subscription had finally paid Emma in full for her Horace Mann statue. Watching from the wings at the Globe Theatre, Emma found it hard to remember that Charlotte was ill and suffering. After two performances of *Macbeth* the same day, George Vandenhoff—lately back from retirement—came off from his dying scene stumbling and groaning like an old woman, but Charlotte took her bows brightly and grandly, as if she had done nothing unusual. Yet a day or so later, Charlotte confessed that the pains in her breast had never been worse, that now at last she could feel a sympathy for Edwin Forrest, who had just retired in New Orleans quavering the words, "I would not lag superfluous on the stage."

The Boston papers saw no decline in her. Meg's crooning, her haggard glee, her terrible death were points "rarely if ever excelled or even equalled." The *Daily Advertiser* tried to sum up her effects in a poem.

> Such is the play her wondrous powers adorn,
> She seems a sybil to the manner born;
> In Katharine to the last she walks a queen
> And startles Macbeth in the midnight scene;
> She stands unrivalled in the dramatic play,
> The noblest, greatest actress of the day,
> With life unblemished, elegant, refined,
> To see her, hear her, is a feast of mind.

Watching Queen Katharine, Annie Fields said that Charlotte's "noble, sympathetic nature" spoke to "every woman's heart there." And Julian Hawthorne, now twenty-five, watched Charlotte's Meg, transfixed at "that wonderful face, those awful eyes!" During the death of Queen Katharine, Thomas Higginson felt as if his own mother were "dying before me. . . . I would have given worlds to be able to look away for a moment, and yet I could not."

But for Charlotte, such praise was no more interesting than a little drama that took place backstage. She had gone one afternoon to see Charley Wiggin, now a successful merchant. In the store, as soon as the floorwalker recognized her, he rushed back to call Mr. Wiggin. When Charley came out, ruddy-faced and white-haired now, he broke into a smile, grasped Charlotte's hands and held them for a moment, then escorted her to his office. Later, when questioned about the visit, Charlotte answered frankly. "When I see him now, rich and respected . . . and think what a good husband he has made, I sigh for what I've lost, and rejoice for what I've gained."

For Charley, the visit reaffirmed a hope that had formed in the back of his mind in April 1866, when the house Charlotte was born in was torn down to make way for a school. Immediately, Charley had broached a plan to the Boston School Committee: the new building should be named for Charlotte Cushman. But the idea had not met with universal enthusiasm. No Boston public school had ever been named for a woman and, said one irate member, a question of moral propriety was involved. To allow the name of an actress to appear "over a temple of learning in our godly city" would be "almost a crime." Since that meeting in 1866, the matter had gone unresolved; for nearly five years the five-story building had stood nameless.

But now, during Charlotte's run at the Globe, Charley reopened the question. The night the School Committee took its final vote,

"To Dare and Do and Be"

Charley rushed up Washington Street to the theatre. As Queen Katharine, Charlotte had already taken her place, ready for the curtain, when he rushed into the wings, waving his hat and whispering: "It shall be called the Cushman School." Then he rushed on stage to grasp her hand.

The news made her happy, but at that moment Charlotte heard the signal to clear the stage. "Get out now, Charley. There's the bell." But Charley kept up his eager chatter, and the drop curtain was rising and the footlights in full view before he left the stage—leaving his tall silk hat where he had dropped it, at the foot of Charlotte's throne.

After the play, Charlotte savored the compliment the School Committee and Boston had paid her. "This from old Puritan stock, which believes that the public school is the throne of the state," was a "greater honor," she said, "than any I could have received," whether as woman or actress.

After Christmas at Hyde Park with Emma's family, Charlotte came back to Boston on January 5, 1872, for the dedication of the new Cushman School.* On the platform among the dignitaries, she delivered her grateful speech. To encourage whatever poor girls might be listening, she assured them that she herself had walked these same streets, a girl as poor as the poorest among them. Whatever she had attained she had won by *giving herself to her work;* hard work was the secret to whatever success her fifty-five years had brought her. To the girls hearing her now, she could say nothing more worthy than to encourage them all to "dare and do and be."

Cheered by all the tributes in Boston, Charlotte could act now or not as her health permitted. She would accept an easier routine, reading from the platform when it suited her. To all managers who now dogged her steps, she gave the same answer. "I cannot work much or long, therefore I am obliged to ask five hundred dollars per night, deposited in advance." If the terms did not frighten them, she would be pleased to hear from them again.

Charlotte had begun her new career as a reader in Providence

---

* Cushman School lasted until 1941, when it was demolished to make room for the Charlotte Cushman Playground. Since then, the North End Branch of the Boston Public Library has been erected on the site.

on December 18, when she had stood a little fearful backstage while Sallie smoothed her skirts and adjusted her ruffle bodice, her hair dressed in a gray pompadour. But when she moved on, she knew at once the old certainty that had long sustained her. She could deliver the crowd's money's worth. Seating herself at a shawl-covered table, she smiled and relaxed a moment, then opened her book. "Ladies and gentlemen, I shall read—I trust for your pleasure, surely for mine, from the second scene in the third act of 'Henry the Eighth.' "

After reading the long scene in which Wolsey faces his downfall, Charlotte turned to passages from *Much Ado About Nothing*. The evening ended with great applause, as the audience told her unmistakably that she had managed to re-create all the important characters, not just the single role she normally acted in a full performance. When booking agents like James Redpath and James H. Roberts beseeched her to add her name to their lists, Charlotte did not demur. Though the audiences were primarily women, proving that American women were more and more hungry for intellectual fare, Charlotte gladly accepted the challenge.

At Jamie's suggestion, she developed a lighter program for some occasions, including pieces like Mrs. Southey's "The Young Gray Head," short pieces from Elizabeth Browning's "Casa Guidi Windows," and some of Burns and Tennyson. Hearing her read "The Young Gray Head" to a packed house at Tremont Temple on January 4, 1872, Thomas Higginson swore he could see "every fibre of thatch on the roof and every bristle on the dog's back." Hearing her read "A Man's a Man for A' That," another listener said he could see Robert Burns himself come into the room among the nobles and gentry and, with a quick shrug and half-laugh, throw down "the gage of humanity among them."

The $3,000 Charlotte got from these first readings in Providence, Boston, and New Haven confirmed her decision to take the platform. With new confidence, she braved the winter rigors of a reading tour west by way of a week's visit in Auburn. Seward's home was a large yellow brick house in the midst of a three-acre lawn. Inside, he had filled it with mementoes from his long public career, many of which Charlotte recognized from his old drawing room on Lafayette Square. Seward looked "pathetically deplorable," with his paralyzed arm and hand. But he was delighted to see her—"as much as the poor soul could demonstrate this."

At Seward's, Charlotte wrote Longfellow to thank him for the book of his poems he had sent her—"And now I am going to ask you something!" Would Longfellow help her adapt Goethe's *Egmont* for an orchestral reading in Boston? In reply, Longfellow sent her a detailed breakdown of the cuttings he would include. When this was all over, he added, he wanted to show her something of his own, a tragedy called *Judas Maccabaeius,* "in which there is a character particularly for you." He would, he said, "be only too happy to have you read anything of mine."

By the time she had ended her swing through Cincinnati, Indianapolis, Chicago, Milwaukee, Philadelphia, and Providence, Charlotte had developed a repertory that ranged from the comedy of Mary Mapes Dodge's "Miss Maloney and the Chinese Question," through the sentiment of Browning's "Hervé Riel" and Macauley's "Horatius," to the religious fervor of Bernard de Cluny's "The Celestial Country." In the terrible weather her good judgment had admonished her repeatedly to go back to Boston or Newport if she hoped to avoid illness from the overheated hotels and unventilated trains, the crush of people who jammed around her begging for autographs. But another wisdom had urged her forward, to combat the fears that always threatened to overcome her whenever she let herself idle.

To husband her strength, she adopted a new policy about autographs. There was perhaps no way to cure the plague entirely, but with her waning energies, she could make it count for something at least. From time to time, she sent a supply of cards bearing her signature to a charitable agency in New York. Then, for its own benefit, The Sheltering Arms could sell the cards for twenty-five cents. Collectors could offer no objection, and she would have a legitimate excuse for admirers who descended on her whenever she left the theatre.

High comedy had never been her long suit, but now, reading to afternoon crowds, usually in ordinary light, she felt a cushion of friendliness surrounding her. Whenever she set her audience roaring with laughter, she paused solemnly, then threw back her head and laughed with them; then just before quiet descended, she ripped through the rest of the lines. But by the time she reached Philadelphia in early April, she was weary and hoarse; she would have cancelled her bookings here and in other cities except for the nagging certainty that it was far better "to wear out," as she wrote Wayman Crow, "than to rust out."

The Academy of Music had been sold out since February for her reading April 4. Later in the month, when Couldock joined her to play Wolsey, the reunion would have worked out better if he had not recently lost a daughter and was now so miserable, acting so much "like an elephantine baby, without intellect or intelligence," that Charlotte would have stopped the show to weep with him, if they had not had a sellout crowd. But bitter humor restored her when an agent approached her to play with Edwin Forrest next season. "Ha! ha! ha! ha!" she wrote Emma Crow.

Before she moved on to Providence the last of May, Charlotte went to visit old Thomas Sully, who at eighty-nine was decrepit now and forgetful—though from time to time in the conversation she saw his eyes light up and then squint in typical fashion as if taking her measure for another portrait. In Providence, playing Meg, she terrified six-year-old George Pierce Baker, who, years later, would clearly recall the evening when "in an early but intense recognition of the genius of Charlotte Cushman I was, for the good of the public, removed shrieking from the theatre."

Relaxing at Addison Childs' at Swampscott, Charlotte relished again the laughs she herself had gotten from the readings. Writing about them to Emma at Hyde Park, she felt a sudden impatience that she was not strong enough to take up her labors immediately. "I read the 'Skeleton in Armor' *well,* and the effect was fine. I made the 'fearful guest' speak in montone, like the ghost in 'Hamlet,' and you cannot think how strange and weird it sounded."

Writing Seward, Charlotte looked back on the season with mixed emotions. Sometimes, she confessed, she had kept engagements when she should have taken to her bed, but "then you know, I am not a philosopher, nor a potentate. I cannot control absolutely everything and I have done the best I could. The rest is with God!" Shopping in New York, she bought black and gold chandeliers to match the drawing room fireplace in the new house in Newport, and carpeting for all the reception rooms—in spite of the fact that Richard Morris Hunt had ignored most of her instructions. She could have cried about it if she had not been too tired to care.

But in June, riding in her open barouche up Newport's Touro Street past the old Synagogue, she did not regret her decision to build here. Coming home to Newport seemed a little like returning to Rome. Both were strong in their ties to the past—Rome to antiquity, Newport to colonial days. Longfellow might even be right in his "Skeleton in Armor" that the "lofty tower" still standing in Touro Park dated back to tenth-century Norse explorers.

In more recent respects, Newport had in common with Rome a certain air. Leisure and wealth and artistic taste poured into its summer cottages from Philadelphia and New York and Boston. Charlotte admitted that investing money in a Newport house for herself was foolish, but for Ned and Emma the future was different. She could honor Emma's wish to live in Newport, to bring up her sons there. Knowing Ned's folly with money, the best Charlotte could do for them was leave them the house, which she would call Villa Cushman. Debt free, it would guarantee his family a home. With her estate invested, with Ned left little management of it, she could rest easier.

But long thoughts did not trouble her as she and Sallie drove up to the house. Through the tall trees up Catherine Street, the Villa's roofs and towering chimneys emerged at last—"so much more than a cottage and almost a chateau." Stepping down, she looked up to the deep shaded porch, then turned for the view toward the open water.

Throughout the summer Charlotte busied herself buying the items needed backstairs in a working household, new horses and trappings for her stable, unpacking the treasures from Rome: her marbles, tapestries, bronzes, her massive antiques that began creaking and popping at night as if resenting being taken so far from Italy. She filled her "red parlor" at the back of the house with her favorite paintings and portraits. Together, she and Emma Stebbins decided the proper colors for their bedrooms upstairs. In her own, she placed her solid brass bed with its silken curtains from 1 Bolton Row, her silk-covered sofas and her claw-footed table under the red chandelier. In the wardrobes, Sallie hung up her costumes.

The party Newport friends gave her when the house was ready opened the social campaign she would command whenever she pleased. When the house was filled, she delighted again in singing or circulating in her reception rooms, injecting a quick conversational thrust here, cracking a joke there.

"This is Liberty Hall," she laughingly welcomed newcomers. "Everyone does here as I please." Watching her dispensing smiles impartially, Colonel J. W. Forney said she resembled a radiant sun, "more like a retired queen than an artist." A neighbor, George H. Calvert, was cheered merely "to see her enter a room."

Yet very soon, she was plagued and distraught, often biting her

359

lips in pain, "so confused and worried, I sometimes find myself wishing I had no house." After her guests had left for the day, she confessed to Emma how hard she had fought to keep the hearty ring in her laughter, especially when so many afternoons and evenings the band concert across the street at the Casino penetrated cruelly into her rooms. Late in the summer, when Emma had gone to Hyde Park to be with her ailing mother, Charlotte wrote frankly about the terrible future she feared. "I pray God in his infinite mercy to take me quickly, that I may not wear out those who love me."

By late September, after Ned and the family had left for a long visit to St. Louis, Charlotte felt suddenly worse than when the tall rooms had echoed to the crush of visitors and the little boys sliding down the banisters or shrieking out on the lawn. "I suppose it is that I am weaker than ever before, and the summer has been a greater strain upon me than I knew." But "this is a confession of weakness; enough of myself."

The time had come to get busy. She was in Portland, Maine, for a reading on October 10 when sad news reached her from Auburn. Seward's death that day only pointed up what wisdom had long ago taught her to do about grief. "Mr. Seward's death has been a fearful blow to me," she wrote Emma Crow, "but thank God I was working when it came!" On October 12, she was in Boston at the Music Hall to read a program of *Macbeth* cuttings and poems of Whittier and Tennyson when a knock came at her door backstage. The white-haired man who stood in her doorway introduced himself as Captain Cornelius Lovell of Cape Cod.

Years ago, said the Captain, he had seen a girl playing with some boys on Long Wharf suddenly fall over the edge and thrash about madly in the water below. He had torn off his coat, dived in, and pulled her out. As an old man now, he had come backstage to say that he was glad to have saved that talented girl who had grown up to give the world so much pleasure.

Charlotte grasped his hands, then turned to the other people in the room and told them the story. "Captain Lovell," she said then, "now what can I do for you?" "Nothing for me personally," Lovell replied, "but I wish you would give a reading for our church." At the thought of what he had done, she gladly consented.

After playing another stand at Booth's in New York, she pushed west in mid-December for Chicago. The curly-haired young Irishman who played Macbeth at Ellsler's Theatre in Cleveland so impressed her that she drew him aside. If James O'Neill determined to "work, work, work," he just might make a brilliant career in the theatre. When he followed her on to Chicago, Charlotte told a reporter that playing with young O'Neill was making this one of her pleasantest engagements—and O'Neill was doubly certain that as an actress Charlotte Cushman got "more out of the language than anyone I have ever listened to." In his long career, especially as the Count of Monte Cristo, James O'Neill remembered her early advice.

West of Cleveland, Charlotte missed connections with the train from Logansport to Chicago. Upset, she begged and cajoled—she was booked for James McVicker's Theatre that night—then finally fired off a telegram to the president of the railroad, who dispatched an engine and car for her. The blustery weather made difficult pulling for an engine headed straight into the wind. The little train made its way slowly forward, but as the blowing increased, the engine gave up at last and stood puffing and stymied in the gale.

About four, a brakeman with his cap tied on with a scarf inched forward to tell the engineer that Miss Cushman wished to see him back in her car. The engineer, a man of some spirit, told the brakeman to report that the engineer must decline the honor, that he would do his best with the train, that nothing else could make the least gain in their headway. But at that moment, the Irish fireman peered out his window and cried, "An' it is herself that is coming now, be jabers!"

When the engineer looked out, he saw Charlotte cling to the sides of the car, with the wind tearing at her, lower her head, grab at her skirts, and push toward the engine. The men leaped out and ran to help her inside the cab. Once in, she put on her grandest tones and began storming about the delay. But the engineer had done his reading.

"Rest assured," he told her. "After 'Hercules' has had time to breathe a little, I think he will take us on again. Working ahead of old Boreas" he was finding to be a harder matter "than any of the immortal labors of his great namesake." At that, Charlotte smiled, then changed her tactics. Couldn't they let her ride in the cab?

Since the rules forbade it, she finally let them hand her down to the ground and escort her back to her car. At last, when the wind died and the train began inching forward, the engineer looked back to see Charlotte lean out her window and wave, then gesture resolutely toward Chicago. When the train arrived at seven, Charlotte came forward to thank the men and get the engineer's name and address. Soon after, tickets for the play reached him.

In the year since the Chicago fire, McVicker had rebuilt his theatre, and now each night Charlotte played to packed houses despite drizzling rain and slush. The critics in both major papers were loud in their praise: on the twenty-fourth of December the Chicago *Times* declared that as Meg Merrilies Miss Cushman "rises to the summit of her great genius. No impersonation can be conceived more terrible, weird, and startling . . . it must stand as the representation of the most sublime and intense acting." On the thirty-first, the eloquence of her face in the sleep-walking scene, "delineating the hidden thoughts and emotions that haunt the inner heart," was so touching and suggestive "that we do not need words to fill out the measure of the meaning."

James McVicker had every cause to be happy. Her price had scared him, but he now took heart in the fact that no run in Chicago had ever drawn such houses. On January 11, 1873, when the run ended, Charlotte could look back with pride on the courage required to complete it. Her throat had plagued her constantly—at times she had no voice at all until some last-minute gargle restored it enough to go on.

Immediately after the curtain on the last night of her run, she answered a written summons to the greenroom, where she found the company assembled. The stage manager asked her to come to the center of the circle; then he read her a short speech.

"We, members of Mr. McVicker's Theatre, desiring to express to you our appreciation, present, through our worthy manager, this circlet of gold, inscribed with the motto that has so endeared you to us, and which is no less engraven on our hearts, namely, 'kind words.' May your happiness here and in the great hereafter be only symboled by this golden circlet, 'endless.' "

Fingering the ring, Charlotte thanked them, then told them how lucky she was that doing with her life what she had most wanted to do, she had managed apparently to bring some joy to others. Leaving the room, she acknowledged the company's smiles and good wishes. But next morning, suddenly depressed by the ceremony's tone and fearing the worst, she sought out a lawyer to draw up a new will. She had too much property now, an estate too complex, to risk uncertainties.

Talking with him, she tasted again the sweet success her career had brought her. She settled on $1,500 annual income for Charlie, who was still in London, $750 each for Rosalie and Mabel (to be increased to $1,000 a year when they married), $1,500 a year for Emma, and $500 for Sallie. In a trust, she put Villa Cushman at Ned's disposal for his family's use. Emma Stebbins and Sallie were to have free quarters in it as long as they lived. Her holdings and her stocks were worth now at least $600,000. The income from these would be Ned's—its use to be subject to the judgment of her trustees.

After Chicago, Charlotte expected to play two weeks in New Orleans. "The greatest living actress, Charlotte Cushman, is coming," shouted the morning *Picayune* on January 7, 1873. Enthusiasm had been building up for a month. With Lawrence Barrett's company at the Varieties Theatre, her appearance would surely be one of the "most notable dramatic events" ever witnessed on the New Orleans stage, said the *Picayune* on the eighteenth.

Sailing down river, Charlotte only hoped she could fulfill the promise. In the fifteen years that had passed since she had played New Orleans, terrible changes had come to the land. She now glimpsed ashes and ruins, charred columns, tree stumps, and broken fences. Cotton fields had become sprawling tangles of weeds. Suddenly sad at the tragic price the war had exacted, Charlotte knew that age and illness had taken in her a similar toll.

At the first rehearsal, when Barrett confessed that he had never played Wolsey, Charlotte offered to run through the lines. Though she had not played the Cardinal for sixteen years, her reading of Wolsey's faltering speech when he knows that he has lost Henry's favor was so poignant that tears came to Barrett's eyes. Her opening crowds were immense; reviews for the most part were glowing. Her Meg, said the *Picayune,* was "grand—one may say terrible. . . . Miss Cushman fairly electrified by her genius." The *Picayune's* man could see no evidence that her magic touch had suffered "in the lapse of years."

After Lady Macbeth the first three nights of her second week, Charlotte had expected to finish her run with three more nights of Queen Katharine; but by Thursday, she knew that her voice and her nerves could not carry the burden. In the hotel's stifling heat she caught cold; she could not sleep; suddenly her mouth broke out in sores. She hoped the audience and the Varieties' company could understand why the benefit ceremony they had planned had to be canceled. One cheerful note in the *Picayune* caught her eye. Busily

363

forging ahead as a sculptress in Rome, Edmonia Lewis had snared two $50,000 commissions. But Charlotte's only real thought now was to move north as quickly as possible where a doctor she trusted might give her relief. She learned only later that the day she and Sallie left for Philadelphia, Isa Blagden had died in Florence; when Isa's own doctor could not be located, a strange physician had dosed her with a medicine she could not tolerate.

The slow trip north was agony, and Sallie could only bathe Charlotte's head and mutter about her foolishness—then assure her that she would be her old self once they reached Philadelphia. By March 1, weak but determined again after her doctor's treatment, Charlotte opened a run in Washington before President Grant and Generals McClellan and Sherman. Sherman came to meet her afterward, but exhausted, she did not meet Grant ("I had no curiosity"); when Mrs. McClellan urged her husband to come backstage, Charlotte found him "common looking."

When a Washington charity approached her to appear for their benefit, she firmly declined. The time had come to protest against the system of making artists "pay so much more than the rest of the community" for charities in which they had no interest "and which had no claim upon them." Such affairs were one-sided, too easy a manner of doing good. Better a house-to-house visitation that would enable every citizen to help the poor of his city than "this cent-per-cent contract for so much money for so much amusement, and the poor thrown in."

In Philadelphia in April, she tried to complete her run at the Walnut, but though her Meg engendered enough excitement in young James Gibbons Huneker to make him call her "a hag spouting fire and fury, a terrible creature, who caused me more than one nightmare," she sent a note to Thomas Hall, the stage manager, explaining that she was simply too weak to continue.

News of Macready's death on April 27—survived by only three of his ten children—quickened Charlotte's memories of his tirades, but she regretted his passing. For all his faults, Macready was still the actor she most truly admired. As mentor and challenger, he had been a singular force in her life. About his Macbeth she could still say that he "grasped its heart and executed it with a splendor." Neither Booth nor Forrest could match him.

For the season, Charlotte had pocketed $66,000. Her work had eased her through months which, however difficult, would have otherwise been impossible. "I try to forget by constant occupation," she wrote Emma at Hyde Park, "that I have such a load near my heart."

When Augustin Daly beseeched her to take on a New York run in the fall, she would not promise to act seven times in one week nor consider any contract. As for Daly's desire to extend her Meg role through more of the play, she refused. "As I give it—it reaches the extent of my power, and if increased would be only beyond it." Any apparent fault in the play could be met by competent actors—all of which prompted her to make an observation that Daly must keep confidential.

Considering the theatre in America, "the trouble now-a-days exists in the actors—they lack respect for the profession—or the characters they represent, think too much of how much money they can get, and how little they can get off with *giving,* in the way of real labour in their art! In a word, they do not forget themselves—and unless one does—he can never be an actor!" Penning her thoughts to Daly, she made herself clear. She had made her position by proving her artistry before the world. Yet never had she willingly, intentionally, downgraded or upstaged other talents. If she ever decided to do Meg for Daly, she and his company would move the town "not by the startling effects of our strong *charcoal sketch* but by the grand strong finished picture as a whole."

Writing Emma, she imagined the troubles her health was bringing those who loved her. "It is wicked of me to say anything about it . . . and yet, and yet, when we regularly *face* our real troubles, I believe they become more endurable." The thought conveyed in one of Emma's last letters from Hyde Park "that anything happening to me would kill you" gave her "much sad thought . . . we must school ourselves for what is inevitable."

All of this helped her laugh at the letter that reached her in Buffalo in December. "I am forty," wrote one H. W. Blair, "have long been struck by you, having long thought that you were unwise to remain unwed. Couldn't I come to see you, and acquaint you with my gentlemanly intentions? I reside in Chicago . . . my work is with pork packers." When Charlotte sent it on to Hyde Park, Emma added a note and returned it. "The man must be a born fool, not for wanting to marry you, but for presuming to have such a thought enter his idiotic brain!"

Late in January 1874, still unwed, Charlotte was back in New York for readings at Steinway Hall. During March she was in Baltimore, where Jamie and Annie Fields heard her from chairs that Charlotte had placed at the edge of the stage. Dressed in black silk and diamonds, Charlotte read, said Annie, like a workaday woman intent on doing her job well. "Now for work, now for having your laughter and your tears," Annie wrote a friend about Charlotte's manner. "Now let us see Charlotte Cushman do her best, and she does it."

In April, she renewed an old friendship in Philadelphia. Adelaide Ristori was appearing in *Elizabetta* and *Marie Antoinette*. Charlotte sat in the director's box, holding lilies of the valley and roses to toss down to her. At the end of the second act, when Ristori returned for a bow, Charlotte lifted the flowers and gestured. At first, Ristori did not recognize her, but approaching the box, she suddenly broke into smiles. "Ah, cara amica!" she cried, throwing her arms out to Charlotte. While the two exchanged a few words, the audience applauded. Next day Ristori called at Charlotte's hotel to gesture her way through excited conversation, since neither had ever mastered the other's language.

In New York in May for more readings, Charlotte felt much better when a course of water treatments gave a sudden upswing to her health. Banking on that, she signed a contract for Booth's Theatre for October, though by now Booth himself, at age forty, was bankrupt and had lost all claim to the handsome house that carried his name. A reporter for *Harpers* begged her in July to write down some personal details—or let herself be interviewed—for a full biographical account that this return to the New York stage would occasion. But Charlotte demurred.

"I wish I had time or strength to tell you something of my early life, but I am far from well, and with my necessary care of myself, and my many duties, I am not able to do anything which would serve you." Perhaps Mary Howitt's 1846 article in England would meet the purpose, if a copy could be found. About the picture *Harpers* wanted. "Don't let me be more libelled than you can help." All her life, pictures had made her "a hag." Now, since bad photographs badly printed would keep alive a mistaken impression—when better truth should focus upon her art—let every care, she begged, be exerted. At fifty-eight, "I am a plain woman but do not like to go down to posterity so much more ugly than my looking glass and even the critics tell me I am."

31

Farewell Miss Cushman

(1874)

Charlotte had never lied to herself; she had always faced facts as she saw them. Now in Boston in October 1874, to read an address at the opening of Beethoven Hall, she decided one afternoon to drive out to Mount Auburn cemetery. Nearly thirty years ago she had written Mary Eliza the somber suggestion that with all the success that was coming to her in England, she ought to be able soon to retire and look ahead to comfortable leisure and eventually to "a quiet corner in some respectable graveyard."

No doubt she ought to be choosing that corner. The attendant in charge suggested a ride up along Mount Auburn's green hills, where at various stops, Charlotte considered the view. "They are all grand," she told the attendant, but wasn't there one lot with an open view over Boston?

There were still a few back of the tower. At last, standing on a corner just under the brow of the tallest hill, Charlotte said quietly, "This is a delightful spot; see, yonder lies dear old Boston." To the east across the Charles stretched open woods, a scatter of farms, and in the far distance the towers and domes of Boston. At the office, she wrote out her check and drove back to town, content.

In earlier times she had grandly tossed out the word "retirement" and sailed off to Europe, determined not to look back, but the word struck her differently now. "Let all who have work to do thank God for it," she wrote Emma Crow. To retire now would be to back up into the grave. When the time came to be old and take her bow, she would try to bend with grace and finality, but on October 14 she received a troubling letter. A Dexter Smith wanted to know when she planned to retire? What was he suggesting? Surely, such a matter was hers to decide. She read his words thoughtfully, then replied: "I can only say that I am about acting a series of engagements in various places, which will probably be the last of my dramatic performances; but with regard to the place where I shall take my final farewell of the stage, or whether I shall ever take any formal farewell, anywhere, it is impossible for me to say."

Before she left for New York, another small scene from the past took place backstage. She had just finished a reading, when the lyceum manager, Major J. B. Pond, knocked at her door. "Miss Cushman, I intended to hand this envelope to you on the platform, but I was so busy in front of the house that I could not get an opportunity. Please pardon me." "That is all right, Major Pond," said Charlotte. "Sit down and have some supper."

In the envelope, Charlotte found a check for $1,000; Pond explained. "Miss Cushman, that $1,000 check of this evening is the interest on twenty dollars that you invested in me in 1857." He then proceeded to tell her about the boy who had escorted her from the theatre to her hotel each night in St. Louis, the callboy who had fallen ill the last night of her run; she had wished young Jimmy Pond an early recovery and slipped a twenty-dollar gold piece into his hand.

On Monday night, October 19, when she began her engagement at Booth's, Charlotte felt the old power surge through her as she swept on stage as Katharine in her velvets and ermine, encompassing the house with one great sweep of her eyes. True, the papers reported later, she had lost some of her "elasticity of limb"; she could not always manage now to conceal the "age" in her voice. But, she was happy to note, the papers saw no decline in her "awe-inspiring presence."

To the audience, that presence still rang through her lines. The intensity of feeling that exploded in the audience was not lost upon Charlotte. Such moments as these were always the high points in the play, when the crowd cried out its response to a job well done. If her heart cried out in 1871, "How have I lived without this through all these years!" how much more urgently her heart cried now, "Without this, could I go on?"

Could she face the months or years—if there were to *be* years— without this nourishment? Noble as the papers found her acting, it was to "a great soul that we would dedicate the thought and feeling of this moment." Only a woman of royal nature, said one paper, could so fill Shakespeare's "massive and tender ideal." In the *Trib-*

une, William Winter found in her life a quality like that "which hallows the lonesome sea, in the gloaming, and on the eve of tempest." We here might call it "genius," but it could not be described.

On the twentieth, John Rankin Towse in the *Post* noted "the sadness of this hour" when New York was seeing the end, not only of a great dramatic career, but of an acting tradition. The front rank of her profession was long ago conceded to Charlotte Cushman, said Towse; she had earned it by genuine hard work, and no profession could afford to lose at any time the impulse and example of such a life. But, observed Towse with words that struck like a bludgeon, too many actors tended to cling to careers too long—as if loathe to acknowledge the fact that the actor's art dies with him—until at last the pit, however painful the justice, must hiss him tottering from the stage.

With that, the word spread through New York that Charlotte meant this engagement at Booth's—in spite of her firm denials—to be her last. Reading the papers, she saw the implications: the public knew she was making herself go on at the cost of terrible suffering; the time had come to bid farewell. Charlotte could not really argue the point. Certainly she could not go on acting and reading forever. If the public wanted to express its appreciation, could she be less than kind? To be honored and sung of in one's harvest years was, after all, to be given a small extra lease on time.

The four-page announcement that Booth's Theatre published on October 31 gave New York the clinching details. On November 7 a great public ceremony was to be given in tribute to Charlotte Cushman. "The illustrious actress appears once again on the stage —for a few nights only—and then to pass away, and professionally, to be seen no more." The reluctant curtain would sweep down, and all that remained of America's greatest tragedienne would be tradition.

But for Charlotte, things were happening too fast either to be understood or tolerated. She would not let herself be hurried off into the wings before she was ready; all emotions aside, she could not ignore her commitments to other cities, her agreements to appear on other stages. New York might call its ceremony a farewell if it pleased, but she herself must consider the affair from a different angle. The time to bid her art an honest good-bye must be hers to decide.

To the President of the Arcadian Club, she phrased her reply carefully. She would accept the Club's wish to "do me honour at Booth's Theatre on the last evening of my present engagement in New York," but she would not call it a formal farewell. She was more explicit to H. D. Palmer, one of the managers at Booth's. In her dressing room, she confronted him head-on: "I see that you have announced my farewell appearance, Mr. Palmer. I did not quite intend that, at this time. I shall not at once retire." Palmer met her objection. "The announcement is only your farewell appearance in New York, Miss Cushman. The public will be deeply interested. There will be a splendid house; and you know, you are not obliged to make it *final!*"

That made a difference of course, but the matter was serious. In forty years she had learned much about theatre managers. From W. E. Burton and Maddox on down, her list carried the names of men who had had to be watched and shrewdly outwitted. Granted the public would be interested, but Charlotte made no attempt to veil her meaning. "Very well, Mr. Palmer. And what are you going to do for me?"

"R. H. Stoddard, the poet is to write an ode for the occasion, which will be read on the stage, after the performance," said Palmer. "And we shall engage the fine elocutionist, Charles Roberts, Jr., of New York University, to read it." The plan had merit. The audience would enjoy the pomp. Charlotte could agree that Stoddard was truly a poet, but . . .

"The venerable William Cullen Bryant," Palmer went on, "has consented to deliver an address." She could play this game from long practice. "I shall, indeed, be honored. Mr. Bryant is a great poet. But—what are you going to do for *me?*"

"The Arcadian Club will send a laurel crown to be presented to you on the stage." All the actors in New York would be invited to assemble around her. Boucicault and Jefferson and Wallack and Gilbert and many others would be there.

"Yes, but . . ."

"And then, of course, *you* will deliver a speech."

"I suppose so," Charlotte agreed. "It would be expected. But what . . ."

Two hundred members of the Arcadian Club, with lighted torches, would escort her in her carriage from the theatre to her hotel, and there would be a band from the New York Militia.

"They are indeed kind, those gentlemen. It will be very pleasant. But, my dear Mr. Palmer, what are you going to do for *me?*"

And after Miss Cushman reached her hotel, she would take her place on the balcony to observe a magnificent fireworks display in her honor.

That would be fine, she liked fireworks. "But Mr. Palmer—*what* are you going to do for ME?"

Her implication was clear. The laurel crown and the speeches were stage effects and good show. The fireworks and the band were spectacle for the crowd. She knew that Palmer understood her.

"Well, Mr. Palmer?"

"Well, Miss Cushman, we are going to give you $1,000 *extra for that night.*"

"Noble boy!" she replied. The money was fine, but other details she would not condone: the white horses and the open carriage, the escort of torches to her hotel. If Palmer carried out this part of his plan, she would remain in the theatre all night.

Throughout the days before November 7, Charlotte continued to think her way through the meaning of the approaching ceremony. She refused to call it farewell, but the program would be legitimate. No one would buy a ticket against his wishes. If the crowd wanted spectacle, spectacle it would get. Her Lady Macbeth would carry all the verve and conviction she had ever felt for the role. And with George Vandenhoff as Macbeth, the audience would receive its money's worth. During this final week, she played to "the finest audiences of the season." For the eight performances, including the Thursday matinee, the box office averaged $3,000.

Much as playing the gypsy hag might have bored her, Meg still gave her a thrill. Playing it even now, no twenty minutes she ever spent on stage quite compared to her twenty minutes of Meg. Exhausting, almost impossibly painful, the part was little more than trash when she looked at it squarely, but the frozen motion, the suspended breath, the frightened eyes it created out front were always new.

After one performance, said one paper, the stormy applause shook the building—until she came back on stage to look one moment upon her triumph, and "calm with her smile this raging sea of admiration." When Miss Cushman retires from the stage, said another, "there can be no question that art will have lost the grandest tragedienne since the days of the great Sarah Siddons."

And *Harpers* still wanted to publish her memoirs. Since Miss Cushman had associated with all the best artists, wrote its editor, since she had witnessed the successes of many young actors, since she had lived near the center of her country's political life, her memories included a veritable roster of bright names. *Harpers'* query tempted her, but when she looked at the labor involved, she declined. Better for writers to write the actual words.

During the week, the New York press used Charlotte's approaching retirement as the focal point for wide-ranging discussion about acting as art. Say what one might, said the *Post,* about the "stilted and pompous" mannerisms of the style she had inherited from Kean and Macready, in Charlotte Cushman it had wonderful points. "What glorious repose there is about it!" What eloquence there was in her manner. "Why, in Miss Cushman's very walk there is power!" In speaking like a queen, her heart dilated—like Macready's—to the stature of majesty.

Though her dignity stamped her a carry-over now into a period when an actress either "raves or rants" to express emotion, Lawrence Barrett observed that Charlotte Cushman had become an actress at a time when one must do more than "carry expensive costumes upon an attractive body and wander through a play." The shallow beauties now taking over the American stage bore about the same relation to a formidable presence like hers that a military march bore "to a symphony of Beethoven." Said the *Spirit of the Times,* only Kate Field, who was due to make her stage debut at Booth's on the fourteenth, seemed to offer any hope. Perhaps as a woman of brains, Miss Field could pick up the gauntlet Miss Cushman was casting down.

In the tributes to Charlotte's nobility on stage, there was, nevertheless, a hint that change was coming. If Towse could label her art "moribund," he could declare as accurately that her art reflected a moribund theory of life. No one could finger the day the change had set in or point to its origin exactly. But in audience reaction to players, one found the audience reflected. The living stage took its measurements inevitably from the living men who watched it.

One paper said it gracefully: it was a sad hour when genius leaves the field and greatness bids adieu to the generation it has "instructed, thrilled, elevated, and honored," especially since Miss Cushman's leaving the stage would empty it of all "majestic power and intellectual character." Looking beyond Charlotte's end, John Gilbert saw the time when Shakespearean tragedies would be impossible to act in America, where so little effort was being made to groom able talents.

The little effort held the clue to the change. The pendulum was swinging toward a sharper realism. It was the age-old pattern, the perpetual question of faith versus reason, of spirit versus mind. The theatre of grandeur, the edifice of poetry, would soon be replaced by the theatre of ordinary life expressing itself in prose. Nobility in man and classic belief in heroism were becoming stage contrivances. If the trend continued, said John Gilbert, audiences soon would prefer to applaud prosaic man and his comfortable resemblance to themselves. There might always be appetite for spectacle, for decorated display and beautiful effects, but the new drama would soon be written in tighter language out of more earthly details.

Charlotte had seen the change coming. "We of the old school endeavored to hold the mirror up to nature, to show virtue her own features, scorn her own image, and the very age and body of the time his form and pressure," she had said before 1869. And even if Charlotte's own audiences remained large, the old acting genre was seeing its houses dwindle. Forrest too had suffered. "We must have been wrong," said Charlotte, "*or* the public."

Wrongly or not, tastes altered; concepts changed. If the actor failed to touch his audience's sensitivities, he failed in the only court of judgment that mattered. Into Katharine of Aragon and Lady Macbeth, Charlotte had poured a personal creed, the distillation of her temperament. As the time approached when she must look back upon them, she saw in them now what the papers and the public were seeing—not only her personal valedictory, but a farewell to a culture's image of itself, the philosophy of an age.

About the ceremony on November 7, she became increasingly nervous. Could she stand the physical strain, the threat of surprises? And for all its origin in humbug, might the ceremony itself strike her too deeply? What would she do if she forgot her speech? To play a role was one thing, but to confront one's self in the heart of it—to be met with praise on her own, apart from her art—for that, she doubted her strength.

Saturday morning's *Tribune* made her feel better. Tonight's ceremony would be recognition, not only of Miss Cushman's genius, said

Winter, but of the honor she had reflected upon her profession by "her noble and stainless character." If she had brought honor to a profession that had always been forced to defend its decency, she could accept, in all humility, the crowd's accolade.

On Saturday Emma made her rest as long as she could in her darkened room at the hotel; then together they entered the flag-draped door at Booth's where she hurriedly dressed for the night's performance.

"The sight in the theatre was magnificent," she wrote Emma Crow later. "I wish the children could have seen it; it was a thing they should have seen, to remember in connection with their 'big mama.'" Under the gas chandeliers, the hall was a welter of flowers, bunting, and flags. Banners festooned the upper circle; red, white, and blue swags draped the balconies. In the lower box at stage right, Charlotte glimpsed William Cullen Bryant and officials of the Arcadian Club. At stage left, a box carried a banner reading "Army and Navy Club." At each end of the stage tall silver fountains sprayed streams of perfumed water. The hall itself was crowded with people representing New York's literature, art, learning, and society—a rare sight in theatres today, said the *Tribune*.

Along with the printed programs, the audience held special souvenirs printed on yellow silk. Two gentlemen who owned a specialty store at Broadway and Twentieth had had a poem inscribed for the occasion.

"Lord and Taylor to Charlotte Cushman on Her
Farewell to the Stage"

And is it true, that we no more shall hear
    The thrilling accents of thy glorious voice?
That we no more shall bend the listening ear,
    And drink those tones which bid the soul rejoice?
. . . .

Thou art a queen! Yes, and far more a queen
    Than was 'bluff Harry's' pure and injured wife
The crown laid on thy brow by genius hath been;
    The sceptre thou dost wield is thine for life.

Charlotte was determined to treat the play seriously, but the audience insisted differently. At the end of her scenes, cheers brought her back to the footlights; ushers handed up armloads of flowers until bouquets formed an unbroken line across the apron. She tried to give her usual strong performance, but tonight the clenched hands of Lady Macbeth trembled from time to time and the occasional breaks in her voice were not mere histrionics.

To Charlotte's surprise, the heavy curtain slowly came down when she finished the sleep-walking scene; the performance was ending where it had ended at Mrs. Siddons' farewell.

> To bed, to bed, there's knocking at the gate . . .
> What's done cannot be undone.

For tonight's festivities, these seemed hardly the words.

Her spirits high but her energies flagging, Charlotte returned to her dressing room, where Sallie quickly exchanged her drab robes for gray silk, white gloves, and diamonds. Nervously, she listened to the band playing out front. For a quick moment she caught Sallie's eye. The ceremony would not honor the loyal woman who had seen her through the long years, but her smile and her hand placed on Sallie's cheek tried to express her feelings. A knock announced that the ceremony was ready.

The stage had been reset as a drawing room. A standing semicircle of people faced forward. At her entrance, the curtain rose slowly, and as the audience caught sight of her, it leaped to its feet cheering. Smiling but feeling suddenly shy, Charlotte took her place beside William Cullen Bryant. Around them stood Governor Dix of New York, Governor-Elect Samuel J. Tilden, New York's Mayor Havemeyer, Cornelius Vanderbilt, her Newport neighbor, W. H. Vanderbilt, Emma's brother Henry, Richard Henry Stoddard, R. B. Roosevelt, Park Goodwin, John Hay, C. Delmonico, Dion Boucicault, Joseph Jefferson—who would follow her at Booth's next week as Rip Van Winkle—John Gilbert, Lester Wallack, John Brougham, and Clara Morris, the rising star who was playing one of Charlotte's old roles, Julia in *The Hunchback,* at the Union Square Theatre.

Professor Roberts stepped forward to read Stoddard's long ode.

SALVE, REGINA

THE race of greatness never dies;
Here, there, its fiery children rise,
Perform their splendid parts,
And captive take our hearts.

375

Men, women of heroic mould,
Have overcome us from of old;
    Crowns waited then, as now,
    For every royal brow
. . . .

To those was given the laurel crown,
Whose lightest leaf conferred renown
    That through the ages fled
    Still circles each gray head.
. . . .

Shakespeare! Honor to him, and her
Who stands his grand interpreter,
    Stepped out of his broad page
    Upon the living stage.

The unseen hands that shape our fate
Moulded her strongly, made her great,
    And gave her for her dower
    Abundant life and power.

To her the sister Muses came,
Proffered their marks, and promised fame;
    She chose the tragic, rose
    To its imperial woes.
. . . .

Salve, Regina! Art and song,
Dismissed by thee, shall miss thee long,
    And keep thy memory green,—
    Our most illustrious queen!

To the applause, Charlotte nodded; then Bryant turned to her. "Madam," he began, "you remember the line of the poet Spenser— 'The laurel, meed of mighty conquerors.' " Well was that line applied in the present instance. The laurel was the proper ornament for the brow of one who had won so eminent and enviable a conquest in the realm of histrionic art. Listening to Bryant, Charlotte felt her hands trembling.

"You have taken a queenly rank in your profession," he continued. "You have carried into one department of it after another the triumphs of your genius; you have interpreted through the eye and ear to the sympathies of vast assemblages of men and women the words of the greatest dramatic writers; what came to your hands in the skeleton form you have clothed with sinews and flesh, and given it warm blood and a beating heart."

Bryant turned to the purple cushion on the stand at his side, to the circle of leaves resting on it. "Receive then," he said, settling it upon her head, "the laurel crown as a token of what is conceded to you, as a symbol of the regal state in your profession to which you have risen and so illustriously hold."

The thousand coronation scenes she had played were a pale show to this. Packed to the walls, the theatre had thrown open the doors and windows so that the crowd standing outside might follow the proceedings. At the crowning, a roar from outside poured in to join the applause.

Now it was time for her own words. In a clear voice that concealed her nervousness and exhaustion, she delivered her speech from memory. "Beggar that I am," she began, "I am even poor in thanks, but I thank you." She paused to adjust the leaves. Then she continued.

"Gentlemen, the heart has no speech; its only language is a tear or a pressure of the hand, and words very feebly convey or interpret its emotions. Yet I would beg you to believe that in the three little words I now speak, 'I thank you,' there are heart depths which I should fail to express better, though I should use a thousand other words. I thank you, gentlemen, for the great honor you have offered me. Thank you, not only for myself, but for my whole profession, to which, through and by me, you have paid this very graceful compliment.

"You would seem to compliment me upon an honorable life. As I look back upon that life, it seems to me that it would have been impossible for me to have led any other. In this I have, perhaps, been mercifully helped more than are many of my more beautiful sisters in art. I was, by a press of circumstances, thrown at an early age into a profession for which I had received no special education or training; but I had already, though so young, been brought face to face with necessity.

"I found life sadly real and intensely earnest, and in my ignorance of other ways of study, I resolved to take therefrom my text and my watchword. To be thoroughly *in earnest,* intensely in earnest in all my thoughts and in all my actions, whether *in* my profession or *out* of it, became my one single idea. And I honestly believe herein lies the secret of my success in life. I do not believe that any success in any art can be achieved without it."

To other actors who would follow her, to younger people now dreaming the dreams she had entertained at the outset, she must say this: "Art is an absolute mistress; she will not be coquetted with or slighted; she requires the most entire self-devotion, and she repays with grand triumphs.

"To my public—what shall I say? From the depths of my heart I thank *you,* who have given me always consideration, encouragement, and patience; who have been ever my comfort, my support, my main help."

But let there be no mistake about the meaning of this grand occasion. It could not be wholly good-bye; other commitments still had to be filled. She might even be back in New York before long, at the reading desk.

"To you, then, I say, may you *fare* well and may I *fare* well, until at no distant day we meet again—*there.* Meanwhile, good, kind friends, goodnight, and God be with you."

In the throng now cheering—she sensed an emotional electricity. When the band began playing "Auld Lang Syne," the cast took up the words, the other actors joined in, and the song welled up in a strong diapason from the waving audience. Adorned in her laurels, she stood before them and accepted the demonstration. Back in her dressing room, a tearful Sallie helped her change for the short carriage ride to the Fifth Avenue Hotel.

Benevolent promises at a time of high tribute are meant, perhaps, to be broken. When Charlotte came through the door on Twenty-Third Street and let herself be handed into a closed carriage, she found herself surrounded by a mass of torches, engulfed in an ovation from a crowd so dense that movement through it was out of the question. Too late now to retreat, she could only settle back in the cushions and meet with a wistful smile the smiles and cheers. Policemen closed in around her carriage to run interference toward Fifth Avenue.

Palmer and his business manager, Joseph Tooker, had hired supers to carry the torches. The fireworks, left over from a recent Tammany Hall celebration, included a colossal rocket that would burst in a gigantic portrait of Boss Tweed. The short trip down the long block between Booth's and the hotel took more than an hour, while the carriage inched through the crowd and the torches flamed around her. When she finally arrived, she was rushed through the covered arcade into the lobby. Crowds in the corridors pressed toward her to grasp her hand, to offer good wishes.

Almost staggeringly tired, she moved out onto an upper balcony facing Madison Square. Below stretched a sea of faces calling up cheer after cheer. There was music from the Ninth Regiment Band, its brasses and drums nearly drowning the shouts. Overhead, a thousand stars began bursting and cannon blasts boomed from the rockets. She waved her greeting, then stood on her balcony, bathed in the colored light of the fireworks. John Gilbert and Palmer and Joseph Tooker stood beside her.

When a thrust of light, bigger than the rest, shot up, a gigantic face blossomed in sparkling pinpoints of light over the Square. "Who is that, Mr. Tooker?" she asked. With a silent apology to Boss Tweed and Tammany, Tooker answered, "That is Shakespeare, Miss Cushman."

The demonstration continued for half an hour; then John Gilbert tapped her shoulder. It was time to go in, lest she take cold from the draft. Again, Charlotte waved her thanks to the crowd, then turned and passed through the tall doors.

Laurence Hutton summed up the affair soon after. Paraphrasing Tennyson's tribute to Macready at the actor's farewell, he wrote:

> Farewell, Miss Cushman, since to-night we part:
> Full-handed thunders often have confest
> Thy power, well used to move the public breast.
> We thank thee with one voice, and from the heart.
> . . . .
> Farewell, Miss Cushman; moral, grave, sublime,
> Our Shakespeare's bland and universal eye
> Dwells pleased, through twice an hundred years on thee.

32

Sidney Lanier and Cushla

(1875)

 On November 14, when the curtain ended her week in Philadelphia, Charlotte was ushered back on stage at the Academy
of Music for more flowers and testimonials. Accepting them, she declared that Philadelphia had always occupied a special place in her
heart. "Here I experienced privately the greatest kindness and hospitality, publicly the utmost goodness and consideration; and I never
come to Philadelphia without the affectionate feeling that I am coming home, and to my family." At that point, sentiment might have
caused her to falter; thirty years had taken their toll of the ties that
once had made Philadelphia unique in her affections. But she held
her poise, and after more fireworks outside, she was ready for Washington.

Reading there, she caught cold, but against Emma's pleas, she determined to fill her dates in the west and end her tour, if her strength
held out, in California. Seeing her read, Jamie Fields thought she
looked "haggard" but said nothing to try to make her quit now.
After the overnight trip to Cincinnati, Charlotte knew she ought to
forgo her commitments. A sudden lurch of the train had broken open
the scars on her breast, and fever and redness soon spread across her
back and down her left arm. Writing Ned, Emma demanded that he
and Emma Crow make Charlotte cancel the rest of her season and
face facts once and for all. Yet the letter was hardly mailed before
Charlotte decided that the pain would really kill her if she did not
get on with her schedule.

In a few days she opened as Meg in Cincinnati. Watching her, a
fifteen-year-old girl named Mary Anderson could almost believe that
Charlotte's terrible shrieks registered real pain—that the ragged old

gypsy on stage who looked "like some great withered tree . . . her eyes blazing under her shaggy brows" was no "creature of this world," but "a mad majestic wanderer from the spirit-land"—until the end of the play when Charlotte reappeared, her face washed clean of greasepaint, to take the applause, like "a sweet-faced old lady, with a smile."

Next day, after rehearsal, Charlotte found Mary and her mother waiting in the hotel parlor. The girl wanted to be an actress. Would Miss Cushman please let her show what she could do? The trite request had come so often, the efforts were usually so bad that Charlotte was tempted to brush on past toward her bed. But something urgent in the girl's eyes stopped her. When Mary said she could do scenes from *Richard III, Hamlet,* and Schiller's *Maid of Orleans,* Charlotte found it a curious selection for such a child. "But begin," she said, "for I am pressed for time."

When Mary had done quick scenes as Joan, she stopped, flushed and excited, waiting for Charlotte's reaction. Watching the girl's beautiful face, the spirit that had enkindled her reading, Charlotte recognized uncommon talent.

"My child," she said slowly, laying her hand on Mary's shoulder, "you have all the attributes to make a fine actress," too much force perhaps at present, "but do not let that trouble you. Better have too much to prune down, than too little to build up."

Hearing the verdict, Mary's mother protested. Surely such a young girl ought not to think about such a difficult and perilous career. "My dear Madam," Charlotte replied gravely, "you will not judge the profession so severely when you know it better. Encourage your child; she is firmly, and rightly, I think, resolved on going upon the stage. If I know anything of character, she will go, with or without your consent."

Saying the words, she felt again an old excitement, the passion that had driven her to prove to Mary Eliza that an ambition this strong must be met. "Be her friend," she said to Mrs. Anderson.

Then she turned to Mary. "My advice to you is not to begin at the bottom of the ladder," enduring the drudgery of small parts in a stock company, under the direction of some coarse nature. Instead, she must get a competent teacher, George Vandenhoff ideally, and "tell him from me that he is to clip and tame you generally. I prophesy a future for you if you continue working earnestly. God be with you." Charlotte's prophecy paid off in full two years later, when Mary Anderson made a stunning New York debut in one of

Charlotte's old roles, Pauline in *The Lady of Lyons*—"The most beautiful woman I ever saw on the stage, or, for that matter, off," wrote George C. D. Odell.

Charlotte had given Mary a word of advice that she herself carefully pondered as she moved on toward Chicago in December. "Remember, each morning we have a fresh reserve of physical magnetism given to us. Exciting amusement and people take it from us. We must hoard it for our audience." Keeping herself in bed between her six reading dates at McCormick Hall helped the time pay off in nearly $6,000. Encouraged by a sudden lift in her energies, she began thinking again of San Francisco. "In California the weather is like our Eastern *June!*" she wrote Denis Alward. But shivering in her warm hotel, she soon despaired of the long journey, even by train.

Returning east, Charlotte played one night at a small town in upstate New York—which gave her wreaths in a little farewell ceremony—and then headed on toward Boston. In Baltimore in January 1875, knowing that she was nearing the end of her strength, another's problems suddenly became more important than her own. Through Gibson Peacock, editor of the Philadelphia *Bulletin,* a young Georgia poet came to her attention, a veteran of bitter fighting at Chickahominy and imprisonment at Fort Lookout in Maryland. Now a flutist with the Peabody Symphony in Baltimore, Sidney Lanier had survived the war, but broken in health, he burned to become a recognized poet, despite the fact that most of his thirty-three years had been, as he said, mostly a matter of "not dying." Reading his verses that had come to her hotel, Charlotte recognized immediately that strong talent lay behind them, and an odd excitement suddenly welled up in her.

A poem like "Corn" was clearly more than fly-by-night inspiration. Without delay, Charlotte called Lanier to her. The pale young man with the high intellectual forehead, deep-set eyes, long nose, and full dark beard entered shyly when Sallie opened the door. But Charlotte quickly put him at ease. Unlike the harsh and tasteless "poetry" of a current writer like Walt Whitman, the delicate sensibility in verses like these, she told Lanier, might have sprung from an Elizabethan. When he told her about his theory that poetic effect was mainly a matter of sounds, she recalled an idea she had in 1840 about an article showing how a union of words and music might indicate the sighing of wind through the trees.

In Sidney, she saw a person who had known all the trials and blocked ambitions that she herself had managed to overcome. Like her, he seemed determined to win out. Listening to him describe the fighting he had seen along the James River, the disease and misery in the military prison, Charlotte felt for the first time the real horrors both armies had undergone. As long as she had strength, she told herself now, she would feed the hope that burned in this young poet's eyes.

Though other guests soon joined them, Charlotte kept her attention strictly on him. Seated beside him on a couch, she told him about the Brownings, how she had always liked Elizabeth better than Robert, about Seward's hopes for a more humane Reconstruction, about the Carlyles, about "many fair things of her own art, of herself, and her adventures," as Sidney told his wife later. She made him promise to send her something to read on the platform. Finally, when Sidney felt he should leave, she detained him, pressing his hand, "saying all manner of handsome things to me," and extracted his word that he would send her more poems. Next day, Lanier was back at her door with his photograph and a handwritten copy of "Corn," bearing a "little Shakespearean dedication to Miss Charlotte Cushman":

> Oh, what a perilous waste, from low to high,
>   Must this poor book from me to you o'erleap:
> From me, who wander in the nights that lie
> About Fame's utmost vague foundations deep,
>   To you, that sit on Fame's most absolute height,
>   Distinctly starred, e'en in that awful light!"

The correspondence between Charlotte and Sidney Lanier soon grew into a regular exchange, a kind of leaven to Charlotte's spirits as she volleyed from one day to the next between bouts with deepening pain. In Lanier, she sensed true genius. Her pleasure in encouraging him was only heightened by his devotion for her. The letters between the young poet and the actress nearly fifty-nine were an outpouring of artistic sensibility and a recognition of themselves as kindred dispositions.

On another tour in February 1875 to Chicago, her letters to the poet helped focus her thoughts on something outside her pain. She forced herself through the two-week run, explaining in a card in the Chicago *Tribune* how embarrassed she was that the New York ovation had seemed to imply that she was saying good-bye to all cities.

In Cincinnati in March she was glad when the *Commercial* said that her voice had still "that mellow force in the lower tones with which no other actress has been gifted," that her Queen Katharine still proved her marvelous range, her skill as a creative artist. If other actors took as much care with Shakespeare's words, said the *Commercial,* the Bard's plays would be almost continuously demanded by audiences, even now. "Her elocution blazes with intelligence."

But by the end of March, she wrote a Philadelphia manager, "I hope my journeys will not make me ill again, but I seem to have come to the end of *work*." Beyond that lay the terrible idleness that she feared now almost as much as pain. When Arthur Cheney, manager of Boston's Globe Theatre, approached her about a Boston farewell similar to New York and Philadelphia's, she consented, grabbing at straws to keep busy. During the week preceding the ceremony, she gave Boston her utmost. Catherine Reignolds-Winslow, who had learned much from her once in New Orleans, saw that the "old fire was as intense as ever," that only Charlotte Cushman had that "ringing voice, the averted head, the magnificent pose, the grandeur of the outstretched arm, the power, even in the pointed finger."

Curtis Guild, editor of the Boston *Commercial Bulletin,* arranged the details of the farewell ceremony. She played an extra matinee on Saturday, May 15, 1875; then that evening after her final *Macbeth* she was escorted back on for Boston's testimonial. As at Booth's, the stage had been set as a drawing room, with a gilt table at center bearing a flower crown and a laurel wreath. At either side stood bronze figures of Mercury and Fortune some seven feet tall. When Charlotte took her place between the bronzes, Guild delivered his speech.

The retirement of one who had so long been recognized as one of the theatre's most distinguished representatives, said Guild, one who had done so much to elevate art, was an event of more than ordinary moment. But when it occurred in the artist's native city, among those who had followed her from the start with hope and admiration, her friends and well-wishers had determined not to permit the occasion to pass without expressing their feelings. Now that Charlotte Cushman was about to "abdicate, not resign," Boston could not part with the great actress of our time without "emotion and tender regard."

Accepting the laurels, Charlotte reminisced a moment about her career, then declared her joy that her season—which might or might not be her last—could conclude in Boston, "which I have always dearly loved, and where I would rather have been born than in any other spot of the habitable globe." Looking back, she could say "without vainglory" that she had never, "by any act of my life, done discredit to the city of my birth." She gestured to right and left and turned full to the audience. "Believe me, I shall carry with me in my retirement no memory sweeter than my associations with Boston and my Boston public. From my full heart, God bless you, and Farewell!"

As the curtain descended, Guild whispered his congratulations for her graceful speech, and Charlotte grasped his hand. "Thanks," she said, "and yours, let me say in the words of Polonius 'was well spoken, with good accent and good discretion.'" As the curtain reached eye level, she cautioned him, "We must step back further, take care of your head, here comes the curtain."

It was Charlotte Cushman's last curtain. On June 2, she filled a reading date in Easton, Pennsylvania, which, against her every will to keep working, proved her last.

Trying to relax at Newport, she found herself plunged more and more into gloom. The children's cries bothered her, and Ned's idleness bothered her more. Lanier's letter of June 17, however, gladdened her spirits. "It is seldom, dear Miss Cushman, that I can bring myself to such a point of daring as to ask that you will stretch out your tired arm merely to take one of my little roses—you whose hands are already filled with the best flowers this world can grow. Does she not (I say to myself) find them under her feet and wear them about her brows, may she not walk in them by day and lie in them by night, nay, does not her life stand rooted in men's regard like one pistil in a great lily?"

Lanier's tone characterized the letters that flourished between them throughout the summer and fall. His very real interest in Charlotte, both as a person and as a judge he respected, flowed through his correspondence. He sent her the manuscript of "The Symphony"; she would be glad to know, he said, that the poem had "met with favor."

Charlotte made her concern about Sidney's health perfectly clear.

"I was so glad to hear from you for I had become anxious that perhaps your work had been too much for you and that your enemy had tried to overtake you again," she wrote on June 23. She had hoped to write him "every day on the hour," but "I have been suffering more than I like to tell you of, and—and—shall I confess it—despair seized me and threw me, and for a time I was demoralized to an hourly weeping."

Unable to face her pain any longer, she had sent for a surgeon in Boston and offered "to lie down again under heroic treatment" to escape the terror of this "gnawing fear near my heart." But the time was past when surgery could help. "The way is still long," the doctor told her, "and if you give way so soon, what is to become of those who love you, for the rest of the way?"

Couldn't Lanier, Charlotte asked, come to see her sometime in the summer, either at Villa Cushman or later at Emma's new cottage in Lenox? About his new poem: " 'The Symphony' reads better every time, and 'The Power of Prayer' is sweet, touching, and strong. No one has ever placed the Southern Negro so faithfully or picturesquely." About his writing dialect poems: "No, a thousand times no, there is no deceit in being able to write such a poem. Only daring to write and publish such a poem so early in your career may make vulgar people wonder, as they always do and will," but he must pursue his own artistic vision and take heart from the fact that already critics like George Calvert in the *Golden Age* were taking him seriously.

In response, Lanier poured out his concern for her pain: "If tender wishes were but medicinal, if fervent aspirations could but cure, if my daily upward breathings in your behalf were but as powerful as they are earnest—how perfect would be your state!" He would visit her, though his trips back and forth to Florida in connection with a guidebook he was writing made it hard to predict just when. "As for you, my dear Queen Catherine, may this velvety night be spread under your feet as Raleigh's cloak was spread for *his* Queen's, so that you may walk dry-shod as to all pain over to the morning—prays your faithful, Sidney Lanier."

Writing Lanier after her birthday on July 23—"many flowers had come from the florists"—Charlotte tried to play down her suffering, but it had been so intense "ever since I stopped work that I have hardly been able to walk beyond my own door." She urged him to guard his own health: "I heard through Peacock that you had been suffering again from hemorrhage. You say nothing of this, let me know how all is with you." She had been turning in her mind the best means she might use to bring Lanier critical attention in England. Struggling to hold firm, she could not help writing her recurring wish to him. "O, if the end could only be any night that I go to sleep," anything to avoid "the sight of my pain to those I love."

In late September, she wrote Lanier from Lenox that "the balmy balsam of this high and dry air" had given her fresh vigor to take hope that "I may weather in some small degree the stone which has torn at me." En route from Newport, she had consulted a young English physician in Boston who, at age twenty-nine, was known already to have done remarkable things "for persons afflicted as I have been." Thornton's manner had given her courage. She would return in mid-October for four or five months of his treatment. Couldn't Lanier come to Boston in the fall? "I feel somehow that we shall be fast friends to the last."

Riding among Lenox's hills in autumn when the maples and birches glowed red and gold in every direction, taking tea on the verandah of the rambling hotel, Charlotte relaxed for long moments. No wonder the Hawthornes had revelled in the Berkshire fall at Tanglewood Cottage. No wonder Fanny Kemble had found such delight among these genial hills when, clad in red riding clothes, she had streaked up the roads like a cardinal flying.

Back in Boston, the Parker House seemed the best place to spend the months her treatments would take. Ushered through the hotel's white marble lobby and corridors, Charlotte was relieved that the large, comfortable rooms Charles Dickens had occupied in 1867 and 1868 were available, that Harvey Parker had preserved them exactly as Dickens had known them, with their heavy dark bedsteads, damask chairs, marble mantel and pictures, and tall pier glass.

Each morning, with the sun rising out of Boston Harbor, she could look out past the gabled end of King's Chapel and its cemetery where Hawthorne had buried Hester Prynne and her scarlet letter. Farther along Tremont Street, she could see directly over the spot where she had made her Boston debut, those decades ago. Farther east and north, she could glimpse the slender tall spire of Second Church. If she had to be ill, there were worse places.

When Lanier arrived in early November, Charlotte had added her own touches to the rooms: her writing table in one corner, her collection of photographs mounted on a purple tack board on the wall, small sculptured pieces, china, glass, and flowers on the mantel. She had had her large easy chair placed by the window where she sat through the day, her swollen left arm strapped to a board, except when she rested in bed in late afternoon.

The morning Lanier sent up a note to say he had arrived, he was in his bath when he heard a tap at his door. Wrapped in a towel, he opened the door to find "the bright face of my good Charlotte Cushman, shining with sweetness and welcome." Too startled to do more than promise to join her for breakfast upstairs, Lanier was dressed before he comprehended fully that Charlotte was up and walking, when he had expected to find her propped weakly on pillows.

But Lanier soon learned that Charlotte's high spirits came and went between sudden periods when, rubbing her aching arm, she must excuse herself and suggest some place of interest Lanier ought to see in town. Every day, she invited people to meet him and hear him play his flute, or she sent him with notes to men who could further his career. Twice, he brought back happy reports from Longfellow and Lowell; both poets had liked his work and encouraged him. Lowell had found him a "shining presence," a man of "genius with a rare gift for the happy word."

Talking with Dr. Thornton, Lanier concluded that the man might really cure her. "I find him not at all a quack," he wrote Peacock, "at least not an ignorant one." At the end of ten days, when Lanier had to return to his work in Baltimore, Charlotte stretched out her good hand. To register his features once and for all, to assure him of her undying regard, she looked at him a long moment. Back at home, Lanier recalled that look and his joy in the visit. It was of "inexpressible value to me as an artist," he wrote later, "besides the pleasure it gave me as a friend."

33

"The Queen, My Lord, Is Dead"

(1876)

Valiantly, Charlotte filled her December days reading and, when she felt able, writing a stream of letters about her health and her never-flagging interests beyond her walls. Mostly, she wrote in her lap, half reclining in front of Charles Dickens' pier glass. In her good moments, her handwriting flowed with the old firm strokes and swirls; in others, it sprawled dully over the page, half-formed and hazed in some fierce clutch of pain.

Her comfort and the weather permitting, she went for short drives, once out of curiosity to a seance in Dover Street conducted by Mrs. Walker, who would falsely advertise herself later as "Miss Cushman's chosen medium." But such ventures were difficult, and Charlotte tried more and more to content herself with the visitors that came crowding to her.

Jamie and Annie Fields came often, and one afternoon Lowell brought along Lord Houghton, now making his first tour of the United States. Charlotte and Dickie Milnes and Lowell filled their quiet talk with recollections of people they had known in London and Rome, though Dickie had grown so deaf that talking with him was an effort. "I have been so glad to have the opportunity to talk of you," Charlotte wrote Lanier after the visit, "though sooth to say the English hide is like that of a rhinoceros, and nothing penetrates far that they do not learn in early days in college." Milnes read her copies of "Corn" and "The Symphony" and promised to write her his impressions of them, then astonished Charlotte by asking in Lowell's presence "Why, Whittier or Longfellow or *'you fellows'* . . . don't write something in the American dialect!!" Since

English critics had always made much of Lowell's *Biglow Papers,* the question seemed stupid or forgetful, to say the least.

Milnes' reference to Whitman dismayed her even more. *Leaves of Grass* was such a "notable and true book," so full of "bold natural truth," said Dickie, that it was strange that Americans did nothing "but jibe and jeer at their one great poet, Whitman." Indignant that anyone could consider Whitman "great," Charlotte stabbed her letter to Sidney with a string of irate exclamation points. How could the same breath mention a crude sensibility like Whitman and an exquisite artist like Lanier?

Charlotte might have tempered her hostility toward Whitman if she had thought again about the long support he had always given her, the fact that he had seen "everything probably that she ever did." Years later, Whitman declared that some aspects of her acting might have been faulty—her Meg Merrilies, for example, had been "too muchly much, as the boys say." But at its best, Charlotte Cushman's acting was "great" and Charlotte was "a great woman—always a great woman," said the poet, "a genius."

But such conversational forays as these with Lowell and Lord Houghton were far from enough to lift Charlotte's burden of distress. Dr. Thornton continued hopeful; by New Year's Day, he promised, "you shall be free from all great pain." But weak and tremulous, her appetite gone for everything but brandy and water, Charlotte was "altogether forlorn," though by some skill retained from the stage, she managed to convince her visitors that she was comfortable. For long periods she sparkled brilliantly; then when quick discomfort suddenly gripped her, a cloud gathered behind her eyes. At such times, she held her posture, her chin lifted imperceptibly, and only Emma, recognizing the sign, knew that Charlotte was suffering. Her eyes filling with tears, Emma found the effect "infinitely touching."

Yet when Thornton insisted that visitors be kept out at times when his patient needed rest, Charlotte would have none of it. "I am more a lover of my kind than most people; hence I must *see* people, and it is useless to attempt to box me up. I cannot be saved in this respect, and it is folly to try."

One day the talk turned to theatre. "You are now alone in your art—your fame has no competitor," someone commented. "Where," he asked, "shall we find an equal to succeed you?" Charlotte replied instantly, "Nobody is indispensable. Madame Janauschek is my equal, and besides she is younger and so handsome."

"The Queen, My Lord, Is Dead"

But as word spread through Boston and across the country that Charlotte was rapidly failing, publishers debated the notion that she was dispensable. They beseeched her while there was still time to prepare some record of her life. "What a pity," one columnist suggested, "that this wonderful woman, who, during her forty years of professional life, has seen everything, and known everybody worth seeing and knowing, contemporaneous with her, should have delayed the work so long." But Charlotte continued to ignore all the pleas. Autobiography was out of her line, and even if modesty had let her consider it, there was no time to make an attempt.

As Christmas approached, Charlotte knew that going home to the Villa was out of the question, and that letting the family come here was equally unthinkable. If she could not be properly merry, she would stay here. In her letter to Emma Crow on Christmas Eve, she was unusually frank. "I grieve for you, dear, more than for myself, though I am a dreadful baby over my pain." At this season especially, her suffering must be causing a comparable pain in all the family, "but the hard places must come in our lives, and perhaps we should not know how to enjoy the pleasures, but for the corresponding glooms." They must all keep up a good heart. "You are loved and thought of as you *would* be, and that must give you courage for the battle which is before you as before us all!"

When Emma Stebbins could force herself to leave Charlotte, she rushed out into Tremont Street for a brisk walk to Brimstone Corner and the Common. But the traffic in the icy streets and the vigor of life rushing past the shop windows disturbed her, and she hurried back inside. Charlotte's rooms bulged with flowers. Harvey Parker sent up a great branch of English mistletoe which she doled out in high humor to her friends. The little boys in Newport had made gifts for her. "Nino's bookmark, so beautifully embroidered, and my darling big boy's [Wayman's] beautiful letter and bookmark," she wrote. The foot-muff from Ned and the handsome headdress from Emma Crow delighted her, though "it is too beautiful for such suffering as mine." And Lanier's letter on New Year's Day touched her almost too deeply.

If this New Year that approaches you (more happy than I, who cannot) did but know you as well as I (more happy than he, who does not) he would strew his days about you even as white apple-blossoms and his nights as blue-black heart's-ease; for then he should be your true faithful-serving lover—as am I

—and should desire—as I do—that the general pelting of time might become to you only a tender rain of such flowers as foretell fruit and of such as make tranquil beds.

But though I cannot teach this same New Year to be the servant of my fair wishes, I can persuade him to be the bearer of them; and I trust he and these words will come to you together; giving you such report, and so freshly from my heart, as shall confirm to you that my message, though greatly briefer than my love, is yet greatly longer than I would the interval were, which stands betwixt you and your often-longing,

S. L.

Replying on January 3, 1876, Charlotte wondered if any other man in the world had ever written such a letter. "I don't believe it possible and in saying this, which was my first word, through tears, after reading it, all the faith and belief in my heart were expressed." Had Lanier seen the appalling reaction in England to Browning's latest efforts? The critics were tearing him limb from limb. Had he heard of the lovely things they were doing for Carlyle in London to honor his eightieth birthday? Gold medals had come from Edinburgh University and from a host of distinguished artists and statesmen.

Reading the January *Atlantic,* Charlotte found momentary distraction from her pain in a Mark Twain article, "A Literary Nightmare." Tongue-in-cheek, Twain wrote that lately a certain popular jingle had kept him awake night after night until he had passed it on to a friend.

> Conductor, when you receive a fare,
> Punch in the presence of the passenjare!
> A blue trip slip for an eight-cent fare,
> A buff trip slip for a six-cent fare,
> A pink trip slip for a three-cent fare,
> Punch in the presence of the passenjare!
> CHORUS:
> Punch brothers! Punch with care!
> Punch in the presence of the passenjare!

That friend in turn had lost sleep until he too had passed it on. "Why did I write this article?" Twain concluded. To warn "you, reader, if you should come across the . . . merciless rhymes, to avoid them —avoid them as you would a pestilence!"

"The Queen, My Lord, Is Dead"

Charlotte tripped the catchy little words on her tongue, but soon, in spite of Thornton's hearty insistence, she busied herself again with plans for her funeral. A request from Lanier brought a brief change in her thoughts. Would "Cushla" write a letter to introduce him to Edwin Booth? In her shaky hand, Charlotte commended Lanier to the actor. "I am too ill to write, and yet I make an effort to send you this word, because I wish to present to your acquaintance what will grow to your friendship—my dearly valued friend, Mr. Sidney Lanier." In him, Booth would find "great cultivation, great refinement of manner, and a knightly soul." To Booth, she added a personal word. "If it should so chance, by God's will that I never see you again, I have made you, here, the sweetest bequest known to your true friend, Charlotte Cushman."

Charlotte's old hostility to Booth was behind her now. The actor had borne his own share of troubles, his losing Mary Devlin, his standing up to the horrors of kinship to John Wilkes, his suffering a bitter marriage to Mary McVicker—after these, he fully deserved her sympathy. Yet, even now, if he counted her a personal friend, he could not have grieved for her approaching end. Of late, he had confided to William Winter his thoughts on dying. Life was little more than a scratch, a temporary ill, to be cured by that "dear old doctor, Death—who gives us a life more healthful, and enduring than all the physicians, temporal or spiritual, can give."

By January 11, she was ready. "What little I can have remaining to me of life after I am cured—if in God's wisdom I am to *be* cured—cannot be worth what I have suffered." Thornton's treatment had culminated; only a few days more should show, he said, a remarkable difference. But in her heart, Charlotte knew that one's feelings in matters like this were sometimes as certain as science. "Ah, please His infinite mercy that if I am ever *well* again, will we not be happy and good, and love him more and more day by day?"

On the thirteenth, William Winter came up from New York bringing a friend, John McCullough, who managed theatres in California. The morning was frigid, but Charlotte received her visitors in a room flooded with sunshine. The face Winter saw was pale, its flesh was drawn taut over the bones, but the blue eyes shone with a luster like "the spectral light of another world." Discussing her illness, Charlotte declared vehemently that she would not die of cancer. "If I thought I had to perish in that way I would not *endure it*—I would myself end my life."

393

Leaving, Winter looked back at her for a moment. With her head held high, she was, he wrote later, "the image of majesty."

On February 12, Charlotte ventured with Sallie into the hall for a brief stroll. Chilly drafts flowed along the floors in streams, and one of these caused her to take cold. Within a few minutes she was sneezing, and she bade Sallie help her back into bed. Too weak to fight off infection, she had a raging fever by nightfall.

The pneumonia was almost painless. Next day, Charlotte was able to write John McCullough, partly to apologize for not being able to see him when he called again at her rooms, partly to [seek] again, after so many efforts, to arrange a journey to the Far West. "I wanted to ask you if next Nov. or Dec. were engaged at your theatre in California. I hope to be able to get well and go there."

That letter, dated February 13, 1876, typified in a sense the hundreds that had flowed from her pen. The last she wrote, it voiced her hopes for a new season, her faith in a possible cure, the chance for more travel.

On February 16, Lanier's sonnet "To Charlotte Cushman" appeared in the March *Lippincott's*. Without her knowledge, Lanier had sent it to the printer: he had hoped it would be a pleasant surprise, but she never saw it.

Look where a three-point star shall weave his beam
Into the slumb'rous tissue of some stream,
Till his bright self o'er his bright copy seem
Fulfillment dropping on a come-true dream;
So in this night of art thy soul doth show
Her excellent double in the steadfast flow
Of wishing love that through men's hearts doth go:
At once thou shin'st above and shin'st below.
E'en when thou strivest there within Art's sky
(Each star must o'er a strenuous orbit fly),
Full calm thine image in our love doth lie,
A Motion glassed in a Tranquillity.
So triple-rayed, thou mov'st, yet stay'st, serene—
Art's artist, Love's dear woman, Fame's good queen!

In her bed, between bouts of coughing, Charlotte bade Sallie bring her the antique ring someone had given her in Rome. It was a jacinth, with tragic and comic masks cut in intaglio. When the time came, she said, Emma must see that Sidney Lanier received it. Through the long hours she remained lucid, as mentally bright as if her body were unaffected. The night of the seventeenth she asked Emma to read her Lowell's poem, "Columbus," a work she had long enjoyed for its strong rolling rhythm. In the dim light, when Emma stumbled over a phrase, Charlotte supplied it from memory. "Endurance is the crowning quality," she said thickly, "And patience all the passion of great hearts," then relaxed as Emma continued.

> These are their stay, and when the leaden world
> Sets its hard face against their fateful thought,
>
> . . . .
>
> The inspired soul but flings his patience in,
> And slowly that outweighs the ponderous globe,
> One faith against a whole earth's unbelief,
> One soul against the flesh of all mankind. . . .

Some hours before dawn on Friday, February 18, Dr. Thornton alerted Ned and Emma Crow who had rushed up from Newport. Lamentably, he told them, his efforts could not arrest pneumonia. A little before seven, Charlotte roused momentarily. Through dull eyes, she recognized the faces circled around her: Sallie, and Emma, and Emma Crow. Quietly, Ned bent down and offered her a sip from her cup. "Come, Auntie," he said, "here is your milk punch." A flicker of amusement played for a moment across her face. "Punch, brothers," she said, half audibly, "punch with care." Then she fell into a deep sleep. She died at ten minutes past nine.

Epilogue

The Passion and the Power

Nine years later, the New York *Tribune* voiced a sadness that the living drama's vivid sounds and gestures die out the moment they are born, leaving the quiet awareness, "Well this great thing has been, and all that is now left of it is the feeble print upon my brain, mine and my neighbors, and when we pass away the impress of the great artist will vanish from the world." If that sadness explains in part the devotion the crowd lavishes upon the actor while he lives, it explains as well their dumb dismay when an actor who has fired them with his supersense of life forever leaves the stage.

By 10 A.M. on February 21, throngs had gathered outside the Parker House to pass in a slow procession beside Charlotte's casket. "The whole city is pouring through the rooms where dear Cushla is lying with the largest, calmest, most majestical face I ever saw," Lanier wrote his wife that morning. The file continued until the pall-bearers carried the bier down and across the frozen street—so jammed that fourteen extra policemen had been called into service —through the portals of King's Chapel.

Once the bearers had placed the coffin at the foot of the pulpit, in front of Charlotte's family and friends and a host of actors representing the profession, flowers were massed upon and around it. The Reverend Henry W. Foote eulogized the woman of genius now lying here who had embodied the highest aims of art. Boston and much of the country had traveled a long road since Charlotte Cushman had first startled her family with the word that she would pursue a career on the stage. In those old days, said the minister, the world had "sneered at the possibility of virtue in dramatic life, and by the sneer and what went with it," had done "its worst to make virtue impossible."

But times had altered; the years had shown in lives like Miss Cushman's that a pure spirit could "go stainless," even in the theatre. Enlightened minds could now see that whatsoever things were true, whatsoever things were lovely, it was a Christian admonition to think on these things, whether one knelt within these hallowed white walls or sat beneath the painted vault of a theatre. By Miss Cushman's efforts, society was purer, the theatre had risen by her example. Let Boston and the world rejoice.

After the Psalm eight students from the Cushman School, at the prompting of Charley Wiggin, placed laurel and pond lilies, forget-me-nots and immortelles on the coffin in tribute to Katharine's famed line, "Saw you not even now a blessed troop invite me to a banquet, whose bright faces Cast a thousand beams upon me, like the sun? They promised me eternal happiness And brought me garlands."

The procession to Mount Auburn wound slowly up Beacon Street to the hill, past the State House where Emma's Horace Mann statue gazed out over Boston Common, past the silent crowds huddling together in the winter wind. A journalist saw the crowd as representative of the many thousands who had formed Charlotte's audience over the years. "No other woman of our day—in America at least—was as well known to so many people."

For two hours the cortege moved through the narrow streets and over the Charles to Cambridge, through the high gates of Mount Auburn where in time the grave stones would read like a cast in Charlotte's play: Mary Devlin and Edwin Booth, James T. and Annie Fields, Harriet Hosmer, Julia Ward Howe, Longfellow and Lowell.

After a prayer, the crowd at the grave stood pondering the life now ended. No one could grieve that Charlotte was now released from suffering, but in her death, what had the country suffered? Winter would write in the *Tribune*: "The greatness of Charlotte Cushman was that of an exceptional because grand and striking personality, combined with extraordinary power to embody the highest ideals of majesty, pathos, and appalling anguish." An inspirational fire, an opulent intellect, an abounding character and genius "were victorious and imperial in Charlotte Cushman." In the New York *Herald* Lawrence Barrett spoke for American actors: "Bigotry itself must stand abashed before the life of our dead Queen, whose every thought and act were given for years to an art which ignorance and envy have battled against in vain for centuries." The New York *Times* borrowed a phrase from Browning: Charlotte Cushman, it was true, was "but an actress," yet her fame would be as enduring

as any conqueror's. In the English-speaking world there was hardly
a place where her name was not a household word. She had lived
and died "a Virgin Queen of the dramatic stage." To the New York
Herald, "Neither Ristori, Madame Janauschek, nor even Rachel
could equal" Charlotte Cushman "in her own realm." In dying, said
Scribner's, the common run of players could be replaced as books
could be reprinted or pictures duplicated. But dramatic genius could
be no more repeated than one lightning flash could match another.
Charlotte's sleepless Queen of Scotland, her weird Queen of the gyp-
sies, her un-queened Queen of Henry VIII—these Queens uniquely
hers—flashed out and passed with her forever. The future would
find it difficult to believe, but Charlotte's art had surpassed that of
her most eminent contemporaries, George Eliot, George Sand, and
Elizabeth Barrett Browning. "They do not stand as high in their
respective professions as she stands on the stage." Agreeing, James
McVicker wrote, "They tasted but gingerly of the world's applause;
she drained the brimming goblet."

On the white slopes of Mount Auburn, however, eloquence and
grief did not go hand in hand. At the edge of the crowd, Lanier
stood fingering the jacinth ring Emma had given him Saturday.
Since Charlotte's death, said Lanier, he was "as one who has lost the
half of his possessions." "I had put out so many leaves and fresh
shoots which only lived in the climate of *her,* that her withdrawal
leaves a sort of winter all in that side of me."

When Emma Stebbins later found her own words, they would
form the first attempt at a Cushman biography, the book that Lanier
and Helen Hunt Jackson both wanted to do. Eight years after the
funeral, Sallie wrote Denis Alward, "the loss of dear Miss Cushman" only those could comprehend who had lived under the shelter
of her wings. "One of the greatest comforts I have is the belief that
she is near me sometimes and helping me." For Charlotte, a remembering nation would unveil a laurel-crowned bust in 1925 at New
York's Hall of Fame for Great Americans, making her one of the
seven women, and the only actress, yet awarded such acclaim.* But

* Charlotte Cushman had been voted into the Hall of Fame in 1915, partly
at the urging of actresses Jane Cowl, Katherine Cornell, and Minnie Mad-
dern Fiske, but the ceremony did not occur until May 21, 1925, when busts of

even that bronze, along with the words it carried, would weather: "To be thoroughly in earnest, intensely in earnest in all my thoughts and all my actions, whether in my profession or out of it, became my single idea."

Fully aware of this, Charlotte had never tried to delay the process of time. She had founded no theatre school to perpetuate her techniques; she had written no words to defend her creed. She might have devoted more effort to putting herself on record, to inscribing her art in the print that would survive her, but she had made her choice decades before the matter occurred to anyone else. Words about Charlotte Cushman were not and never could be the woman who had breathed fire into Shakespeare's titanic figures. Corrosive time would win out, and she knew it.

An anonymous sonneteer said it for her immediately after her death:

> For thee of earnest spirit and great heart,
> In a fair time a fair and kindly death
> Rounds a life nobly consecrate to art,
> Nor lacking praiseful tributes of man's breath
> For us, like music ended; a dead voice
> That sounded sweet in our ears of yesternight,
> The passion and the power wherein men's souls rejoice
> Are with the player buried out of sight.
> Within our ears an unreturning tone
> Of calm, majestic dignity still rings;
> A reverent memory remains alone,
> Sad sense of loss in sorrowful words that sings.
> Yet, even as Art to Death her daughter gives,
> Death bows to Art, for Art eternal lives.

With pen in hand, the best Charlotte could do was record in a lifelong correspondence her ranging curiosities, the flashes of a mind enlivened by her period's concerns, the dictates of a heart athirst for love. Her life was her spokesman. In the end, her stardom in it was more than talent, more than strength and self-knowledge, integrity and courage. She rose a star out of the darkness of her time, sailed

---

John Marshall, William T. Sherman, Asa Grey, and Harriet Beecher Stowe were also unveiled. The Cushman bust, by Francis Grimes, had been financed by popular subscription. Otis Skinner delivered the address; John Drew as President of the Players Club presented the bust; and Dr. Allerton Seward Cushman unveiled it. (Printed program of the ceremony.)

399

across the heavens through her bright particular orbit, and at its end, sank slowly down.

One summer day years after her death, William Winter stood recollecting the vivid impressions which the name on the grave's tall obelisk rekindled. A gardener looked up from clipping the grass and, pointing to the stone, voiced a comment that might serve for Charlotte Cushman's epitaph and measure.

"She was considerable of a woman, for a play-actress."

Reference Matter

Abbreviations

Abbreviations for library names are those used in the National Union Catalogue.

CCP	Charlotte Cushman Papers, Library of Congress
CSmH	Huntington Library
CtY	Yale University Library
CU-B	University of California at Berkeley Library
DFo	Folger Shakespeare Library
LNHT	Tulane University Library
LU	Louisiana State University Library
MB	Boston Public Library
MBHi	Massachusetts Historical Society Library
MCR	Radcliffe College Library
MdBJ	Johns Hopkins University Library
MH-H	Houghton Library, Harvard University
MH-T	Harvard College Library Theatre Collection
MoSHi	Missouri Historical Society Library
NjP	Princeton University Library
NNC	Columbia University Library
NNHi	New York Historical Society Library
NNP	Players Club Library
NN-T	New York Public Library Theatre Collection
NRU	University of Rochester Library
PPCc	Charlotte Cushman Club Library
PPHi	Pennsylvania Historical Society Library
PU	University of Pennsylvania Library
ScEN	National Library of Scotland
TxU	University of Texas in Austin Library
TxU-T	Hoblitzelle Theatre Collection, University of Texas at Austin
MW	Milwaukee Public Library

$\mathcal{N}otes$

page

2   "cannot fail them"—Robert Cushman, *The Sin and Danger of Self Love
    Described in a Sermon Preached at Plymouth, In New England 1621*
    (Plymouth, Massachusetts: Nathaniel Coverly, 1785), p. iv.

4   figure in Boston—Harold and James Kirker, *Bulfinch's Boston: 1787–
    1817* (New York: Oxford University Press, 1964), p. 220.
    the entire city—ibid., p. 215.

5   "born a tomboy"—quoted in Emma C. Stebbins, *Charlotte Cushman:
    Her Letters and Memories of Her Life* (Boston: Houghton, Osgood,
    1878), p. 13; hereafter cited as Stebbins.
    "anything with tools"—Stebbins, p. 13.

6   to her father—Stebbins, p. 8.
    dying of cancer—CCP, *4,* 1158.

7   "my mother's children"—CCP, *2,* 457.
    "for a young lady!"—Stebbins, p. 14.
    expressing her grief—Stebbins, p. 14.

8   throughout its interior—Richard Moody, *Edwin Forrest: First Star of
    the American Stage* (New York: Knopf, 1960), p. 72.
    his Brooklyn *Eagle*—Howard Taubman, *The Making of the American
    Theatre* (New York: Coward-McCann, 1965), p. 83.
    Kean on stage—Glenn Hughes, *A History of the American Theatre
    1700–1950* (New York: Samuel French, 1951), p. 155.

9   and good alike—Mary A. Livermore, *The Story of My Life: Or the
    Sunshine and Shadow of Seventy Years* (Hartford, Connecticut:
    Worthington, 1898), p. 85.

10 Street during 1828—James Henry Wiggin, "A House and a Name,"
    The Bostonian, 1 (October, 1894): 87.

11 on October 30—Alan S. Downer, *The Eminent Tragedian: William
    Charles Macready* (Cambridge: Harvard University Press, 1966),
    p. 110.
    transitions of his eyes—London *Globe,* quoted in J. C. Trewin, *Mr.
    Macready: A Nineteenth-Century Tragedian and His Theatre* (Lon-
    don: Harrap, 1955), p. 43.
    from his eyes—Walt Whitman, "Dramatics and the True Secret of
    Acting," Brooklyn *Eagle,* August 20, 1846.
    reaches of passion—James E. Murdoch, *The Stage: Or Recollections of
    Actors and Acting from an Experience of Fifty Years: A Series of
    Dramatic Sketches* (Philadelphia: Stoddart, 1880), p. 97.

Notes

page

12 her ruling passion—Stebbins, p. 16.

"to the theatre"—James Parton, *The World's Famous Women: A Series of Sketches of Women Who Have Won Distinction by Their Genius and Achievements as Authors, Artists, Actors, Rulers, or within the Precinct of the Home* (New York: Alden, n.d.), p. 19.

13 attracting attention—Stebbins, p. 15.

CHAPTER TWO

16 "of human hopes"—quoted in Ralph L. Rusk, *The Life of Ralph Waldo Emerson* (New York: Scribner's, 1949), p. 136.

"duly keep"—from the introductory poem to Emerson's essay, "Compensation," published in 1841.

"his own esteem"—Rusk, *Life of Emerson,* p. 158.

"plump, round, rosy"—recollections of an unidentified old man who knew Charlotte Cushman, quoted in an untitled newspaper clipping at NN-T.

17 "got from below"—Emerson quoted in Rusk, *Life of Emerson,* p. 159.

church each Sunday—Rusk, *Life of Emerson,* p. 141.

18 enjoy the theatre—James Henry Wiggin, "Some Interesting But Little Known Facts About Charlotte Cushman," *Coming Age* (March, 1900): 225.

"Farewell, My Love"—Clara Erskine Clement, *Charlotte Cushman* (Boston: Osgood, 1882), p. 3.

19 surprised even him—John Paddon quoted in Boston *Transcript,* April 13, 1885.

"of her glory"—Frances Trollope, *Domestic Manners of the Americans* (New York: Knopf, 1949), p. 337.

20 a troubling dilemma—Mary Howitt, "The Miss Cushmans," *The People's Journal, 2* (July 18, 1846): 31.

21 perhaps, began—Walt Whitman, *New York Dissected: A Sheaf of Recently Discovered Newspaper Articles by the Author of the Leaves of Grass,* ed. Emory Holloway and Ralph Adimari (New York: Wilson, 1936), pp. 18–19.

22 "fortune I coveted"—CCP, *15,* E. Stebbins's ms. of Charlotte Cushman's recollections.

23 "cheerfully die tomorrow"—quoted in New York *Sunday Morning News,* January 3, 1836.

intellectual universe—W. S. Tryon, *Parnassus Corner: A Life of James T. Fields: Publisher to the Victorians* (Boston: Hougton Mifflin, 1963), p. 24.

24 recognized talent—Clara Fisher Maeder, *Autobiography of Clara Fisher Maeder* (New York: Dunlap Society, 1897), p. xv.

core of her life—Howitt, "The Miss Cushmans," p. 30.

25 "make her happy"—CCP, *10,* 3013.

astonished to comment—Gamaliel Bradford, "Charlotte Cushman," *Biography and the Human Heart* (Boston: Houghton Mifflin, 1932), p. 110.

26 "reading this letter"—CCP, *14,* 3932.

audiences to tears—Oral Sumner Coad and Edwin Mims, Jr., *The*

Notes

    American Stage (New Haven: Yale University Press, 1929), p. 98.

    moving the hands—Maeder, *Autobiography,* p. 92.

27 New York since 1824—Wallace Brockway and Herbert Weinstock, *The Opera: A History of its Creation and Performance: 1600–1941* (New York: Simon and Schuster, 1941), p. 94.

28 to the Tremont Theatre—Wiggin, "A House and a Name," p. 87.

    "flexible, and sweet"—quoted in Edward G. Fletcher, "Charlotte Cushman's Theatrical Debut," *Studies in English,* The University of Texas Publication No. 4026 (Austin, Texas, July 8, 1940): 167.

29 "success was brilliant"—Boston *Daily Atlas,* April 11, 1835, quoted in Fletcher, "Theatrical Debut," p. 168.

    showed much promise—*Atlas,* April 18, 1835, quoted in Fletcher, "Theatrical Debut," p. 169.

    "his fortune—perhaps"—*Spirit of the Times,* April 18, 1835.

30 "the substantial cause"—Paddon, Boston *Transcript,* April 13, 1835, quoted in Fletcher, "Theatrical Debut," p. 171.

    "for her success"—ibid., p. 174.

    on the first occasion—*The Pearl,* quoted in Fletcher, "Theatrical Debut," p. 173.

    "beside Mrs. Wood"—quoted in Fletcher, "Theatrical Debut," p. 175.

31 side of morality—Charles Durang, *The History of the Philadelphia Stage between the Years 1749 and 1855* (published serially in the Philadelphia *Dispatch,* May 7, 1854 through July 8, 1860, and arranged as an unpublished scrapbook by Thompson Westcott), *4, 174.*

    and marry him—New York *Sunday Dispatch,* quoted in Celia Logan, untitled newspaper clipping in MH-T.

CHAPTER THREE

33 "unkindness to me"—CC to Sam Judd, New Orleans, June 1, 1836, at NNHi.

    several Italian musicians—Mrs. John Drew, *Autobiographical Sketch of Mrs. John Drew* (New York: Scribner's, 1899), p. 73.

35 arriving each autumn—Tyrone Power, *Impressions of America: During the Years 1833, 1834, and 1835* (Philadelphia: Carey, Lea, and Blanchard, 1836), *2,* 145.

36 city with gas—*Spirit of the Times,* November 19, 1836, p. 316.

    had erected it—Robert Tallant, *The Romantic New Orleanians* (New York: Dutton, 1950), p. 191.

    could match it—Moody, *Edwin Forrest,* p. 182.

    even a veteran—Catherine Mary Reignolds-Winslow, *Yesterdays with Actors* (Boston: Cupples and Hurd, 1887), p. 25.

38 had other resources—Murdoch, *The Stage,* p. 235.

    "taste nor skill"—quoted in John S. Kendall, *The Golden Age of the New Orleans Theatre* (Baton Rouge: Louisiana State University Press, 1952), p. 126.

39 transplant from England—Nelle Smither, "Charlotte Cushman's Apprenticeship in New Orleans," *Louisiana Historical Quarterly, 31* (October, 1948): 978.

    "with success"—*Bee,* April 12, 1836.

page
40 "not a singer"—quoted in Stebbins, p. 22.

"badly stage-struck"—Clara Fisher Maeder in New York *Dramatic Mirror,* February 13, 1897, clipping at MH-T.

"the lower one"—CC to Stebbins, CCP, *15,* 3997.

"you must succeed"—quoted in *The New York Times,* February 19, 1876, p. 6.

41 with a kiss—Lewis C. Strang, *Players and Plays of the Last Quarter Century* (Boston: Page, 1903), p. 112.

as an actor—Moody, *Edwin Forrest,* p. 49.

42 character on stage—H. Barton Baker, *The London Stage: Its History and Traditions from 1576 to 1888* (London: Allen, 1889), *2,* 162.

43 "a competent teacher"—quoted in Smither, "Apprenticeship," p. 979.

over the shoulders—Howitt, "The Miss Cushmans," p. 32.

44 "pantheress let loose"—*The New York Times,* February 19, 1876, p. 7.

45 "on the stage"—untitled contemporary newspaper clipping at MH-T.

"members of the company"—quoted in Stebbins, p. 23.

to straight drama—*Bee,* April 25, 1836, p. 2.

her special powers—James Rees, *The Dramatic Authors of America* (Philadelphia: Zieber, 1845), p. xi.

to her salary—Smither, "Apprenticeship," p. 980.

46 by the twenty-fifth—CC to Judd, June 1, 1836, at NNHi.

CHAPTER FOUR

48 reception than this—Stebbins, p. 26.

his kindly nature—Coad and Mims, *American Stage,* p. 91

49 passion almost electric—*The New York Times,* February 19, 1876, p. 7.

could be drawn—Charles W. Sandford to CC, New York, July 30, 1836, in CCP, *13.*

50 useful articles—*Spirit of the Times,* February 26, 1876, p. 65.

51 "This is Miss Cushman"—New York *Mirror,* August 20, 1836.

"a general favorite"—*New Yorker, 1* (August 27, 1836) : 367.

"for three years"—*Spirit of the Times,* August 27, 1836, p. 220.

52 "attractive young lady"—New York *Mirror,* August 20, 1836.

words with blows—George Vandenhoff, *Leaves from an Actor's Note-Book: With Reminiscences and Chit-Chat of the Green Room and the Stage, in England and America* (New York: Appleton, 1860), p. 196.

53 "all our hearts"—*Spirit of the Times,* September 17, 1836, p. 244.

"of the manager"—CC quoted in Stebbins, p. 27.

54 down in flames—*Spirit of the Times,* October 1, 1836.

"afflatus within me"—CC quoted by Celia Logan in New York *Sunday Dispatch,* n.d., clipping at MH-T.

CHAPTER FIVE

56 herself in New York—E. Burke Fisher to Francis C. Wemyss, New York, September 27, 1836, at MH-T.

57 of the building—Moody, *Edwin Forrest,* p. 51.

night, October 11—H. P. Phelps, *Players of a Century: A Record of the Albany Stage: Including Notices of Prominent Actors Who Have Appeared in America* (Albany, N.Y.: McDonough, 1880), p. 199.

forgot to appear—Eleanor Ruggles, *Prince of Players: Edwin Booth* (New York: Norton, 1953), p. 8.

"lanky girl"—Phelps, *Players of a Century,* p. 201.

58 "as she deserves"—*Spirit,* October 22, 1836, p. 284.

a practical move—CC, "Extracts from My Journal: The Actress," *The Lady's Book and Magazine of Belles Lettres, Fashions, Music, etc., 14* (February, 1837): 70–73.

"glory of man"—quoted in Richardson Wright, *Forgotten Ladies: Nine Portraits from the American Family Album* (Philadelphia: Lippincott, 1928), p. 215.

59 "all a bam"—*Spirit,* October 22, 1836, p. 284.

"in love with her"—quoted in *Spirit,* November 19, 1836, p. 313.

"of bright eyes"—quoted in *Spirit,* November 19, 1836, p. 319.

60 "at the Capitol"—CC quoted in Stebbins, p. 28.

the other actors—Stebbins, p. 24.

61 "dear, darling sister"—CCP, *10,* 3008.

62 November 4, 1836—George Combe to CC, Edinburgh, Scotland, February 7, 1846 at ScEN.

fortunes had taken—Howitt, "The Miss Cushmans," p. 47.

Alexander the Great (footnote)—Phelps, *Players of a Century,* pp. 203–04.

63 "national jealousy"—quoted in Moody, *Edwin Forrest,* p. 147.

"the compliment"—December 18, 1836, quoted in *Spirit,* February 4, 1837, p. 402.

64 "reward the Man"—CC's holograph in CCP, *15.*

"kept from harm"—quoted in Geraldine Jewsbury to Emma Stebbins, February 6, 1877, CCP, *11,* 3462.

"in my art"—CC to Emma Crow Cushman, May 24, 1862, CCP, *2,* 457.

65 "ever I saw"—quoted in David Belasco, "Women and the Stage," *Ladies Home Journal, 37* (November, 1920): 13.

attempted the role—Charles E. L. Wingate, *Shakespeare's Heroes on Stage* (New York: Crowell, 1896), p. 303.

"enthusiastic applause"—Albany *Advertiser,* quoted in Phelps, *Players of a Century,* p. 204.

66 "than the Albanians"—ibid.

Augustus had written—CCP, *10,* 3012.

"over my soul"—CC to Emma Crow Cushman, May 24, 1862, CCP, *2,* 457.

CHAPTER SIX

68 "cross-bearer"—William Winter, *Shadows of the Stage* (Boston: Macmillan, 1893), p. 208.

"learn it thoroughly"—CCP, *15,* 4000.

season in September—Stebbins, p. 29.

69 "by a girl"—quoted in George C. D. Odell, *Annals of the New York Stage* (New York: Columbia University Press, 1931), *4,* 147.

70 if she liked—*Harper's Weekly* (March 4, 1876): 193.

"fight against fate"—quoted from CC's acting version included in F. C. Wemyss, *The Modern Standard Drama: A Collection of the*

page

Most Popular Acting Plays, with Critical Remarks, also the Stage Business, Costumes, etc. (New York: William Taylor, n.d.), pp. 8–59. CC's own *Guy Mannering* promptbooks are in CCP.

71 staff, staring—Reignolds-Winslow, *Yesterday with Actors*, p. 20.

72 "all over me"—quoted in Stebbins, p. 149.
have been made—*Harper's Weekly* (March 4, 1876) : 193.
"dramatic nondescript"—Murdoch, *The Stage*, p. 240.
"melodramatic monstrosity"—Strang, *Players and Plays, 1,* 110.
as Meg Merrilies—T. Allston Brown, *A History of the New York Stage: From the First Performance in 1732 to 1901* (New York: Dodd, Mead, 1903), *1,* 243.

73 "or our currency"—Philip Hone, *The Diary of Philip Hone 1828–1851,* ed. Allan Nevins (New York: Dodd, Mead, 1927), *1,* 265.

74 *Speed the Plough*—Strang, *Players and Plays,* p. 101.
"worthy of you"—quoted in Stebbins, p. 34.
"*Man,* in these !"—CC holograph at MH-H.
"for a pedestrian"—Jules Zanger, *Captain Frederick Marryat: Diary in America* (Bloomington: Indiana University Press, 1960), p. 12.

75 *Free Press* to call—CC to J. S. Baggs, August 8, 1837, at CSmH.
a Sheridan play—Durang, *History of the Philadelphia Stage, 4,* 153.
"meal-bag together"—Thomas Chandler Haliburton, *The Clockmaker: Or, the Sayings and Doings of Sam Slick of Slickville* (New York: Lea and Blanchard, 1843), p. 39.

76 "if possible"—CCP, *13,* 3565.
a perpetual game—Lydia Maria Child, *Letters from New York* (New York: Francis, 1844), p. 68.
to avoid starvation—ibid, p. 13.
tracery and ornament—quoted in Joseph Jay Rubin and Charles H. Brown, *Walt Whitman of the New York Aurora: Editor at Twenty-Two* (State College, Pa.: Bald Eagle Press, 1950), p. 18.

77 outside of London—quoted in *Spirit,* February 27, 1836.
"loss of reason"—Howitt, "The Miss Cushmans," p. 47.

78 ingenue roles—William Davidge, *Footlight Flashes* (New York: American News, 1866), pp. 171–72.
so little scope—Odell, *Annals, 4,* 190.

79 "retroussé"—Joseph N. Ireland, *Records of the New York Stage from 1750 to 1860* (New York: Morrell, 1867), *2,* 162.

80 "a great eminence"—quoted in Garff B. Wilson, *A History of American Acting* (Bloomington: Indiana University Press, 1966), p. 22.
"surges of the sea"—William Winter quoted in Moody, *Edwin Forrest,* p. 405.
"Hercules himsel' "—quoted in John Coleman, *Fifty Years of an Actor's Life* (London: Hutchinson, 1904) *1,* 335.
"untempered brutality"—Strang, *Players and Plays, 1,* 74.
"Shakespeare more"—quoted in Moody, *Edwin Forrest,* p. 403.
"of a Man !"—quoted in Coleman, *An Actor's Life, 1,* 334.

81 "bones of his kindred"—quoted in Moody, *Edwin Forrest,* p. 96.
"snow she died !"—quoted in ibid, p. 98.
"brusque characters"—New York *Herald,* September 30, 1837.

82 "unknown young woman"—quoted in Stebbins, pp. 31–32.

of his support—James Grant Wilson, *The Life and Letters of Fitz-Greene Halleck* (New York: Appleton, 1869), p. 467.

83 "given due recognition"—Adrien de Montfort, "Amateurs and Actors: Random Recollections of the Stage," *Spirit of the Times, 91* (April 1, 1876) : 180.

blocking her way—William James Stillman, *The Autobiography of a Journalist* (Boston: Houghton Mifflin, 1901), p. 361.

"the old continent"—quoted in Meade Minigerode, *The Fabulous Forties 1840–1850: A Presentation of Private Life* (New York: Putnam's, 1924), p. vii.

84 "native music sung"—*Spirit,* July 28, 1838, p. 185.

CHAPTER SEVEN

86 "interesting and prominent"—James Rees, *The Life of Edwin Forrest: With Reminiscences and Personal Recollections* (Philadelphia: Peterson, 1874), p. 379.

"more genius"—Brooklyn *Eagle,* August 14, 1846, recalling earlier performances.

louder applause—*Spirit,* June 30, 1838, p. 153.

"brilliant"—*Spirit,* August 25, 1838, p. 217.

"does not play it"—New York *Weekly Herald,* December 22, 1838, quoted in Jennie Lorenz, "Charlotte Cushman: A Study in Acting" (M.A. thesis, State University of Iowa, 1929), p. 296.

87 "and good benefits"—*Spirit,* December 22, 1838, p. 353.

"beauty of that performance!"—Brooklyn *Eagle,* August 14, 1846.

88 greedy opportunist—Herbert Marshall and Mildred Stock, *Ira Aldridge: The Negro Tragedian* (New York: Macmillan, 1958), p. 31.

"break my engagement"—Annie H. Brewster, "Miss Cushman," *Blackwood's Edinburgh Magazine, 124* (August, 1878) : 173.

89 to the theatre—untitled newspaper clipping at MH-T.

"where they might"—Charles Dickens, *Oliver Twist,* preface to 1867 London edition.

"tip off a stick"—Brewster, "Miss Cushman," p. 174.

honor and decency—Vandenhoff, *An Actor's Note-Book,* p. 195.

90 play in her face—CC's promptbook for *Oliver Twist* at MH-T.

91 "spoke through blood"—Lawrence Barrett describing a later performance, quoted in Clement, *Charlotte Cushman,* p. 25.

"in the play"—*Spirit,* February 9, 1839, p. 409.

"on the Park boards"—Brooklyn *Eagle,* August 14, 1846.

play, *The Genoese*—Durang, *History of the Philadelphia Stage, 4,* 174.

92 a popular play—John Howard Payne to CC, CCP, *13,* 3635.

"to see them"—ibid.

"my promise good"—Payne to CC, 86 Frankfurt Street, Saturday, n.d., at NNC.

93 talents be known—Chapman quoted in Philadelphia *Times,* February 19, 1876.

page

coaxing Sir Peter—Laurence Hutton, *Plays and Players* (New York: Hurd and Haughton, 1875), p. 229.

94 "prospects before her"—*Spirit,* August 25, 1838, p. 217.
"scold and a vixen"—*Spirit,* March 28, 1840, p. 48.
talented sisters—*Spirit,* May 9, 1840, p. 120.

95 "part she played"—quoted in Lorenz, *Charlotte Cushman,* p. 221.
actor with blood—J. M. D. Hardwick, *Emigrant in Motley* (London: Rockliff, 1954), p. 8.

96 one more money—Howitt, "The Miss Cushmans," p. 47.

CHAPTER EIGHT

97 "in my heart"—CC to Judd, July 23 [1840] at MCR.
eight years before—Margaret Armstrong, *Fanny Kemble: A Passionate Victorian* (New York: Macmillan, 1938), p. 159.

98 wrote Sam Judd—CC to Judd, October, 1840, at MCR.
in her career—Durang, *History of the Philadelphia Stage, 4,* 172.
Nicholas Nickleby—ibid., p. 173.
"up her mind"—quoted in W. T. Price, *A Life of Charlotte Cushman* (New York: Brentano's, 1894), p. 49.
"bloomed and flourished"—Durang, *History of the Philadelphia Stage, 4,* 173.

99 "once a favorite"—CC to Judd, October, 1840.
"inferior" to her—Armstrong, *Fanny Kemble,* p. 176.

100 found her "marvelous"—Frank Preston Stearns, *The Life and Genius of Nathaniel Hawthorne* (Boston: Lippincott, 1906), p. 231.
"acquaintance," Fanny wrote—Fanny Kemble to CC, CCP, *9,* 2763.
"to visit me"—Kemble to CC, CCP, *9,* 2759.
"opportunity of seeing"—Francis Courtney Wemyss, *Twenty-Six Years of the Life of an Actor and Manager: Interspersed with Sketches, Anecdotes and Opinions of the Professional Merits of the Most Celebrated Actors and Actresses of Our Day* (New York: Burgess, Stringer, 1847), *2,* 344.
"on every tongue"—Wemyss, *Modern Standard Drama, 10,* 3.

101 "going to close"—CC to Mrs. William Creswick, January 23, 1841, at MH-T.
far from well—ibid.
"and Burton himself"—New York *Herald,* January 23, 1841.
"heartily disappointed"—CC to Mrs. Creswick, February 7, 1841, at MCR.

102 "therefore refuses"—CC to Judd, February 3, 1841, at MCR.
"in show pieces"—quoted in Odell, *Annals, 4,* 468.
fetch her in style—Wemyss, *Twenty-Six Years, 2,* 352.
"for a time"—CC to Judd, n.d., at MCR.

103 "life your Father"—Babbit to CC, June 13, 1841, in CCP, *9.*
the staring eyes—CC to Mrs. Creswick, July 9, 1841, at MH-H.
"skill and attention"—playbill for this performance, at TxU-T.
"in the whole cast"—*Spirit,* September 4, 1841, quoted in Odell, *Annals, 4,* 530.
"poutingly"—CC to Park Benjamin, October 13 [1841], at MH-T.

Notes

104 over the lawn—playbill for this performance, at TxU-T.
"greatly against her"—W. T. W. Ball in Clement, *Charlotte Cushman,* p. 162.

104 "anything finer"—Walt Whitman, "Specimen Days," in *Leaves of Grass and Selected Prose,* ed. John Kouwenhoven (New York: Modern Library, 1950), p. 572.
"beginning to end"—quoted in Floyd Stovall, "Walt Whitman and the Dramatic Stage in New York," *Studies in Philology, 50* (July, 1953): 531.
"loud-talking Amazonian"—*New World,* about October 16, 1841, quoted in Price, *Life of Charlotte Cushman,* p. 47.
"does the rheumatism"—New York *Daily Herald,* October 14, 1841, quoted in Lorenz, *Charlotte Cushman,* p. 61.

105 "of more importance"—CC to Benjamin, October 13 [1841], at MH-T.
"and his 'notice' "—New York *Herald,* October 16, 1841.
cowardly attack—*Herald,* October 18, 1841.
"witless ape"—*Aurora,* March 24, 1842, quoted in Rubin and Brown, *Walt Whitman,* p. 111.
"to obtain this"—CC to Noah M. Ludlow and Sol Smith, October 29, 1841, at MoSHi.
"flowing elocution"—untitled newspaper clipping in Joseph N. Ireland's scrapbook of New York stage actors and actresses at CtY.

106 "Nor even Somivel's"—Field's holograph, displayed on walls of the "Dickens Room" at the Parker House, Boston.
"Atlantic between them"—*Life, Letters, and Speeches of Charles Dickens: With Biographical Sketches of the Principal Illustrations of Dickens's Work* (Boston: Houghton Mifflin, 1894), *2,* 419.
"Miss Charlotte Cushman"—New York *Sun* (weekly edition), March 26, 1842.
"lights under bushels"—quoted in Rubin and Brown, *Walt Whitman,* p. 92.

107 "present glooms"—CC to Campbell P. White, at NNHi.
"filling up"—*Weekly Herald,* June 17, 1842.
his side of the house—Olive Logan, *Before the Footlights and Behind the Scenes* (Philadelphia: Parmelee, 1870), pp. 506–07.

108 "New Yorkers in six"—CC to W. H. Chippendale, August 2, 1842, in CCP, *2.*
"and very nice"—CC to Chippendale, September 11, 1842, at MH-T.

CHAPTER NINE

109 "generous sentiment"—CC holograph in CCP, *1,* 15.
"Walnut St. wardrobe"—CCP, *9,* 2793–94.

110 the most good—Vandenhoff, *An Actor's Note-Book,* p. 195.
"the Far West"—Howitt, "The Miss Cushmans," p. 48.

111 "C. S. Cushman"—CC to Chippendale, Philadelphia, October 29, 1842, at MH-T.
laws were laws—*Actors and Actresses of Great Britain and the United States: Macready and Forrest and Their Contemporaries,* ed.

page

Brander Matthews and Laurence Hutton (Boston: Page, 1900), p. 150.

"respectability"—*Herald,* November 14, 1842, quoted in Lorenz, *Charlottte Cushman,* p. 18.

Enchanted Isle—Brewster, "Miss Cushman," p. 171.

112 were irritating—Durang, *History of the Philadelphia Stage, 5,* 211.

of the calls—Walter M. Leman, *Memories of an Old Actor* (San Francisco: Roman, 1886), p. 179.

"to overestimate"—quoted in Stebbins, p. 34.

to another seat—Diary of Joseph Sill, Sunday, April 16, 1843, printed in Philadelphia *Public Ledger,* February 27, 1927, at PPHi.

"button-hole society"—Leman, *Memories of an Old Actor,* p. 180.

113 *"I am beautiful"*—CC to Thomas Sully, n.d., at MH-T.

she owed him?—Edward Biddle and Mantle Fielding, *The Life and Works of Thomas Sully: 1783–1872* (Philadelphia: Biddle and Fielding, 1921), p. 131.

114 a special treasure—original at DFo.

"epicene"—Vandenhoff, *An Actor's Note-Book,* p. 218.

115 her "assistant"—Wemyss, *Twenty-Six Years, 2,* 337.

wrongly emphasized—Leman, *Memories of an Old Actor,* p. 170.

off the stage—Drew, *Autobiographical Sketch,* p. 98.

116 and other actors—Matthews and Hutton, *Macready and Forrest,* p. 9.

"the eye alone"—quoted in Downer, *The Eminent Tragedian,* p. 33.

"mischief for me"—Brewster, "Miss Cushman," p. 172.

"my little dear"—contemporary untitled newspaper clipping at MH-T.

saw them together—ibid.

117 "make me a gown"—quoted in *Spirit,* February 26, 1876.

"on the stage"—quoted in William Toynbee, *The Diaries of William Charles Macready: 1833–1851* (New York: Chapman and Hall, 1912), *2, 233*

"and I will"—quoted in Brewster, "Miss Cushman," p. 173.

"to give it"—Toynbee, *Diaries of Macready, 2, 230.*

"Charlotte Cushman"—CC to [Macready] My Dear Sir, n.d., at NNC.

"the common room"—quoted in Toynbee, *Diaries of Macready, 2,* 234–35.

"powerful and clever"—quoted in ibid., p. 230.

"was only kind"—quoted in ibid., p. 239.

118 "forget-me-not!"—*Knickerbocker* (October, 1843): 364.

with Macready—Stebbins, p. 33.

"to stand up!"—Drew, *Autobiographical Sketch,* p. 94.

119 "by his imagination"—Trewin, *Mr. Macready,* p. 80.

indescribable "splendor"—CC quoted in George T. Ferris, "Players of Yesterday," *The Theatre, 10* (September, 1909): 82.

fugitive impression—Lawrence Barrett, *Charlotte Cushman: A Lecture,* Publications of Dunlap Society, No. 9 (New York, 1889), p. 17.

audience dissolved—Murdoch, *The Stage,* pp. 104–06.

120 *"where I please!"*—Mrs. Bancroft, *Gleanings from 'On and Off the Stage'* (London: George Routledge, 1892), p. 244.

"something into it"—Edward Fitzgerald, *The Letters of Edward Fitzgerald to Fanny Kemble* (New York: Macmillan, 1895), p. 55.
"up into prose"—quoted in Richard Findlater, *Six Great Actors: David Garrick et al.* (London: Hamish Hamilton, 1957), p. 127.
to her acting—Dutton Cook, *Hours with the Players* (London: Chatto and Windus, 1881), 2, 197.
"colloquial whisper"—quoted in Alan S. Downer, "Players and Painted Stage: Nineteenth Century Acting," *PMLA, 61* (June, 1946) : 544.
121   "anticipate my thought"—quoted in Findlater, *Six Great Actors,* p. 125.
"of her calling?"—Toynbee, *Diaries of Macready, 2,* 241.
"sent to me, etc."—quoted in Clement, *Charlotte Cushman,* pp. 26–27.
cheered "enthusiastically"—*Spirit,* December 9, 1843, p. 492.
"very double person"—Toynbee, *Diaries of Macready, 2,* 242.
"for many years"—*Spirit,* December 16, 1843, p. 504.
"him play second"—quoted in Stebbins, p. 32.
"fixed Miss Cushman"—Toynbee, *Diaries of Macready, 2,* 243.,
122   "or Da Vinci"—CC to [Macready] My Dear Sir, [December, 1843], at NNC.
"of knowing you"—Macready to CC, December 24, 1843, in CCP, *12,* 3536.
"thee, Dr. Fell!"—Toynbee, *Diaries of Macready, 2,* 244.

CHAPTER TEN

123   "revered the same"—*Anglo-American, 2* (January 6, 1844), in Stowe's notes at MCR.
124   "depth and power"—Leman, *Memories of an Old Actor,* p. 122.
"for *four weeks*"—CC to Chippendale, December 27, 1843, at MH-T.
"Magreedy"—Trewin, *Mr. Macready,* p. 229.
"fickleness and infidelity"—Toynbee, *Diaries of Macready, 2,* 242.
"difficulty is past"—CCP, *9,* 2817.
125   "children from me"—Kemble to CC, in CCP, *9,* 2753.
"enquiry for me"—CCP, *9,* 2770.
"for the better"—CCP, *9,* 2768.
"dare not take"—CCP, *9,* 2753.
her for desertion—Armstrong, *Fanny Kemble,* pp. 281–82.
126   "praised by her"—CC's diary is at NNC.
"appetite for my dinner"—CC's diary, January 11, 1844.
"insect in amber"—Macready to CC, March 13, 1844 in CCP, blue box.
127   eternal fidelity—Rosalie Sully to CC, May 11, 1845, in CCP, *14,* 3970.
"Yours, Charlotte"—CCP, *8.*
128   "future affluence"—CC to [Mr. Gregg], My Dear Sir, at NNC.
*"per se—*agh!"—quoted in Odell, *Annals, 5,* 86.
so far received—James Willis Yeater, "Charlotte Cushman: American Actress" (Ph.D. diss., University of Illinois, 1959), p. 131.
"of being foreigners"—quoted in Downer, *The Eminent Tragedian,* p. 268.
129   with cheers—William T. W. Ball, in Clement, *Charlotte Cushman,* p. 164.

sailed for England—Stebbins, p. 30.

130 "figure in America"—original in Matthews and Hutton, *Macready and Forrest, 4,* no. 6, at MH-T.

"never get over"—quoted in Brewster, "Miss Cushman," p. 175.

131 "fifth acts together"—Vandenhoff, *An Actor's Note-Book,* pp. 196–97.

"performers of America"—*Spirit,* October 26, 1844, p. 420.

herself and Sallie—CC's diary, October 26, 1844.

132 "voyage from home"—CC's diary, October 27, 1844.

"a manly heart"—penciled in CC's diary, back of title page.

CHAPTER ELEVEN

133 "did I leave home"—CC's diary, October 27, 1844.

134 "than I expected"—CC's diary. Dates of entries are not always easy to determine since she seldom confined herself to the small notebook's printed spaces.

"Long Wharf, more wet"—CC to her mother, quoted in Stebbins, p. 47.

"his fifth rib"—quoted in J. W. T. Ley, *The Dickens Circle: A Narrative of the Novelist's Friendships* (New York: Dutton, n.d.), p. 162.

"nobody sees it"—quoted in Edwin Percy Whipple, *Charles Dickens: The Man and His Work* (Boston: Houghton Mifflin, 1912), pp. 208–09.

135 "soda bottle"—quoted in M. A. DeWolfe Howe, *Memories of a Hostess: A Chronicle of Eminent Friendships Drawn Chiefly from the Diaries of Mrs. James T. Fields* (Boston: Atlantic Monthly Press, 1922), p. 136.

"I have taken her"—CCP, *I,* 16.

137 "heaped densely together"—Nathaniel Hawthorne, *The English Notebooks of Nathaniel Hawthorne; Based upon the Original Manuscripts in the Pierpont Morgan Library* (New York: Russell and Russell, 1962), p. 535.

"were so kind"—CC to her mother, Liverpool, December 2, 1844, in CCP, *I,* 18.

140 "dove-like softness"—Trewin, *Mr. Macready,* p. 168.

141 rebuff on Macready—Strang, *Players and Plays, I,* 90.

"begin with Emilia"—quoted in *Reminiscences of the Life of the World-Renowned Charlotte Cushman, Compiled from Various Records, by Mrs. Dr. Walker, her Chosen Medium: Together with Some of her Spirit Experiences, Expressions of Regret, etc.* (Boston: Tenny, 1876), p. 27.

"obdurate as Shylock"—quoted in Vandenhoff, *An Actor's Note-Book,* p. 198.

142 "my own terms."—quoted in Stebbins, p. 46.

143 "the Queen's box"—CC's diary, February 6, 1845.

"a passionate explosion"—London *Times,* February 14, 1845, p. 6, quoted in Yeater, "Charlotte Cushman," p. 77.

benches in the pit—London *Era,* August 5, 1905, clipping at MH-T.

144 "a grave voice"—Westland Marston, *Our Recent Actors: Being Recollections Critical, and, in Many Cases, Personal, of Late Distin-*

guished *Performers of Both Sexes* (London: Low, Marston, Searle, Rivington, 1888), *2*, 66.

"nearly as deep"—London *Era,* August 5, 1905, at MH-T.

"horrible enlightenment"—London *Times,* February 14, 1845, p. 6.

145   embodiment of despair—ibid.

the slate of her guilt—London *Times,* June 24, 1854, p. 10.

"tremblingly sweet refrain"—London *Era,* August 5, 1905.

career was assured—Stebbins, p. 52.

"you've got 'em"—quoted in Col. Forney, in untitled contemporary newspaper clipping, at MH-T.

146   "a demented brain"—Coleman, *An Actor's Life, 1,* 295.

CHAPTER TWELVE

147   "J. M. Maddox"—CCP, *12,* 3564.

148   "most brilliant one"—quoted in Stebbins, p. 53.

"her superior"—Stebbins, p. 51.

"acquisition to our stage"—quoted in *Spirit,* March 22, 1845.

"gift is Miss Cushman's"—quoted in Clement, *Charlotte Cushman,* p. 37.

"had amongst us"—quoted in *Spirit,* March 22, 1845.

"inelegancies"—quoted in Yeater, "Charlotte Cushman," p. 55.

"rude and violent"—ibid.

149   "tragedienne of her time"—Odell, *Shakespeare: From Betterton to Irving* (New York: Benjamin Blom, 1963), *2,* 251.

"make it complete"—CCP, *1,* 20.

snakelike hiss—Moody, *Edwin Forrest,* p. 216.

"of the public"—*Age and Argus,* quoted in *Spirit,* March 22, 1845.

interest in her—Marston, *Our Recent Actors, 2,* 74.

150   "go to Hell!"—Maud Morgan, *Strings of Memory: The Autobiography of Maud Morgan* (n.p., 1938), p. 9.

"of the evening"—February 22, 1845, p. 125, quoted in Lorenz, *Charlotte Cushman,* p. 344.

under the applause—London *Literary Gazette,* March 1, 1845, p. 141, quoted in Yeater, "Charlotte Cushman," p. 53.

"would sound badly"—CCP, *1,* 20.

"not meet them"—CCP, *1,* 21.

was "a butcher"—quoted in Phelps, *Players of a Century,* p. 203.

151   "him with me"—CCP, *1,* 20.

"you think I do"—CCP, *1,* 21.

"then and there"—a London paper quoted in Stebbins, p. 54.

152   Beatrice, and Portia—Price, *Life of Charlotte Cushman,* pp. 62–63.

"weeping in an audience"—quoted in *Spirit,* April 5, 1845, p. 66.

"admirable a manner"—April 18, 1845, quoted in Lorenz, *Charlotte Cushman,* p. 247.

"nobleman over here"—CCP, *1,* 28.

"sick of it"—CCP, *1,* 22.

"rush to rehearsal"—CCP, *8,* 2499.

153   "they can be"—CCP, *1,* 27.

"painful to me"—CCP, *1,* 2n.

"the civilized world"—CCP, *1,* 28.

154 bright talk around him—*The Correspondence of Thomas Carlyle and Ralph Waldo Emerson: 1834–1872* (Boston: Osgood, 1883), *1,* 199.

"at my age"—quoted in "Rogers, Samuel," *Dictionary of National Biography,* p. 141.

"like him consumedly"—CC to Mackey, March 14 [1845], at DFo.

156 "Christ had said"—quoted in Alethea Hayter, *A Sultry Month: Scenes of London Literary Life in 1846* (London: Faber and Faber, 1965), p. 38.

"Falstaffian mask"—*The Education of Henry Adams: An Autobiography* (Boston: Houghton Mifflin, 1961), p. 124.

"genius for head"—James Pope-Hennessy, *Monckton Milnes: The Years of Promise: 1809–1851* (New York: Farrar, Straus, 1955), p. 114.

Lieutenant Disraeli—CCP, *8,* 2499.

"intensity of feeling"—CCP, *9,* 2661.

157 "The Avenging Child"—CCP, *8,* 2499.

"but they did"—ibid.

"a skipper at sea"—*The Autobiography and Letters of Mrs. M. O. W. Oliphant* (New York: Dodd, Mead, 1899), pp. 38–39.

a glass of beer—J. R. D., in *The New York Times,* September 30, 1851, p. 1.

"kneel" at her feet—"H. W.," quoted in Stebbins, p. 17.

158 "which explained all"—CCP, *14,* 3970.

"Infatuation had failed—*Illustrated London News,* May 3, 1845.

"will bring me up"—CCP, *1,* 28.

"hold you long"—quoted in Stebbins, p. 50.

"of our lives"—quoted in Stebbins, p. 50.

CHAPTER THIRTEEN

160 "been done before!"—Charles Cushman to Emma [Stebbins], quoting CC, in CCP, *8,* 2499.

rest of the hour—Cuthbert Bede, "Miss Cushman: A Reminiscence," *Belgravia, 29* (May, 1876): 333.

blood turn "cold"—CCP, *11,* 3467.

"Rachel ever achieved"—untitled contemporary newspaper clipping at NN-T.

161 challenge to the world—CCP, *10,* 2970.

"I have ever met"—CC to Coleman, June, 1845, at MH-T.

"at every turn, 'on!' "—CC to Mrs. Jameson, July 5 [1845], at MH-T.

"glorious creature"—quoted in A. G. L'Estrange, *The Friendships of Mary Russell Mitford as Recorded in Letters from her Literary Correspondents* (London: Hurst and Blackett, 1882), *2,* 88.

"think of you"—quoted in Frederick G. Kenyon, *The Letters of Elizabeth Barrett Browning* (London: Smith, Elder, 1898), *1,* 307.

"summer brightness"—Vera Watson, *Mary Russell Mitford* (London: Evans, n.d.), p. 261.

162 "of great genius"—quoted in Henry Chorley, *Letters of Mary Russell Mitford* (second series, London: R. Bentley, 1872), *1,* 220

"long for them"—CC to Mrs. Howitt, London, n.d., at DFo.

163 "three pounds and *a half*"—Marston, *Our Recent Actors, 2,* 68.

"you cannot perform"—ibid., pp. 72–73.

164 "a boy of twelve"—quoted in Trewin, *Mr. Macready,* p. 171.

"Only an Actress!"—quoted in *The Letters of Robert Browning and Elizabeth Barrett Barrett 1845–1846* (New York: Hooper, 1898), *1,* 154.

"name Miss Cushman"—Toynbee, *Diaries of Macready, 2,* 300.

"told won't go"—CC to Mrs. Creswick, August 11, 1845, at CSmH.

"perfect inconsistency"—Toynbee, *Diaries of Macready, 2,* 300–01.

165 "melting mood"—playbill for Theatre Royal, Hull, England, September 3, 1845, in CCP, *15.*

"away with you"—quoted in Lester Wallack, *Memories of Fifty Years* (New York: Scribner's, 1889), pp. 76–77.

166 "vain struggling"—quoted in Lawrence and Elizabeth Hanson, *Necessary Evil: The Life of Jane Welsh Carlyle* (New York: Macmillan, 1952), pp. 260–61.

"in love with"—ibid., p. 263.

"protection and strength"—CCP, *9,* 3463.

"exquisitely sad"—CCP, *11,* 3442.

167 "don't deserve it"—CCP, *11,* 3444.

"as she does"—CCP, *11,* 3455.

"effective performance"—G. Jewsbury to E. Stebbins, February 6, 1877, in CCP, *11,* 3468.

"for a nose"—Coleman, *An Actor's Life, 1,* 293

"internal fire"—ibid., p. 294.

168 "comeliness in Charlotte Cushman"—ibid., p. 295.

"her *debut* here"—ibid., pp. 296–97.

"strength in them?"—ibid., p. 303.

169 "feminine loveliness"—quoted in Roger Manvell, "Ellen Terry's Lady Macbeth," *The Listener, 77* (February 2, 1967): 159.

"in them" publicly—Coleman, *An Actor's Life, 2,* 362–63.

"in her skull?"—Frances Ann Kemble, *Records of Later Life* (New York: Holt, 1882), pp. 459–60.

170 "I have made"—CC to George Combe, November 21, 1845, at ScNE.

"thing as Romeo"—CC to Benjamin Webster, March 21 [1846], at MH-T.

171 "like an owl!"—quoted in Coleman, *An Actor's Life, 1,* 310.

"one you are"—quoted in J. H. Stoddart, *Recollections of a Player* (New York: Barnes, 1903), pp. 34–35.

"piece of business"—ibid., p. 19.

"have ever seen"—Glasgow *Dramatic Review,* December 3, 1845, p. 273.

172 "varied and alive"—quoted in ibid., p. 274.

CHAPTER FOURTEEN

173 "was not married"—CC to unnamed person, n.d., at MH-T.

"virtuous society"—Combe to CC, December 25, 1845, at ScEN.

"the slander boldly"—CC to unnamed person, n.d., at MH-T.

page

174 "names is false"—Combe to CC, Edinburgh, December 25, 1845.

175 "a lazy company"—CC to Webster, Tuesday noon, at MH-T.

to leave the cast—Stebbins, pp. 58–59.

"to be a *boy*"—quoted in N. M. Ludlow, *Dramatic Life as I found It: A Record of Personal Experience, etc.* (St. Louis, Mo.: Jones, 1880), p. 316.

"maiden modesty"—*John Bull*, January 3, 1846, p. 12.

"dangerous young man"—quoted in Elizabeth M. Puknat, "Romeo Was a Lady: Charlotte Cushman's London Triumph," *New York Theatre Annual, 9* (1951): 66.

"in actual life"—Marston, *Our Recent Actors, 2,* 76.

marry her sister—quoted in "Charlotte Cushman," *The Nation, 19* (November 12, 1874): 314.

the ringing applause—*John Bull*, January 3, 1846, p. 12.

176 "ardent human being"—quoted in Stebbins, p. 60.

"Miss O'Neil"—quoted in Stebbins, pp. 60–61.

"how to go on"—quoted in Stebbins, p. 63.

"considerable merit"—*John Bull*, January 3, 1846, p. 12.

"at 1/4 before 10?"—note from Samuel Rogers to CC, at CSmH.

"with Miss Cushman"—Jane Welsh Carlyle to Babbie [January 19, 1846], at ScEN.

177 "a week as 'Romeo'"—*Illustrated London News*, January 24, 1846, p. 59.

"storm was on"—quoted in *Spirit*, July 4, 1846.

"black forever"—Robert Browning to Elizabeth Barrett Barrett, January 31, 1846, in *Letters of Robert Browning and Elizabeth Barrett Barrett, 1,* 443.

"by the ultimate result?"—Combe to CC, February 7, 1846, at ScEN.

178 "think of it"—quoted in Marston, *Our Recent Actors, 2,* 77–78.

"but the mind"—quoted in Bede, "Miss Cushman," p. 338.

179 "the mother's favorite"—CCP, *11,* 3466.

"as Daniel Webster's"—Washington *Union*, July 13, 1846, quoted in Hershel Parker, "Gansevoort Melville's 1846 London Journal," *Bulletin of the New York Public Library, 69* (December, 1965; January, 1966; February, 1966): 634.

"when I left"—quoted in ibid., *70* (January, 1966): 38.

180 "escorting Miss Susan"—quoted in ibid., p. 44.

"for some time"—quoted in ibid., p. 48.

thirty performances—Wemyss, *Modern Standard Drama, 10,* 5.

181 "forbid the bans!"—quoted in George Vandenhoff, *Dramatic Reminiscences; Or, Actors and Actresses in England and America* (London: Cooper, 1860), p. 292.

"aslape in the cheer!"—quoted in ibid.

"bore it down"—quoted in Coleman, *An Actor's Life, 2,* 346.

182 "if he *dared!*"—quoted in Moody, *Edwin Forrest,* p. 227.

"It is Forrest"—quoted in Toynbee, *Diaries of Macready, 2,* 329.

"Bra-vo, Char-let!"—quoted in *Harper's Weekly*, March 4, 1876, p. 193.

"mere scenic illusion"—quoted in New York *Herald,* May, 2, 1846, p. 138.

"choose to assert"—CC to Combe, April 1, 1846, at ScEN.

183 "and a *woman*"—quoted in New York *Sunday Dispatch,* September 6, 1846.

CHAPTER FIFTEEN

184 "bursts of passion"—Glasgow *Dramatic Review, 50* (May 20, 1846): 398.

185 "*beau ideal* of a woman"—untitled clipping from Liverpool *Journal,* at MH-T.

"proprieties bite dreadfully"—CCP, *11,* 3461.

"regal paradises"—Sophia Hawthorne, quoted in Rose Hawthorne Lathrop, *Memories of Hawthorne* (Boston: Houghton Mifflin, 1897), p. 235.

186 "my next speech"—quoted in Fred Belton, *Random Recollections of an Old Actor* (London: Tinsley Brothers, 1880), pp. 204–06.

187 "unescapable woman"—CC to unnamed person, quoted in Stebbins, p. 84.

"hair's breadth of it!"—quoted in Hayter, *A Sultry Month,* p. 155.

"brimstone of a creature"—Elizabeth Drew, *The Literature of Gossip: Nine English Letterwriters* (New York: Norton, 1964), p. 197.

"Hell"—ibid., p. 211.

"Carlyle's wife"—quoted in Hayter, *A Sultry Month,* p. 155.

188 "it is always true"—Howitt, "The Miss Cushmans," p. 30.

"yourself upon it"—quoted in Stebbins, p. 75.

"doing their duty"—H. H. [Helen Hunt Jackson], *Bits of Travel* (Boston: Roberts, 1891), p. 299.

"the morning air"—quoted in *Letters of Charles Dickens,* ed. Walter Dexter (Bloomsbury, England: Nonesuch Press, 1938), *2,* 279–80.

"I ever tried"—quoted in John Nichol, *Thomas Carlyle* (New York: Harper and Brothers, 1904), pp. 110–11.

"front and ruffles"—Margaret Howitt, *Mary Howitt: An Autobiography* (Boston: Isbister, 1889), *2,* 37.

189 "in any hemisphere"—quoted in *The Gathering of the Forces: Editorials, Essays, Literary and Dramatic Reviews and Other Material Written by Walt Whitman as Editor of the Brooklyn Daily Eagle in 1846 and 1847* (New York: Putnam's, 1920), p. 344.

"Theatre Royals"—in Brooklyn *Eagle,* August 14, 1846.

"professionally with me!"—Toynbee, *Diaries of Macready, 2,* 348.

190 "Shakespeare ever drew"—quoted in Clement, *Charlotte Cushman,* p. 51.

"green room all over"—quoted in Hanson, *Necessary Evil,* p. 236.

"I am not head"—quoted in ibid., p. 106.

"have gone mad"—quoted in ibid., p. 156.

"the butt-end"—quoted in ibid.

191 "been more explicit"—quoted in Anne Ritchie, *Records of Tennyson, Ruskin, and Browning* (New York: Hooper, 1893), p. 157.

page

"to talk with Carlyle"—Ralph Waldo Emerson, "Carlyle," in *The Complete Essays and Other Writings of Ralph Waldo Emerson* (New York: Random House, 1950), p. 925.

"her husband is there?"—Margaret Fuller to Emerson, November 16, 1846, in R. W. Emerson, W. H. Channing, and J. F. Clarke, *Memoirs of Margaret Fuller Ossoli* (Boston: Roberts Brothers, 1884), *2*, 187

"rose water imbecilities"—Carlyle in his diary, March 13, 1872, in William Allingham, *A Diary* (London: Macmillan, 1907), p. 208.

"life and death"—Emerson, *Margaret Fuller Ossoli, 2,* 187.

"he gets among them"—Fitzgerald, *Letters to Fanny Kemble,* p. 9.

192 captured in marble—Adam Badeau, *The Vagabond* (New York: Rudd and Carleton, 1859), p. 44.

"effort together"—quoted in Clement, *Charlotte Cushman,* p. 53.

"rescue her from this?"—quoted in Hayter, *A Sultry Month,* p. 146.

"rejoiced"—Elizabeth Barrett Browning to Mrs. Martin, August 7, 1847, quoted in Kenyon, *Letters of Elizabeth Barrett Browning, 1,* 338.

"compete with her"—London *Theatrical Times, 1* (September 5, 1846): 98.

193 " 'danger' before"—Liverpool *Journal,* January 2, 1847.

"unprofitable affair"—Liverpool *Mercury,* January 18, 1847.

"practicing *steadily*"—Liverpool *Mercury* supplement, January 8, 1847.

"very great desire"—CCP, *10,* 2930.

CHAPTER SIXTEEN

195 "any other country"—*Pennsylvanian,* June 15, 1847.

"may retire forever"—*Spirit,* June 12, 1847, p. 179.

"hand or foot or eyelash"—Chorley to CC, May 8, 1847, in CCP, *10,* 2955.

196 "may attain a century"—*Theatrical Times,* July 31, 1847, p. 243.

"an untried work?"—Elizabeth Barrett Browning to Mary Mitford, February 8, 1847, quoted in Kenyon, *Letters of Elizabeth Barrett Browning, 1,* 321.

"our next campaign"—*Theatrical Times, 2* (August 14, 1847): 252.

"as I am doing!"—quoted in *The New York Times,* May 26, 1878, p. 10.

197 half a million—Lathrop, *Memories of Hawthorne,* p. 267.

"as something amusing"—*Spectator,* October 9, 1847.

"for the civility"—Toynbee, *Diaries of Macready, 2,* 373.

"frigid mannerisms"—quoted in a note by L. B. Stowe at MCR.

"off the stage"—untitled contemporary newspaper clipping at MH-T.

198 "true friends!"—Toynbee, *Diaries of Macready, 2,* 373.

"of her success"—*Spectator,* October 9, 1847.

"to get on"—CC to Povey, October 17, 1847, at NNP.

"to witness it"—London *Examiner,* October 9, 1847, quoted in Yeater, "Charlotte Cushman," p. 55.

"the theatre myself"—quoted in Fitzgerald, *Letters to Fanny Kemble,* p. 177.

Notes

199 "to the world"—London *Athenaeum* (1854): 447.

"bonnet-strings"—Chorley to CC, October 28, 1847, in CCP, *10,* 2951.

"duplicity and meanness"—William Winter, *Shakespeare on the Stage* (New York: Moffat, Yard, 1911), p. 556.

200 grunt of relief—Henry Austin Clapp, *Reminiscences of a Dramatic Critic* (Boston: Houghton Mifflin, 1902), p. 88.

"the source of tears"—ibid., p. 90.

201 good to the part?—referred to by Chorley to CC, October 28, 1847, in CCP, *10,* 2951.

"are my critics?"—Toynbee, *Diaries of Macready, 2,* 374.

"histrionic poetry"—quoted in Price, *Life of Charlotte Cushman,* pp. 150–51.

"you played the part"—Chorley to CC, October 28, 1847, in CCP, *10,* 2951.

202 "none in England"—CC to Povey, October 17, 1847, at NNP.

"multitude thought of me"—Toynbee, *Diaries of Macready, 2,* 376.

"go to hell"—ibid., p. 375.

"more deliberate judgment"—Macready to CC, November 2, 1847, in CCP, *12,* 3538.

"of the sublime"—*Theatrical Times, 2* (November 13, 1847): 355.

"a very pleasing actress"—ibid., August 21, 1847, p. 258.

offended the ear—ibid., November 13, 1847, p. 355.

203 "had been *talked*"—quoted in Leonard Huxley, *Jane Welsh Carlyle: Letters to Her Family, 1839–1863* (Garden City, N.Y.: Murray, 1924), pp. 303–04.

"and good sense"—Elizabeth Davis Bancroft, *Letters from England 1846–1849* (New York: Scribner's, 1904), p. 156.

"reserve about acting"—Charles and Frances Brookfield, *Mrs. Brookfield and Her Circle* (New York: Scribner's, 1906), p. 251.

"Will it wash?"—George W. Bell to Charles Cushman, in CCP, *9,* 2661.

"to Dr. Muspratt"—CC to Mrs. Howitt, December 5, 1847, at PU.

204 "to Mrs. Mowatt"—Anna Cora Mowatt, *Autobiography of an Actress; or, Eight Years on the Stage* (Boston: Ticknor, Reed, and Fields, 1854), pp. 273–75.

"of genteel comedians"—quoted in Mary Caroline Crawford, *The Romance of the American Theatre* (New York: Little Brown, 1940), p. 450.

CHAPTER SEVENTEEN

205 "one of his poems"—quoted in Hanson, *Necessary Evil,* p. 357.

"sleep interrupted it"—ibid., p. 358.

206 "visit it was"—quoted in Ralph L. Rusk, *The Letters of Ralph Waldo Emerson* (New York: Columbia University Press, 1939), *4,* 5.

"Quite possible"—untitled newspaper clipping from Philadelphia *Bulletin,* at MH-T.

in "her" roles—Kemble, *Records of Later Life,* p. 630.

"a deeper fall"—Toynbee, *Diaries of Macready, 2,* 386

"(to look well)"—Jewsbury to CC [February, 1848] in CCP, *11,* 3438.

page

207   social ornament—Dr. W. F. Hardie, "The Muspratts and the British Chemical Industry," *Endeavor, 14* (January, 1955): 32.

"what I am"—quoted in Stebbins, p. 79.

"and *no more!*"—CC to Coxin, April 28, 1848, in CCP.

208   "you come home again"—quoted in Trewin, *Mr. Macready*, p. 216.

"heap of filth"—Toynbee, *Diaries of Macready, 2,* 399.

"mischief in America!"—ibid., p. 388.

"expenses were paid"—ibid., p. 397

disinterest in London theatre—Downer, *The Eminent Tragedian,* p. 288.

and the like—*Spirit,* July 29, 1848, quoted in Downer, *The Eminent Tragedian,* p. 373.

"for want of room"—Toynbee, *Diaries of Macready, 2,* 400.

209   candles held over head—Trewin, *Mr. Macready,* p. 154.

210   "immature growth"—quoted in Susanne Howe, *Geraldine Jewsbury: Her Life and Errors* (London: Allen and Unwin, 1935), pp. 105–110.

"circulation in families"—quoted in Hanson, *Necessary Evil,* p. 358.

set of chessmen—Mrs. Victor B. Cushman to Lyman Beecher Stowe, March 18, 1942, at MCR.

perhaps even "eminence"—*Theatrical Times, 3* (October 21, 1848): 411.

"by no means uncommon"—Elizabeth Barrett Browning to her sister Arabel, October 22, 1852, at NN.

211   "a lofty position"—January 27, 1849, *4,* 23.

"It was perfection"—Hull *Advertiser,* March 9, 1849, at MH-T.

212   "from the stage"—quoted in Trewin, *Mr. Macready,* p. 218.

"proved a liar!"—quoted in Charles Haynes Haswell, *Reminiscences of an Octogenarian of the City of New York: 1816–1860* (New York: Harpers, 1896), p. 452.

"the English hog!"—quoted in Trewin, *Mr. Macready,* p. 220.

Washington Irving—William K. Northall, *Before and Behind the Curtain; or, Fifteen Years' Observations among the Theatres of New York* (New York: Burgess, 1851), p. 142.

"him to remain"—Haswell, *Reminiscences,* p. 453.

213   "Three cheers for Ned Forrest!"—Northall, *Before and Behind the Curtain,* p. 140.

"den of the aristocracy!"—quoted in Moody, *Edwin Forrest,* p. 277.

people lay dead—Downer, *The Eminent Tragedian,* p. 306.

land she came from—*The New York Times,* quoted in New York *Weekly Yankee,* June 23, 1849.

"in the case of Mr. Forrest"—*Illustrated London News,* June 2, 1849, p. 369.

"raving madman"—quoted in Dickens, *Life, Letters and Speeches, 2,* 156 (Dexter edition).

"safe and unharmed"—quoted in Moody, *Edwin Forrest,* p. 270.

214   "of her time"—Marston, *Our Recent Actors, 2,* 66.

CHAPTER EIGHTEEN

215   "go to heaven"—New York *Weekly Yankee,* August 4, 1849.

page
216 "Hurray for Our Charlotte!"—quoted in *Spirit*, September 15, 1849, p. 360.
"altogether beyond her"—CC to James T. Fields, September 29, 1849, at MH-T.
217 "other means being open"—CC to Chippendale, September 20, 1849, at MH-T.
"subordinate parts!"—quoted in Armstrong, *Fanny Kemble*, p. 318.
218 right for it—Richard Henry Stoddard, *Recollections Personal and Literary* (New York: Barnes, 1903), p. 184.
"contentious tempers"—Whitman in Brooklyn *Eagle*, February 12, 1847, quoted in Whitman, *Gathering of the Forces*, p. 315.
219 faces greeted her—*Spirit*, October 13, 1849, p. 408.
220 "intellectual jewels"—ibid.
"emphatically *Our Charlotte*"—New York *Weekly Yankee*, October 20, 1849.
"through the senses"—Alfred Ayres quoted in Wilson, *History of American Acting*, p. 51.
220 "the purest character"—*Spirit*, October 13, 1849, p. 408.
"half her influence"—Barrett, *Charlotte Cushman*, p. 14.
"they ought to come"—quoted in Stebbins, p. 150.
Meg her "greatest"—*Spirit*, January 20, 1849, p. 420.
221 "my finest characters"—quoted in Marston, *Our Recent Actors, 2,* 78.
"Cush-mania"—*Weekly Yankee*, November 3, 1849.
"Cushmania, Before and After"—cartoon clipping in Durang, *History of the Philadelphia Stage, 5,* facing p. 242.
her vivid splendor—Leon Edel, *Henry James: The Untried Years 1843–1870* (Philadelphia: Lippincott, 1953), p. 100.
"doing it myself"—quoted in Bradford, *Biography and the Human Heart,* p. 121.

CHAPTER NINETEEN

222 "anti-American"—cited in New York *Weekly Yankee*, December 15, 1849.
"attitudinizer"—quoted in Stowe's note, at MCR.
turned away hundreds—Durang, *History of the Philadelphia Stage, 5,* 302.
"her poor sisterhood"—ibid., *4, 176.*
223 content with her victory—William Corbyn to Ludlow and Smith, November 2, 1849, at MoSHi.
224 "well-puffed star"—Walt Whitman, quoted in Glenn Hughes, *A History of the American Theatre 1700–1950* (New York: Samuel French, 1951), p. 147.
"ungraceful in the extreme"—quoted in *Spirit*, December 8, 1849, p. 493.
"less acting better"—quoted in Edward Wagenknecht, *Longfellow: A Full-Length Portrait* (New York: Longmans, Green, 1955), p. 185.
225 "intelligent forehead"—Frederika Bremer, *America of the Fifties: Letters of Frederika Bremer* (London: American Scandinavian Foundation, 1924), p. 49.

page

"him surely come"—Julia Ward Howe to CC, January 19 [1849], in CCP, *11*, 3363.

226   "peculiar class of people"—CC to William Fredericks [January, 1850], at MH-T.

"arrest or stoppage"—Corbyn to Ludlow and Smith, December 13, 1849, at MoSHi.

CHAPTER TWENTY

228   "touching their sympathies"—*Daily Picayune,* February 12, 1850, p. 2.

"in writing!"—quoted in Coad and Mims, *American Stage,* p. 176.

229   to greater receipts—C. W. Couldock to J. F. Pray, March 27, 1850, in CCP, *10,* 2980.

"remarkably well"—*Daily Picayune,* February 12, 1850.

Portnam Square rooms—referred to by Chorley to CC, March 7, 1850, in CCP, *10,* 2933.

bought him easily—Longfellow's journal, ms. at Longfellow House, Cambridge, Massachusetts.

"not over-courteous"—CC to J. C. Adams, April 19 [1850], at NN.

230   "peculiarly fine"—Aloysius I. Mudd, "The Theatres of Washington from 1835 to 1850," *Records of the Columbia Historical Society, 6* (1903) : 261.

"free list entirely"—quoted in Wilson, *History of American Acting,* p. 48.

231   "in the land"—*Spirit,* May 18, 1850, p. 156.

"view of the stage"—*Literary World, 7* (September 7, 1850) : 195.

"than in this country"—Longfellow's journal.

their bright friends, the Carlyles—Whittier to CC, November 10, 1868, CCP, *14,* 3907.

"very agreeable" visit—Longfellow's journal.

"in that respect"—CC to Mrs. Mann, at MBHi.

232   "not this fall"—CC to Fredericks, September 15, 1850, at MH-T.

$5 per head—*Literary World, 7* (September 7, 1850) : 195.

"might be excited"—CC to Fredericks, September 19 [1850], at MH-T.

233   "shame and disgust"—untitled contemporary newspaper clipping at MH-T.

farewell some months hence?—CC to Fredericks, November 8, 1850, at MH-T.

234   "damn fool head off!"—quoted in Clara Morris, *Life on the Stage: My Personal Experiences and Recollections* (New York: McClure, Phillips, 1901), p. 131.

"cleverest young man I have seen"—CC to Fredericks, January 5, 1851, at MH-T.

236   bleak crumpled reflection—this Clarke report is from an untitled newspaper clipping by Celia Logan at MH-T, quoting an undated article in the New York *Sunday Dispatch* by Don Piatt, and from a letter from Kathryn M. Miller to Lyman Beecher Stowe, dated January 15, 1941, in Stowe's notes at MCR.

"worn out with it"—CC to Fredericks, January 5, 1851, at MH-T.

237   brains—or feelings?—ibid.

      white children, or else—Bede, "Miss Cushman," pp. 338–39.

238   hard on her nerves—E. Dunbar to Chloe Dunbar [March 10, 1851] at LU.

      "nights to me"—CC to Sol Smith, February 25, 1851, at MoSHi.

      "those actors"—quoted in Matthews and Hutton, *Macready and Forrest,* p. 11.

239   "challenged even Rachel"—*Tallis's Dramatic Magazine* (February, 1851): 103.

      burst into cheers—Mrs. John Greene, *Married Life on the Stage,* quoted in Durang, *History of the Philadelphia Stage, 5,* 218.

      "forget your business"—untitled contemporary newspaper clipping at MH-T.

240   with her heels—Clement, *Charlotte Cushman,* pp. 68–69.

      "reed-like Meg Merrilies"—Chicago *Daily Journal,* July 31, 1851, quoted in Napier Wilt, "The History of the Rice Theatres" (Ph.D. diss., University of Chicago, 1923), p. 154.

      "to act with novices"—CC to J. B. Wright, September 30, 1851, in Locke Collection Scrapbook, *139,* at NN-T.

      "my return from Europe"—CC to Wright, October 14, 1851, quoted in untitled newspaper clipping from Boston *Evening Transcript,* July 22, 1916, at MH-T.

      her legally adopted son—CC to Mitchell, November 29, 1851, at NjP.

241   "as of disappointment"—Longfellow's journal, November 5, 1851.

      "to do it myself!"—quoted in Clement, *Charlotte Cushman,* p. 68.

242   "It was grand"—Harriet Hosmer to Miss Carr, January, 1852, quoted in Cornelia Carr, *Harriet Hosmer: Letters and Memories* (London: Moffat, Yard, 1913), p. 17.

      "in so short a time"—ibid.

      doors might open—Lydia Maria Child, "Harriet E. Hosmer, a Biographical Sketch," *The Ladies' Repository, 21* (January, 1861).

      "my best friend"—Lydia Maria Child, quoted in James Parton et al., *Eminent Women of the Age: Being Narratives of the Lives and Deeds of the Most Prominent Women of the Present Generation* (Hartford, Conn.: Betts, 1868), p. 596.

243   near the White House—CC to Seward, January 18, 1852, at NRU.

      "yours very truly, Charlotte Cushman"—CC to Chippendale, February 23, 1852, at MH-T.

      "retirement from the Stage"—playbill in CCP, *15.*

244   "she wishes it"—Hawthorne to Greenwood, April 17, 1852, typescript in collection of Norman Holmes Pearson at CtY.

      "my Penates"—CC to Longfellow, June 13, 1852, at MH-T.

      "that milks me"—quoted in Durang, *History of the Philadelphia Stage, 6,* 363.

245   "weary beyond description"—CC to James Brown, May 15, 1852, at MH-T.

      "ever forget that?"—New York *Empire City* clipping, 1852, at DFo.

      "from the profession"—*Spirit,* May 8, 1852, p. 144.

Notes

page

246 found her "beautiful"—George Eliot to Sara Hennell, quoted in Gordon S. Haight, *The George Eliot Letters* (New Haven: Yale University Press, 1955), *2*, 40.

247 "actress ever lived"—CC to Grace Greenwood, July 9, 1852, at NNC.

"truth and inspiration"—Madame de Marguerittes, "Mademoiselle Rachel and Miss Cushman," *Sharpe's London Journal, 15* (June 1, 1852): 13–14.

249 "she survived it"—Hawthorne, *English Notebooks*, p. 616.

"morn to dewy eve"—Greenwood to unidentified person, inserted in CSmH copy of Parton, *Eminent Women, 1* (extra-illustrated edition).

"a bit of marble"—quoted in Child, "Harriet Hosmer," p. 4.

250 "bower of curls"—quoted in Samuel Longfellow, *The Life of Henry Wadsworth Longfellow: With Extracts from his Journals and Correspondence* (Boston: Ticknor, 1886), *2*, 309.

shy and self-conscious—CC to Stebbins, quoted in Stebbins, p. 169.

"I must say!"—Elizabeth Barrett Browning to John Kenyon, quoted in Kenyon, *Letters of Elizabeth Barrett Browning, 2*, 89.

251 "always golden"—quoted in Gardner B. Taplin, *The Life of Elizabeth Barrett Browning* (New Haven: Yale University Press, 1957), p. 266.

"a little more, perhaps"—Elizabeth Barrett Browning to Arabel, October 22, 1852, at NN.

253 "she shall learn!"—quoted in Child, "Harriet Hosmer," p. 4.

255 "world has ever seen"—quoted in Coleman, *An Actor's Life, 1,* 306.

the same offer—Child, "Harriet Hosmer," p. 5.

suspect herself—Margaret Farrand Thorp, *Female Persuasion: Six Strong-Minded Women* (New Haven: Yale University Press, 1949), p. 156.

256 "I shall not"—Story to Lowell, February 11, 1853, quoted in Gertrude Reese Hudson, *Browning to His American Friends: Letters between the Brownings, the Storys, and James Russell Lowell 1841–1890* (London: Barnes and Noble, 1965), p. 255.

"first woman who ever had"—ibid., pp. 272–73.

257 "display my gratitude"—Lowell to Frances G. Shaw, Rome, 1851, quoted in Charles Eliot Norton, *Letters of James Russell Lowell* (New York: Harper, 1893), *1,* 193.

the finished picture—original now in the Cushman family collection.

"I ever saw"—quoted in Henry James, *William Wetmore Story and His Friends: From Letters, Diaries, and Recollections* (New York: Grove, 1957), *1,* 269.

"such modern art, certainly"—quoted in William Clyde de Vane and K. L. Knickerbocker, *New Letters of Robert Browning* (New Haven: Yale University Press, 1950), p. 74.

"soul and body together"—Elizabeth Barrett Browning to Mrs. Jameson, December 21, 1853, quoted in Kenyon, *Letters of Elizabeth Barrett Browning, 2,* 148.

"it so abounds"—quoted in Parton, *Eminent Women,* p. 160.

"place for an artist"—quoted in Margaret Farrand Thorp, *The Literary Sculptors* (Durham, N.C.: Duke University Press, 1965), p. 28.

page

258 "the capricious sea"—quoted in Parton, *Eminent Women,* p. 161.
      "come tonight too?"—Elizabeth Barrett Browning to CC, in CCP, *9.*
259 "to please you"—quoted in *Spirit,* February 26, 1876.
260 "to crush me"—CC to Greenwood, June 15, 1854, at NNC.

CHAPTER TWENTY-TWO

261 "Us off the stage"—Edmund Knowles Muspratt, *My Life and Work*
      (London: John Lane, 1917), p. 16.
262 "to be an actress"—Sophia Hawthorne to her mother, quoted in
      Lathrop, *Memories of Hawthorne,* p. 262.
      "fate matrimonial"—CC to Hawthorne [January 1, 1854], quoted in
      Stowe's notes, at MCR.
      tiny gold charms—Lathrop, *Memories of Hawthorne,* p. 261.
263 "but I loved her"—Julian Hawthorne, *Hawthorne and His Circle* (New
      York: Harper, 1903), pp. 149–50.
      "captive your soul"—Julian Hawthorne, *Memoirs of Julian Hawthorne*
      (New York: Macmillan, 1938), pp. 262–63.
      "(that is, in my house)"—Hawthorne to Ticknor, January 6, 1854,
      typescript in collection of Norman Holmes Pearson, at CtY.
      "strikes us, increased"—*Illustrated London News,* January 28, 1854,
      quoted in Lorenz, *Charlotte Cushman,* p. 275.
      "artistic excellence"—CC to Greenwood, June 15, 1854, at NNC.
      "highest rank of tragedy"—quoted in Price, *Life of Charlotte Cushman,*
      pp. 102–03.
264 "wonderfully startling"—Henry Morley, *The Journal of a London
      Playgoer from 1851 to 1866* (London: Routledge, 1866), p. 81.
      "dependent upon her"—CC to Greenwood, June 15, 1854, at NNC.
      played "finely"—quoted in Chorley's notice, *Athenaeum,* March 18,
      1854, p. 348.
265 "a young man would"—Elizabeth Barrett Browning to Miss Mitford,
      March 19, 1854, quoted in Kenyon, *Letters of Elizabeth Barrett
      Browning, 2,* 166.
      "works show him"—Browning to Forster, April 2, 1854, quoted in De
      Vane and Knickerbocker, *New Letters of Robert Browning,* p. 75.
      "manner as possible"—quoted in Charles Osborne, "Henry the Eighth
      and Padding: A Recollection of Miss Cushman," *Era Almanach*
      (1879): 111.
266 " 'Thy will be done' "—quoted in Stebbins, pp. 94–95.
267 " 'Horders, please, mem' "—quoted in Stebbins, pp. 108–09.
      "realism of the scene"—quoted in Laurence Irving, *Henry Irving: The
      Actor and His World* (New York: Macmillan, 1952), p. 76.
      "a painted fire"—quoted in Erroll Sherson, *London's Lost Theatres of
      the Nineteenth Century: With Notes on Plays and Players Seen
      There* (London: John Lane, 1925), p. 129.
268 "*Donnerwetter,* it's a woman!"—Richard Wagner, *My Life* (New
      York: Dodd, Mead, 1935), p. 634.
      "describe to you"—CC to Page, August 22, 1855, in Howell Collection.
      "by Titian"—Lowell to D. F. Briggs, September 18, 1856, quoted in
      Norton, *Letters of Lowell, 1,* 274.

page

269 "little store of art"—CC to Sophia Hawthorne, September 15, 1855, in NN Berg Collection.

"happier influences"—CC to Page, August 22, 1855.

270 "Ristori is a woman"—quoted in clipping from Brooklyn *Eagle,* pasted in copy of Stebbins at WM.

"were very unwell"—CC to Carrick, November 16 [1856], at ScEN.

271 "to do in the world"—George Eliot to Sara Hennell, March 2, 1858, quoted in Haight, *Letters of George Eliot, 2,* 439.

"thoughtful she is"—Harriet Hosmer to Wayman Crow, July 25, 1857, in Carr, *Harriet Hosmer,* p. 83.

273 "so much risk"—CC to Chippendale, August 4, 1857, at CSmH.

CHAPTER TWENTY-THREE

275 "of popular interest"—quoted in Murdoch, *The Stage,* p. 239.

"more delicate"—*Tribune,* September 29, 1857, quoted in Odell, *Annals, 7,* 8.

"destiny is fulfilled"—*Spirit,* October 10, 1857, p. 420.

"by emphasis alone"—ibid.

276 "Cooke, Kean, and Macready"—quoted in Stebbins, p. 217.

"as well as passion"—untitled contemporary newspaper clipping at DFo.

twenty-seven cents—Hughes, *The American Theatre,* p. 186.

277 "is better"—CC to Dear Sir, October 9, 1857, at CtY.

"like Charlotte Cushman"—quoted in *Spirit,* November 21, 1857, p. 484.

"This I want done"—CC to Julia Ward Howe (date illegible), at MH-T.

278 "about womankind"—Howe to CC, September 20 [1857], in CCP, *11,* 3364.

returned Julia's play—Julia Ward Howe, *Reminiscences: 1819–1899* (Boston: Houghton Mifflin, 1899), p. 240.

"would have been filled"—quoted in Laura E. Richards and Maud Howe Elliott, *Julia Ward Howe: 1819–1910* (Boston: Houghton Mifflin, 1925), p. 102.

279 curls to his lips—Emma Crow Cushman's memoirs, p. 2, in CCP, *15.*

280 "faithfully by my side"—Major J. B. Pond, *Eccentricities of Genuis: Memories of Famous Men and Women of the Platform and Stage* (New York: Dillingham, 1900), p. 316.

"true and devoted"—CC to Emma Crow, February 3, 1858, in CCP, *1,* 49.

281 "look better"—*Daily Picayune,* February 10, 1858.

where she belonged—Reignolds-Winslow, *Yesterdays with Actors,* p. 20.

282 "without limit"—quoted in Gamaliel Bradford, *Union Portraits* (Boston: Houghton Mifflin, 1916), p. 228.

"seldom enjoy"—Seward to CC, May 25, 1858, in CCP, *13,* 3700.

"almost visibly"—quoted in Stebbins, p. 139.

"greatest living actress"—playbill at TxU-T.

"strength and power"—quoted in *Spirit,* June 12, 1858.

283 "stage struck fit"—Ednah D. Cheney, *Louisa Mae Alcott: Her Life, Letters, and Journals* (Boston: Prang, 1889), p. 99.

"the purification of the stage"—Louisa Mae Alcott, *Jo's Boys and How They Turned Out* (Boston: Little, Brown, 1944), p. 157.

"would be *for me*"—quoted in Lilian Whiting, *Kate Field: A Record* (Boston: Little, Brown, 1899), p. 76.

284 "nailed to the masthead"—quoted in Boston *Journal,* February 18, 1876.

"her doing so"—*The New York Times,* July 7, 1858, p. 4.

CHAPTER TWENTY-FOUR

287 "at night in Rome"—quoted in Parton, *Eminent Women,* p. 597.

"thrown in my way"—CC to Emma Crow, March 8, 1859, in CCP, *1,* 110.

288 "breathable air"—Elizabeth Barrett Browning to Ruskin, June 3 [1859] quoted in Kenyon, *Letters of Elizabeth Barrett Browning, 2,* 316.

"stain it beforehand"—Hawthorne, *Passages from the French and Italian Note-Books of Nathaniel Hawthorne* (Boston: Osgood, 1871), *1,* 162.

"there it is"—quoted in Thorp, *Literary Sculptors,* p. 48.

289 "faithful care"—quoted in Albert Ten Eyck Gardner, *Yankee Stone-cutters: The First American School of Sculpture 1800–1850* (New York: Columbia University Press, 1945), p. 48.

"watching them"—quoted in Thorp, *Literary Sculptors,* p. 111.

"to flay him"—Hawthorne, *French and Italian Note-Books, 1,* 160.

"commonplace prosperity"—Hawthorne, *The Marble Faun* (Columbus: Ohio State University Press, 1968), p. 3.

"never made a scratch"—quoted in Thorp, *Literary Sculptors,* p. 157.

290 "man-ism"—CC to Emma Crow Cushman, January 15, 1863, in CCP, *2,* 616.

"till all is blue"—quoted in Annie Fields, *Authors and Friends* (Boston: Houghton Mifflin, 1896), p. 168.

"they were women?"—quoted in Edward Wagenknecht, *Harriet Beecher Stowe: The Known and the Unknown* (New York: Oxford University Press, 1965), p. 131.

"on in spirit"—Harriet Hosmer to unnamed person, March, 1861, in Carr, *Harriet Hosmer,* pp. 171–72.

"harmonious tune"—Lydia Maria Child, *Lettters from New York* (New York: Francis, 1844), p. 252.

"of much fun"—quoted in Whiting, *Kate Field,* p. 90.

291 "bitter against us"—quoted in ibid., pp. 95–96.

292 "eternal drama"—quoted in Clement, *Charlotte Cushman,* p. 53.

"by the good God"—quoted in Stebbins, p. 142.

293 "the *studio* way"—CC to Story, at TxU.

one particular lion—CC to Julia Wheeler, April 16, 1871, quoted in Stowe's notes at MCR.

"his spirit in"—Hawthorne, *French and Italian Note-Books, 2,* 11–12.

294 "she is dying?"—CC to Emma Crow, May 12, 1859, in CCP, *1,* 114.

"accomplished"—Liverpool *Daily Post,* May 11, 1859.

295 "ever had before"—CC to Emma Crow, October 18, 1859, in CCP, *1,* 120.

page

"Boston once more"—quoted in Stebbins, p. 160.

"birth or education"—CC to Kate Field, December 22, 1859, at MB.

296 "Capital of Italy"—CC to Field, February 14, 1860, at MB.

"'men I have known'"—CC to Emma Crow, February 8, 1860, in CCP, *I*, 130.

297 "Rome, you know!"—quoted in Willa Cather, *Not Under Forty* (New York: Knopf, 1936), p. 66.

"waiting her there"—Annie Field's diary, March 1, 1860, at MBHi.

"Brava! Brava!"—quoted in Stebbins, p. 97.

298 "obligations to you?"—CCP, *9*, 2751.

recommended the lawyer—Ruggles, *Prince of Players*, p. 96.

299 "happy, darling?"—CC to Emma Crow, April 5, 1860, in CCP, *I*, 141.

CHAPTER TWENTY-FIVE

300 "ashamed to say"—CC to Miss Dorr, September 15, 1860, in CCP.

301 frightened her now—CCP, *I*, 137.

302 "as 'Our Charlotte'"—*The New York Times*, October 1, 1860, p. 5.

so "superbly"—ibid., October 26, 1860, p. 5.

"not been invited"—CCP, *I*, 197.

"I can like best"—CC to Sir [1860 or 1861], at MH-T.

303 "'of the Union'"—CC to Wayman Crow, November 6, 1860, in CCP, *I*, 206.

304 "respect for Union"—ibid.

"a foot hold"—ibid.

"old Auntie's notions"—CC to James T. Fields, September 20, 1860, at CSmH.

305 "am and have been"—CC to Annie Fields, November 27 [1860], at CSmH.

"seem but twenty-eight"—quoted in Stebbins, p. 139.

a "mere willow"—untitled contemporary newspaper clipping at MH-T.

"bigger than I am"—quoted in Richard Lockridge, *Darling of Misfortune: Edwin Booth 1833–1893* (New York: Century, 1932), p. 96.

"big as a codfish!"—quoted in Winter, *Shakespeare on the Stage*, p. 480.

306 "Scotch sorceress"—[Paul Akers], "Our Artists in Italy, William Page," *Atlantic Monthly, 7* (February, 1861): p. 134.

"bottom of the page?"—CC to Annie Fields, December 25, 1860, at CSmH.

"amazed at myself"—CC to Emma Crow, January 29, 1861, in CCP, *I*, 235.

"to meet your wishes"—copy of playbill in CCP, *15*.

307 "so strong an arm"—*The New York Times*, February 26, 1861, p. 4.

308 thousand dollars in gold—CC to Emma Crow, February 26, 1861, in CCP, *I*, 241.

"the home of the brave"—playbill at MH-T.

309 "with *stems*"—CC to Emma Crow Cushman, May 9, 1861, in CCP, *I*, 248.

"Harpers or anybody"—James Fields to CC, May 14, 1861, in CCP, *II*, 3293.

"all right next fall"—CC to James Fields [May 15, 1861], at CSmH.

"to our children"—CC to Algernon Chase, May 2, 1861, in Stowe's note at MCR.

310   "will raise the statue"—CC to James Fields, June 26, 1861, at CSmH.

"a million half-alive women"—Higginson's journal, quoted in Mary Thacher Higginson, *Letters and Journals of Thomas Wentworth Higginson 1846–1906* (Boston: Houghton Mifflin, 1921), p. 244.

311   "mission and came away"—CC to Seward, July 9, 1861, in Nicolay Papers at DLC, quoted in David C. Mearns, "Charlotte Cushman's 'True and Faithful' Lincoln: Some Documents with Some Observations," *Lincoln Herald, 59* (summer, 1957), p. 4.

312   "both to love her"—CC to Emma Crow Cushman, July 26, 1861, in CCP, *1,* 298.

"the Lotus-Eaters"—Hawthorne to Stebbins, June 24, 1861, typescript in collection of Norman Holmes Pearson at CtY.

CHAPTER TWENTY-SIX

313   "laugh who win"—CC to Emma Crow Cushman, August 8, 1861, in CCP, *1,* 309.

314   "than his duties"—CC to Emma Crow Cushman, October 28, 1861, in CCP, *1,* 336.

"will grow upon him"—CC to Emma Crow Cushman, date illegible, in CCP, *2,* 499.

"to care for a woman"—CC to Emma Crow Cushman, October 28, 1861, in CCP, *1,* 336.

"law for us"—CC to Emma Crow Cushman, August 30, 1861, in CCP, *1,* 316.

"ever shall"—CC to Emma Crow Cushman, August 16, 1861, in CCP, *1,* 312.

"largest good of all"—quoted in Stebbins, pp. 178–79.

315   "tell it him again?"—Emilia Hawkes Venturi to CC, December 15, 1861, in CCP, *11,* 3251.

"kiss your hands"—CC to Jane Carlyle, January 28, 1862, at ScEN.

"of me *by you!*"—Jane Carlyle to CC, January 31, 1862, CCP.

316   "to write or to talk"—CC to Emma Crow Cushman, February 6, 1862, in CCP, *2,* 383.

"your faithful friend"—CC to Seward, December 4, 1861, at NRU.

"our *women workers!*"—ibid.

"develop well"—CC to Emma Crow Cushman [spring, 1862], CCP, *1,* 349.

her mother's name—CCP, *2,* 409.

317   the baby to rear?—CCP, *2,* 445.

"for God's"—CC to Emma Crow Cushman, May 24, 1862, in CCP, *1,* 457.

Rotterdam for shipment—CC to James Fields, March 15, 1862, at CSmH.

318   herself to applaud—Stillman, *Autobiography,* p. 363.

"open and malignant"—ibid., p. 360.

319   "they can well bear"—CC to Emma Crow Cushman [May 1, 1862], in CCP, *2,* 443.

"I know it"—CC to Emma Crow Cushman, May 7, 1862, in CCP, *2,* 448.

"my time or actions"—CC to Jane Carlyle, July 15, 1862, at ScEN.

failed to call—Browning to Isabella Blagden, July 19, 1862, quoted in Edward C. McAleer, *Dearest Isa: Robert Browning's Letters to Isabella Blagden* (Austin: University of Texas, 1951), p. 111.

"doing things in America"—CC to Emma Crow Cushman, first week of October, 1862, in CCP, *2, 471.*

"My soul aches for it"—CC to James Fields, November 21, 1862, at CSmH.

320 "to one of them"—ibid.

321 "Three cheers for Charlotte Cushman!"—Humphrey H. Swift, an eyewitness, to William Winter, October 7, 1906, at DFo.

"for 'sair e'en' "—CC to Seward, June 19, 1863, at NRU.

"to look further"—Seward to CC, June 20, 1863, in CCP, *13,* 3692.

remain in the room—Emma Crow Cushman, "Charlotte Cushman, a Memoir," in CCP, *15.*

322 "Sallie do?"—CCP, *10,* 2921.

"continue until then"—quoted in CC to Seward, August 2, 1863, at NRU.

"shining upon us"—Seward to CC, July 25, 1863, in CCP, *13,* 3963.

"and be glad"—CC to Seward, July 21, 1863, at NRU.

323 "over a weak woman"—CC to Emma Crow Cushman, February 7, 1863, in CCP, *2,* 530.

"lives for effects"—Annie Field's diary, September 20, 1863, quoted in Howe, *Memories of a Hostess,* p. 220.

"sleep is thrilling"—ibid., September 26, 1863.

to Rebel Sympathizers—Joseph George, Jr., "The Night John Wilkes Booth Played Before Abraham Lincoln," *Lincoln Herald, 59* (summer, 1957): 12.

"of the present age"—Washington *Daily Chronicle,* October 16, 1863, p. 2.

edged in ribbon—CC's copy of the program is in CCP, *15.*

324 "like the Arc de Triomphe"—Emma Crow Cushman's memoirs, CCP, *15, 5.*

tickets for $20—*The Diary of George Templeton Strong* (New York: Macmillan, 1952), p. 37.

"success of the year"—*Tribune,* October 23, 1863, p. 5.

two reigning stars—*Spirit,* October 31, 1863, p. 144.

surgical incision (footnote)—cf. Francis Wilson, *John Wilkes Booth: Fact and Fiction of Lincoln's Assassination* (Boston, Houghton Mifflin, 1929).

325 "save the fight!"—quoted in Morris, *Life on the Stage,* p. 98.

dying in battle—CC's reading copy in CCP, *15.*

"in the national struggle"—*The New York Times,* November 9, 1863.

CHAPTER TWENTY-SEVEN

326 "the old story"—Browning to Blagden, February 19, 1867, quoted in McAleer, *Dearest Isa,* p. 255.

327 "her own hands"—Story to editor of *Athenaeum,* December 19, 1863.

"namely, separation"—CC to Emma Crow Cushman, January, 1864, in CCP, *2,* 619.

frightened speechless—CC to Emma Crow Cushman, January, 1864, in CCP, *2,* 613.

"how beautiful they are"—CC to Emma Crow Cushman, January 22, 1864, in CCP, *2,* 617.

"an inferior calibre"—ibid., 620.

"chiselers"—CC to Emma Crow Cushman, March 3, 1865, in CCP, *3,* 759.

"I say it of all!"—CC to Story, April 1, 1864, at TxU.

328 "revolving around her"—quoted in James, *William Wetmore Story,* *2,* 127.

"ideas for himself"—CC to Field, August 26, 1864, at MB.

"a pure poet's heart"—CC to Fanny Seward, undated, quoted in Stebbins, p. 199.

"down to Camelot"—ibid.

"no acting can reach it"—CC to Emma Crow Cushman, quoted in Stebbins, p. 172.

329 "true and faithful!"—CC to Emma Crow Cushman, March 4, 1865, in CCP, *3,* 758.

"to recognize bondage"—CC to Fanny Seward, April 11, 1865, quoted in Stebbins, p. 191.

"glorious, free"—ibid.

330 "dread and fear"—CC to Emma Crow Cushman, April 28, 1865, in CCP, *3,* 781.

"to a public"—CC to Emma Crow Cushman, May 6, 1865, in CCP, *3,* 785.

saw it all—J. C. Derby, *Fifty Years among Authors, Books, and Publishers* (New York: Carleton, 1884), pp. 79–80.

"would say but cannot"—quoted in Stebbins, pp. 200–01.

"to have a name!"—CC to Field, August 23, 1865, at MB.

331 "noble, self-sacrificing"—CCP, *3,* 788.

"worst thing I ever saw"—quoted in Thorp, *Literary Sculptors,* p. 91.

"home to stay?"—Seward to CC, September 8, 1865, in CCP, *13,* 3704.

CHAPTER TWENTY-EIGHT

333 "she is happy"—Blagden to Field, October 27, 1865, at MB.

"spring in me"—CC to Ann Stevenson Lemon, January 13, 1866, at PPCc.

"unless seen"—ibid.

334 "longer with me"—CC to Seward, May 18, 1866, at NRU.

"my social duties"—CC to Seward, July 3, 1866, at NRU.

335 "in a public way"—CC to Field, September 29, 1866, at MB.

"beautiful in nature"—Fanny Seward to CC, July 12, 1866, at NRU.

"altar of *your country*"—CC to Seward, November 23, 1866, at NRU.

"something from Miss Stebbins"—CC to James Holland Beal, May 23, 1867, at MH-H.

"else to fight"—CC to Elizabeth Peabody, July 23, 1869, at MBHi.

"struggled and suffered"—quoted in Thorp, *Literary Sculptors,* p. 94.

336 "cultivated people"—CC to president of Boston YMCA, May 1, 1867, in CCP, *3,* 901.

"to be my proxy"—Seward to CC, July 17, 1867, in CCP, *13,* 3699.

"like sea-birds"—CC to Emma Crow Cushman, July 27, 1867, in CCP, *3,* 919.

337 "proud republic of America"—quoted in Joseph Rossi, *The Image of America in Mazzini's Writings* (Madison: University of Wisconsin Press, 1954), p. 73.

"by such a proceeding"—quoted in Leo Francis Stock, "An American Consul Joins the Papal Zouaves," *Catholic World, 132* (November, 1930) : 149.

"want him dismissed"—quoted in Rossi, *Image of America,* p. 74.

"lesson well learned"—CC to Seward, February 29, 1868, at NRU.

338 "for seven months"—CC to Lemon, December 30, 1867, at PPCc.

"delightfully human nature"—Peabody to Stebbins, quoted in Stebbins, pp. 139–40.

339 "no changes in me"—quoted in Whipple, *Charles Dickens,* p. 179.

"possibly help it"—CC to Annie Fields, July 15, 1868, at CSmH.

"have remarked it"—CC to Algernon Chase, July 13, 1868, quoted in Stowe's note at MCR.

340 "away from them?"—CC to Emma Crow Cushman, July 13, 1868, in CCP, *3,* 979.

"no whole, no harmony"—CC to Emma Crow Cushman, September 12, 1868, in CCP, *3,* 1032.

"my home in Newport"—CC to William F. Bridges, August 23, 1865, at MCR.

341 "under the tables and chairs"—Emma Crow Cushman's memoirs, p. 18, in CCP, *15.*

"by not coming"—quoted in Mrs. George W. Childs, *Talks with a Friend Recalling Those I Have Met and Entertained, also Incidents of Former Days* (typescript at PPHi), pp. 24–26.

342 "her trouble if possible"—quoted in Clement, *Charlotte Cushman,* p. 90.

"with dread and fear"—CC to Peabody, July 23, 1869, at MBHi.

"discovered it"—ibid.

"sweet and lovely?"—CC to James Fields, July 7, 1869, at CSmH.

343 "sedative of a kiss"—Blagden to CC, July 16 [1869], in CCP.

CHAPTER TWENTY-NINE

344 "for a day or two"—quoted in Clement, *Charlotte Cushman,* p. 91.

"be lifted up again"—Stebbins to Emma Crow Cushman, August 26, 1869, in CCP, *13.*

"Your loving Auntie"—CC to Ned Cushman, August, 1869, in CCP, *4,* 1179.

"would na say so"—Stebbins to Emma Crow Cushman, September 11, 1869, in CCP, *13.*

"will trust in Him"—CC to Emma Crow Cushman, August, 1869, in CCP, *8.*

345 "very well, lately"—quoted in Clement, *Charlotte Cushman,* p. 92.

page

"buried Caesars"—CC to Seward, March 26, 1870, at NRU.

"end my days"—ibid.

"sooner or later"—CC to Seward, May 10, 1870, at NRU.

346   "help her endure"—Stebbins to Emma Crow Cushman, July 24, 1870, in CCP, *13*.

"last Thursday"—CC to Dear Friend [c. June 12, 1870], at PPHi.

347   "great in art"—Marston, *Our Recent Actors, 2,* 82.

"betimes, or never"—Hawthorne, *Marble Faun,* p. 461.

"ever to leave"—CC to Dear Friend, September 13, 1874, at CSmH.

348   swirls of snow—Maud Howe Elliott, *This Was My Newport* (Cambridge, Mass.: Mythology, 1944), p. 83.

to be amused—Mary Higginson, *Letters and Journals of Thomas Wentworth Higginson,* p. 244.

"when to retire!"—CC to Annie Fields, January 5, 1871, at CSmH.

349   "not be justified"—CC to Emily Warren, March 29, 1871, quoted in Stowe's note, at MCR.

"to stand pat"—CC to James Fields, March 30, 1871, at CSmH.

"wiser and nobler"—Annie Field's dairy, April 27, 1871, quoted in Howe, *Memories of a Hostess,* p. 221.

"not overdo myself"—CC to Booth, July 25, 1871, at NNP.

350   "as a *finality*"—CC to Booth, July 12, 1871, at NNP.

"to do so"—CC to Dr. Bliss, July 25, 1871, at MH-T.

"can make money"—CC to Emma Crow Cushman, May 25, 1871, in CCP, *5,* 1477.

CHAPTER THIRTY

351   "all these years!"—quoted in Wingate, *Shakespeare's Heroes,* p. 235.

"to resist the fetters?"—Seward to CC, October 8, 1871, in CCP, *13,* 3716.

352   "little of 'decay' "—*The New York Times,* September 26, 1871, p. 4.

"a radiant light"—William Winter, *Other Days: Being Chronicles and Memories of the Stage* (New York: Moffat, Yard, 1908), p. 159.

"in a generation"—New York *Standard,* September 27, 1871, p. 2.

"unfaltering intelligence"—John Rankin Towse, *Sixty Years of the Theatre: An Old Critic's Memoirs* (New York: Funk and Wagnalls, 1916), p. 197.

"reserved power"—John D. Stockton, "Charlotte Cushman," *Scribner's Monthly, 12* (June, 1876): 265.

such "little men"—Winter, *Shakespeare on the Stage,* p. 503.

"incarnate power"—Winter, *Other Days,* p. 153.

"age or illness"—Winter, *Shakespeare on the Stage,* p. 502.

"each other hereafter"—Seward to CC, October 8, 1871, in CCP, *13,* 3715.

353   dignity and grace—untitled contemporary newspaper clipping at MH-T.

"left the stage"—untitled contemporary newspaper clipping at MH-T.

"want me the more"—CC to Emma Crow Cushman, October 27, 1871, in CCP, *5,* 1534.

"of genius"—Blagden to CC, n.d., in CCP, *9,* 2639.

page

"superfluous on the stage"—quoted in Montrose J. Moses, *The Fabulous Forrest: The Record of an American Actor* (Boston: Little, Brown, 1929), p. 320.

354 "or even equalled"—a critic's pencillings on a Globe Theatre playbill, November 28, 1871, at CU-B theatre collection.

"a feast of mind"—*Daily Advertiser* supplement, December 9, 1871, in CCP, *15*.

"woman's heart there"—Annie Fields's diary, November 13, 1871, quoted in Howe, *Memories of a Hostess,* p. 222.

"awful eyes!"—Julian Hawthorne, *Memoirs,* p. 263.

"yet I could not"—Thomas Wentworth Higginson to Harriett Prescott, quoted in Mary Thacher Higginson, *Thomas Wentworth Higginson: The Story Of His Life* (Boston: Houghton Mifflin, 1914), pp. 130–31.

355 "what I've gained"—quoted by Celia Logan in untitled contemporary newspaper clipping at MH-T, quoting from an article in New York *Sunday Dispatch.*

355 "There's the bell"—quoted in James Henry Wiggin, "A House and a Name," pp. 87–97.

"I could have received"—CC to unnamed friend, December 31, 1871, quoted in Stebbins, p. 238.

"do and be"—quoted in Stebbins, p. 240.

"deposited in advance"—CC to Henry A. Willard, November 22, 1871, at NN-T.

356 "'Henry the Eighth'"—quoted in Mrs. Roger A. Pryor, *My Day: Reminiscences of a Long Life* (New York: Macmillan, 1909), p. 359.

"the dog's back"—quoted in Mary Higginson, *Lettters and Journals of Thomas Wentworth Higginson,* p. 265.

"humanity among them"—quoted in clipping from *Harper's, 9,* 1876, at MH-T.

"demonstrate this"—CC to Emma Crow Cushman, January, 1872, in CCP, *5, 1579.*

357 "anything of mine"—Longfellow to CC, January 24, 1872, in CCP, *12, 3528.*

"than to rust out"—CC to Wayman Crow, May 22, 1872, in CCP, *5, 1649.*

358 "ha! ha!"—CC to Emma Crow Cushman, May 5, 1872, in CCP, *5, 1638.*

"shrieking from the theatre"—quoted in Wisner Payne Kinne, *George Pierce Baker and the American Theatre* (Cambridge: Harvard University Press, 1954), p. 5.

"weird it sounded"—quoted in Stebbins, p. 247.

"The rest is with God!"—CC to Seward, June 2, 1872, at NRU.

359 "as I please"—quoted in Stebbins, p. 249.

"her enter a room"—quoted in Stebbins, p. 299.

360 "I had no house"—quoted in Stebbins, p. 250.

"those who love me"—quoted in Stebbins, p. 249.

"enough of myself"—quoted in Stebbins, p. 246.

page

"when it came"—CC to Emma Crow Cushman, November 18, 1872, in CCP, *6,* 1692.

"for our church"—quoted in John Bouve Clapp, "Charlotte Cushman, Our Greatest Actress," Boston *Evening Transcript,* July 22, 1916, section 3, p. 6.

361 "work, work, work"—quoted in Arthur and Barbara Gelb, *O'Neill* (New York: Harper, 1962), p. 25.

"have ever listened to"—quoted in Wilson, *History of American Acting,* p. 51.

"coming now, be jabers!"—untitled contemporary newspaper clipping at NN-T and untitled clipping from the *Christian Register* at MH-T.

362 "intense acting"—Chicago *Times,* December 24, 1872, p. 3.

"of the meaning"—Chicago *Times,* December 31, 1872, p. 8.

" 'endless' "—quoted in Stebbins, p. 147.

363 to Barrett's eyes—Willie Seymour in an interview with Susan Rice, in Boston *Evening Transcript,* in clipping dated 1925 at MH-T.

"electrified by her genius"—quoted in Kendall, *Golden Age,* p. 432.

364 could not tolerate—W. Bracken to CC, January 31, 1873, in CCP, *9.*

"common looking"—CCP, *6,* 1751.

"poor thrown in"—quoted in Stebbins, p. 155.

"one nightmare"—James Gibbons Huneker, *Steeplejack* (New York: Scribner's, 1922), *1,* 84.

"with a splendor"—quoted in "Charlotte Cushman, Actress and Woman, *Theatre Magazine* (September, 1909), clipping at NN-T.

365 "near my heart"—CC to Stebbins, June 26, 1873, quoted in Stebbins, p. 248.

"as a whole"—CC to Daly, July 7, 1873, quoted in Joseph Francis Daly, *The Life of Augustin Daly* (New York: Macmillan, 1917), p. 134.

"what is inevitable"—CC to Stebbins, November 26, 1873, quoted in Stebbins, p. 254.

"idiotic brain!"—Blair to CC, December 1, 1873, in CCP, *9,* 2703.

366 "she does it"—Annie Fields to Laura, March 2, 1874, at CSmH.

"cara amica"—quoted in Stebbins, p. 271.

"tell me I am"—CC to Mrs. Booth, July 27, 1874, at MH-T.

CHAPTER THIRTY-ONE

367 "some respectable graveyard"—CC to her mother, May 1, 1845, quoted in Stebbins, p. 50.

"dear old Boston"—untitled contemporary newspaper clipping at NN-T.

"thank God for it"—quoted in Emma Crow Cushman's memoirs in CCP, *15.*

368 "for me to say"—CC to Dexter Smith, October 24, 1874, in untitled newspaper clipping at MH-T.

"in me in 1857"—Pond, *Eccentricities of Genius,* p. 316.

369 "to be seen no more"—quoted in *The Republic,* n.p., n.d., in CCP, *15.*

370 "engagement in New York"—CC to Algernon Sullivan, quoted in Clement, *Charlotte Cushman,* p. 125.

Notes

371 "Noble boy!"—quoted in Winter, *Other Days*, pp. 162–64.
"sea of admiration"—untitled contemporary newspaper clipping in Ireland, scrapbook of New York actors and actresses at CtY.

372 "Sarah Siddons"—untitled contemporary newspaper clipping at MH-T.
"symphony of Beethoven"—Henry Austin Clapp, "Dramatic Critic," p. 352.

373 "intellectual character"—untitled contemporary newspaper clipping in Ireland, scrapbook at CtY.
"*or* the public"—quoted by George W. Bell to Ned Cushman, May 20, 1876, in CCP, *9*, 2661.

374 "their 'big mama' "—quoted in Stebbins, p. 265.
"is thine for life"—CC's copy of the poem in CCP, *15*.

376 "Our most illustrious queen!"—quoted in Stebbins, pp. 259–62.

377 "a beating heart"—Bryant's holograph in CCP, *15*.

378 "God be with you"—CC's holograph in CCP, *15*.

379 "Shakespeare, Miss Cushman"—quoted in Winter, *Other Days*, pp. 165–66.
"an hundred years on thee"—Hutton, *Plays and Players*, p. 233.

CHAPTER THIRTY-TWO

381 "with a smile"—Mary Anderson, *A Few Memories* (New York: Harper, 1896), p. 38.
"God be with you"—quoted in ibid., p. 41.

382 "for that matter, off"—Odell, *Annals, 10*, 373.
"for our audience"—quoted in Anderson, *Few Memories*, p. 269.
nearly $6,000—Pond, *Eccentricities of Genius*, p. 315.
"Eastern *June!*"—CC to Alward, December 15, 1874 at PPCc.
little farewell ceremony—New York *Mirror*, January 1, 1885.
wind through the trees—CC to Harrington, July 15, 1840, at MB.

383 "e'en in that awful light!"—Lanier to his wife, January 29, 1875, at LNHT.

384 good-bye to all cities—Chicago *Tribune*, February 12, 1875.
"has been gifted"—Cincinnati *Commercial*, March 2, 1875, p. 8.
as a creative artist—ibid., March 6, 1875, p. 5.
"the end of *work*"—CC to Pugh, March 29, 1875, at DFo.
"the pointed finger"—Reignolds-Winslow, *Yesterdays with Actors*, p. 28.
"emotion and tender regard"—quoted in Clement, *Charlotte Cushman*, p. 132.

385 "and Farewell!"—CC's holograph at DFo.
"here comes the curtain"—Guild's "Reminiscence" holograph, Boston, August 9, 1883, at MBHi.
"in a great lily?"—Lanier to CC, June 17, 1875, at MdBJ.

386 "rest of the way?"—CC to Lanier, June 23, 1875, at MdBJ.
"your faithful, Sidney Lanier"—Lanier to CC, July 31, 1875, at MdBJ.

387 "is with you"—CC to Lanier, August 3, 1875, at MdBJ.
"to the last"—CC to [Lanier] Dear Friend, September 29, 1875, at TxU.

as Dickens had known them—James W. Spring, *Boston and the Parker House: A Chronicle of Those Who Have Lived on that Historic Spot Where the New Parker House Now Stands in Boston* (Boston: Whipple, 1927), p. 188.

388 "sweetness and welcome"—Lanier to Peacock, November 4, 1875, in Charles R. Anderson and Aubrey H. Starke, *The Centennial Edition of the Works of Sidney Lanier* (Baltimore: Johns Hopkins University Press, 1945), *9,* 267.

"the happy word"—quoted in Edwin Mims, *Sidney Lanier* (Boston: Houghton Mifflin, 1905), p. 190.

"ignorant one"—Lanier to Peacock, November 10, 1875, in *Letters of Sidney Lanier: Selections from His Correspondence 1866–1881 with Portraits* (New York: Scribner's, 1899), p. 22.

"gave me as a friend"—Lanier to Lady Clare, November 30, 1875, at LNHT.

CHAPTER THIRTY-THREE

389 "days in college"—CC to Lanier, December 12, 1875, at MdBJ.
390 "great poet, Whitman"—quoted in Lathrop, *Memories of Hawthorne,* p. 311.

"a genius"—quoted in Horace Traubel, *With Walt Whitman in Camden: January 21–April 7, 1889* (Carbondale: Southern Illinois University Press, 1959), pp. 189–90.

"all great pain"—CC to Lanier, December 12, 1875, at MdBJ.

"folly to try"—quoted in Stebbins, p. 282.

"so handsome"—quoted in Boston *Press,* February 19, 1876.

391 "the work so long"—untitled contemporary newspaper clipping at TxU-T.

"before us all!"—CC to Emma Crow Cushman, December 24, 1875, quoted in Stebbins, p. 279.

392 "your often-longing, S.L."—Lanier to CC, December 30, 1875, quoted in Mims, *Sidney Lanier,* p. 191.

"heart were expressed"—CC to Lanier, January 3, 1876, at MdBJ.

393 "your true friend, Charlotte Cushman"—CC to Booth, January 11, 1876, at NNP.

"spiritual, can give"—quoted in Charles Townsend Copeland, *Edwin Booth* (Boston: Small, Maynard, 1901), pp. 149–50.

"what I have suffered"—CC to Lanier, January 11, 1876, at MdBJ.

"day by day?"—quoted in Stebbins, pp. 281–82.

"of another world"—Winter, *Other Days,* p. 176.

394 "image of majesty"—William Winter, *The Wallet of Time: Containing Personal, Biographical, and Critical Reminiscence of the American Theatre* (New York: Moffat, Yard, 1913), *1,* 170.

"well and go there"—CC to John McCullough, February 13, 1876, at MH-T.

Lanier received it—Lanier to his father, February 26, 1876, quoted in Anderson, *Centennial, 9,* 326.

395 "punch with care"—untitled contemporary newspaper clipping at NN-T.

Notes

page

396   "from the world"—New York *Tribune,* August 16, 1885.

"face I ever saw"—quoted in Anderson, *Centennial, 9,* 324.

397   could "go stainless"—Henry W. Foote quoted in Stebbins, p. 291.

"to so many people"—John D. Stockton, "Charlotte Cushman," *Scribner's Monthly, 12* (June, 1876) : 263.

"imperial in Charlotte Cushman"—New York *Tribune,* February 19, 1876.

"in vain for centuries"—quoted in Winter, *Other Days,* p. 177.

398   a household word—*The New York Times,* February 19, 1876, p. 6.

"in her own realm"—quoted in Price, *Life of Charlotte Cushman,* p. 176.

"stands on the stage"—Stockton, "Charlotte Cushman," p. 265.

"the brimming goblet"—newspaper clipping entitled "Charlotte Cushman, J. H. McVicker's Recollection of the Great Actress," at NN-T.

"of his possessions"—Lanier to his wife, February 26, 1876, in Anderson, *Centennial, 9,* 328.

"that side of me"—Lanier to his wife, February 27, 1876, in ibid.

"helping me"—Sallie Mercer to Dennis R. Alward, December 26, 1884, at MH-T.

399   "Art eternal lives"—"Charlotte Cushman, February 18, 1876," in New York *Sunday World,* clipping at MH-T.

400   "for a play-actress"—quoted in Winter, *Wallet of Time, 1,* 159.

440

Bibliographical Note

The only previous attempt at a serious biography of Charlotte Cushman was Emma Stebbins' *Charlotte Cushman: Her Letters and Memories of Her Life* (1878). Books by C. E. Clements, W. T. Price, and Mrs. Dr. Walker, all written before 1900, purported to be biographies; actually they are echoes of the Stebbins biography or expanded essays about Charlotte Cushman.

Charlotte Cushman's career is so fully documented in letters, diaries, journals, memoirs, scrapbooks, and memorabilia, as well as the public press, that space limitations preclude my indicating all the sources behind this biography. While my source notes (pp. 403–40) specify most of the books and newspaper articles, the primary materials I used seem to merit special comment.

The Charlotte Cushman Papers in the Manuscripts Division of the Library of Congress formed the major base of my study. In the hundreds of letters contained in these fifteen leather-bound volumes and supplementary boxes—donated to the Library by the Cushman family—is preserved most of the record Charlotte left of herself. The collection includes the memoir written by Emma Crow Cushman as well as numerous letters addressed to Charlotte, scrapbooks, photograph albums, and similar materials. The Folger Shakespeare Library has a rich assemblage of portraits, photographs, and drawings of Charlotte in her stage roles and copies of her most important acting scripts. The Harvard Library Theatre Collection is rich in letters, pictures, promptbooks, playbills, and scrapbooks. Its most valuable items are bound into an extra-illustrated copy of Joseph N. Ireland's *Records of the New York Stage: From 1750 to 1860,* forty-eight large volumes packed with manuscript letters, clippings, and pictures. The Yale Bienecke Library has a similarly valuable copy of Ireland. Charlotte's diary for 1844–45 is one of the several uniquely helpful items in the Butler Library at Columbia. The Robinson Locke scrapbooks in the New York Public Library's theatre collection make it especially valuable. The University of Rochester Library holds the most important items in the Seward-Cushman correspondence. The Johns Hopkins University Library owns most of the Cushman-Lanier correspondence. The Hoblitzelle Theatre Collection at the University of Texas at Austin contains a rich trove of letters, clippings, and playbills. The James T. and Annie Fields collection at the Huntington Library contains letters to and from the major names figuring in Charlotte's career. The National Library of Scotland holds most of the Cushman–Jane Carlyle correspondence.

In addition to these public repositories, the Players Club has letters, playbills, and the best Cushman costumes and stage properties still in existence. The Charlotte Cushman Club in Philadelphia holds important Cushman letters and memorabilia. The Cushman family collection contains painted portraits, sculptures, letters, and more photograph albums.

For the privilege of using these materials, for the courtesy attendant upon their being made available to me, I am grateful.

J. L.

Index

443

Index